Counter-terrorism Financing

Nijhoff Law Specials

VOLUME 98

The titles published in this series are listed at *brill.com/nlsp*

Counter-terrorism Financing

International Best Practices and the Law

By

Nathalie Rébé

BRILL
NIJHOFF

LEIDEN | BOSTON

Library of Congress Cataloging-in-Publication Data

Names: Rébé, Nathalie, author.
Title: Counter-terrorism financing : international best practices and the law / Nathalie Rébé.
Description: Leiden ; Boston : Brill | Nijhoff, 2020. | Series: Nijhoff law specials, 0924-4549 ; vol. 98 | Includes bibliographical references and index. | Summary: "In Counter-Terrorism Financing: International Best Practices and the Law, Nathalie Rébé, offers a new comprehensive framework for CTF worldwide and reviews the strengths and weaknesses of current regulations and policies. Both accessible, interesting and engaging in how it approaches chronic problems of Counter-terrorism Financing, this book provides general understanding of this topic with a literature review and a gap-analysis based on CTF experts' advices, as well as a very detailed analysis of current international regulatory tools. Nathalie Rébé's 'all-in'one' CTF manual is innovative in this field and provides answers for the international community to fight terrorism financing together more effectively, using a set of standards which promotes strong and diligent cooperation between countries concerning reporting, information exchange and gathering, as well as enforcement"-- Provided by publisher.
Identifiers: LCCN 2019038552 (print) | LCCN 2019038553 (ebook) | ISBN 9789004409668 (hardback) | ISBN 9789004409675 (ebook)
Subjects: LCSH: Terrorism--Finance--Prevention. | Terrorism--Finance--Law and legislation--Criminal provisions. | Terrorism--Prevention--Law and legislation.
Classification: LCC KZ7220 .R43 2020 (print) | LCC KZ7220 (ebook) | DDC 344.05/325--dc23
LC record available at https://lccn.loc.gov/2019038552
LC ebook record available at https://lccn.loc.gov/2019038553

Typeface for the Latin, Greek, and Cyrillic scripts: "Brill". See and download: brill.com/brill-typeface.

ISSN 0924-4549
ISBN 978-90-04-40966-8 (hardback)
ISBN 978-90-04-40967-5 (e-book)

This book is printed on acid-free paper and produced in a sustainable manner.

I dedicate this book to my family and friends for their constant support and unconditional love. They helped me overcome all the obstacles I had to face over the past 10 years of my international academic career

Contents

Acknowledgements

First and foremost, I would like to express my deepest gratitude to Dr. Robert Munro for his continuous encouragement and support of my study and research. He guided me through all the stages of this work.

I have appreciated all his help and advice, as well as his patience, motivation and thorough knowledge of my topic. I could not have imagined having a better mentor.

Second, I would like to express my heartfelt gratitude to Dr. William Byrnes for his trust in my capabilities and patience over the years despite the numerous obstacles I have encountered.

I am also greatly indebted to Dr. Dionysios Demetis for his precious help as an international expert and academic scholar and his valuable feedback, advice, and reassurance during our meetings when we discussed my subject in London.

I also owe my sincere gratitude to INTERPOL Expert on Counter-terrorism François PERRENOUD, for his great involvement in my work, as well as to Delphine SCHANTZ, United Nations Expert Counter-terrorism Executive Directorate for her immense knowledge. I would also like to pay my sincere thanks to my numerous contacts at the Basel Institute on Governance for their help and precious expertise.

I hereby send my most sincere thanks to the numerous professionals that have been a continual source of support, as well as a springboard for ideas, through our ongoing discussions on various AML/CTF related topics. They comforted me in the choice of my career path in CTF and law.

I also want to ardently thank my beloved family for their loving consideration and great confidence in me all through this year. This book would not have been possible without the infallible support and encouragement of my dear family and friends.

Acronyms and Abbreviations

AML	Anti-Money Laundering
AML/CTF CI	AML/CTF Compliance Index
ANF	Al-Nusra Front
ARS	Alternative Remittance System
ASOP	Alliance for the Safety of Our People
ASOPICI	Alliance for the Safety of Our People 'Intercontinental CTF Initiative'
ATM	Automated Teller Machine
BCBS	Basel Committee on Banking Supervision
CDD	Customer Due Diligence
CHIPS	Clearing House Interbank Payments System
CIP	Customer Identification Program
CTR	Currency Transaction Report
CTF	Counter-terrorism Financing
DD	Due Diligence
DNPBP	Designated Non-Financial Businesses and Professions
EDD	Enhanced Due Diligence
EU	European Union
FARC	Revolutionary Armed Forces of Colombia
FATF	Financial Action Task Force
FAU	Financial Analysis Unit
FBI	Federal Bureau of Investigation
FI	Financial Institution
FIEA	Financial Information Exchange Agreement
FinCEN	Financial Crimes Enforcement Network (US Treasury Department)
FINRA	Financial Industry Regulatory Authority
FISA	Finance Industry Standards Association (UK)
FIU	Financial Intelligence Unit
GCIT	Grave Crime of International Terrorism
GDP	Global Domestic Product
GFIU	Global Financial Intelligence Unit
IAEA	International Atomic Energy Agency
IMF	International Monetary Fund
INCSR	International Narcotics Control Strategy Report
INTERPOL	International Criminal Police Organization
IPS	Investor Portfolio Securities
IRS	Internal Revenue Service
ISIL	Islamic State of Iraq and the Levant

ISP	Internet Service Provider
KYC	Know Your Customer
ML	Money Laundering
MLAT	Mutual Legal Assistance Treaty
MSB	Money Service Business
NGO	Non-Governmental Organization
NPO	Non-Profit Organization
NPT	New Payment Technology
NSL	National Security Letter
OECD	Organization for Economic Co-operation and Development
OFAC	Office of Foreign Assets Control
PEP	Politically Exposed Person
RBA	Risk Based Approach
SARI	Stolen Asset Recovery Initiative
SAR	Suspicious Activity Report
SIM	Subscriber Identification Module
STR	Suspicious Transaction Report
SWIFT	Society for Worldwide Interbank Financial Telecommunication
TF	Terrorism Financing
UN	United Nations
UNCAC	United Nations Convention Against Corruption
UNODC	United Nations Office on Drugs and Crime
UNTOC	United Nations Convention against Transnational Organized Crime
WB	World Bank
WCO	World Customs Organization
WHO	World Health Organization
WMD	Weapon of Mass Destruction

Introduction

Terrorism has been on everybody's mind since the multiple deadly attacks nations have had to face over these past decades. Most countries are discussing internal strategies and regulations to minimize this grave problem. However, it seems more than evident that this issue will not be solved any time soon. Multiple factors require further consideration in order to design a somewhat perfect tool to Counter-terrorism. Definitions, criminalization, political will and international criminalization remain key issues that need to be addressed if there is to be an effective policy. One particularly pressing matter is the need to find adequate solutions for combatting terrorism-financing, which is a major challenge given its underground and anonymous nature. Moreover, these schemes are various, with the participants and their accomplices knowing how to adapt to new laws and financial systems worldwide to avoid being investigated. In addition, they are adept at stopping the raising of the red flags put in place by countries, financial institutions and international organizations.

The aim of this work is to create a tool to enhance Counter-terrorism Financing (CTF) monitoring, while taking privacy concerns into account. The international community clearly understands the importance of fighting Terrorism Financing (TF) to prevent major future terrorist attacks from occurring. However, despite there being a general awareness of the gravity of the TF problem, detection of its activities, prevention, and enforcement have only slowly progressed in past decades. To achieve stronger international measures, a new tool is necessary to deal with problems that have not been addressed so far. This study will involve developing a new Counter-terrorism Financing Convention model that could be used by participating countries at the international level. This will be achieved through an in-depth analysis of the current CTF regulations worldwide to identify the current successes and failures so as to able to construct an effective new convention model.

To build a new model, one must first understand the current situation regarding CTF, how TF can be detected and prevented as well as how new regulation could be enforced at a worldwide level. Thereafter, recommendations and warnings will be considered to identify the limits of such a new framework for TF monitoring. For, it has to be acknowledged that such a new tool will always face obstruction by parts of the international community, political pressure, miscommunication between the main actors involved in CTF, misuse and slow application while dealing with paperwork and procedures. Hence, all these

 | DOI:10.1163/9789004409675_002

issues will be addressed in this book. This work will be based upon a literature review as well as secondary and empirical data regarding CTF, which will be analyzed to promote the perspective that a new tool is needed by highlighting the current gaps in this domain. The reader will be provided with a visual map of current gaps in several areas of CTF through consideration of current regulations and tools along with experts' opinions and knowledge from diverse professions dealing with CTF on a daily basis.

Firstly, an overview is provided of the current situation concerning CTF. The purpose and *modus operandi* of terrorism will be clarified, moreover, the struggle to define it and its financing will be explained, since this issue represents a major obstacle to the accomplishment of a new model. Counter-terrorism regulations and international agencies specialized in CFT will also be covered. Detecting TF has always been an international concern. A general classification of TF methods will be laid down to demonstrate how money is gathered by potential terrorists and their accomplices. The main problems encountered while trying to detect TF activities will be demonstrated by analysing schemes found in annual reports, such as the Egmont Group 100 cases from financial intelligence units. These methods include: private donations, the wire transfer system, cash couriers and non-profit organizations, but also risky value transfer systems, such as Hawala and alternative remittance systems.

Terrorism financing risks faced by financial institutions will be introduced, along with the CTF red flags provided by the main international regulators concerning TF. The main cases as delivered by Financial Intelligence Units Reports will be discussed in terms of defining the indicators of TF and actions required by FIUs to cope with their suspicions.

Preventing TF already encompasses several known compliance measures operating worldwide. In this investigation, the way institutions model TF risk will be overviewed, offering a clarification on the use of Counter-terrorism risk models, risk assessment and risk-based supervision. Well-known tools used by professionals to prevent TF, such as enhanced due diligence, especially in the case of politically exposed persons, which are closely watched, in addition to suspicious activity reports, currency transaction reports, and national security letters will also be analyzed. Financial intelligence units and the Egmont Group also play a key role in the prevention of TF and will be discussed later as well as how their work could be enhanced to achieve better TF monitoring between nations.

Secondly, the main threats to the success of the New Counter-terrorism Financing Convention will be debated. Issues, such as cross-border activities, third party reliance, anonymity and employee participation in ML schemes, will also be clarified for the purpose of this endeavor. Matters regarding the main blockages to the effectiveness of the Convention, such as the emergence of new ML/TF activities, like new payment technologies, along with the key challenges at the international level, including international cooperation between actors and agencies, political involvement, international privacy laws and civil liberties will be examined. Privacy in tracing and detecting TF schemes remains one of the key elements to consider including in a new tool that could interest nations enough to agree to changing their ways of dealing with TF monitoring. Moreover, one of the main issues regarding the practicality of the Convention that needs to be taken into consideration is the ineffectiveness of the current enforcement system mechanisms, including cross-border enforcement. The asset recovery system will be explained in terms of the process of locating, freezing and recovering assets linked to TF activities.

Thirdly, existing Counter-terrorism tools with regard to CTF, including international Counter-terrorism regulations, agencies and financial institutions' recommendations, financial services best practice rules and countries' legislative contributions will be discussed. This study will offer a critical evaluation of these legal tools to underline the importance of the creation of a new convention model. The gaps in the current legal system, observed in the previous chapters about asset recovery, privacy and civil liberties will be disclosed. Experts from different professions dealing with CTF have been interviewed and their responses reveal where they feel problems occur as well as how they could be fixed at their level. A gap analysis is then provided by means of a visual map to recognize where a new model should intervene.

Fourthly, the new CT proposal will be presented along with recommendations of ways to strengthen worldwide detection, prevention and enforcement. These will be particularly targeted at areas of concerns including actor involvement and cooperation at the domestic and international levels, collaboration with the private sector and Global Financial Unit development.

Lastly, questions for further consideration should be discussed. They include interrogations such as: How to lower the barriers to the implementation of a new Convention and promote international cooperation between the main actors involved in fighting Terrorism Financing, whilst supporting International Privacy Rights and Civil Liberties?

This study will provide a significant contribution to the area of international legal compliance by identifying risks that have not been acknowledged in previous researches and legislations, to offer the international community a new tool to fight TF. Privacy and civil liberties represent serious threats to the achievement of a new model and frequently leave the international community sceptical about the means utilized to catch terrorists in the financing process of their illegal endeavor. Accordingly, the proposed tool will give a special focus to privacy and civil liberties when dealing with TF monitoring issues.

PART 1

Counter-terrorism Financing Worldwide Overview

Introduction to Part 1

To start with, this work will provide a comprehensive summary of the current situation regarding CTF worldwide. This part is divided into three chapters as follows.

Chapter 1 will highlight the purpose and *modus operandi* of terrorism, provide current definitions of terrorism and Terrorism financing, introduce existing international tools and regulations and discuss the actors responsible for preventing TF.

Chapter 2 will deal with detection issues regarding TF. The main differences between Terrorism financing (TF) and Money-laundering (ML) will be explained and an over-all classification of TF methods will be provided. The basic methods of ML employed by Terrorists and their accomplices drawn from FIU case reports and specialised agencies' red flags will be discussed. Moreover, the risks faced by financial institutions will also be listed in this Chapter.

Chapter 3 will demonstrate how institutions model terrorism-financing risk and incorporate counter-terrorism risk models, risk-assessment and risk-based supervision within their existing compliance efforts to prevent and report TF worldwide. Other elements of deterrence, including enhanced due diligence, suspicious activity reports, Currency Transaction Reports, and national security letters will be discussed in this chapter. In addition, the work of the Egmont Group and financial intelligence units will also be explained.

This overview of the current CTF situation is essential for understanding the circumstances in which terrorists evolve and how they are able to launder money and/or gather sources of funding to finance their illicit activities.

 | DOI:10.1163/9789004409675_003

CHAPTER 1

What Is the Current Situation Concerning Counter-terrorism Financing?

This chapter not only explains the purpose and *modus operandi* of terrorism, for it also provides consideration of the thorny issue of defining terrorism as well as current definitions of TF. Actors responsible for preventing terrorism-financing will also be introduced. In addition, this chapter will offer a list of all the existing international tools and regulations that will be reviewed in Chapter 7, criticized in Chapter 8 and utilized to build up the new Counter-terrorism Compliance model in Chapter 10.

A Terrorism's Purpose and *Modus Operandi*

Terrorism represents a daily threat at the international level. Whilst hijackings, bombings, and assassinations worldwide may appear to be isolated events, such terrorism is, in fact, an instrument of statecraft, domination, oppression, revolution or rebellion that relies on violence as a way to promote social, political and religious change.[1] Terrorist organizations target and attack innocent people in order to create a situation of fear within a group or a population. Far from being random violence, its advocates promote a violent strategy centered on targeting specific victims. The psychological impact of terrorism is often much more serious than the related physical consequences. Terrorists use propaganda through action and media exposure to increase the number of their followers and their influence. In general, the purpose of terrorist attacks is to create a widespread feeling of vulnerability and to deliver a public statement aimed at provoking anger or revenge, while conveying a message to people who are not directly attacked. Different types of terrorism include domestic, international, as well as non-state terrorism, covering settings such as: maritime terrorism, aircraft terrorism, economic terrorism, cyberterrorism and Weapon of Mass Destruction (WMD) terrorism.

Terrorism does not necessarily require big amounts of money to finance the illicit actions, but necessitates organization and a specific hierarchical and

1 Kerby Anderson, *Terrorism*, Probe Ministries, 1992, http://www.leaderu.com/orgs/probe/docs/terror.html.

 | DOI:10.1163/9789004409675_004

task specific structure along with good secure internal communication between actors, which often makes them hard to detect by national and international authorities. While the 9/11 terrorist attack on the United States World Trade Center cost between $400,000 and $500,000, of which approximately $300,000 was deposited into U.S. bank accounts of the 19 hijackers, the CIA estimates that prior to 9/11 it cost Al-Qaida about $30 million per year to sustain its activities.[2] Expenses included funding operations, maintaining its training and military equipment, contributing to the Taliban and their high-level officials as well as to related terrorist organizations. The Bali, Madrid and London attacks cost significantly less, i.e. the Bali nightclub attack cost about $50,000, the train bombing in Madrid in 2004 is believed to have cost between $10,000 and $15,000 and the London attacks on the tube system about $2,000.[3] Terrorists have begun to rely increasingly on cash, to avoid a paper trail, for instance, the 2005 London attacks were funded entirely in this way.

Cyberterrorism principally requires specific knowledge and little or no source of financing compared to Maritime and aircraft terrorism, or acquiring WMDs for terrorism purposes. After the successes of recent terrorist attacks, terrorists could be tempted to use WMD as instruments of aggression, which would lead to mass murder. WMD terrorism requires huge sums of money to be donated or schemed to finance the necessary materials to build the instrument of terror. Whilst there has been no nuclear/radiological incident and limited bio-chemical incidents known to date, WMD terrorism is still considered by international regulators to be a major concern.

A new kind of terrorism started being introduced in Europe in the years 2013–2016: isolated religious fundamentalist actors deciding to act on their own, in the name of a foreign leader, with a budget of €10,000 to €30,000, according to Michel Sapin,[4] French Finance Minister.[5] This new type of "isolated," "low-cost" terrorism needs to be strongly considered in the establishment of a new CTF tool, as these terrorists can derive their money from delinquency and organized crime to finance their activities in the name of a terrorist cause.

2 John Roth et al., National Commission on Terrorist Attacks Upon the United States, *Monograph on Terrorist Financing, Staff Report to the Commission,* 2004, available from https://govinfo.library.unt.edu/911/staff_statements/911_TerrFin_Monograph.pdf.

3 Eben Kaplan, Council on Foreign Relations, *Tracking Down Terrorist Financing,* 4 April 2006, available from https://www.cfr.org/backgrounder/tracking-down-terrorist-financing.

4 Michel Sapin's statement, when he was France's Finance Minister in 2015.

5 John Irish, *France to Press U.S. on "Low-Cost" Terror Financing,* Reuters, 17 December 2015, http://www.reuters.com/article/us-mideast-crisis-financing-france-idUSKBN0U02MZ20151217.

Accordingly, typical ML schemes need to be considered and watched to identify suspicious behaviours.

B The Struggle to Define Terrorism

The international community adopted a series of conventions that define and criminalize several types of terrorist activities. The United Nations has established 14 anti-terrorism conventions and hence, international terrorism can be regarded as a treaty crime at the global level. Moreover, many terrorist acts are covered by international treaties on maritime navigation, aircraft and airports, internationally protected persons, plastic explosives, nuclear material and terrorism funding. Despite the numerous, though similar, already proposed definitions of terrorism offered by the international community, dealing with general violence and the threat of it, politicians, jurists and scholars do not seem to be close to reaching an agreement as to what the legal biding definition of the crime of terrorism should be. Former chief of the UN Treaty Section and Ambassador of Sri Lanka P. Kohona rightfully mentioned that: *"One knows terrorism when one sees it"*.[6]

Whilst it is a severe crime, according to many, there is, as yet, no clear definition and thus, it has not been possible to punish this wrong doing at the international level, even if the crime itself seems obvious to anyone who sees it. By bypassing the definitional consideration, the 14 anti-Terrorism conventions sidestep the issue. Hence, a definition of terrorism is necessary, so that "terrorist" acts of violence can be legitimately condemned. Terrorism is a controversial definition to agree upon. Words chosen to define terrorism are crucial. The question of legitimacy of the use of violence for political reasons, either by states or by self-determination and revolutionary groups, is known to be the main reason why the definition has not yet been established, whereby there are disagreements at the international level regarding these matters and hence no agreed comprehensive definition of terrorist acts. Dr. Rohan Perera, Chair of the Ad Hoc Committee to Eliminate Terrorism stated that: *"The only way to reach a consensus on the issue is to follow the path of adopting an operational or a criminal law definition of terrorism, rather than a generic definition"*.[7] The danger of defining terrorism lies in the fact that the use of the term could be made in ways that endanger democracy, erode civil liberties, and risk promoting it.

6 Thalif Deen, *U.N. Remains Deadlocked on Defining Terrorism*, 23 November 2010, available from http://www.ipsnews.net/2010/11/un-remains-deadlocked-on-defining-terrorism/.

7 Deen, *supra*.

Several countries, The United Nations, as well as numerous experts, do not wish to see an agreement on the definition, since they consider that it would eradicate the possibility and legitimacy of fighting state sponsored oppression and tyranny. As pointed out by Gerald Seymour in Harry's Game in 1975: *"One man's terrorist is another man's freedom fighter."*[8] Depending on the interests that best suit specific states at particular times, the term terrorism can be used to describe acts of violence carried out by one's enemy. A proposed definition of terrorism will, thus, need make a distinction between "freedom fighters" and "State sponsored terrorism" since use of violence in the situations such as fight over self-determination and national liberation ought to be considered as a different issue.

For the purpose of this study, the problems with defining terrorism will temporarily be put aside to focus on TF itself, but it should be borne in mind that international conventions defining TF will remain inconsistent until the term "Terrorism" is defined according to the "*nulla poena sine lege*" principle, which makes enforcement impossible, for it is a crime that cannot be legitimately agreed upon. Until then, TF at the international level should be associated with other Hague International core crimes, such as crimes against humanity and war crimes or national legislation-related crimes considered to be unlawful, such as tax evasion.

C Defining Terrorism Financing

A New Counter-terrorism Financing Model must start with a definition of TF in order to be coherent. Many legal instruments and recommendations offered by international organizations fail to highlight the foremost concern remaining with defining TF, which is that despite terrorism being a term that has been defined by the international community, countries and international tribunals,[9] as abovementioned, it remains undefined in International Criminal Law.

The Appeal Chamber of the Tribunal for Lebanon established indicators of *opinio juris*, such that the customary international law definition of terrorism consists of the following three key elements:

8 Gerald Seymour, *Harry's Game: A Novel* (1975).

9 Interlocutory Decision on the Applicable Law: Terrorism, Conspiracy, Homicide, Perpetration, Cumulative Charging, Case No. STL-11-01/I (Feb. 16, 2011), (last visited 5 June 2014), http://www.stl-tsl.org/x/file/TheRegistry/Library/CaseFiles/chambers/20110216_STL-11-01_R176bis_F0010_AC_Interlocutory_D....

(i) the perpetration of a criminal act (such as murder, kidnapping, hostage-taking, arson, and so on), or threatening such an act;
(ii) the intent to spread fear among the population (which would generally entail the creation of public danger) or directly or indirectly coerce a national or international authority to take some action, or to refrain from taking it;
(iii) when the act involves a transnational element.

The first definition of TF appeared in the Convention for the Suppression of the Financing of Terrorism in 1999, where it is considered an offence within the scope of the Convention and according to Article 2.[10] That is, person can be considered guilty of TF according to Article 2 paragraph 1 of the Convention:

10 Article 2 of the Convention for the Suppression of the Financing of Terrorism (1999) states that:
"1. Any person commits an offence within the meaning of this Convention if that person by any means, directly or indirectly, unlawfully and wilfully, provides or collects funds with the intention that they should be used or in the knowledge that they are to be used, in full or in part, in order to carry out:
(a) An act which constitutes an offence within the scope of and as defined in one of the treaties listed in the annex; or
(b) Any other act intended to cause death or serious bodily injury to a civilian, or to any other person not taking an active part in the hostilities in a situation of armed conflict, when the purpose of such act, by its nature or context, is to intimidate a population, or to compel a government or an international organization to do or to abstain from doing any act.
2.
(a) On depositing its instrument of ratification, acceptance, approval or accession, a State Party which is not a party to a treaty listed in the annex may declare that, in the application of this Convention to the State Party, the treaty shall be deemed not to be included in the annex referred to in paragraph 1, subparagraph (a). The declaration shall cease to have effect as soon as the treaty enters into force for the State Party, which shall notify the depositary of this fact;
(b) When a State Party ceases to be a party to a treaty listed in the annex, it may make a declaration as provided for in this article, with respect to that treaty.
3. For an act to constitute an offence set forth in paragraph 1, it shall not be necessary that the funds were actually used to carry out an offence referred to in paragraph 1, subparagraphs (a) or (b).
4. Any person also commits an offence if that person attempts to commit an offence as set forth in paragraph 1 of this article.
5. Any person also commits an offence if that person:
(a) Participates as an accomplice in an offence as set forth in paragraph 1 or 4 of this article;
(b) Organizes or directs others to commit an offence as set forth in paragraph 1 or 4 of this article;

> ...if that person by any means, directly or indirectly, unlawfully and willfully, provides or collects funds with the intention that they should be used or in the knowledge that they are to be used, in full or in part, in order to carry-out.[11]

TF, therefore, consists of soliciting, collecting or providing funds intended to be used to support terrorist acts or organizations, with the intention that they are to be used for this specific purpose. The sources of funding can be both legal and illicit.[12] Article 2 of the Convention for the Suppression of the Financing of Terrorism specifies knowledge and intention requirements and indicates that a person still commits an offence even if:

> ...the funds are not used to carry out an offence in (a) and (b) above; a person attempts to commit an offence as described above; a person participates as an accomplice in an offence as above; and a person organizes or directs others to commit an offence as above, or contributes to the commission of one or more offences as above by a group of persons acting with a common purpose, where the contribution is intentional and is made with the aim of furthering the criminal activity or criminal purpose of the group, where such activity involves the commission of an offence as above, or is made in the knowledge of the intention of the group to commit an offence as above.[13]

This Article holds that to be found guilty of TF, a person shall demonstrate knowledge and intention to further the criminal activity as well as be aware of the intent of the group to commit the offence. Moreover, The United Nations Convention for the Suppression of the Financing of Terrorism confirms that,

---

(c) Contributes to the commission of one or more offences as set forth in paragraphs 1 or 4 of this article by a group of persons acting with a common purpose. Such contribution shall be intentional and shall either:

(i) Be made with the aim of furthering the criminal activity or criminal purpose of the group, where such activity or purpose involves the commission of an offence as set forth in paragraph 1 of this article; or

(ii) Be made in the knowledge of the intention of the group to commit an offence as set forth in paragraph 1 of this article."

11 U.N. GAOR 54/109 *International Convention for the Suppression of the Financing of Terrorism*, 9 December 1999, available from http://www.un.org/law/cod/finterr.htm.

12 International Monetary Fund, *Anti-Money-Laundering/Combating the Financing of Terrorism—Topics*, 2000, available from http://www.imf.org/external/np/leg/amlcft/eng/aml1.htm.

13 GAOR 54/109, *supra*.

according to Article 2, a person cannot be found guilty of TF, if his personal funds or identity were used without his approval to perpetrate a terrorist act or, if the funds were said to be collected from him for another purpose.

D International Specialized Agencies Fighting TF

At this point of the study, it is essential to identify the main agencies fighting TF worldwide in order to foresee who will be in charge of enforcing the new CTF tool. It is also important to elicit where blockages could take place among the main players that could slow down the enforcement process ultimately leaving criminals enough space to escape detection and punishment mechanisms. Actors in charge of deterring TF, including: international bodies; government agencies; industry players; charities; scholars; and research institutes, work together to deter and regulate terrorism and TF. The diagram (Figure 1) below provides a visual overview of the leading actors dealing with CTF on a daily basis (An in-depth description of how these agencies interact will be provided in Chapter 4, Part C).

The United Nations plays a key role in CTF since it provides international conventions and resolutions that countries party to it should respect to avoid difficulties. The United Nations Office on Drugs and Crime (UNODC) is the branch most familiar with Anti-money-laundering and CTF as it is tasked with dealing with crimes and their financing. The European Union with the Council of Europe also provides regulations to be applied by EU countries. National

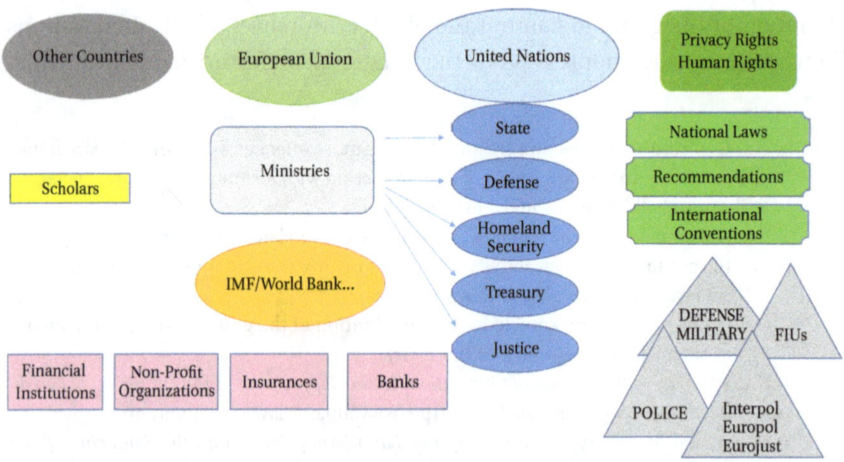

FIGURE 1 International specialized agencies fighting terrorism financing, 2014

regulators oversee validating drafts of national regulations related to TF and national laws most often involve creating a domestic set of rules to follow based on the guidelines provided by institutions such as the IMF, The World Bank, the OECD's FATF Recommendations,[14] the E.U. Moneyval, The Wolfsberg Standards, The Basel Institute, and many others. At the national level, countries can choose to implement Articles from international conventions specific to this matter, or follow the example of other countries' Counter-terrorism financing national laws. Ministries of State, Defense, Homeland Security, the Treasury and Justice worldwide incorporate units specialized in Counter-terrorism responsible for communication with other countries and international agencies. They also draft new laws to keep up to date with recently observed AML/TF trends.

At the defense level, national police forces, intelligence sections and the military work closely together with international structures, such as INTERPOL, Europol, Eurojust, the Egmont Group and its financial intelligence units in charge of finding terrorists, as well as tracing the financing methods and actors involved before and after terrorist attacks take place. A few Non-Profit Organizations also cooperate with National and International structures. They regularly create internal guidelines and AML/CTF rules to follow in order to avoid being used by terrorist organizations to finance their operations. NPOs also collaborate to detect insiders that could assist terrorists, dissimulate money or hide their tracks. Such organizations include: the Red Cross, the World Health Organization (WHO), and financial institutions (insurance companies, banking and financial services) facing Terrorist Financing threats through their contractual relationships and daily operations.

Annex 1 illustrates the United States departments and agencies involved in combating terrorism. Generally, the Department of State incorporates the Bureau of Economic and Business Affairs, the Office of the Coordinator for Counter-terrorism and the Bureau of International Narcotics and Law Enforcement Affairs. The Department of Defense includes the Secretary of Defense, the Central Intelligence Agency and the Naval Intelligence Office. The Department of Homeland Security helps fight terrorism, with the Bureau of Immigration and Customs Enforcement providing surveillance and information that could be useful for tracking terrorists crossing borders and catching them. Most countries have national governmental agencies similar to the U.S. Department of Treasury, the Internal Revenue Service (IRS), the Office of Foreign

14 FATF Recommendations and Reports specific to ML/TF methods can be found listed in the Bibliography.

Assets Control (OFAC), the Office of International Affairs, the Financial Crimes Enforcement Network, and the Executive Office of Terrorist Financing and Financial Crime. They also have a Department of Justice which usually comprises a Bureau of Investigation, the Bureau of Alcohol, Tabacco, Firearms, Explosives, Criminal Division, and Drugs Enforcement.

E Current Counter-terrorism Financing Regulations

For the purpose of this study, current regulatory tools and recommendations with regard to CTF will be critically analysed in-depth in Chapters 7 and 8. A comprehensive, but non-exhaustive, list of regulatory instruments that will be used later within the scope of this study encompassing international Counter-terrorism regulations, agencies and financial institutions' recommendations, financial services best practice rules and countries' legislative contributions is provided below. Only an examination of the current and previous CTF tools, can lead to a comprehensive assessment of the successes and failures in this field. Given the occurrence of terrorist events, the UN Security Council has argued that defeating international terrorism is essential for the preservation of international peace and security, demanding that there should be the surrender to justice of persons accused of terrorist acts.[15] United Nations resolutions and conventions aimed at the suppression of general terrorism offences are also dedicated to stopping terrorists' sources of funding and the organization frequently urges nations party to its conventions to prevent the financing of terrorism activities.

In the 1990s, CTF started to be dealt with by the Council of Europe and the OECD's Financial Action Task Force (FATF). FATF has constantly worked on improving its recommendations to help various financial sectors recognize the red flags associated with associated with ML and TF. In 1999, after discussing the matter of TF in several terrorism-related conventions, the United Nations issued an International Convention specifically aimed at its suppression. Since then, various nations have implemented Counter-terrorism legislations at the domestic level, most of them in the aftermath of the 9/11 events, to prevent such crimes going unpunished. They also contained sets of rules and strategies for preventing similar events from occurring again. In 2005, the IMF

---

15 Robert Cryer et al., *An Introduction to International Criminal Law and Procedure* 341 (2nd ed. 2010).

introduced a new legislation model on ML and TF, while the Council of Europe implemented the Convention on Laundering, Search, Seizure, and Confiscation of the Proceeds from Crime and on the Financing of Terrorism. In the same year, Third EU Directive was born. Since then, improvements have been made to FATF. Recommendations and agencies have published many ML/TF crime based guidelines, specifically targeting banks and Financial Institutions.

Following numerous mass-killing terrorist events in Europe starting in 2013, the United Nations issued Security Council Resolutions urging an international fight against terrorism, in particular, targeting the financing of well-known terrorist cells, such as Al-Qaida and the Islamic State. In light of the considerable threat faced by Europe, the European Union decided to provide within the fourth version of the EU Directive, its own version of the "terrorism" definition, so long avoided at the international level so as to be able to prosecute individuals carrying out terrorist acts in its territory. At the European level, a Proposal for a Directive of the EU Parliament and the Council on combatting Terrorism was issued in 2015.

Terrorists and criminals have become increasingly aware of the gaps within the current international system for tracking and punishing persons involved in TF, thus always looking for new ways to fool the system.

The three following lists of tools provide a timeline that demonstrates the international response to terrorism and TF activities over the years. The documents were chosen according to their relevance to the field of terrorism and reflect the evolution of the field. TF has been increasingly referred to in recent years, having growing importance within conventions and advisory tools. With the purpose of analyzing of the regulatory tools and recommendations at the national, international and institutional levels in Chapter 7, three types of regulations and advisory guidelines will be reviewed:

1. International Counter-terrorism related regulations offered by the United Nations and the Security Council, along with the Security Council Resolutions;
2. Current advisory tools provided by agencies and financial institutions pertaining to organized crime, corruption, and TF;
3. A list of countries' most significant legislative contributions relating to terrorism and TF, including the European Union Conventions.

As abovementioned, the United Nations has issued 14 Conventions related to terrorism. Even though several of these instruments appear off topic and do not mention the word "Terrorism" within the title of the legislative tool itself, these offer a good comprehension of the evolution of the TF legal framework.

First, the list of international Counter-terrorism related regulations offered by the United Nations and its Security Council includes:

1963 Convention on Offences and certain other acts committed on board aircraft[16] (No: 10106)
1970 Convention for the Suppression of Unlawful Seizure of Aircraft[17] (No: 12325)
1971 Convention for the Suppression of Unlawful Acts against the Safety of Civil Aviation[18] (No: 14118)
1973 Convention on the Prevention and Punishment of Crimes against Internationally Protected Persons[19] (Annexed to General Assembly resolution 3166 (XVIII))
1973 United Nations Convention on the Law of the Sea[20] (resolution 3067 (XXVIII))
1979 International Convention against the Taking of Hostages[21] (No: 21931)
1979 Convention on the Physical Protection of Nuclear Material[22]
1988 Protocol for the Suppression of Unlawful Acts of Violence at Airports Serving International Civil Aviation, supplementary to the Convention for the Suppression of Unlawful Acts against the Safety of Civil Aviation[23]

---

16 U.N. International Civil Aviation Organization, *Convention on Offences and Certain Other Acts Committed on Board Aircraft*, 14 September 1963, *U.N.T.S.*, No. 10106, available from http://treaties.un.org/doc/db/Terrorism/Conv1-english.pdf.

17 U.N., *Convention for the Suppression of Unlawful Seizure of Aircraft*, 16 December 1970, *U.N.T.S. 1973*, available from http://www.refworld.org/docid/3ddcaa774.html.

18 U.N., *Convention for the Suppression of Unlawful Acts Against the Safety of Civil Aviation*, Montreal, 23 September 1971, *U.N.T.S.*, vol. 974, no. 1-14118, available from http://www.un.org/zh/terrorism/pdf/1971E.pdf.

19 U.N., *Convention on the Prevention and Punishment of Crimes against Internationally Protected Persons, U.N.T.S. 1973*, available from http://legal.un.org/ilc/texts/instruments/english/conventions/9_4_1973.pdf.

20 U.N. GAOR resolution 3067 (XXVIII), *Convention on the Law of the Sea*, 19 November 1973, available from http://www.un.org/depts/los/convention_agreements/texts/unclos/unclos_e.pdf.

21 U.N., *International Convention against the Taking of Hostages*, New York, 17 December 1979, available from http://www.unodc.org/documents/treaties/Special/1979%20International%20Convention%20against%20the%20Taking%20of%20Hostages.pdf.

22 International Atomic Energy Agency, *Convention on the Physical Protection of Nuclear Material*, 26 October 1979, available from https://www.iaea.org/publications/documents/conventions/convention-physical-protection-nuclear-material.

23 U.N., *Protocol for the Suppression of Unlawful Acts of Violence at Airports Serving International Civil Aviation, supplementary to the Convention for the Suppression of Unlawful Acts against the Safety of Civil Aviation*, 24 February 1988, *U.N.T.S 1990*, available from http://www.refworld.org/docid/3ddcac634.html.

1988 Convention for the Suppression of Unlawful Acts against the Safety of Maritime Navigation[24] (No: 29004)
1988 Protocol for the Suppression of Unlawful Acts against the Safety of Fixed Platforms located on the Continental Shelf[25]
1988 The United Nations Convention Against Illicit Traffic in Narcotic Drugs and Psychotropic Substances[26]
1991 Convention on the Marking of plastic explosives for the purpose of Detection[27]
1997 International Convention for the Suppression of Terrorist Bombings[28]
1999 International Convention for the Suppression of the Financing of Terrorism[29]
1999 United Nations' Model Legislation on Laundering, Confiscation and International Cooperation in Relation to the Proceeds of Crime[30]
2000 UN Convention against Transnational Organized Crime[31]
2004 The United Nations Convention Against Corruption[32]

---

24 International Environmental Agreements (IEA) Database Project, *Convention for The Suppression of Unlawful Acts Against the Safety Of Maritime Navigation*, 10 March 1988, available from http://iea.uoregon.edu/treaty-text/1988-unlawfulactssafetymaritimenavigationentxt.

25 Admiralty and Maritime Law Guide, International Conventions, *Protocol for the Suppression of Unlawful Acts against the Safety of Fixed Platforms Located on the Continental Shelf*, 10 March 1988, available from http://www.admiraltylawguide.com/conven/fixedplatforms1988.html.

26 U.N. Commission on Narcotic Drugs and the Economic and Social Council, *United Nations Convention Against Illicit Traffic in Narcotic Drugs and Psychotropic Substances,* 25 May 1988, available from http://www.unodc.org/pdf/convention_1988_en.pdf.

27 U.N. International Explosives Technical Commission, *Convention on the Marking of Plastic Explosives for the Purpose of Detection,* 1 Mar. 1991, available from http://www.un.org/en/sc/ctc/docs/conventions/Conv10.pdf.

28 U.N. GAOR, *International Convention for the Suppression of Terrorist Bombings*, A/52/653, 25 November 1997, available from http://www.un.org/law/cod/terroris.htm.

29 U.N. GAOR resolution 54/109 *International Convention for the Suppression of the Financing of Terrorism,* 9 December 1999, available from http://www.un.org/law/cod/finterr.htm.

30 International Money-Laundering Information Network, Global Programme Against Money-Laundering, *Model legislation on laundering, confiscation and international cooperation in relation to the proceeds of crime,* 1999, available from http://www.imolin.org/imolin/en/ml99eng.html.

31 U.N. GAOR 55/25, *Convention on Transnational Organized Crime and the Protocols Thereto,* Article 14, 15 Nov. 2000, available from https://www.unodc.org/documents/middleeastandnorthafrica/organised-crime/united_nations_convention_against_transnational_organized_crime_and_the_protocols_thereto.pdf.

32 U.N. Office on Drugs and Crime, GAOR 58/4, *Convention Against Corruption*, New York, 31 October 2003, available from https://www.unodc.org/documents/brussels/UN_Convention_Against_Corruption.pdf.

2005 International Convention for the Suppression of Acts of Nuclear Terrorism[33]

2005 Protocol of 2005 to the Convention for the Suppression of Unlawful CTs Against the Safety of Maritime Navigation[34]

2010 Convention on the Suppression of unlawful Acts relating to International Civil Aviation[35]

It is also important to highlight the Security Council Resolutions pertaining to this study:

2001 United Nations Security Council Resolution 1373[36,37]
2004 United Nations Security Council Resolution 1566[38,39]
2014 United Nations Security Council Resolution 2170[40,41]
2014 United Nations Security Council Resolution 2178[42,43]

---

33 U.N., *International Convention for The Suppression of Acts of Nuclear Terrorism*, (2005), available from https://treaties.un.org/doc/db/Terrorism/english-18-15.pdf.

34 U.S. Dep't. of State, Bureau of International Security and Nonproliferation, *Protocol of 2005 to the Convention for the Suppression of Unlawful Acts Against the Safety of Maritime Navigation*, LEG/CONF.15/22, 1 November 2005, available from https://www.state.gov/t/isn/trty/81728.htm.

35 U.N., *Protocol Supplementary to the Convention for the Suppression of Unlawful Seizure of Aircraft*, Beijing, 10 September 2010, available from https://www.icao.int/secretariat/legal/Administrative%20Packages/Beijing_protocol_EN.pdf.

36 U.N. SCOR, *Resolution 1373*, S/RES/1373, 28 September 2001, available from http://www.un.org/en/sc/ctc/specialmeetings/2012/docs/United%20Nations%20Security%20Council%20Resolution%201373%20(2001).pdf.

37 The Security Council Resolution 1373 (2001) was adopted under Chapter 7 of the Charter and provided for the implementation of a Counter-Terrorism Committee.

38 U.N. SCOR, *Resolution 1566*, S/RES/1566, 8 October 2004, available from https://www.scribd.com/document/63963034/UNSCR-1566-2004.

39 The Security Council Resolution 1566 (2004) offers a potential description of "terrorism."

40 U.N. Meetings Coverage and Press Releases, *Security Council Adopts Resolution 2170 (2014) Condemning Gross, Widespread Abuse of Human Rights by Extremist Groups in Iraq, Syria*, SC 11520, 15 August 2014, available from http://www.un.org/press/en/2014/sc11520.doc.htm.

41 United Nations Security Council Resolution 2170 imposes the asset freeze, travel ban and arms embargo on six individuals associated with Al-Qaida, Islamic State in Iraq and the Levant.

42 U.N. SCOR, *Resolution 2178*, 24 September 2014, available from http://www.un.org/en/sc/ctc/docs/2015/SCR%202178_2014_EN.pdf.

43 United Nations Security Council Resolution 2178 deals with States affected by foreign Terrorist Fighters: including preventing inter-States travel ban by foreign terrorist fighters, law enforcement, terrorism-financing, regional and international cooperation and countering violent extremism, including social media.

Second, there is the list of current advisory tools provided by agencies and financial institutions relating to organized crime, corruption, and TF pertinent to this analysis:

1990 The FATF 40 Recommendations[44]

1997 Convention on Combating Bribery of Foreign Officials in International Business Transactions (OECD)[45,46]

2001 Basel Committee on Banking Supervision, Customer Due Diligence[47]

2002 Basel Committee on Banking Supervision, Sharing of financial records between jurisdictions in connection with the fight against terrorist financing[48]

2002 Wolfsberg AML Principles for Correspondent Banking[49]

2003 FATF Recommendations[50]

2003 Basel Committee on Banking Supervision, Consolidated KYC Risk Management[51]

2005 IMF Model Legislation on Money-laundering and Financing of Terrorism[52]

---

44 Financial Action Task Force (FATF) on Money-Laundering, *The Forty Recommendations*, (1990), available from http://www.fatf-gafi.org/media/fatf/documents/recommendations/pdfs/FATF%20Recommendations%201990.pdf.

45 Organisation for Economic Co-Operation and Development (OECD), *OECD Convention on Combating Bribery of Foreign Public Officials in International Business Transactions*, 17 December 1997, available from http://www.oecd.org/corruption/oecdantibriberyconvention.htm.

46 And related Documents (into force since 1999), revised recommendations were adopted in 2009.

47 Bank for International Settlements, *Customer Due diligence for banks—final document*, October 2001, available from http://www.bis.org/publ/bcbs85.htm.

48 Bank for International Settlements, *Sharing of Financial Records Between Jurisdictions in Connection with the Fight Against Terrorist Financing* (April 2002), http://www.bis.org/publ/bcbs89.htm.

49 Wolfsberg, *Anti-Money-Laundering Principles for Correspondent Banking*, (last visited 5 July 2014), http://www.wolfsberg-principles.com/pdf/standards/Wolfsberg-Correspondent-Banking-Principles-2014.pdf.

50 Financial Action Task Force (FATF) on Money-Laundering, *The Forty Recommendations*, 20 June 2003, available from http://www.fatf-gafi.org/media/fatf/documents/recommendations/pdfs/FATF%20Recommendations%202003.pdf.

51 Bank for International Settlements, *Consolidated KYC Risk Management—Consultative Document*, August 2003, available from http://www.bis.org/publ/bcbs101.htm.

52 U.N. Office on Drugs and Crime, *Model Legislation on Money-Laundering and Financing of Terrorism*, 1 December 2005, available from http://www.imf.org/external/np/leg/amlcft/eng/pdf/amlml05.pdf.

2008 The Wolfsberg Group on PEPs[53]

2009 IMF Model Provisions on Money-laundering, Terrorist Financing, Preventive Measures and Proceeds of Crime[54]

2011 IMF Compliance with the AML/CTF International Standard: Lessons from a cross country Analysis[55]

2012 FATF Recommendations[56]

2012 Revised Wolfsberg Principles[57]

2013 FATF International Best Practices[58,59]

2013 Methodology for assessing Compliance with the FATF Recommendations and the Effectiveness of AML/CTF Systems[60]

2014 Basel Committee on Banking Supervision, Sound Management of Risks related to Money-laundering and Financing Terrorism[61]

2015 FATF Report on Financing of the Terrorist Organization Islamic State in Iraq and the Levant (ISIL)[62]

---

53 Wolfsberg, *Frequently Asked Questions ("FAQ's")*, (last visited 5 July 2014), available from http://www.wolfsberg-principles.com/pdf/Wolfsberg_PEP_FAQs_(2008).pdf.

54 U.N. Office on Drugs and Crime, *Model Provisions on Money-Laundering, Terrorist Financing, Preventative Measures and Proceeds of Crime,* April 2009, available from http://www.imolin.org/pdf/imolin/Model_Provisions_Final.pdf.

55 Verdugo-Yepes, Concepcion, Compliance with the AML/CFT International Standard: Lessons from a Cross-Country Analysis, International Monetary Fund, July 2011, available from http://www.imf.org/external/pubs/ft/wp/2011/wp11177.pdf.http://www.imf.org/external/pubs/ft/wp/2011/wp11177.pdf.

56 Financial Action Task Force (FATF), *International Standards on Combating Money-Laundering and the Financing of Terrorism & Proliferation,* February 2012, http://www.fatf-gafi.org/media/fatf/documents/recommendations/pdfs/FATF_Recommendations.pdf.

57 Wolfsberg, *Anti-Money-Laundering Principles for Private Banking*, (last visited 5 July 2014), available from http://www.wolfsberg-principles.com/pdf/Wolfsberg-Private-Banking-Prinicples-May-2012.pdf.

58 Financial Action Task Force (FATF), *International Best Practices: Targeted Financial Sanctions Related to Terrorism and Terrorist Financing* (*Recommendation 6*), 2012, available from http://www.fatf-gafi.org/publications/fatfrecommendations/documents/bpp-fin-sanctions-tf-r6.html.

59 Targeted Financial Sanctions Related to Terrorism and Terrorist Financing (Recommendation 6).

60 Financial Action Task Force (FATF), *Methodology for Assessing Technical Compliance with the FATF Recommendations and the Effectiveness of AML/CFT Systems,* November 2017, available from http://www.fatf-gafi.org/media/fatf/documents/methodology/FATF%20Methodology%2022%20Feb%202013.pdf.

61 Bank for International Settlements, *Sound Management of Risks Related to Money-Laundering and Financing of Terrorism* (January 2014), http://www.bis.org/publ/bcbs275.htm.

62 Financial Action Task Force (FATF), *Report on Financing of the Terrorist Organization Islamic State in Iraq and the Levant* (ISIL), (2015), available from http://www.fatf-gafi.org/media/fatf/documents/reports/Financing-of-the-terrorist-organisation-ISIL.pdf.

2015 FATF Report on Emerging Terrorist Financing Risks[63]
2016 IMF Working Paper on Islamic Finance and Anti-money-laundering and Combatting the Financing of Terrorism[64]
2016 FATF Guidance on the criminalization of Terrorist Financing[65]

Third, the list of countries' most significant legislative contributions related to terrorism and TF, including the European Union Conventions consists of the following:

1990 Council of Europe's Convention on Laundering, Search, Seizure and Confiscation of the Proceeds from Crime[66]
1996 Commonwealth Model Law for the Prohibition of Money-laundering & Supporting Documentation[67]
1996 The Financial Transactions Reporting Act (New Zealand)[68]
1999 Organization of African Unity combating Terrorism[69]
1999 Convention of the Islamic Conference on Combating International Terrorism[70]
2000 UK Terrorism Act[71]

63 Financial Action Task Force (FATF), *Emerging Terrorist Financing Risks*, October 2015, available from http://www.fatf-gafi.org/media/fatf/documents/reports/Emerging-Terrorist-Financing-Risks.pdf.

64 Nadim Kyriakos-Saad et al., *Islamic Finance and Anti-Money-Laundering and Combating the Financing of Terrorism* (*AML/CFT*), 2016, available from https://www.imf.org/external/pubs/ft/wp/2016/wp1642.pdf.

65 Financial Action Task Force (FATF), *Criminalising Terrorist Financing* (*Recommendation 5*), October 2016, available from http://www.fatf-gafi.org/media/fatf/documents/reports/Guidance-Criminalising-Terrorist-Financing.pdf.

66 Council of Europe, Treaty Office, *Convention on Laundering, Search, Seizure and Confiscation of the Proceeds from Crime*, http://www.coe.int/web/conventions/full-list/-/conventions/treaty/141.

67 *Commonwealth Model Law for the Prohibition of Money-Laundering*, 1996, http://www.imolin.org/pdf/imolin/Comsecml.pdf.

68 Parliamentary Counsel Office, New Zealand Legislation, *Financial Transactions Reporting Act 1996, No 9*, 1 April 2017, available from http://www.legislation.govt.nz/act/public/1996/0009/latest/DLM373804.html.

69 Organization of African Unity, *Convention on the Prevention and Combating of Terrorism,* (*1999*), 14 July 199, available from http://treaties.un.org/doc/db/Terrorism/OAU-english.pdf.

70 Convention of the Islamic Conference on Combatting International Terrorism, available from www.oic-cdpu.org/en/getdoc/?dID=13.

71 Terrorism Act 2000, available from http://www.legislation.gov.uk/ukpga/2000/11/contents.

2001 Anti-terrorism, Crime and Security Act[72]
2001 USA Patriot Act[73]
2002 Inter-American Convention against Terrorism[74]
2002 UK Proceeds of Crime Act[75]
2002 Terrorism Suppression Act (New Zealand)[76]
2005 Council of Europe Convention on Laundering, Search, Seizure, and Confiscation of the Proceeds from Crime and on the Financing of Terrorism[77]
2005 Serious Organised Crime and Police Act[78]
2005 Third EU Directive[79]
2006 United Kingdom Terrorism Act[80]
2006 Anti-money-laundering and Counter-terrorism Financing Act (2006)[81]
2007 Australia, Anti-money-laundering and Counter-terrorism Financing Rules Instrument 2007 (No. 1)[82]

---

72 Anti-terrorism, Crime and Security Act, 2001, c. 24, http://www.legislation.gov.uk/ukpga/2001/24/pdfs/ukpga_20010024_en.pdf.

73 Financial Crimes Enforcement Network, *USA Patriot Act*, FinCEN.gov, (last visited 5 July 2014), https://www.fincen.gov/resources/statutes-regulations/usa-patriot-act.

74 U.N. GAOR, *Inter-American Convention Against Terrorism*, AG/RES 1840, 3 June 2002, available from http://www.oas.org/xxxiiga/english/docs_en/docs_items/AGres1840_02.htm.

75 Proceeds of Crime Act 2002, available from http://www.legislation.gov.uk/ukpga/2002/29/contents.

76 Terrorism Suppression Act 2002, No 34, 1 March 2017, available from http://www.legislation.govt.nz/act/public/2002/0034/latest/DLM151491.html.

77 Council of Europe Treaty Office *Council of Europe Convention on Laundering, Search, Seizure, and Confiscation of the Proceeds of Crime and on the Financing of Terrorism*, 15 May 2005, available from http://conventions.coe.int/Treaty/en/Treaties/Html/198.htm.

78 Serious Organised Crime and Police Act 2005, available from http://www.legislation.gov.uk/ukpga/2005/15/pdfs/ukpga_20050015_en.pdf.

79 European Union, *Directive 2005/60/EC of the European Parliament and of the Council of 26 October 2005 on the prevention of the use of the financial system for the purpose of money-laundering and terrorist financing*, 26 October 2005, available from http://eur-lex.europa.eu/legal-content/EN/TXT/?uri=CELEX%3A32005L0060.

80 Terrorism Act 2006, available from http://www.legislation.gov.uk/ukpga/2006/11/section/1

81 Australian Government Federal Register of Legislation, *Anti-Money-Laundering and Counter-terrorism Financing Act 2006 No. 169*, 2006, available from https://www.legislation.gov.au/Details/C2006A00169.

82 Australian Government Federal Register of Legislation, *Anti-Money-Laundering and Counter-Terrorism Financing Rules Instrument 2007 (No. 1)*, 10 April 2007, available from https://www.legislation.gov.au/Details/F2007L01000/Html/Text.

2008 UK Counter-terrorism Act[83]
2015 Fourth EU Directive[84]
2017 EU Directive on Combating Terrorism[85]
2017 The Parliament of the Commonwealth of Australia Anti-money-laundering and Counter-terrorism Financing Amendment Bill (2017)[86]
2018 Fifth EU Directive[87]

The three lists of current regulatory and advisory tools provided above will be reviewed and analyzed in this work in the context of TF. Further details about related topics encompassed by most of the existing tools will also be provided. It is important to cover these matters within a new convention model while considering the inclusion of topics such as privacy, civil liberties, asset freezing, confiscation of assets and asset recovery tools, as well as specific international cooperation and enforcement measures drawn from current counter-terrorism instruments. These extracts will be customized to best fit the new proposed CTF tool.

83 Counter-Terrorism Act 2008, c. 28, available from http://www.legislation.gov.uk/ukpga/2008/28/pdfs/ukpga_20080028_en.pdf.

84 European Union, *Directive (EU) 2015/849 of the European Parliament and of the Council of 20 May 2015 on the prevention of the use of the financial system for the purposes of money-laundering or terrorist financing, amending Regulation (EU) No 648/2012 of the European Parliament and of the Council, and repealing Directive 2005/60/EC of the European Parliament and of the Council and Commission Directive 2006/70/EC*, 20 May 2015, available from http://eur-lex.europa.eu/legal-content/EN/TXT/?uri=CELEX%3A32015L0849.

85 European Union, Directive (EU) *2017/541 of the European Parliament and of the Council of 15 March 2017 on combating terrorism and replacing Council Framework Decision 2002/475/JHA and amending Council Decision 2005/671/JHA*, 15 March 2017, available from https://eur-lex.europa.eu/legal-content/EN/TXT/PDF/?uri=CELEX:32017L0541&from=EN.

86 Anti-Money-Laundering and Counter-Terrorism Financing Amendment Bill 2017, available from http://parlinfo.aph.gov.au/parlInfo/download/legislation/bills/r5952_aspassed/toc_pdf/17177b01.pdf;fileType=application%2Fpdf.

87 European Union, *Directive (EU) 2018/843 of the European Parliament and of the Council of 30 May 2018 amending Directive (EU) 2015/849 on the prevention of the use of the financial system for the purposes of money-laundering or terrorist financing, and amending Directives 2009/138/EC and 2013/36/EU*, 30 May 2018, available from https://eur-lex.europa.eu/legal-content/EN/TXT/PDF/?uri=CELEX:32018L0843&from=EN.

CHAPTER 2

Can Terrorism Financing Be Detected?

Disassembling Terrorist organizations to prevent future terrorist attacks starts with detecting, tracking and dismantling the financial structure supporting these terrorist networks.[1] Funding is vital to terrorists' plots to support the existence and operations of their structures and networks. Some terrorists' acts do not require enormous amounts of money to be perpetuated. Trails of this type of financing can most often be located, tracked, and exploited to deter TF. To locate and follow the money, conduct productive investigations, and identify potential criminals and their accomplices, it is essential to find evidence of contribution and participation in illicit activity

This chapter will focus on understanding how money is found or donated and processed to achieve its end goal of financing a terrorist event or network and what main obstacles can prevent the monitoring process. This chapter is divided into three parts as follows.

Part A discusses the main differences between Terrorism Financing (TF) and Money-laundering (ML), explaining how they comprise similar types of schemes to collect and conceal illicit funds as well as their sources for supporting terrorist undertakings.

Part B provides a repertoire of general TF and ML techniques gathered from the 100 FIU ML cases provided by the Egmont Group and numerous financial institutions' reports.

Part C introduces the TF risks faced by financial institutions, as well as providing a comprehensive overview of TF Red Flags. A list of indicators of TF activities and evaluation of actions taken by FIUs is also provided.

In general, this chapter illustrates how financial support is collected by potential terrorists and their collaborators, whilst also highlighting the main problems encountered by financial institutions while trying to detect these TF activities.

---

1 John S. Pistole, *Terrorism Financing: Origination, Organization, and Prevention*, *FBI*, 2003, available from http://www.fbi.gov/news/testimony/terrorism-financing-origination-organization-and-prevention.

 DOI:10.1163/9789004409675_005

A The Links between Terrorism Financing and Anti-money-laundering

To understand how TF works, it is necessary to understand the regular money-laundering process. Money-laundering refers to converting money arising from criminal activities, so called "dirty money", into revenues that seem to originate from legitimate sources, to disguise the criminal origin of the money, thus making it more complicated to trace, i.e. "cleaning the money." The aim of effective ML is to hide criminals' participation or suppress their linkage to the money, and therefore to the perpetration of criminal activities to avoid prosecution and potential confiscation of launderers' profits. By laundering money, criminals can benefit from the proceeds of their crime and re-invest them into further criminal activities. The three stages of laundering money include placement, layering and integration. Launderers introduce the money from criminal activities into the financial system, layer the funds to hide their source and integrate the funds by bringing them back to the same account so that they seem to be coming from a legitimate source. They can also be integrated into legitimate businesses, other accounts or be used to fund for future crimes.[2]

Terrorism financing resembles traditional ML in that it involves using the three main stages of ML, i.e. placing, layering and integrating the money into the international financial system to conceal the source of the funds. It is taken that TF works like ML but in reverse. Terrorists and their accomplices use the same methods to acquire their funding. Organized criminals do the same to disguise their funds. Instead of placing, layering and integrating money to dissimulate criminal earnings as legitimate funds, as money-launderers do, terrorist financers integrate then layer both legitimate and illegitimate funds to disguise their origins, then, making use of them to perpetrate terrorism acts. Terrorist organizations' proceeds originate from a wide range of sources, usually coming from both legitimate and illicit sources of funding. That is, whilst ML funds are always of illegal origin, TF related funds can arise from both lawful and illegitimate sources. The principal objective of individuals and organizations financing terrorism is to disguise the nature and funding of their activities. Terrorist financers will want to cover the unlawful origin of the funds and still increase the profits for the sponsoring organization. Individuals involved in ML and TF schemes do not necessarily know the unlawful end of that income. Terrorists, just as petty criminals and organized criminal groups,

2 New Zealand Ministry of Justice, *Justice Sector & Policy*, available from http://www.justice.govt.nz/policy/criminal-justice/aml-cft/about.

rely on a specific infrastructure and network to assist them with the funding of their operations, to gather the equipment required and provide them with the services necessary for the end goal such as the laundering of the funds used in financing the terrorist activity or deriving from it.

There are two distinctive forms of TF with the first being financial support originating from donations, fundraising and community solicitation from individuals, organizations or states. The second form of TF comes from the income generated by various legal or illegal types of activities. Lawful activities include schemes such as real estate investments or merchandise trading, whilst unlawful ones include criminal activities like smuggling, fraud, kidnapping, and extortion.

The determining difference between ML and TF is that financial transactions are monitored and investigated differently, because the process is reversed. However, as many indicators between ML and TF overlap, determining the crime at stake and reporting it effectively in a SAR is a difficult task for a compliance officer. This can complicate the investigation work as the crime might not be reported correctly. ML investigations are aimed at linking the money to a criminal act that already took place and depriving the criminals and their accomplices from the profits they made from illicit activities. Whilst the purpose of TF investigations is to prevent crimes from taking place and to stop individuals from acquiring funds that could sponsor upcoming criminal activities. When monitoring potential terrorist financial transactions, a special focus should be put on the intentions of those engaging in those observed. Both AML and CFT approaches use the financial trail to detect the various components of the criminal or terrorist network. Both strategies aim at catching or stopping the criminal or terrorist organization through its financial activities. A strong mechanism should be in place to detect suspicious financial transfers and ensure proper detection of TF endeavours.

B Traditional Terrorism Financing Methods

Terrorist groups require capital to plan their operations and human capital, just as any start-up relies on equity and investment. For this, terrorist financers resort to diverse funding sources. Criminals and terrorists tend to operate in non-transparent worldwide business markets, where they can take advantage of close networks in vulnerable sites to earn, transfer, and collect their illicitly acquired assets as anonymously as possible. Most terrorist groups heavily depend on illegal activities to finance their operations. As previously mentioned in this chapter, there are three phases to disguising funds for financing terrorist activities. First, terrorist financers must earn assets and TF's income most often relates to lucrative crimes. Second, terrorists use schemes and structures that allow them to transfer, hide or launder their financial resources. Third, they use products that are bought and sold in businesses that are expected to sustain their price over time as well as being simple to purchase and trade in parallel to the traditional banking system.[3] Cash schemes, merchandising and movable assets laundering, wire transfers, both national and international, investments, white collar crimes, secret banking systems, private donations and charities, gaming and new payment technologies are the patterns discussed in Part B of this chapter so as to provide a general overview of the traditional techniques used by launderers and terrorist financers.

i) *Cash Schemes*

There are many ways to finance terrorist events, some of which are sophisticated and complicated. Whilst conventional money-laundering techniques are still predominant for acquiring funds, as explained earlier, the process works on reverse. Typical TF includes numerous traditional ML stratagems such as: cash withdrawals, cash smuggling, bulk cash, cash couriers, checks schemes, smurfing, and money mules, as well as a variety of alternative financing mechanisms that are used to earn, move and store terrorists' assets. The aim of these techniques is to mix dirty proceeds of crime with money of legal origin by using various financial transactions to insert the money into the regular financial system or to distribute the funds as discreetly as possible to avoid authorities' appraisal.

Currency smuggling is one of the oldest strategies for concealing money traceability for illegal purposes and is still prevalent in the case of TF. The aim of bulk cash smuggling is to evade financial transparency reporting requirements.[4] Currency smuggling consists of moving funds across borders to disguise their source and ownership by mail, courier or body packing by making use of a messenger or by international transport to pass on the dirty money to a country overseas in which money market regulations are less developed or offer secret banking. Examples of cash smuggling can be found internationally, most often linked to drug trafficking or other crimes, where money is exchanged against illegal business and services. In January 2018, a Jet Airways flight attendant was caught trying to smugly $500,000 in cash out of India to

3 U.S. GAO, *Terrorist Financing: U.S. Agencies Should Systematically Assess Terrorists' Use of Alternative Financing Mechanisms*, GAO-04-163, November 2003, available from http://www.gao.gov/new.items/d04163.pdf.

4 U.S. GAO, *Terrorist Financing: U.S. Agencies Should Systematically Assess Terrorists' Use of Alternative Financing Mechanisms*, GAO-04-163, November 2003, available from http://www.gao.gov/new.items/d04163.pdf.

Hong Kong.[5] The alleged handler collected money from metal dealers in Delhi and sent it via air hostess to foreign destinations. The money was then used to purchase gold abroad, which was then sent to India illegally. Cash can also be smuggled across borders in cars' glove departments, or through belts of cash attached to a person.

Terrorist organizations make use of bulk cash smuggling to move large amounts of currency as this money can easily be converted without a traceable paper trail. On the one hand, bulk cash smuggling avoids the involvement of third parties from financial institutions that might report the suspicious transaction, thus leaving the criminal with full control over the movement of the money. On the other hand, the drawbacks of this method are that cash smuggling entails the risk of courier loss or theft, as well as that of getting caught at customs border searches. Cash is also difficult to hide because of its weight. Despite the emergence of new ML/TF techniques, which never cease to evolve with time, means and technology, the use of 'bureaux de change' to smuggle cash across national borders to dispose of criminal proceeds and mask the origin and ownership of tainted funds continues to increase significantly.[6]

"Smurfing" or nominal partnership is known to be one of the easiest methods to collect money on the same account, to finance terrorist activities. It refers depositing small amounts every day at several financial institutions taking into account that each deposit should not exceed the legal reporting amount to the domestic government that would draw the attention of the banks. A high value transaction is thus split into numerous smaller ones. The money collected from these diverse institutions will then be successively transferred to a main central account.[7] This strategy is a team effort to avoid suspicion that involves several actors. Another ML/TF technique consists of exchanging transactions by purchasing foreign currency and transferring it to offshore accounts.[8]

ii) *Merchandising and Movable Assets Laundering*

Merchandise laundering has also been identified as another main source of illicit proceeds. Smuggling goods and contraband is often considered as one of the most frequently used ML/TF schemes. Selling merchandise that is

5 BBC News, *Jet Airways India Flight Attendant Held for Smuggling Money*, 9 January 2018, http://www.bbc.com/news/world-asia-india-42617388.

6 U.S. Dep't. of the Treasury, Financial Crimes Enforcement Network, (last visited 5 July 2015), http://www.fincen.gov/news_room/rp/advisory/html/advissu4.html.

7 New Zealand Ministry of Justice, *Justice Sector & Policy*, available from http://www.justice.govt.nz/policy/criminal-justice/aml-cft/about.

8 Justice Sector, *id.*

purchased by buyers out of the banking system masks the layers. The money collected therefore becomes clean. Terrorists acquire assets through illicit trade in various goods, such as: selling counterfeits; precious commodities smuggling, including diamonds, gold, jewellery and art treasures, weapons, cigarettes, oil, illicit drugs, commercial products/purchases, human beings and petty crime. Assets, such as real estate, cars, and boats are commonly bought with bulk cash with another identity, then sold back to deposit the now legitimately cleaned funds in someone else's account.[9] Illegal profits derived from drugs and cigarettes laundering represent another source of revenue for terrorists. In fact, cigarettes are commonly used as currency in many Eastern European countries according to a European Commission Anti-Fraud Office official.[10] Illegal Internet cigarette sales and the trade in counterfeit cigarettes therefore offer great opportunities to terrorism financers.

Terrorism financers want to smuggle bulk cash or convert their assets into commodities. For that matter, they resort to Money Mules to carry commodities which can be hidden and sold easily across borders without detection. Internationally traded assets that can be used as forms of currency, such as gold or diamonds are also preferred by terrorist financers as they are not bound by ordinary financial reporting requirements.[11]

Terrorists are mostly encouraged by ideological factors rather than profit itself. Financers may use legitimate systems to finance their activities, as well as illicit transactions involving assets they unlawfully acquired. Commodities smuggling, to be sold with a high profit margin is another source of funding for terrorists.[12] Terrorists store assets in cash or commodities, that can be used later on as forms of currency that are expected to retain value over longer periods of time. Commodities are easy to buy and sell outside the formal banking system. Trade-based money-laundering is the use of trade to legitimize, disguise, relocate, and convert huge quantities of illicit cash into assets and remains an efficient way to move assets or settle accounts.

Trade in diamonds, gold and gems are particularly attractive to terrorist organizations since they have money value, are easily hidden and transferred. Diamonds are often traded fraudulently by terrorists as they are easy to smuggle and because they are untraceable, of relatively low weight, and display high value. Smuggling routes for rough diamonds are well established, making diamonds a precious commodity to be passed on to countries that have permeable

9 Justice Sector, *supra.*
10 Justice Sector, *supra.*
11 Terrorist Financing, *supra.*
12 Terrorist Financing, *supra.*

borders and no rule of law. Diamonds are current means of payment for crimes and arms deals to purchase material required to accomplish future terrorist events.

Money arising from the sale of gold can easily be legalized, making gold purchase one of the most effective mechanisms to clean illegal money and finance terrorist activities. Although gold used in trade often has no valid paper trail, gold still grants an opportunity for moving terrorist assets by being smuggled through geographical borders as it can be altered and materialized in many forms to camouflage the item, then resold in form of bars, fragments or jewellery. Gold is also regularly used as a hedge against inflation.

Opportunities to legalize unlawful revenues can be accessed by legal export-import among different countries to cover the TF scheme, or by the barter trade system of commercial products. Terrorist organizations attempt to penetrate the classic economic flow system by exerting authority over substantially profitable industrial sectors such as the energy business and a range of industrial and commercial activities, natural resources and commodities. Agricultural products including wheat and barley as well as other natural resources such as oil, natural gas, phosphate, cement, sulphur also represent a prospect for terrorists to finance their activities without catching local authorities' attention.[13] Terrorist organizations get access to and control of roads to smuggle oil after covering their own energy needs and collect profit by selling the remaining oil at their disposal to the local black market and export crude oil and/or refined products.[14]

One of the oldest methods of money-laundering is the purchase of art treasures and jewellery. The money obtained through these items is displayed as legal, as if they were the estate of a deceased relative of the seller. Certificates can be obtained by selling the goods through auctions, covering the launderers' trails and making the valuable legitimately owned by the person selling it. Terrorist financers can purchase art treasures and jewellery at an auction, and resell them later to clear up the origin of money, then valuables can be sold at a higher price to collect money and sponsor future activities of their terrorist groups. Objects are also easy to transfer, smuggle and their value is deemed not to change over the years.

---

13 Jean-Charles Brisard & Damien Martinez, *Islamic State: The Economy-Based Terrorist Funding* (October 2014), http://cat-int.org/wp-content/uploads/2016/06/White-Paper-IS-Funding_Final.pdf.

14 Brisard, *id.*

iii) *Wire and International Transfers*

Terrorism financing activities also comprise: Wire transfers, International transfers, money remittance providers and money orders. International transfers are money transfers abroad made through traditional bank transfer money remitting services, internet payment services and bank accounts as well as e-currency. Wire transfers provide cash to financers that is easy to move. It is hard to disguise the traces in wire transfers schemes due to the transparency. According to Title 31 of the Code of Federal Regulations,[15] a wire transfer system is:

> a system through which an unconditional order to a bank to pay a fixed or determinable amount of money to a beneficiary upon receipt, or on a day stated in the order, is transmitted by electronic or other means through the network, between banks, or on the books of a bank.[16]

According to FinCEN, there are three wire transfer systems, namely: Fedwire, CHIPS, and S.W.I.F.T.[17] These systems offer the comparable features of a widely distributed network of users, high dollar value and real time systems. Wire transfers should be filtered for OFAC, CFSP and other lists algorithmically. Institutions check for ML/TF behaviours in those transactions, yet scrutiny may not be successful or effective. Fedwire rooms are not as closely monitored as cash transactions and the transactions are approved in a fast manner without the client having to state the purpose.[18]

Wire transfers, international transfers and money orders therefore strongly rest on the widespread use of reliable family and ethnic connections. Money orders are schemes often used by immigrant workers to transfer funds to their home countries and in those lacking secure banking systems, they can serve as capital to finance terrorist events.

---

15 Prohibition on Funding of Unlawful Internet Gambling, 31 C.F.R. §§ 132.2 (2012), available from https://www.law.cornell.edu/cfr/text/31/132.2.

16 U.S. Legal, *Wire Transfer System Law and Legal Definition*, (last visited 5 July 2014), http://definitions.uslegal.com/w/wire-transfer-system/.

17 Federal Reserve System Division of Banking Supervision and Regulation, *Bank Secrecy Act Examination Manual*, September 1997, available from http://www.federalreserve.gov/boarddocs/supmanual/bsa/7-00bsaman.pdf.

18 U.S. Dep't. of the Treasury, Financial Crimes Enforcement Network, *Notice to Customers: A CTR Reference Guide*, available from http://www.fincen.gov/whatsnew/pdf/CTRPamphletBW.pdf.

iv) *Investments*

Examples of investments representing major sources of cash flow for terrorist financers are: fictitious business organizations and transactions, shell companies, acquisitions of sports clubs or players and loans/financing tax evasions, real estate transactions, and also insurance frauds. It should be mentioned that the FATF glossary does not yet refer to taxation or excise evasion, although it is known to be a major source of illicit funds for criminals financing their activities.

Terrorists and their accomplices can finance their activities using fictitious transactions and establishing business organizations, with real business purposes and cash intensive branches (e.g. restaurants, money services, casinos), or even fictitious companies hiding their money transfers and origin. Companies used for these schemes might have no business activity, assets and/or liability apart from invoicing. These so-called shell companies' aim is to provide a motive for payments received by accomplices to cover the money trail, whereby these businesses retain numerous bank accounts in various countries. Thus, money flows into different locations making it hard to define its real origin.[19] Covering companies or phony companies are generally controlled by terrorists and launderers when owners are not easily identifiable. Cash allegedly deriving from the business's operations can be incorporated unnoticeably into the system since it derives from both revenues and expenses, or is simply "dirty money."

Booking data are frequently forged in such schemes and techniques of over/undercharging with false prices that do not reflect the market value offer criminals an open window to cash money to finance illicit activities without getting authorities' attention. Fictitious businesses' money can be provided or collected by outsiders, with no real link to the company, it being layered with third parties and therefore, disguising its origins. Companies can, at some point, get out of the business by selling it, thus making the revenue legal for the criminal selling the business. As abovementioned, the acquisition of sports clubs and the purchase and sale of professional sportsmen among various sport categories is also a way to move enormous amounts of funds and legalize it such that it can later be used to finance illicit actions or legalize dirty money.

Loans from banks, relatives, or even self-financing loans are investments that may be linked to TF and ML. In fact, loans are often referred to by criminals

---

19 Council of Europe, *Committee of Experts on the Evaluation of Anti-Money-Laundering Measures and the Financing of Terrorism*, available from http://www.coe.int/t/dghl/monitoring/moneyval/typologies/MONEYVAL(2012)6_Reptyp_flows_en.pdf.

in cases of investigation of sudden wealth. The dirty money can be transferred to a bank in another country, a financial haven, or invested into properties, businesses, or financial instruments. Some felons also clean money by using governmental institutions such as by making tax account overpayments. That is, when a person or company pays a large amount to the tax office that is not due. The administration will realize the "error" and it will send the money back to a legitimate bank account, thereby cleaning the money without a clue about the scheme's end purpose.

Real estate transactions and assuring real estate are stratagems frequently used by criminals to acquire extra money or clean their funds. Ownership of real estate, such as off-shore companies, often remains vague or anonymous. The money-laundered might therefore be invested later on into real estate. Increasing the real estate's value through renovation using that dirty money, will lead to a higher selling price and this is also a convenient way for criminals to earn extra cash in large amounts. An owner can also sell himself his estate with a different identity and when the transaction fails, retrieve the relatively big down payment he has invested in the purchase as clean money. Moreover, a real estate company could get an investment trust unit and guarantee interest payment for an investor, who might acquire credit only with difficulties. The investor will be covered by the insured real estate credit for the loan, and credit balance certificate, if the borrower could not perform his payment duty.

v) *White Collar Crimes*

White collar crimes, such as: tax, fraud, corporate crimes, corruption, bribery, intellectual property crimes and drug are commonly related with TF, as they facilitate the collection and movement of significant amounts of money. Extortion, kidnapping for ransom and political corruption are also substantially profitable activities for obtaining funds. Key sources of criminal proceeds also include corruption and bribery, including the embezzlement of public funds. Multinational companies owned by Western groups already operating in certain countries might be constrained by the payment of protection money to certain terrorist groups. This might be the only way to ensure the security of the enterprise in the foreign country. The company would therefore be participating in the financing of criminal endeavours and sponsoring future terrorist attacks. For instance, the Revolutionary Armed Forces of Colombia (FARC) have frequently used this scheme to finance their terrorist group's activities and demanded that international corporations pay protection money to remain in a secure business environment, while operating in their country.[20]

20 Brisard, *supra.*

vi) *Secret Banking Systems, Private Donations and Charities*

Various strategies to finance terrorism exist, they include secret banking systems, as well as private donations and the use of structures such as charitable organizations that collect large sums of money under the name of their charities to redistribute funds to terrorists. Alternative remittance systems, which are also called underground or parallel banking, are generally connected with ethnic groups from Africa, Asia, China, or the Middle East. These informal networks of remitters have different names depending on their country of origin, such as Hawala, Hundi, black market Peso exchange, "Poey Keran," "Chit System" and "Fei Ch'ien."[21] An alternative remittance network can be built among countries outside of the legitimate banking system to transfer value between them by using correspondent businesses in another country, such as an established shop. Businesses which are not principally involved in the money business such as nonbank money services businesses and other business entities are often involved in these unlawful structures. These businesses are frequently undocumented and unregulated. Typically built on an organized system of trust and close business contacts (family, tribal), coded information, such as receipts, couriers and faxes, are frequently used in this type of system followed by a confirmation of money transfers by telephone. Money-launderers or terrorist financers can then collect the money or value by providing a document, which carries the connected identifiable number related to the transaction. Secret banking systems have been established by criminal groups primarily due to political disorder and distrust in banks and habitually consist of transactions to isolated areas with no formal banking system or to countries with weak financial rules.

Some terrorist organizations use a well-known form of informal banking system referred to as hawala to move their assets. Hawala, comes from the Arabic language and means remittance or transfer. Within an informal banking system, funds are transferred with the purpose of collecting (in the same form or not) an equivalent value to be paid to a third party in another country. Regulatory policies and practices related to hawala and other alternative remittance systems are under review in most of the countries concerned by this system. While it is legal in some countries and perceived as a part of the "grey" economy, it constitutes an illegal AML/CTF scheme in others. The purpose of these activities is to avoid the financial regulations in place and to bring out the dirty and/or clean money from another country or to settle for goods purchased

21 International Centre for Asset Recovery, *Alternative Remittance Systems*, (last visited 5 July 2014), available from http://www.assetrecovery.org/kc/node/22849190-bd32-11dc-bb7d-ebf2eb5e792a.0;jsessionid=70C2FBB8CEDA3B036D3C64D31E733234.

abroad. Hawala offers a fast, cost-effective and less bureaucratic method than moving funds through officially recognized banking systems. Persons can move funds out of the reach of the traditional financial sector, making it a convenient way to finance operations for criminals desiring to remain in the shadow. In general, the hawala scheme is attractive to both legitimate and non-legitimate customers due to the lack of a paper trail and anonymity offered.

The system is non-transparent and liquid by nature, but since the market is two-directional, it can only function well if the countries have commercial contacts and their operations can balance over time. The hawala system has received close scrutiny by regulators and the international community since the terrorist events of September 11, especially since expatriates are believed to have accessed this informal banking system to finance them by sending money to relatives in their home country.[22] More recently, private and state sponsored donations, as well as institutional donations (principally from NGOs) coming from Gulf States, such as Saudi Arabia, Kuwait and Qatar, have contributed to raising funds to finance the terrorist activities of the Islamic State.[23]

Terrorist organizations have also earned funds using systems such as charitable organizations to move their assets, taking advantage of the industry's non-transparent nature. According to the Financial Action Task Force 2002–2003 Report on Money-laundering Typologies, some charitable organizations were established with a stated charitable purpose, yet are serving as a direct source of income to earn funds for terrorist organizations or could have been set up as a cover for moving funds to support international terrorist activities.[24] Charities, non-profit organizations and small cash-intensive businesses are the most predominant legitimate sources of reported fund raising and donations linked to terrorism-financing.[25] Funds can be used with or without the knowledge of the donor or charitable organization. Yet, they offer a ready source of substantial funds collected between people sharing from similar ethnic, religious, or geographic backgrounds, or with similar interests and values. In some countries, charitable giving is a religious duty.[26] Moreover, terrorists can exploit contributions that are originally intended for legitimate humanitarian purposes due to lack of controls by international

---

22 Terrorist Financing, *supra*.

23 Brisard, *supra*.

24 Terrorist Financing, *supra*.

25 Financial Action Task Force (FATF), *Global Money-Laundering & Terrorist Financing Threat Assessment*, July 2010, http://www.fatf-gafi.org/media/fatf/documents/reports/Global%20Threat%20assessment.pdf.

26 Terrorist Financing, *supra*.

authorities to make sure donations are used according to their intended purpose.

vii) *Gambling*

Gambling in casinos, amusement arcades, gambling machines, the purchase of a winning lottery ticket and horse-races or even greyhound races provide criminals with a great alibi to disguise money's source when authorities ask about its origin. Casino owners can be implicated in the financing schemes since criminals can agree with them to falsify prize certificates to a higher amount. This explains why some criminal organizations decide to purchase their own casino to avoid negotiations with casino owners. Criminals can also increase their proceeds through casinos by gambling part of their money and redeeming the rest of their chips in form of a casino cheque or transfer.[27] As the declaration of income originating from amusement arcades and gambling machine operations is made by estimation, funds are less easy to keep track of.[28] Launderers can make animal racing bets with dirty money for all probable outcomes and redeem more money than the prize, thus obtaining a "cleaned" legal earning.

viii) *New Payment Technologies*

The emergence of new payment technologies is increasing fast, in response to online purchases through the internet's demand and supply. Online intermediaries can fund others' accounts or facilitate payments with wire transfers, money orders, cash, or credit cards. Criminals are now using the cyberspace to move and clean their funds. Internet payment services, on-line banking, e-cash, virtual money/e-currency, digital precious metals (e-gold/silver), on-line gaming, on-line auction, on-line football pool sides, virtual casinos, and purchases through the internet are becoming increasingly menacing for TF investigators, as they are more difficult to detect than other TF methods. Numerous jurisdictions have denoted the proliferation of internet-based frauds.[29] Access to online services and bank accounts represents a great opportunity for criminals since it is almost impossible to track communication access and utilization as it could involve public terminals like in a library or an internet café, for example. Nowadays, creating an email or opening an online account is

---

27 Justice Sector, *supra.*

28 Financial Action Task Force (FATF), *Money-Laundering Using New Payment Methods*, October 2010, available from http://www.fatf-gafi.org/media/fatf/documents/reports/ML%20using%20New%20Payment%20Methods.pdf.

29 Wojciech Filipkowski, *Cyber Laundering: An Analysis of Typology and Techniques*, 3.1 Int. J. Crim. Just. Sci., 15–27, 2008, available from http://www.sascv.org/ijcjs/wojciech.html.

becoming an easy task for skilled lawbreakers, who can take advantage of free and anonymous services without personal contact.

Illegal purchases through the Internet are often used at the integration or layering stage of financing schemes. These purchases include illegal items, phony pharmaceutical products, as well as escort services, child pornography, online gambling, firearms, prescription drugs, tobacco sales, or stolen credit cards. On-line auction sites are also preferred tools for launderers and terrorist financers to purchase or sell expensive goods. Gambling in virtual casinos, on-line football pools, as well as internet games, provide an anonymous way for launderers to finance terrorist activities. These can be performed at any place in the world and they exploit the lack of regulation in this domain. Moreover, virtual money is accessible and can be easily transferred from any location worldwide, making it hard to trace for international authorities.

Mobile payments, prepaid cards, stored value cards, smart cards, as well as gambling, and lotteries are also closely studied by international organizations, offering ML/TF recommendations. There are different ways to misuse mobile payment services and to finance terrorist activities including the use of prepaid mobile accounts, which function the same way as prepaid cards and electronic purses. Mobile payments can be exploited as an extension of old-fashioned payment methods as mobile phones can provide access to online accounts and a means for transactions from payment cards or current bank accounts as well as for securities accounts services. Mobile devices can be used as a typical pre-paid card since money can be deducted from the telephone owner's prepaid account just like a credit/debit card. There are two kinds of transactions, pre-paid ones or those charged directly to the phone's bill.

Smart Money is the mobile prepaid payment of services ordinarily co-branded by banks and telecom providers. Regarding it, payments are approved against a prepaid account at the partner bank from the mobile provider or can be linked to Master Card accounts and it is thus possible to use Smart Money prepaid cards to transfer money abroad. In the case of TF, criminals can send money to cross-border relatives, who can then collect cash from an ATM. Tele-com companies can be used as an intermediary to function without a bank partner where monies are transmitted using G-cash. There are various ways to utilize mobile phones to launder money or finance terrorist activities, but it seems obvious that this is a non-exhaustive list that might include other strata-gems which will be invented by criminals in the future as technology evolves fast.

The distinction between ML and TF techniques seems quite ambiguous. However, Money-Laundering schemes shall be used to earn and pass on mon-ey to finance terrorists in a discrete manner. Typical laundering activities help terrorist financers to collect and disguise funds even when the money originally comes from a legitimate owner or business. As for the illegitimately acquired funds, they frequently derive from activities that are similar to/part of organized criminals' activities, which explains the similitude in the financing *modus operandi*. It is necessary to comprehend the above cited methods used by criminals and terrorists to finance unlawful events to discover potential gaps in the system and threats linked to these specific activities.

C Terrorism Financing Risks Faced by Financial Institutions

Financial institutions face multiple threats dealing with terrorist financers. The main concern of such institutions is to be accused of being accomplices of TF by local law authorities, resulting in possible fines, loss of reputation, degraded image and potential company shutdown. These reasons signal the need for enhanced due diligence and continuous awareness of the clues leading to the belief that TF might arise from a certain transaction or product.

According to the *International Standards on Combating Money-Laundering and the Financing of Terrorism & Proliferation* provided by the Financial Action Task Force[30] in 2012, financial institutions should detect and evaluate the money-laundering or terrorism-financing risks that could arise owing to:

> ...the development of new products and new business practices, including new delivery mechanisms, and the use of new or developing technologies for both new and pre-existing products.[31]

The FATF 2012 Report also states that financial institutions should take appropriate measures to manage and mitigate risks related to the launch of new products, business practices or the use of new or developing technologies and fulfil appropriate risk assessment.[32]

The Australian Anti-money-laundering and Counter-terrorism Financing Rules Instrument 2007 (No. 1) provides 11 examples of risks faced by a financial institution linked to TF, which are:

---

30 Financial Action Task Force (FATF), *International Standards On Combating Money-Laundering and the Financing of Terrorism & Proliferation*, February 2012, http://www.fatf-gafi.org/media/fatf/documents/recommendations/pdfs/FATF_Recommendations.pdf.

31 FATF (2012c), *supra*.

32 FATF (2012c), *supra*.

1. The nature of the other financial institution's business, including its product and customer base;
2. The domicile of the other financial institution;
3. The domicile of any parent company of the other financial institution;
4. The existence and quality of any anti-money-laundering and counter-terrorism financing regulation in the other financial institution's country of domicile;
5. The existence and quality of any anti-money-laundering and counter-terrorism financing regulation in the country of domicile of any parent company of the other financial institution—where the parent company has group-wide controls and where the other financial institution operates within the requirements of those controls;
6. The adequacy of the other financial institution's controls and internal compliance practices in relation to anti-money-laundering and counter-terrorism financing;
7. The ownership, control and management structures of the other financial institution and any parent company, including whether a politically exposed person has ownership or control of the other financial institution or any parent company;
8. The other financial institution's financial position;
9. The reputation and history of the other financial institution;
10. The reputation and history of any parent company of the other financial institution;
11. Whether the other financial institution has been the subject of an investigation, or any criminal or civil proceedings relating to money-laundering or terrorism-financing.[33]

i) *CTF Red Flags*

According to FinCEN of the U.S. Department of the Treasury, when a single factor signals that a transaction is unusual and possibly "suspicious," it is called a "red flag." TF reds flags have been under review by many international players involved in CTF, which provide knowledge derived from the extensive databank of case studies on the field and by dealing with professionals. It is crucial for financial institutions to recognize the signs of possible ML and TF schemes, although the existence of a red flag is not necessarily evidence of criminal activity. Management's task is not to determine whether the transactions are to

33 Australian Government Federal Register of Legislation, *Anti-Money-Laundering and Counter-Terrorism Financing Rules Instrument 2007 (No. 1)*, 10 April 2007, available from https://www.legislation.gov.au/Details/F2007L01000/Html/Text.

do with money-laundering, terrorist financing, or a particular crime and/or the occurrence of an insurance specific designated offence.[34] When encountering red flags during a transaction or customer interaction, CTF professionals should undertake additional scrutiny and report the suspicious activity so that competent authorities can focus on conducing further investigations to determine whether the activity is suspicious, and discover this activity's business or legal purpose. According to internal procedures, when an employee of the firm detects a suspicious activity, he or she will notify the compliance representative within the firm. The company's AML compliance supervisor will decide whether or not the activity is suspicious and if so, how to investigate the case by gathering additional information internally or from third-party sources, contacting the government, freezing the account and/or filing a SAR-SF.[35]

Suspicious indicators and red flags might not be applicable to all jurisdictions, but are provided to deliver to the private sector, law enforcement and regulators a general idea of the types of activities that can be mistrustful. Account openings, payment and settlement of premiums, special types of transaction and product, claims, risk enhancing factors, and post-inception of policy are general categories of financial transactions that represent major risks of including red flags and ML/TF potentially suspicious activities indicators.[36] According to FINRA, red flags that signal possible ML or TF include, but are not limited to: customers' insufficient or suspicious information, efforts to avoid reporting and recordkeeping, certain fund transfer activities, certain deposits or dispositions of physical certificates, certain securities transactions, transactions involving penny stock companies, transactions involving insurance products, activity inconsistent with business and other suspicious customer activity.[37] Another popular scheme for avoiding reporting or recordkeeping requirements is to use multiple persons or locations so as to break one transaction into two or more. Customers conducting transactions just below

---

34 Federal Financial Institutions Examination Council, *Bank Secrecy Act/Anti-Money-Laundering Examination Manual*, available from https://www.ffiec.gov/bsa%5Faml%5Finfobase/pages_manual/manual_online.htm.

35 Financial Industry Regulatory Authority (FINRA), *Anti-Money-Laundering Template for Small Firms*, 1 Jan. 2010, available from http://www.finra.org/industry/anti-money-laundering-template-small-firms.

36 Council of Europe, Committee of Experts on the Evaluation of Anti-Money-Laundering Measures and the Financing of Terrorism, 30 January 2018, available from http://www.coe.int/web/moneyval.

37 FINRA, *supra*.

relevant thresholds or using two or more locations or cashiers in the same day in order to break one transaction, as well as clients offering bribes or tips, or openly acknowledging criminal conduct, are current suspicious activity indicators and should be closely watched or reported.[38]

ii) *Cases from FIU Reports*

The "FIU's In Action report" is the product of an initiative by the Egmont Group to gather 100 cases from amongst its members that display indicators of TF activities and actions considered or taken by FIUs as a result of these red flags. The main categories of indicators of TF contained in the report are: concealment within business structures, misuse of legitimate businesses, use of false identities, documents, straw men, exploitation of international jurisdictional issues, the use of anonymous asset types and the effective use of intelligence exchanges. In cases where several indicators occur, it could be concluded that these indicators may be a warning sign of unusual activity linked to ML or TF, yet the listed activities may not necessarily be indicative of a patent crime, but rather, simply the customer's legitimate business transactions. The FIU's in action report is a comprehensive list of Red Flags which is the product of an initiative by the Egmont Group to gather 100 cases from their entity that displays indicators of Terrorist Financing activities and actions considered or taken by FIUs. Examples of these red flags can be found in Annex 2 "FIU's in action," 100 cases from the Egmont Group.

According to the "FIU's In Action report", actions taken by FIUs to respond to terrorism-financing indicators consist of: cross referencing with national and international law enforcement data bases; document business history, a document timeline showing opening and closing of "representative" office; exchange of intelligence with foreign FIUs or with other FIUs through Egmont, liaising with foreign FIUs to recover citizens' funds, examining financial records for evidence of fund movement or for signs of travel expenses, as well as potential clues to the help locating suspects. FIUs have identified assets of suspects and possible fraud techniques. Identification of related business interests by targets or false documentation has also been examined. The re-emergence of a known financial criminal in the financial services sector or a likely jurisdiction to be used for fund destination are considered to be TF

38 U.S. Dep't. of the Treasury, Financial Crimes Enforcement Network, *Red Flags,* (last visited 5 July 2015), available from http://www.fincen.gov/financial_institutions/msb/materials/en/prevention_guide.html#Red Flags.

indicators.[39] The cases highlighted by the Egmont "FIU's In Action report" demonstrates that money frequently crosses national borders, which underlines the importance of intelligence and international cooperation in correctly tracing criminal money flows.

39 FIUs in Action, *100 Cases from the Egmont Group*, (last visited 5 July 2014), http://www.u4.no/recommended-reading/fius-in-action-100-cases-from-the-egmont-group/.

CHAPTER 3

Existing Compliance Measures to Prevent Terrorism Financing

The aim of Chapter 3 is to identify existing CTF compliance measures worldwide. Since the observed countries comprise different CTF initiatives and rely upon diverse penalties and procedures, only general tools will be discussed in this chapter. This chapter is divided into two parts as follows.

Part A describes how institutions model terrorism-financing risk by reviewing Counter-terrorism risk models, risk-assessment and risk-based supervision. In this part, internationally used tools for identifying, reporting and preventing TF worldwide are presented, including: customer due diligence, know your customer procedures, customer identification programs, enhanced due diligence for politically exposed persons, currency transaction reports, national security letters and suspicious activity reports.

Part B introduces the Egmont Group and explains the purpose of financial intelligence units (FIUs) worldwide. Later, Chapter 11 will provide proposals for enhancements to strengthen FIUs' work and thus, accomplish better TF monitoring amongst nations.

This chapter describes the compliance measures already in place for CTF and the actors in charge of prevention.

A Internationally Used Tools to Detect and Report TF

Increased globalization of business operations requires an international cross sectorial effort to recognize and monitor ML and TF operations. That is, it is important to identify and apprehend terrorist financers and TF entities. The effectiveness of CTF tools relies on their identification and the reporting guidelines provided to CTF specialists, and in the adoption and implementation of comprehensive CDD policies, and procedures. Without suitable due diligence provided towards new and existing customers, banks could face operational, reputational, and legal risks, which might result in substantial financial costs.[1] Customer Due Diligence (CDD), Suspicious Activity Reports (SARs), Currency

1 Bank for International Settlements, *Sharing of Financial Records Between Jurisdictions in Connection with the Fight Against Terrorist Financing* (April 2002), http://www.bis.org/publ/bcbs89.htm.

 | DOI:10.1163/9789004409675_006

Transaction Reports (CTR) and National Security Letters (NSL) are current procedures used under different names in most countries to prevent ML/TF. Comparison with Governments' Terrorist lists is also required to spot terrorism-financing. Reports should be made to local FIUs or law enforcement authorities when there is reasonable suspicion. Enhanced Due Diligence (EDD) works as a determining factor, especially in the case of politically exposed persons that have the means to finance crime. Their ideology and power could constitute a main threat that should be closely monitored.

Current compliance measures operating worldwide, such as Customer Identification programs (CIPs), require Financial Institutions (FIs) to ascertain whether a potential or existing customer is on any federal government list of known or suspected terrorists or Specially Designated Nationals (SDNs). This should be done within a reasonable timeframe after an account is requested, preferably before it is opened and at least, soon after. FIs should also check the OFAC list, which includes groups, entities and companies owned, controlled by, or acting on behalf of individuals suspected of being terrorists or narcotics traffickers in targeted countries. It is prohibited to deal with SDNs, regardless of their location and all their assets should be blocked. The OFAC Specially Designed Nationals and Blocked Persons List comprises approximately 5,500 names linked with sanctions targets and also keeps additional sanctions lists with other prohibitions.[2] There is an overlap between the SDN lists from various nations and sometimes a person can appear on one list and not another. Hence, these should be accessed regularly to ensure the validity of the information collected on a particular individual.

i) *How Institutions Model Terrorism Financing Risk*

The most important thing to consider before implementing specific CTF measures, is to determine how institutions model the risk itself and which models they would like to follow to deter CTF. Risk assessment and risk supervision also plays a key role to understand the strengths and weaknesses of risk models already in place at the institutional level.

a Counter-terrorism Risk Models

A risk-based approach to combating the financing of terrorism, according to the FATF means:

> ...that countries, competent authorities and financial institutions, are expected to identify, assess and understand the Money-laundering/

2 U.S. Dep't. of the Treasury, *Resource Center*, 15 March 2017, available from https://www.treasury.gov/resource-center/sanctions/Programs/Pages/faq_10_page.aspx.

> Terrorism Financing risks to which they are exposed and take AML/CTF measures commensurate to those risks in order to mitigate them effectively.[3]

The Basel Committee on Banking Supervision underlined the importance of the directing of ML/TF risk assessments within its 2014 "Sound Management of Risks related to Money-laundering and Financing of Terrorism" document. Per the Basel Committee:

> Sound risk management requires the identification and analysis of ML/TF risks within the bank and the design and effective implementation of policies and procedures that are commensurate with the identified risks. In conducting a comprehensive risk assessment to evaluate ML/TF risks, a bank should consider all the relevant inherent and residual risk factors at the country, sectoral, bank and business relationship level, among others, in order to determine its risk profile and the appropriate level of mitigation to be applied.[4]

The Risk-Based Approach (RBA) is fundamental, because it recognizes the wide variability among countries' potential exposure to TF and calls on country-level policy makers to identify, assess, and understand their own specific risks. The RBA is particularly critical in the crafting of a financial inclusion friendly AML/CTF regime as it affords the flexibility to tailor risk mitigation policies to the specific nature, levels, and types of relevant risk of concern to the AML/CTF regime, as required to apply it. The starting point of the RBA is the risk assessment of AML/CTF to determine those faced by the bank or financial institution. Institutions should implement close monitoring of higher risk customers' profile, products and services, as well as the geographies the bank has business with, depending on the type of risks detected.

The FATF confirms that this exercise should be performed and described in the BSL/AML risk assessment:

> when assessing ML/TF risks, countries, competent authorities and financial institutions should analyze and seek to understand how ML/TF risks they identify affect them; the risk assessment therefore provides the basis

3 Financial Action Task Force (FATF), *Guidance for a Risk-Based Approach: The Banking Sector*, October 2014, available from http://www.fatf-gafi.org/media/fatf/documents/reports/Risk-Based-Approach-Banking-Sector.pdf.

4 Bank for International Settlements, *Sound Management of Risks Related to Money-Laundering and Financing of Terrorism* (January 2014), http://www.bis.org/publ/bcbs275.htm.

> for the risk-sensitive application of Anti Money-laundering/Combating Terrorism Financing measures.[5]

The application of the RBA to transaction monitoring scenarios can be achieved by taking specific measures to manage false positive alerts of low-risk customers better, thereby being able to allocate more time to reviewing potential positive alerts.

It must be clear that this risk-based approach does not exempt the FIs from implementing controls to mitigate low risks identified in the risk assessment, as explained by FATF in the Guidance for a risk-based approach to the banking sector:

> a risk based approach does not exempt countries, competent authorities and financial institutions from mitigating Money-laundering/Terrorism Financing risks where these risks are assessed as low.[6]

b Risk Assessment

To apply a risk-based approach to AML/CTF monitoring, it is essential to evaluate risk elements as additional parameters to the AML/CTF detection scenarios. The first part of risk-assessment is to determine risks related to clients, products and services, countries and channels. The second phase when assessing threats to the company, is to evaluate its internal control environment including risk assessments, policies and procedures, such as KYC, CDD, EDD, SAR, controls, training as well as other management information and record-keeping/retention requirements. The third phase is to align the residual risk with strategical and tactical actions, along with risk appetite.

The three key issues FIs need to look at through a systematic approach to risk assessment are: geographical risk, business and entity risk along with product and transaction risk. Risk factors frequently include the nature, scale, and complexity of the business, distribution channels, jurisdictional and regulatory issues, size of transactions, target markets as well as the number and profile of the customers. To determine whether stronger measures are required, risk should be computed by assigning specific scores to each known factor and when the total is a high count, additional scrutiny and actions must be considered.

---

5 Financial Action Task Force (FATF), *Guidance for a Risk-Based Approach: The Banking Sector* October 2014, available from http://www.fatf-gafi.org/media/fatf/documents/reports/Risk-Based-Approach-Banking-Sector.pdf.

6 FATF (2014), *supra*.

Risk assessment is essential to arrive at a comprehensive understanding of a bank's ML/TF risk setting. Financial institutions covered by CTF regimes apply the RBA per the 2012 FATF recommendations. The risk assessment conducted will depend on the level of risk of the countries in which the company operates, the given market's specific nature as well as the levels and types of relevant risk. Despite it being challenging and costly in nature, RBA affords the flexibility to tailor risk mitigation policies. The aim of applying an RBA is to identify high risk situations and cope with them accordingly, where regular recommendations from FATF might not be secure enough. Countries with lower identified risks can adopt less restrictive measures than required by the FATF AML/CTF measures. To mitigate TF risks, countries should require FIUs and DNPBPs to detect and evaluate existing risks to deter them. Risk indicators resulting from the sum of the risk management/risk-based approach comprise: client base stability, integration of IT systems, expected account/client growth, expected revenue growth, recent compliance employee turnover, reliance on a third party, recent/planned acquisitions, recent/planned introductions of new products and/or services, national risk assessment, recent relevant enforcement actions, recent projects and initiatives related to compliance matters.

The results of the sum of the risk management/risk-based approach are indispensable in numerous areas of TF prevention including identifying and remedying gaps in AML/CTF policies, procedures and controls, to decide on the development and formulation of risk appetite and on the implementation of control efforts, allocation of resources etc. It also supports ensuring senior management is up to date with what the key risks are, control gaps, and remediation efforts, while facilitating the key decision makers with strategic decision-making associated with entering or exiting certain markets or sectors. The results also ensure that regulators are attentive to risks, controls gaps and remediation efforts, as well as assisting senior management to warrant that resources and priorities are aligned with encountered risks

c Risk-Based Supervision

A few risk-based supervisory models exist, yet no specific model is known to be obligatory regarding International Advisory Institutions' standards. The aim of an effective RBS model is to enumerate potential ML/TF risks faced by the financial sector and to provide mitigatory perspectives, while offering proper communication and coordination mechanisms with related authorities and supervisory agencies. AML/CFT supervision can form part of the wide-ranging supervision or it can be separate. The Council of Europe's perspective distinguishes four types of risks that should be supervised: countries risk, customers, transactions/products/services, and levels of compliance. Country risks should incorporate a list of high-risk or non-cooperative countries or jurisdictions identified by the FATF. Countries against which the UN, the EU or other regional or international organizations have imposed sanctions or restrictive measures are also to be closely watched by compliance supervisors. The number and types of customers an entity works for determines the level of ML/FT risk applicable and certain types of customers can increase the ML/TF risk. Companies with more complex structures, including non-residents, customers from high-risk countries and private banking clients are frequently perceived as high-risk, while small enterprises and domestic retail should be inherently less risky for risk-based supervisors. The types of transactions, services and products offered by an entity can be varied and diverse. Moreover, anonymity represents a high-risk of being used for ML/TF with non-face to face transactions. Cash intensive products and services, as well as international transactions are also deemed potentially riskier than other types. Finally, the compliance level is determined by policies, internal controls and procedures, which should be adequate and implemented, whereby employees must be made well-aware of risks.

ii) *Identification*

Identification instruments include mechanisms such as: customer due diligence, know your customer procedures, as well enhanced due diligence related to PEPs and customer identification programs. The importance of identification is to prevent financial institutions from being abused by criminals, who use or attempt to use, the bank's products and services for illicit purposes, thereby adhering to safe and sound banking practices.

a Customer Due Diligence (CDD)

Effective CDD policies, procedures, and processes refers to the efforts required to understand a customer's profile and the expected activity given his or her occupation or business operations. For the aim should be to predict their behavior and consists of verifying customers' identities by collecting identification evidence (such as a national identification card, a passport, utility bills, etc.). By assessing the risks associated with customers, the bank can consequently forecast the kinds of transactions a customer is expected to participate in.[7] Information gathered by the bank during the CDD procedure helps the

7 Federal Deposit Insurance Corporation fdic, Bank Secrecy Act and Anti-Money-Laundering, 20 February 2009, available from http://www.fdic.gov/regulations/examinations/bsa/index.html.

bank distinguish between lower-risk customers and higher-risk customers starting with the account opening. CDD procedures contribute to the detection of potentially suspicious transactions. Specifically, CDD is a framework that assists banks in monitoring their lower-risk customers by complying with regulatory requirements and to report suspicious activity. Any change relevant to the customer's risk profile, such as unexpected account activity, a change in business operation or a different work activity, should be considered to reassess the customer risk rating. Senior management approval is often required to decide whether the requirements are met and the client can keep a relationship with the financial institution after verification of the source of wealth and the source of the funds involved.

In the event of potential TF activities being spotted, EDD should be carried out as the risks associated with a customer are high, that depending on the industry he works in, the country he transacts in, or if he is a politically exposed person. Verification requirements differ among countries' procedures. The United States Federal Financial Institutions Examination Council's Bank Secrecy Act Anti-money-laundering Examination Manual recommends that during a CDD evaluation concerning businesses, banks should collect, both at account opening and during the relationship, pertinent information regarding their customers, including the reason for opening this account, the source of wealth of the client, occupation or type of business, beneficial owners, signatories or guarantors, financial statements, banking references, domicile and proximity to the bank. A description of the customer's business operations, its anticipated volume of currency and total sales, as well as a list of major customers and suppliers he or she deals with and whether international transactions are expected frequently, should be part of the CDD process for banks. Clients should also explain changes in any account activity.[8] As due diligence is an ongoing process, banks should take all appropriate measures to ensure account profiles are current, and that monitoring respects high-risk standards. They should determine the riskiness of a client based on his or her customers' business activities, volume and type of transactions.

b Know Your Customer (KYC)

Know your customer, is the procedure for identifying customers based on guidelines aiming at preventing banks from being exploited by criminals

8 Federal Financial Institutions Examination Council, *Bank Secrecy Act/Anti-Money-Laundering Examination Manual*, available from https://www.ffiec.gov/bsa%5Faml%5Finfobase/pages_manual/manual_online.htm.

deliberately or involuntarily for ML or TF purposes. Financial institutions, sellers, intermediaries and insurance companies should make sure they have made reasonable effort to take the necessary steps provided by guidelines to identity beneficial ownership of accounts, source of funds, the nature of the customer's business, and the relationship between operations in the account and the customer's business. Identity and address are key components of KYC and should be frequently updated in the financial institutions' records.

c Enhanced Due Diligence (EDD)

Enhanced due diligence should apply to higher-risk customers that pose higher ML or TF threats. Accordingly, banks' procedures and due diligence policies need to be enhanced, for this is crucial to identifying any anticipated transactions carrying future terrorist impact. Customers' documentation should be reviewed carefully at the opening of any high-risk account and ought to be revised later, following enhanced regular monitoring procedures over the term of the relationship between the customer and the bank.[9]

According to the U.S. Bank Secrecy Act, EDD is:

> A rigorous and robust process of investigation over and above (KYC) procedures, that seeks with reasonable assurance to verify and validate the customer's identity; understand and test the customer's profile, business and account activity; identify relevant adverse information and risk assess the potential for money-laundering and / or terrorist financing to support actionable decisions to mitigate against financial, regulatory and reputational risk and ensure regulatory compliance.[10]

Even though EDD has not been internationally defined, the USA PATRIOT Act provides that institutions:

> ...shall establish appropriate, specific, and, where necessary, enhanced, due diligence policies, procedures, and controls that are reasonably designed to detect and report instances of money-laundering through those accounts.[11]

---

9 FFIEC, *supra*.

10 Federal Deposit Insurance Corporation FDIC, *Bank Secrecy Act*, (last visited Jul 5, 2014), FDIC, http://www.fdic.gov/regulations/examinations/bsa/bsa_13.html.

11 U.S. Patriot Act, *SEC. 312*, (last visited 5 July 2014), http://ithandbook.ffiec.gov/media/resources/3356/con-usa_patriot_act_section_312.pdf.

Hence, EDD should comprise the designation of a compliance officer, ongoing training for employees, AML/CTF audit procedures, suspicious activity reporting requirements and CDD procedures.[12] EDD measures can apply to private banking, correspondent account, and offshore banking institutions. Unfortunately, as regulatory definitions differ among countries and their jurisdictions, they remain inconsistent.

d Politically Exposed Persons (PEPs)

1 *Defining PEPs*

A PEP is a banking term used to manage the risks associated with customers belonging to a specific category defined through the bank's practice or international regulatory instruments that might have the capacity to move, hide or store money. These specific customers might do so, with or without knowledge monies or assets are associated with: corruption, money-laundering or terrorism-financing. Identifying PEP customers is a substantial part of all banks' AML controls.[13] Specific precautions should be taken by them in the assessment of risk when opening and managing private banking accounts associated with a PEP.[14]

PEPs are known to be Natural Persons and the definition of PEPs differs from one source to another as there is no internationally agreed-upon definition.[15] Common definitions for domestic and international PEPs are needed on a national level to prevent PEPs from abusing the power they are given by their functions and would help identify these people, their close relatives and associates.

The Financial Action Task Force (FATF) defines PEPs as:

> … individuals who are or have been entrusted with prominent public functions in a foreign country, for example Heads of State or of government, senior politicians, senior government, judicial or military officials,

---

12 Connie M. Friesen, *US and UK Anti-Money-Laundering Requirements Compared*, International Law Office, 5 September 2008, available from http://www.internationallawoffice.com/newsletters/detail.aspx?g=5e143642-6dd9-4b32-8d4e-cab33d724eea.

13 Council of Europe, *Committee of Experts on the Evaluation of Anti-Money-Laundering Measures and the Financing of Terrorism, Politically Exposed Persons—COE*, 2018, available from http://www.coe.int/t/dghl/monitoring/moneyval/Web_ressources/WB_PEPs_en.pdf.

14 FFIEC, *supra*.

15 Council of Europe, Committee of Experts on the Evaluation of Anti-Money-Laundering Measures and the Financing of Terrorism, 30 January 2018, available from http://www.coe.int/web/moneyval.

> senior executives of state owned corporations, important political party officials. Business relationships with family members or close associates of PEPs involve reputational risks similar to those with PEPs themselves. The definition is not intended to cover middle ranking or more junior individuals in the foregoing categories.[16]

Organizations need a better way to identify PEPs to deter TF linked to public assets stolen, or extorted by prominent public office holders, or grand corruption, including: bribes, extortion, ML and taking or accepting use of money or items for personal use, among other things.

According to the World Bank, as part of its Stolen Asset Recovery Initiative, the following examples are provided to help institutions define PEPs. They include: heads of state, government and cabinet ministers, influential public servants in nationalized industries and government administration, senior judges, senior party functionaries, senior and/or influential officials, public servants and military leaders and people with similar functions in international or supranational organizations, members of ruling royal families as well as senior and/or influential representatives of religious organizations (if these functions are connected with political, judicial, military or administrative responsibilities).[17]

In addition, the following could still be considered risky by financial institutions and hence, fall within the definition of PEPs: heads of supranational bodies, e.g. UN, IMF, WB, members of parliament or national legislatures, senior members of the diplomatic corps, e.g. ambassadors, chargés d'affaires or members of boards of central banks as well as holders of public functions not meeting the above-referenced standards of seniority, prominence or importance.[18]

Individuals defined as PEPs should be assessed using appropriate risk factors, but may be excluded from the definition, when the they operate in areas where the risk of corruption or abuse is measured as moderately low, whereby they do not have the facility to control or divert funds. Beyond the limited scope of PEP definitions, some organizations also consider PEP family members to be part of the definition, requiring enhanced monitoring, including: the mother or father, child, spouse or common-law partner, spouse's or common-law

16 Financial Action Task Force (FATF), *Glossary*, (last visited 5 July 2014), http://www.fatf-gafi.org/glossary/0,3414,en_32250379_32236930_35433764_1_1_1_1,00.html#34285860.

17 Wolfsberg, Anti-Money-Laundering Principles, (last visited 5 July 2014), http://www.wolfsberg-principles.com/faq-persons.html.

18 Wolfsberg, *Frequently Asked Questions* ("*FAQ's*"), (last visited 5 July 2014), available from http://www.wolfsberg-principles.com/pdf/Wolfsberg_PEP_FAQs_(2008).pdf.

partner's mother or father and brother, sister, and half-brother or half-sister of an individual designated.

Recommendation 6 of the FATF 40 Recommendations states that banks should, on the subject of PEPs, in addition to performing normal CDDs measures: have appropriate risk management systems to determine whether the customer is a politically exposed person, obtain senior management approval for establishing business relationships with such customers, take reasonable measures to establish the source of wealth and source of funds, and conduct enhanced ongoing monitoring of the business relationship.[19]

2 *PEP Affiliated Risks*

The risk specific context of PEPs regarding CTF is rather different than for general financial crimes, in particular, because state sponsored terrorism is a sensitive issue. Frequently, either governments finance terrorism, or foreign companies provide them different types of support, which was the case for the French Group Lafarge, HSBC, and the Swiss private bank Edmond de Rothschild. Mr. Olsen, former chief executive of LafargeHolcim, who resigned in April 2017, ran the world's largest cement maker and five other top officials are being investigated to determine whether the company contributed to financing terrorism, while operating in Syria. Lafarge's managers are accused of having financed Syrian plant and paid armed groups to allow employees to move to and from the factory so that it could continue operating. Difficulty of doing business in war-torn regions, especially in the energy and industrial sectors, might have pushed the company into attempting to maintain profitability and a presence there, despite the growing danger to its employees.[20] On January 15, 2018, in a letter addressed to the judges, Eric Chevalier, the French ambassador in Syria (at the time the facts occurred), admitted that he met with Lafarge's directors summer 2012. This confession left public opinion with the impression that France did advice the Lafarge group to pay terrorists.

HSBC's neglected AML policies and allowed Mexican drug money, Iranian terrorist funds, and even suspicious Russian money to enter the U.S. for a few years. It also provided U.S. dollar financing and services to banks in Saudi Arabia and Bangladesh that were tied to terrorist organizations. HSBC did not block transactions involving terrorists, drug lords, and rogue regimes, whilst also failing to conduct AML due diligence before opening accounts for HSBC

---

19 MENAFATF, (last visited 5 July 2014), www.menafatf.org/Linkcounter.asp?rid.

20 Liz Alderman, *France Investigates Lafarge Executives for Terrorist Financing*, N.Y. Times, 8 December, 2017, https://www.nytimes.com/2017/12/08/business/lafarge-syria-eric-olsen.html.

affiliates. Moreover, the bank did not monitor $60 trillion in wire transfers and account activity nor a backlog of 17,000 unreviewed account alerts regarding potentially suspicious activity.[21]

In June 2017, Luxembourg's financial regulator, the Commission de Surveillance du Secteur Financier (CSSF), imposed an administrative penalty against the Swiss private bank Edmond de Rothschild of nearly €9m overfailings regarding its handling of funds linked to sovereign wealth fund 1Malaysia Development Berhad.[22] That is, it held that Edmond de Rothschild failed to take proper AML and CTF precautions. Falcon Bank, BSI Bank, Credit Suisse and UBS were all found to have links with the same account.

PEPs represent a certain risk in TF schemes, as they have access to big amounts of money to be used for their political campaigns, or to budgets created for certain national or regional projects. It seems easy for them to disguise and move part of the money they can access by illegal means, without raising much suspicion from local authorities they might control. Hence, PEPs should be identified and closely watched by banks from the account opening throughout the relationship with financial institutions. Resources should be examined in order to ascertain the identity of the customer and beneficial owner of accounts, his or her country of residence, or determine if the customer is a PEP. Banks should obtain sufficient information to decide on the acceptability of accounts considered "high-risk," and establish whether the account, the trust, personal investment company or foundation is beneficially owned by a PEP, his close family or a close associate. If this is the case, the account should be subject to the control framework appropriate for high-risk accounts.

To disguise the ownership of corrupt assets, PEPs frequently use others to launder their illicit funds and finance their activities. Hence, the definition of a PEP should include close associates and family members of the PEP, as these people often undertake transactions and apply for goods and services on behalf of the prominent public official. Since SDNs lists are public, the validity of the entire list detection process can be questioned, as it seems evident for a person listed who is comprised in the watchlist will ask their non-listed associates to conduct transactions for them and thus, avoid detection. Once a

---

21 Agustino Fontevecchia, HSBC Helped Terrorists, Iran, Mexican Drug Cartels Launder Money, Senate Report Says, Forbes, 16 July 2012, available from https://www.forbes.com/sites/afontevecchia/2012/07/16/hsbc-helped-terrorists-iran-mexican-drug-cartels-launder-money-senate-report-says/#69ad011a5712.

22 Kirsten Hastings, *Rothschild Fined €9m Over 1MDB Failings,* Fund Selector Asia, 22 June 2017, https://fundselectorasia.com/rothschild-fined-eur9m-1mdb-failings/.

bank or financial institution foresees a future high-risk customer, officers are advised to utilize electronic tools to compare the names of their future customer with the databases of known PEPs, as well as consulting relevant reports and databases on corruption risk published by specialized national, international, non-governmental and commercial organizations, to decide whether they should proceed with accepting their potential customer.[23] The Dow Jones Watchlist is an effective example of a tool for identifying PEPs, their relatives and close associates.

Per Recommendation 6 of the Financial Action Task Force, financial institutions should, in relation to politically exposed persons, in addition to performing normal due diligence measures:

> ...have appropriate risk management systems to determine whether the customer is a politically exposed person, obtain senior management approval for establishing business relationships with such customers, take reasonable measures to establish the source of wealth and source of funds, conduct enhanced ongoing monitoring of the business relationship.[24]

Many problems related to PEPs/EDD have been observed by international financial institutions. For instance, as different definitions of PEPs exist at the national and international level, regulatory controls remain weak to nonexistent. Moreover, since there are no formal procedures in place to identify PEP customers at the account opening stage and at later ones of the banking relationship, there is an obvious lack of applications of EDD measures related to PEPs. Lack of leadership from banks, governments and related institutions is a major factor explaining the existing gaps regarding due diligence obligations related to PEPs. Hence, many banks' policies are not being reviewed, and they are outdated. Banks fail to understand their own PEP definition and thus, have difficulties classifying and declassifying customers as being so. Therefore, they cannot apply broader EDD measures to political connections, which fall outside their local definition of PEPs.

---

23 Central Bank of Ireland, (last visited 5 July 2014), http://www.centralbank.ie/regulation/processes/anti-money-laundering/Documents/IFIA%20Draft%20AML%20Procedures.

24 Financial Action Task Force (FATF), *Measures to be Taken by Financial Institutions and Non-Financial Business and Professions to Prevent Money-Laundering and Terrorist Financing*, 2006, available from http://www.un.org/en/sc/ctc/docs/bestpractices/fatf/40recs-moneylaundering/fatf-reco6.pdf.

Other key issues related to PEP/EDD are linked to poor employee training such that the wrong steps are used to identify PEPs, offshore company structures are often misunderstood, undocumented CDD processes often take place and a difficulty in distinguishing between sources of wealth and lack of funds.[25] The difficulty encountered by institutions and compliance entities is to establish whether individuals or legal entities qualify as PEPs. To aid and assist the identification of PEPs, a new Convention should include relevant definitions. PEPs' close relationships should also be part of these definitions. The origin of wealth plays a key role and therefore, any new convention should contain a request to disclose its source. While some jurisdictions focus on foreign political figures, others limit the definition to the national level or include regional PEPs. Moreover, the definition "Politically Exposed Person" in various legal instruments and recommendations from countries and international institutions frequently does not include political parties.

Per the federal agencies and FinCEN, despite banks' requirement to follow reasonable measures to ascertain the status of an individual, these dispositions might not uncover all close associations.[26] PEPs' close business relationships should also face additional controls, at least once a year, to ensure that individuals subject to PEPs' specific measures are accurately reported.

According to FINTRAC:

> Heightened scrutiny has to be applied whenever the Politically Exposed Persons/families/ associates is the contracting party of the Bank or the beneficial owner of the assets concerned, or has power of disposal over said assets by virtue of a power of attorney or signature authorization.[27]

Depending on the country, governments have different definitions of public officials. Hence, as titles alone do not provide sufficient information to determine whether a public official is in fact a PEP, importance, prominence and seniority of that person should be considered. The Wolfsberg principles observed that relevant factors financial institutions should refer to in order to

---

25 U.K. Financial Services Authority, *Banks' Management of High Money-Laundering Risk Situations*, June 2011, available from www.fsa.gov.uk/pubs/other/aml_final_report.pdf.

26 FFIEC, *supra*.

27 Reports Analysis Centre of Canada, (last visited 5 July 2014), http://fintrac.gc.ca/publications/brochure/06-2008/1-eng.asp.

determine whether or not an individual should be considered as one could include:

> examining the official responsibilities of the individual's function, the nature of the title (honorary or salaried political function), the level of authority the individual has over governmental activities and over other officials, and whether the function affords the individual access to significant government assets and funds or the ability to direct the awards of government tenders or contracts.[28]

Banks and other financial institutions are subject to corruption, bribery and ML by PEPs that can conduct illegal activities through their financial circuits, as it was the case in high-profile cases over the past few years. PEPs represent different levels of risk, depending on numerous factors, which should be considered, such as the purpose of the account, the current or anticipated activity, products and services used, and the size or complexity of the account relationship, as well as the geographic location, industry, or sector, position, and level or nature of influence or authority.[29]

3 *Risk Mitigation and Management*

PEP controls are designed to draw attention to reputational and legal risks to mitigate the stronger ML risks related to this specific type of customers. The access, control or influence of a PEP over corporate or government accounts, the level of involvement of actors related to these people (such as intermediaries part of the industry or sector of business activities), remain a strong concern for banks, as well as the inappropriate use of corporate vehicles or legal entities to conceal ownership of PEPs.[30]

As a PEP's entourage is known frequently to aid and abet him or her in executing his or her financial operations on their behalf, failure to know family members, relatives, partners or changes that occur to his/her occupational or social status, should push banks into monitoring these people as well. An increasing factor of ML/TF behavior by PEPs can be encountered when the individual gets promoted, after an election or through marriage. A PEP's regular account should be closely watched on a yearly basis to discover new facts related to the account owner, which could be relevant to flagging financial crimes. PEPs continue to be monitored for several years after they cease to

28 Frequently Asked Questions "FAQ's," *supra*.

29 FFIEC, *supra*.

30 FFIEC, *supra*.

"hold power." Enhanced CDD is important, as customers might fail to submit valuable information or give insufficient or misleading information.[31]

Banks should regularly check public sources of information relating to the accountholder and any beneficial owners of legal entities. According to the U.S. Bank Secrecy Anti-money-laundering Compliance Examination Manual, banks should follow specific practices to moderate threats posed by PEPs. These measures need to include: the identification of the accountholder and beneficial owner, including the nominal and beneficial owners of companies, trusts, partnerships, private investment companies, or other legal entities that are accountholders, to seek information directly from the account holder and beneficial owner regarding possible PEP status, the identification of the accountholder and beneficial owner's country of residence and the level of risk for corruption and ML associated with these jurisdictions, obtaining information regarding employment, including industry and sector and the level of risk for corruption associated with the industries and sectors, to check references, as appropriate, to determine whether the account holder and beneficial owner is or has been a PEP, checking the account holder and beneficial owner's source of wealth and funds, to obtain information on immediate family members or close associates either having transaction authority over the account or benefiting from transactions conducted through the account, to determine the purpose of the account and the expected volume and nature of account activity, and to make reasonable efforts to review public sources of information.[32]

Private online databases, such as the World-Check's PEP risk intelligence, provide a service used by most FIUs to review thousands of profiles of these people, which are updated monthly with new profiles, as new public data become available. The inclusion of a database where PEPs would remain more than a year after being removed from their position is subject to discussion, for the influence of the person concerned does not disappear on the day they exit their function.

In sum, management should be involved in the decision to open a PEP account, whereby it should evaluate the risks and take appropriate steps for monitoring.[33] Financial institutions should, with regard to PEPs, have appropriate risk management measures to determine whether the customer is one, as well as design and implement policies, procedures, and processes regarding PEPs that provide for appropriate scrutiny and monitoring. After determining

31 MENAFATF, *supra.*

32 FFIEC, *supra.*

33 FFIEC, *supra.*

the source of wealth and funds, senior management should approve the client.

e Customer Identification Programs (CIPs)

Customer identification consists in identifying customers and verifying information provided by them through reliable documentary and non-documentary methods, provided within reasonable and practical risk-based procedures implemented by the bank. The CIP must include account opening procedures and should ensure that customers' information is periodically updated according to their risk category. Each document provided by the customer does not need to be verified, yet banks must authenticate sufficient information to ascertain that they know the "true" identity of their customers.

Bank CIP procedures need to define when they intend to use documents, non-documentary methods or both. Banks are required to identify customers before opening accounts, collecting data, including: their names, dates of birth, addresses and identification number. For certain products or customers, banks might require additional verification and the creation of a customer profile to confirm that the account is not being used for any terrorist activities. The information collected should include evidence, such as: the purpose and reason for opening the account, the customer's financial and social status, sources of wealth or income, the expected origin of the funds to be used within the relationship, details of occupation, expected monthly remittance, expected monthly withdrawals, the nature of the business activity, information about his or her clients' business and their location, amongst other things.[34] Non-documentary methods to verify customers' identity are not required by banks, but they may include: contacting a customer, obtaining a financial statement, public database or other source, checking information provided by the customer with information obtained through a consumer reporting agency, as well as matching references with other financial institutions.[35]

CIP procedures do not apply to: products or services for which a formal banking relationship is not established with a person (such as check cashing, funds transfer or the sale of a check or money order), accounts opened in order to participate in an employee benefit plan, or any account that the bank acquires (including accounts as a result of a purchase of assets, acquisition, merger or assumption of liabilities).[36] Record-keeping and retention

34 Federal Bank, *KYC Norms*, http://www.federalbank.co.in/kyc-norms.

35 Federal Deposit Insurance Corporation, *Bank Secrecy Act, Anti-Money-Laundering, And Office of Foreign Assets Control Introduction to the Bank Secrecy Act* §8.1 (December 2004), available from https://www.fdic.gov/regulations/safety/manual/section8-1.html.

36 U.S. SEC, *Joint Final Rule: Customer Identification Programs for Mutual Funds*, 9 June 2003, available from https://www.sec.gov/rules/final/ic-26031.htm.

requirements for banks usually apply the following for five years after the record was made.[37]

f Comparison with Governments' Terrorist Lists

As part of the CIP procedure, financial institutions should check whether a potential or existing customer is listed among the federal government's list of known or suspected terrorists or terrorist organizations within a reasonable time in relation to the account opening or even earlier. Banks might be required to follow specific instructions regarding their clients, provided by Specially Designated Nationals (SDNs)[38] lists. Groups and entities suspected of being terrorists or narcotics traffickers, as well as individuals and companies owned or controlled by, or acting for or on behalf of, targeted countries, appear on the OFAC list. Nationals from the country mentioned in the list are usually prohibited from dealing with persons designated by their government's terrorist list. Moreover, the assets of such individuals and companies are retained by their National Treasury Department.

iii) *Reporting*

Current internationally used mechanisms, include currency transaction reports, national security letters or procedures carrying similar effects and most importantly Suspicious Activity Reports (SARs), which are aimed at reporting potentially doubtful financing actions detected by CTF actors. Inconsistent account activities with the customer's identification and lifestyle must be reported in order to predict future terrorist attacks.

a Currency Transaction Reports (CTRs)

Threats posed by ML and other financial crimes to the financial industry involving monetary transactions are many, mainly because there is no general prohibition against handling large amounts of currency within national borders. Currency transaction reporting involves the reporting of large currency transactions with regard to national and institutional statutory and regulatory compliance requirements.[39] Transactions subject to reporting requirements individually or by aggregation most often comprise: automated teller machine transactions, deposits and withdrawals, monetary instrument purchases, fund transfers paid for in currency, purchases of certificates of deposit, denomination exchanges, loan payments and individual retirement accounts. Banks should

---

37 FFIEC, *supra*.

38 U.S. Dep't. of the Treasury, *Resource Center*, 15 March 2017, https://www.treasury.gov/resource-center/sanctions/Programs/Pages/faq_10_page.aspx.

39 FFIEC, *supra*.

file CTR for currency transactions exceeding a certain amount defined by their national legislation, conducted through, or to the bank by, or on behalf of, one person. Transactions that aggregate this amount conducted through the financial institution during a single business day should be considered as one, if it is known to be by or on behalf of the same person.

Financial institutions need to acquire personal identification information concerning the person involved in large amount transactions, which can include documents such as an identification card, passport, or a document delivered by the appropriate government proving the person's identity. The filing of a CTR is required to detect the transfer of huge amounts of money, regardless of the reasons for the currency transaction and even, if the person responsible for the transaction does not own an account at the financial institution. "Exempt persons," such as retail or commercial customers meeting specific criteria, might not be reported, if meeting certain criteria. In the case of moving large amounts of currency across international borders, customs declarations are often required when reaching a minimum amount, as defined by the country's national policies on that matter.

Currency transaction reports should be governed by a time frame for filing and meeting record retention requirements. For example, in the United States, FinCEN mandates that CTRs must be filed within 15 days after the date of the transaction and copies must be retained for five years from the date of the report.[40] Further, financial institutions must collect the required information under consideration of the customers' right to financial privacy.[41]

b National Security Letters (NSLs)

It is important to mention the use of NSLs by the U.S. local Federal Bureau of Investigation and other federal government authorities conducting counterterrorism and counterintelligence investigations to collect data regarding potential terrorists. NSLs are written investigative demands or extraordinary search procedure issued to a specific entity or organization. NSLs give the FBI the power to demand the disclosure of information records and data concerning certain individuals. NSLs can only request non-content data information, such as: financial records from financial institutions, financial records of broker-dealers, (including open and closed checking and savings accounts), from banks, private bankers, credit unions, thrift institutions, brokers and

40 FFIEC, *supra*.

41 U.S. Dep't. of the Treasury, Financial Crimes Enforcement Network, *FinCEN Educational Pamphlet on the Currency Transaction Reporting Requirement*, available from https://www.fincen.gov/fincen-educational-pamphlet-currency-transaction-reporting-requirement.

dealers, investment bankers and companies, credit card companies, insurance companies, travel agencies, casinos, and others. Transactional records, information from credit bureaus, full credit information reports (including names and addresses of all financial institutions with which the consumer has an account), and information necessary to identify a consumer (name, address, former addresses, and past and current employers) can also be requested by appropriate authorities using NSLs.[42]

Further, telephone and electronic historical communications records of calls made and received from land lines, cell phones, and other sources, of a specified phone number, along with billing records associated with that number from telephone companies and Internet service providers, can be accessed through the use of NSLs. E-mail records, including e-mail addresses and screen names associated with the requested account as well as the e-mail addresses and screen names of those who have contacted that account are also available by filling an NSL. Finally, investigation can also include examining billing records and methods of payment for each account.[43]

NSLs are highly confidential discretionary letters, which contain an order precluding disclosure of the letter existence and hence, the examiners are not permitted to review or sample a specific NSL. They do not necessitate probable cause or need judicial oversight. Entities are proscribed from letting anyone know about their receipt of an NSL and consequently, no bank, broker-dealer, officer, employee or agent of the institution, can reveal to a person that any government authority or the FBI has sought or obtained access to records. Financial actors receiving NSLs must take appropriate measures to ensure the confidentiality of the letters and have policies and procedures in place for processing and maintaining discretion regarding them.[44]

c Suspicious Activity Reports (SARs)

The aim of SARs is to report potential unlawful transactions that flow through the bank. It is clear that nowadays, banks cannot detect and report all suspicious transactions arising in their institution. Hence, examiners should put emphasis on assessing a bank's policies, procedures, and processes concerning the identification, evaluation, and reporting process of any suspicious activity, to determine the effectiveness the its filing decisions. Taking the example of U.S law again, to determine when logically SARs should be filed, federal

42 Electronic Privacy Information Center (EPIC), National Security Letters, available from http://epic.org/privacy/nsl/.

43 FFIEC, *supra*.

44 FINRA, *supra*.

regulations require banks, bank holding companies, and their subsidiaries to file an SAR when there are:[45]

1) Criminal violations involving insider abuse in any amount.
2) Criminal violations aggregating $5,000 or more when a suspect can be identified.
3) Criminal violations aggregating $25,000 or more regardless of a potential suspect.
4) Transactions conducted or attempted by, at, or through the bank (or an affiliate) and aggregating $5,000 or more, if the bank or affiliate knows, suspects, or has reason to suspect that the transaction:
   - May involve potential money-laundering or other illegal activity (e.g., terrorism-financing).
   - Is designed to evade the BSA or its implementing regulations.
   - Has no business or apparent lawful purpose or is not the type of transaction that the particular customer would normally be expected to engage in, and the bank knows of no reasonable explanation for the transaction after examining the available facts, including the background and possible purpose of the transaction.[46]

According to the Bank Secrecy Act, a deposit, a withdrawal, a transfer between accounts, an exchange of currency, an extension of credit, a purchase or sale of any stock, bond, certificate of deposit, or other monetary instrument or investment security, or any other payment, transfer, or delivery by, through, or to a bank, constitutes a transaction.[47]

To summarize, TF cases were found to include the following types of suspect financial transactions: large cash deposits into accounts of non-profit organizations, large numbers of deposits of checks drawn from legal trust accounts followed by withdrawals, deposits of U.S. postal money orders or cash, followed by large cash withdrawals or issuance of checks or purchase of bank drafts payable to foreign money service business(es).[48] Activities deemed suspect, must be reported by banks, insurance companies, casinos, money service providers, securities broker-dealers and futures commission merchants. Reporting requirements depend on countries and their specific laws concerning TF and ML suspect behaviors. In the United States, SARs mainly apply to

---

45 FFIEC, *supra*.

46 FFIEC, *supra*.

47 FFIEC, *supra*.

48 Reports Analysis Centre of Canada, *Money-Laundering and Terrorist Financing Typologies and Trends in Canadian Banking*, May 2009, available from http://www.fintrac.gc.ca/publications/typologies/2009-05-01-eng.asp.

activities involving funds or assets meeting specified dollar thresholds, while in the United Kingdom banks must submit reports when they know or "have reasonable grounds to know" or suspect an individual or entity they are doing business with might be carrying out transactions linked to financial crime.[49]

Numerous transactions can raise flags during the initial detection phase, nevertheless, this does not instantly mean the transaction should be reported on the basis of this inconsistent activity. Additional control parameters should be considered to review the issue to determine whether the transaction should be reported to authorities and subject to an SAR filling. Inheritance funds, real estate investment or a gift would be typical inconsistent activities that might not necessarily be part of a financial scheme. Banks should establish reviewing procedures, which consider facts and circumstances that might underline real suspicious transactions, and therefore, incorporate policies, and processes to identify and monitor unusual activities by utilizing effective compliance programs. Banks with offices abroad should implement procedures to ensure that they notify authorities as per local regulations.

Financial institutions and banks tend to file a SAR to be safe, even if the facts do not, after further observation, prove this necessity. Moreover, notification to law enforcement does not relieve institutions from filling a SAR.[50] The local authority that should be notified is typically the office of the Revenue Service Investigation Division or FBI homologue in the country in which the SAR is filled. Evaders know that lawyering multiple times different amounts of funds could allow them to evade the system, as well as CTR filling requirements related to ML/TF, tax evasion and other financial crimes. Banks must use monitoring systems, either manual or automated, if not both, and assign trained staff to identify, research and report suspicious activities as per the volume of transactions and risk profile of the bank. Whilst large banks encompass distinct functions among different departments in monitoring, smaller banks or institutions might use no more than one or two employees to complete similar tasks, such as managing alerts, research activities, review monitoring reports, as well as SAR decision making, completion, and filing. Responsibilities among the institution should be well described so to address clearly the duties of each employee. Monitoring and reporting systems include identification of unusual activities, employee identification, referrals, law enforcement inquiries and transaction system output. Banks should implement training schemes and procedure to ensure that the personnel who observe transactions daily are doing the job correctly.

---

49 Connie M. Friesen, *US and UK Anti-Money-Laundering Requirements Compared*, International Law Office, 5 September 2008, available from http://www.internationallawoffice.com/newsletters/detail.aspx?g=5e143642-6dd9-4b32-8d4e-cab33d724eea.

50 FFIEC, *supra*.

Surveillance monitoring systems refer to intelligent systems and rule-based systems that often use computer programs purchased or developed in-house, which are automated and can identify several patterns of suspect activity or deviations from expected financial behaviors and transactions, such as deposits, withdrawals, funds transfers, ATM transactions or automated clearing house transactions from a bank's core data processing system by using different sets of rules. Institutions should tailor appropriate parameters and filters pertaining to the activity of the individual and business activity the institution tries to control. Transactions data, such as information on the customer or business account type and category, should be stored in the system for review to identify gaps, such as financial crimes, ML/TF or tax evasion criteria.

Whilst organizations need to review a customer's transactions or account activities to decide whether to file an SAR or not, many transactions could raise flags and yet be legitimate.[51] Once research and analysis have been completed, banks and financial institutions should get an individual, board or committee, to review the findings to decide whether to file one. SAR filing on continuing activities should be carried out over a certain period and cooperation should continue with law enforcement. Management is in charge of deciding when to terminate a relationship with a customer or employee subject to the filing. SAR disclosure is prohibited to persons involved in the transaction that has been reported and no one related to the bank should inform the person involved in this report. Whether SARs may be shared with head offices and controlling companies in the country of origin or abroad shall be determined by inter-agency guidance provided to agencies for this type of event.[52] A branch, or agency of a foreign bank, can share SARs with its head office or controlling companies, whether domestic or foreign.[5]

B The Egmont Group and Financial Intelligence Units

The Egmont Group and the Financial Intelligence Units (FIUs) are undeniable actors in the detection of TF and the 2012 FATF Recommendation 29 requires the latter to become members of the former. In 2013, the Egmont Group had 139 member FIUs (2013)[53] and that number is expected to grow as over 190

51 U.S. Dep't. of the Treasury, Financial Crimes Enforcement Network, *Suggestions for Addressing Common Errors Noted in Suspicious Activity Reporting*, 10 Oct. 2007, available from https://www.fincen.gov/resources/statutes-regulations/guidance/suggestions-addressing-common-errors-noted-suspicious.

52 FFIEC, *supra*.

53 Egmont Group, *About*, 2018, (last visited 5 July 2014), https://egmontgroup.org/.

countries, which are FATF and FSRBs members, have promised to implement FATF's AML/CFT standards. To enhance international cooperation in the fight against ML and the financing of terrorism, the Egmont Group of Financial Intelligence Units was created by a group of FIUs, which met at the Egmont Arenberg Palace in Brussels (Belgium), with a view to establishing an informal network of FIUs for the stimulation of international co-operation. It meets regularly to find ways to promote the development of FIUs and to cooperate, especially in the areas of information exchange, training and the sharing of expertise. The Egmont Group is a gathering of FIUs with the objective of promoting awareness and application of domestic programs concerning ML and TF, as well as increasing worldwide cooperation in this field.

The Egmont Group is an operational organization fostering information exchange and international cooperation. The revised *Egmont Charter* (*2013*), *Egmont Principles for Information Exchange* and *Operational Guidance for FIUs* offers a basis for the Egmont Group's work and promotes international exchange between FIUs, as well as guidelines to reinforce international cooperation. Its functions are as follows:

> to expand and systematize international cooperation in the reciprocal exchange of information; to increase the effectiveness of FIUs by offering training and promoting personnel exchanges to improve the expertise and capabilities of personnel employed by FIUs; to foster increased coordination and support among the operational divisions of member FIUs; to promoting the operational autonomy of FIUs; and the establishment of FIUs in conjunction with jurisdictions with an AML/CFT program in place, or in areas with a program in the early stages of development.[54]

The structure of the Egmont Group comprises the heads of FIUs, the Egmont Committee, the working groups, the regional groups and the secretariat. The Egmont Group's decision-making body is composed of heads of FIUs reaching decisions by consensus on the Group's membership, structure, budget and principles daily through the Egmont Secure Web (ESW) and through open email as well as yearly, at the Egmont Group Annual Plenary meeting.

The Egmont Group and its secretariat are funded by their members on the basis of voluntary contributions from members and membership fees. Whilst countries are not obligated to be part of the Egmont Group, member parties

54 Egmont, *id.*

must sign the Egmont's Charter as well as comply with the Group's regulations and principles, whilst committing themselves to working according to its founding documents. Since there is no existing Treaty or Convention binding the Egmont Group to its members, there is no punishment or sanction mechanism for non-compliance. Internal compliance procedures are provided by the Egmont Group for its member FIUs. The key strength to FIUs' cooperation relies the fact that members the Egmont Group can cooperate notwithstanding the political relationships between represented countries.

Unclassified information is released to the public and the organization's stakeholders via the Egmont Group's public website. Moreover, the Egmont's Annual Report discloses the group's undertakings and other improvements during the reporting period. As the use of intelligence and investigative techniques represents a strong tool for detecting and disrupting the activities of terrorists and terrorist organizations,[55] FIUs are central offices that serve as national centers for gathering, examining and disseminating financial intelligence relevant to ML, the financing of terrorism, associated predicate offences and SARs.[56] An FIU gathers financial disclosure information to investigate or/and prosecute these violations. FIUs process collected information, then deliver it to the appropriate government authority to support national Counter-terrorism efforts. The FIU should have access to additional information from reporting entities on a timely basis, to be able to gather required financial, administrative and law enforcement information.[57]

The creation of FIUs is a major step for international cooperation. This collaboration is based on local laws, current local law enforcement, as well as local counter terror financing laws. There is also a need for an authority that will collect, access and share financial information.[58] Recommendation 29 requires OECD signatory countries to establish FIUs (FIU) and be part of the Egmont Group. In its Interpretive Note, FATF Recommendation 29[59] states that countries are using *the Egmont Group statement of purpose* and its *Principles for Information Exchange Between Financial Intelligence Units for Money-Laundering*

55 Egmont Group, *Money-Laundering and the Financing of Terrorism*, (last visited 5 July 2014), https://egmontgroup.org/en/content/money-laundering-and-financing-terrorism.

56 New Zealand Police, *Financial Intelligence Unit (FIU)*, (last visited 5 July 2014), http://www.police.govt.nz/advice/businesses-and-organisations/fiu.

57 FATF (2012c), *supra.*

58 Egmont Group, *Financial Intelligence Units (FIUs)*, (last visited 5 July 2014), http://www.egmontgroup.org/about/financial-intelligence-units-fius.

59 FATF (2012c), *supra.*

and Financing of Terrorism Cases[60] for guidance on the role, functions and information exchange mechanisms between units internationally. There seems to be general confusion over the acronym FIU, which could easily be mixed up with "Financial Investigative Units," which are police units established for the purpose of investigating financial and white-collar crime and this does not necessarily entail collaboration with the Egmont Group and its prerogatives. To avoid confusion, numerous countries have instigated the acronym "FAU" as for Financial Analysis Unit. Using the term analysis instead of intelligence also eradicates the negative connotation of the latter word by focusing on the function of the units instead of the material dealt with by these national police units.[61] In some countries, FIUs and FAUs are combined and FIUs are more police-oriented. The two primary functions of FIUs are detection and law enforcement. Acting through international and regional initiatives, they deliver regulatory oversight, whilst also providing support to the efforts of multiple law enforcement or judicial authorities with concurrent or competing jurisdictional authority to investigate TF. FIUs often act as a safe intermediary between the private financial sector and law enforcement as well as judicial authorities.

According to the Egmont Group, there are four existing FIU models, namely: judicial, law enforcement, administrative and hybrid.[62] The judicial model relates to FIUs that are part of governments' juridical branches and enforcing judiciary powers, which also deal with SAR disclosure received by the investigative agencies of a country from its financial sector. Examples of the judicial model's competencies include: accounts seizing and freezing, detention of persons, as well as conducting searches and interrogation among other powers.[63] The law enforcement model supports the efforts of various law enforcement or judicial authorities implementing and enforcing current local laws on CTF with conflicting jurisdictional power for investigating it. The administrative model is an independent administrative authority collecting and utilizing information from the financial sector, to then send it to judicial or law local enforcement authorities for prosecution. Finally, the hybrid model includes elements of at least two or more of the FIU models.[64]

---

60 Egmont Group, *Egmont Group of Financial Intelligence Units Principles for Information Exchange Between Financial Intelligence Units,* 28 Oct. 2013, available from https://sic.gov.lb/intorg/EG%20Principles%20for%20Information%20Exchange%20(2013).pdf.

61 U.S. Dep't. of State, *Money-Laundering,* (last visited 5 July 2014), http://www.state.gov/1997-2001-NOPDFS/policy_remarks/1998/980611_winer_mlaundering.html.

62 Egmont FIUs, *supra.*

63 Egmont FIUs, *supra.*

64 Egmont FIUs, *supra.*

PART 2

Main Threats to the Accomplishment and Success of a New Counter-terrorism Financing Convention

Introduction to Part 2

The second part of this book covers the main threats to the accomplishment and success of a New Counter-terrorism Financing Convention. It is divided into three chapters as follows.

Chapter 4 will review key challenges at the international level. The main problems encountered when trying to detect TF activities, such as anonymity, cross-border activities, third party reliance, and employee participation in ML schemes will be addressed. The main obstacles to the accomplishment of a new CTF Convention assessed in this chapter are: the emergence of new money-laundering terrorism-financing activities, including new payment technologies, international cooperation between actors and agencies as well as political pressure against the establishment of a new international TF tool.

Chapter 5 will take into consideration issues regarding the practicality of the Convention, such as the ineffectiveness of the current enforcement system mechanisms, including cross-border enforcement matters. Moreover, asset recovery legal tools will be reviewed to demonstrate how those linked to TF activities are located, frozen and recovered.

Chapter 6 will highlight potential conflicts between a new CTF tool and human rights, such as international privacy laws and civil liberties. Privacy in tracing and detecting TF schemes, as well as the inclusion of a surveillance clause into a new CTF tool to monitor financers' endeavors are strongly argued by the International community.

In sum, the purpose of Part 2 is to provide an overview of the challenges at the international level that need to be acknowledged and incorporated into a new CTF tool. The difficulties encountered while trying to detect wrongful conduct should be considered, even if they cannot be totally overcome at present.

 | DOI:10.1163/9789004409675_007

CHAPTER 4

Key Challenges at the International Level

In this chapter, the main threats to the accomplishment and success of a New Counter-terrorism Financing Convention are discussed. Key challenges at the international level encountered while trying to identify TF endeavours are clarified in order to pin down the main blockages faced when striving to detect TF schemes.

Part A describes the barriers that could prevent TF from being detected. The main risk factors encountered while trying to detect ML and TF activities that are overviewed in this section include: anonymity, cross-border activities, cross-border transport of prepaid cards and intermediaries, exploitation of the non-face-to-face nature of certain transactions, employee participation in ML/TF schemes, third party funding and reliance (including strawmen and nominees).

Part B highlights the problems associated with the emergence of new payment technologies. The internet and mobile payment technologies offer a good place for terrorist financers to hide their identities and carry out exchange across borders undetected. That is, these rapidly developing technologies have been increasing the difficulties for authorities in discovering their schemes and shutting them down.

Part C explains the key obstacle to the establishment and functioning of a new CTF Convention at the international level, which is the lack of international cooperation between actors and agencies.

Part D provides insight into political involvement, which can act as an impediment to the implementation and enforcement of an effective international detection mechanism. That is, political pressure can hinder international reporting of TF activities, thus making it difficult for domestic authorities to recognize and report actors involved in major TF schemes.

Using the information collected in Chapter 2 B, defining types of terrorist financing activities, and Chapter 3 A, providing more information on international identification and reporting methods utilised by financial institutions, it is now possible to draw the first conclusions on how the system gets abused and where solutions should be found at the international level to prevent terrorists from going undetected and therefore, unpunished. Problems linked to TF detection are reviewed, along with new payment technologies, international cooperation issues and political pressure, in order to shed light on what could be incorporated effectively into a new CTF tool and what cannot until actors are ready to accept changes aimed at benefiting the international TF fight.

 | DOI:10.1163/9789004409675_008

A Main Problems Encountered While Trying to Detect TF Activities

Part A identifies the common obstacles that might prevent TF plots from being discovered and reported. Anonymity, cross-border activities, third party reliance, and employee participation in ML schemes are the main problems discussed in this chapter to provide a better understanding at these issues to be considered and taken into account when building the new CTF tool.

i) *Anonymity*

One of the main concerns of the authorities while tracing dirty money or funds used to finance terrorist activities is anonymity, for there are many cases in it can be used to evade the system. An anonymous person or a fake identification card holder therefore represents a significant threat. False or stolen identities obtained through theft of personal data can also be exploited to open unlimited numbers of accounts, to be accessed at anytime, anywhere in the world, to manage financial operations and transfers to other anonymous persons. Shell companies can also be set up in the name of a nominee dealing with a company's bank accounts often having an address and a letterbox.

There are many risks associated with TF arising from wire transfer operations. Despite all the international efforts and more stringent measures taken in the past few years, the purpose of transactions and personal knowledge of the customers are almost never known, especially when wires are made through companies such as Western Union or non-banking institutions, where no account is required. Terrorists can receive wire transfers of small amounts of money with fake identification or by providing so little information on themselves that is it nearly impossible for regulators to track them and punish them. Third parties can help financers transmit the money from their illicit activities by sending small amounts or at least smaller amounts than allowed by current regulations and manage to still send a big amount using several senders or donate money through wire transfers. Hence, money can be deposited in the banking system or extracted anonymously by criminals or their accomplices without in-depth scrutiny. In view of the current situation, it is still very hard for FIUs and reporting sections of banks and financial institutions to track all the small transactions, connect people that could take part in terrorism and its financing, and to understand the process of the financing of their operations.

The online world has created a gigantic playground for terrorists and organized criminal groups, one in which the nature of internet transactions has made anonymity prevalent. The exploitation of the non-face-to-face phenomenon of new payment methods offers many possibilities to wrongdoers, such as opening accounts and using banking and electronic payment systems anonymously and freely, providing them with access to services for their own accounts or those of others, from various unknown locations with a moving IP, or from an internet café, a fast food restaurant or public library's free internet facilities. Given the explanation of Chapter 2 Part B regarding methods of financing, an individual with a user name and password, cannot just open online banking accounts, for he or she can create them off-shore, participate in trade, sell and buy assets as well as collect money through online casinos, betting offices, online auctions etc.

Communication between financers can take place through the creation of an email account used from any public location, making exchanges, access and utilization almost untraceable, thus without giving any hints on which specific individuals to watch. The expansion of online transactions endangers banking procedures and financial units' work, as the KYC principle required by banks through their compliance efforts cannot be satisfied, leaving doubt as to the person they are in communication with via the internet or through the real phone identity. Illicit proceeds gained from fraud following identity theft or from stealing money from bank accounts or credit/debit cards through phishing or hacking methods, as well as clean donated money are often transferred anonymously from one person to another through the use of new payment technology products. Clearly, there are still loopholes for criminals to abuse financial institutions and the system in general, the main problem being identity in that the increase of internet operations is rapidly reducing the need for personal contact. Anonymity, owing to today's technologies, is making it increasingly more difficult for authorities to track TF and ML activities. Banks and financial institutions, as well as Internet service providers should thus pay more attention to anonymity and take specific measures to prevent new schemes. They should also ensure that KYC procedures are well applied.

Prepaid cards for mobile phones represent a big legislative gap so far. They provide a great deal of anonymity for launderers and financers of illegal activities since they can be purchased without knowing the real identity of the buyer. Phones can also be used as e-purses, utilizing the prepaid value from the SIM card to transfer money. In many cases, prepaid cards or IPS accounts are used as transit accounts and once the funds have been transferred, they get cashed at ATMs or spent to buy other goods by criminals and their associates. As many schemes to fund prepaid cards or other accounts are initiated from bank accounts or credit cards of legitimate customers, banks and authorities do not directly detect that the transactions do not originate from a legitimate customer and thus, constitute suspect activity. Money becomes untraceable through multiple operations, electronic transfers, and purchases which increase the layering. The frequency of operations, makes it much more complicated to determine the identity of the wrongdoers. Identification, verification and monitoring systems fail to detect most suspicious activities as they seem to carry a legitimate purpose, while contributing to illegal activities. Moreover, the anonymity of online transactions makes it unlikely that the operation will be reported. In sum, the non-face to face nature of the Internet makes deterring TF a difficult task.[1]

ii) *Cross-border Activities*

Cross-border activities means the involvement of multiple jurisdictions, which makes it a difficult task for law enforcement to track and recover criminal assets. Once funds have crossed international borders via money mules or by other means, it becomes complicated to trace, identify the leading financer and transfer coordinators. Some jurisdictions are particularly advantageous for criminals regarding transfers to accounts of establishments residing in offshore zones.[2] Cases involving cross-border transport of prepaid cards are not rare as there is no obligation to declare them when crossing borders and the likelihood to be caught is not as important since customs officers cannot easily differentiate regular cards from prepaid ones given both types have very similar aspects.[3]

Cross-border activities in the 21st century are mainly linked to our "borderless" Internet world. Shell companies are often associated with offshore jurisdictions, which tend to be regulated differently or less, thus making them attractive for criminals.[4] Even a regular shell company scheme like those utilized in the traditional financial system becomes a simple task for financers and criminals hiding funds using Internet based payment services providers. Shell companies are known vehicles for cybercrime schemes, ML and TF. When transactions are performed via the banking system, it is complicated to detect the shell element in a company while running the suspicious activity report. As the transfers involve using new technology and go through less regulated new payment services, shell companies can remain concealed from suspicion while receiving large amounts of transfer. Geographic origin of suspect funds or transactions is among the best reasons for reporting such activity, but

1 Financial Action Task Force (FATF), *Money-Laundering Using New Payment Methods*, October 2010, available from http://www.fatf-gafi.org/media/fatf/documents/reports/ML%20using%20New%20Payment%20Methods.pdf.

2 Council of Europe, *Committee of Experts on the Evaluation of Anti-Money-Laundering Measures and the Financing of Terrorism*, available from http://www.coe.int/t/dghl/monitoring/moneyval/typologies/MONEYVAL(2012)6_Reptyp_flows_en.pdf.

3 FATF (2010c), *supra*.

4 COE (2012), *supra*.

when cross-border movement of prepaid cards is involved, funds are generally withdrawn in a different jurisdiction to where the card was loaded.

iii) *Third-Party Involvement*

Third-Party involvement in ML/TF schemes can occur at many levels. Employees can participate by providing voluntary or malicious assistance to criminals. Reliance on third-party for CDD, as well as for data collection and retention can provide access to important information to external workers. Third-parties can also fund crimes by becoming simple intermediaries.

a Employee Participation in the Financing Schemes

Terrorism Financers takes advantage of the systems in place, of the help provided by employees in schemes, wilfully or recklessly, as well as the contribution of third parties, whether aware or not of their participation in ML and TF activities.[5] Employees have been found in many cases accomplices and guilty of facilitating the laundering and acquisition of illicit proceeds. Moreover, they can be blackmailed, corrupted or even infiltrated into the system in place to facilitate transactions for launderers. Market players frequently involved in aiding terrorist financers and launderers include program managers, banks, payment networks, distributors and payment processing facilities.

b Third-Party Reliance

Banks are under specific circumstances allowed to make arrangements with another financial institution or other third party to perform some or all elements of their customer identification procedures. Reliance on another financial institution permits a bank and its affiliates to perform part or all its CIP on its behalf when a customer opens an account at the bank. The other financial institution must certify it has implemented the bank's related AML program each year and perform the CIP required by the bank. The use of third parties to perform CIP on a bank's behalf is permitted. This allows the bank to leave the verification of the identity of its customer to a third party acting as its agent. The bank is responsible for the third party's compliance with the bank's CIP requirements and hence, it should implement adequate controls and review procedures to ensure compliance.

Depending on the jurisdiction, responsibility regarding third-party reliance can differ. In the United States, the difference in determining responsibility for CIP relies on the terms "reliance on another financial institution" or "delegation to third parties". The bank will remain responsible for a third party's

5 FATF (2010c), *supra*.

reliance on its CIP's requirements, while it will not be held responsible for another financial institution's failure to fulfill adequately its CIP program's responsibilities. In the United Kingdom, banks can officially delegate, but not rely on third parties to perform their CIP and CDD duties in the US sense. Third parties must consent to the delegation and comply with the set record-keeping requirements. In the UK, banks remain liable for third parties' compliance with CDD. Financial institutions, tax advisers, accountants, auditors, legal professionals and insolvency practitioners are potential third parties.[6]

c Third-Party Funding

One of the issues encountered while trying to detect terrorist financers is the reliance criminals can have on others to fund their activities anonymously. A third-party can fund accounts or prepaid cards by cash, P2P (person-to-person) transfers or simply bank transfers. Internet Service Providers and mobile payment services also allow third-party funding, which can be exploited by criminals with the use of straw men or financial agents/financial mules. Funds can also be acquired from unwilling victims by third parties to be redistributed to the financing of terrorism. Family, friends and private parties can get involved in illegal transactions by transferring funds to criminals via mobile phones. In fact, the greater the number of people involved in the scheme, the better the layering process. If a third party is tricked into sending money or layering it, the predicate offence becomes difficult to link legally to the following phase of prosecuting the individual, who had no intention or knowledge of the wrongdoing he or she was part of.

B The Emergence of New Payment Technologies

In March 2008, the International Narcotics Control Strategy Report (INCSR) affirmed that:

> ... there are already indications that money launderers and those that finance terrorism will avail themselves of the new m-payment systems.

According to the Task Force's report:

6 Connie M. Friesen, *US and UK Anti-Money-Laundering Requirements Compared*, International Law Office, 5 September 2008, available from http://www.internationallawoffice.com/newsletters/detail.aspx?g=5e143642-6dd9-4b32-8d4e-cab33d724eea.

> ... the mission of the task force was to identify, in partnership with private industry and the public, consumer issues raised by emerging electronic money technologies and to explore the extent to which innovative responses were being developed that are consistent with the needs of the developing market.

Transnational criminal organizations have taken advantage of technological innovation and globalization to expand their illicit business and inventiveness. Terrorist financers are now turning to new methods to stay one step ahead of law enforcement. Our interconnected world offers new and innovative methods for electronic cross-border funds transfer, which can serve their illicit endeavors. By conquering and controlling the "cyber space," criminals have access to nearly every tool available to further their enterprises and dirty activities. The Internet includes extensions of established payment systems as well as new payment methods, which operate differently from traditional monetary transactions and represents new ML/TF concerns, as criminals can anonymously exploit new opportunities to evade the system and make high value transactions without paper trails or legal accountability.[7] With new technologies, new detection and tracing methods are required to deter TF activities.

Using Internet based financial services is possible at all stages of the ML process. Cyber-payments include different typologies, such as internet payment services (e.g. mobile payments, micro-payments or digital precious metals), stored value cards or smart cards, and on-line banking.[8] The 2006 FATF report identified several risk factors and characteristics shared by most new payment methods, which cause hazard in that most operators are located abroad and benefit from different jurisdictions that are not regulated enough as far as ML/TF is concerned.[9] The Internet is used as a distribution channel for financial instruments, such as cards, where there is no face-to-face contact with the customer.

The main new payment methods' risk factors related to their misuse for ML and TF purposes are the absence of credit risk, the speed of transactions, the exploitation of the non-face-to-face nature the account, cross-border transport of prepaid cards, third party funding (including strawmen and nominees), and complicit NPM providers or their employees.[10] The absence of credit risk

7 *Money-Laundering*, September 2007, available from http://www.justice.gov/usao/eousa/foia_reading_room/usab5505.pdf.

8 Wojciech Filipkowski, *Cyber Laundering: An Analysis of Typology and Techniques*, 3.1 Int. J. Crim. Just. Sci., 15–27, 2008, available from http://www.sascv.org/ijcjs/wojciech.html.

9 Filipkowski, *supra*.

10 FATF (2010c), *supra*.

exists with new payments methods, as funds are usually prepaid, and the nature of the business relationship does not require service providers to obtain full and accurate information. Moreover, the speed of the transactions makes them difficult to monitor. The non-face to face nature of NPM business relationships and transactions are identified in the "specific 36 ML/TF risks" of FATF Recommendation 8.[11]

The Internet is ideal for commerce. It is therefore the perfect platform for money-laundering and terrorism-financing activities to be conducted, as transactions fall outside the existing regulatory definitions. There is also a general lack of record keeping or suspicious transaction reporting by the technology provider, and an inadequacy of audit trails for law enforcement which make the internet ideal for financial criminals.[12] The Council of Europe has provided a red flags and indicators list to help recognize potential suspect transactions under new payments methods schemes.[13]

Many financial institutions provide legitimate retail banking services through the Internet, while other entities offer ML services camouflaged as real investments or offshore accounts. It is therefore important to determine which business is an authentic financial service. The term cyberpayment refers to the systems that allow their users to move funds electronically through the internet. When an encryption software is used, the appropriate key is generated by the browser software, allowing rightful access to online accounts. Banks permit users to make payments and transfer funds from one account to another, but it is impossible to verify with certitude which Internet user has made such transactions as a personal identification code can be easily given to another person, fake IDs can be used to open a account, and different persons can in fact access the account simultaneously from anywhere in the world. Internet transfers happening almost at the same time, fast-moving funds and multiple withdrawing from ATMs, make any TF scheme very hard to keep track of. Since access is obtained through the ISP, it is almost impossible for institutions to verify where the transfer took place. Financial intermediaries, such as PayPal, can also be abused by launderers, acting as non-bank Internet-based agents for persons and organizations that want to trade or transfer funds by setting up a prepaid account, which can be funded from a bank account, or a debit or credit card to purchase goods or transfer funds.[14]

---

11 Anti-Money-Laundering, (last visited 5 July 2014), http://www.antimoneylaundering.ukf.net/papers/solicitor.htm.

12 Anti-Money-Laundering, *id.*

13 COE (2012), *supra.*

14 Filipkowski, *supra.*

The phone is a device which can be utilized to move funds instead of a computer. Transactions via mobile phone can be initiated using a SIM card linked to that bank account, yet anyone can access another person's mobile and initiate payments. The lack of regulation concerning new payment technologies also represents huge money-laundering risks and loopholes for criminals to abuse the system. Banks and securities companies can reduce risks by implementing regulations and surveillance procedures similar to internet banking.

KYC an EDD measures are also used for new subscribers, but the security policies are still weak. Similarly to Internet banking, the non-face to face relationship between the customer and the service provider issuing the account represents a major threat. Mobile payment providers' reputation is at stake when it comes to ML/TF risks, as classified in the World Bank 2008 paper, which identifies and categorizes risk associated with each type of these services, according to its level. Money can be stored in a phone and funds can be withdrawn from a mobile provider's account, and later on transferred or utilized to make payments. This can hinder traces of illegal activities and makes it difficult to notice, or/and report suspect transactions, as well as to identify the person moving funds.

Regulators and law enforcers concerns about prepaid cards, might be related to the fact that they solely rely on mobile payment providers to play the role of financial institutions. Mobile payment providers should therefore monitor mobile payment services which allow non-bank account holders to initiate payments of bills or services.

Once a mobile phone is used as a prepaid card or an electronic purse, terrorist financers and launderers can easily transfer funds and escape ML/TF's regular identification procedure, thereby preserving anonymity. The velocity of loads and reloads, the acquisition of multiple cards for the same account, and control of the number of ATM withdrawals make prepaid cards an ML tool of choice for criminals to finance their illicit activities and render the verification by law enforcement almost impossible without the use of software specifically designed to detect payment fraud. An increasingly regulated prepaid cards market would greatly reduce criminal activities in this regard and promote the legitimate usage of such a service.

Very few statutes and regulations address e-money systems at the international level in that the current law enforcement framework mainly relies on geographic borders and traditional law enforcement techniques, which are becoming obsolete or simply inefficient when dealing with NPT. Primary law enforcement issues concerning e-money relate to the need to revise regulatory regimes, to ensure adequate and accurate records of the transactions and persons involved, to find better ways to detect stored value cards and to ascertain their legitimate owners' identity and to monitor such fast and voluminous transactions daily so as to be able to track unusual financial activities that could be linked to ongoing or future crimes.[15] The FATF Recommendations require all entities or persons involved in certain financial activities and services including transferring money or value, or issuing and managing means of payment, to be subject to AML/CTF obligations and oversight. Since the majority of NPT providers are financial institutions, they should be regulated and supervised according to Recommendation 23 or Special Recommendations.[16]

Intermediaries may be subject to regulatory requirements depending on the jurisdiction they belong to and may have to report and monitor transactions. Hence, it is important to determine whether an entity in the chain of contribution to an online payment service is an intermediary, or rather, qualifies to be designated as a financial institution.[17] The fact that e-money systems are operated in multiple counties and currencies, implies that multiple jurisdictions are involved, and that law enforcement must determine the prevailing one. Very few Internet based NPT cases of ML and TF have been identified to date, but this does not mean that such activities are not taking place. Internet enabled transfer of value methods can bypass the banking system and the use of Bitcoins has grown significantly over the last 8 years, increasing from an average of 100 daily transactions in 2009 to 282,000 in August 17, 2017.[18] There are over 900+ cryptocurrencies, most of which can permit instant transfers and are accepted all over the world by big companies as payment methods. Several cyber-laundering techniques also offer almost complete privacy. Companies such as Samurai, DarkWallet and BitcoinFog have worked on creating a Bitcoin "dark wallet" that makes transactions untraceable and anonymous. Cryptocurrencies can be created and exchanged via a decentralized network of computers, thereby avoiding banks and governments' involvement. Criminals can hide their transactions, send bitcoins anywhere, convert them into cash, and deposit them in banks, or the other way around. Europol claims that

15 Organisation for Economic Co-Operation and Development (OECD), (last visited 5 July 2014), www.oecd.org/dataoecd/31/50/34043689.pdf.

16 Financial Action Task Force (FATF), *Money-Laundering Using New Payment Methods*, October 2010, available from http://www.fatf-gafi.org/media/fatf/documents/reports/ML%20using%20New%20Payment%20Methods.pdf.

17 U.S. Dep't. of the Treasury, Financial Crimes Enforcement Network, *FATF-VIII Money-Laundering Typologies Exercise Public Report*, November 1996, available from http://www.fincen.gov/news_room/rp/files/fatf.pdf.

18 Micah Zenko, Politics, Power, and Preventive Action & Center for Preventive Action, *Bitcoin for Bombs*, Council on Foreign Relations, 17 August 2017, available from https://www.cfr.org/blog/bitcoin-bombs.

cryptocurrencies are increasingly utilized to finance terrorism.[19] Since e-currencies are becoming a "parallel" financial system that eludes the traditional control mechanism, they require a central authority.[20]

The Panama Papers and recent terrorist attacks prompted many countries into introducing better rules concerning TF. In 2017, the Australian Government amended their legislation relating to combating ML and TF by incorporating NPT vocabulary into the existing bill, including gambling and e-currencies.[21] The UK Treasury plans to regulate bitcoin and other cryptocurrencies, with traders being required to disclose their identities.[22] The EU has agreed to implement stricter rules against ML and TF concerning exchange platforms for bitcoins and other virtual currencies as well as bringing in more transparency to improve prevention.[23] Under the EU new regulations, bitcoin exchange platforms and "wallet" providers will be required to identify their users.[24] As abovementioned, bitcoins and e-currencies can help fund terrorists' attacks. In 2017, a 27-year-old Pakistani-Born US resident, Zombie Shahnaz, was charged with conspiracy to commit ML of Bitcoins and other cryptocurrencies as well as bank fraud to help ISIS. The accused fraudulently obtained more than $85,000 through a bank loan and credit cards to buy cryptocurrencies, then planned to travel to Syria.[25] The accused reportedly made several wire transactions to individuals and shadow entities in China, Pakistan and Turkey

---

19 Samuel Haig, *Europol and Interpol to Increase Measures Against BTC Laundering*, Bitcoin.com 30 January, 2018, https://news.bitcoin.com/105481-2/.

20 Edoardo Saravalle & Elizabeth Rosenberg, *Bitcoin Can Help Terrorists Secretly Fund Their Deadly Attacks*, Fox News, 9 January 2018, available from http://www.foxnews.com/opinion/2018/01/09/bitcoin-can-help-terrorists-secretly-fund-their-deadly-attacks.html.

21 Anti-Money-Laundering and Counter-terrorism Financing Amendment Bill 2017, available from http://parlinfo.aph.gov.au/parlInfo/download/legislation/bills/r5952_aspassed/toc_pdf/17177b01.pdf;fileType=application%2Fpdf.

22 Julia Kollewe, *Bitcoin: UK and EU Plan Crackdown Amid Crime and Tax Evasion Fears*, The Guardian, 4 December 2017, https://www.theguardian.com/technology/2017/dec/04/bitcoin-uk-eu-plan-cryptocurrency-price-traders-anonymity.

23 Alissa de Carbonnel, *EU Agrees Stricter Bitcoin Rules Against Money Laundering, Terrorist Financing*, Reuters (15 December 2017), http://uk.businessinsider.com/r-eu-agrees-stricter-bitcoin-rules-against-money-laundering-terrorist-financing-2017-12?IR=T.

24 Francesco Guarascio, Foreign Exchange Analysis, *EU Agrees Clampdown on Bitcoin Platforms to Tackle Money-Laundering*, Reuters, 15 December 2017, https://www.reuters.com/article/uk-eu-moneylaundering/eu-agrees-clampdown-on-bitcoin-platforms-to-tackle-money-laundering-idUSKBN1E928M.

25 Barnes, Joe, *Bitcoin Warning: ISIS Using Cryptocurrency to Fund Reign of Terror as Bitcoin Price Soars*, Sunday Eexpress, 17 Dec. 2017, available at https://www.express.co.uk/finance/city/893151/Bitcoin-price-latest-news-ISIS-terror-cryptocurrency.

to evade reporting and hid the identity of the launderer and receivers along with the source and destination of the money. In November 2017, ISIS website Akbar al-Muslimin sought donations in Bitcoins for its website and there is strong possibility that the money obtained would be utilized for TF. A few countries, such as Russia and Venezuela, have also attempted to bypass international sanctions by creating their own systems. While Venezuela created the "petro," its own digital money, Russia has striven to legalize the trading of e-currencies.[26]

C International Cooperation between Actors and Agencies

Reviewing Figure 1, provided within Chapter 1, the International Specialised Agencies Fighting Terrorism Financing Diagram (by the researcher, 2014), it is held that this offers a clear understanding of the relationship between actors and agencies. All the main actors are expected to respect certain privacy and human rights, including national regulations in force in this domain, UN treaties, EU laws as well as international conventions and policies. Defense-military, police, FIUs and INTERPOL-Europol-Eurojust cooperate with both ministries and main actors while obeying by national laws and international conventions, taking into account recommendations and respecting privacy and human rights. Ministries of State, Defense, Homeland Security, Treasury, Justice take into consideration institutions recommendations and work under the auspices of the EU and UN main guidelines. Ministries' regulations directly impact departments of State, Defense, Homeland Security, Treasury and Justice. These institutions also follow advices provided by financial Institutions, nonprofit organizations, insurance companies and banks.

The IMF, the World Bank and other international institutions' work regarding CTF is followed by the EU, the UN, other countries and ministries regulations. This directly impacts departments of State, Defense, Homeland Security, Treasury, Justice. These institutions' advice is being considered by Financial Institutions, Non-Profit Organizations, Insurance Companies and Banks.

Scholars inspire EU and UN core policies with their work underlining and explaining multiple problems that should be solved at the International level regarding CTF and provide solutions and topics of further work for decision makers.

26 Travis J. Tritten, *The Dark Side of Bitcoin: Terror Financing and Sanctions Evasion*, Washington Examiner, 16 January 2018, available from http://www.washingtonexaminer.com/the-dark-side-of-bitcoin-terror-financing-and-sanctions-evasion/article/2646118#!.

The European Union, the United Nations and other countries have similar issues and consider National Laws, Recommendations by Institutions, International Conventions, Privacy Rights, Human Rights, and interact with ministries to regulate local and International law enforcement to manage and ensure cooperation among them.

Financial institutions, non-profit organizations, insurance companies and banks cooperate with law enforcement to share information while providing information on suspect transactions and accounts according to the policies in place. These institutions need to ensure privacy and human rights and take into consideration International Organizations' recommendations and work. International cooperation is a key to CTF. The United Nations Resolution 2178[27] urges member states to improve international, regional, and sub-regional cooperation. Also, when appropriate, they are being encouraged to conclude bilateral agreements to prevent the travel of foreign terrorist fighters from or through their territories. In addition, the resolution promotes the sharing of information for the purpose of identifying foreign terrorist fighters, along with the sharing and adoption of best practices, and improved understanding of the patterns of travel by these fighters. Since the internet is a worldwide instrument, international cooperation is a key element to preventing terrorists from exploiting technology, resources and communications to incite terrorism and its financing. Terrorists can utilize the internet to collect or launder funds and benefit from the almost complete anonymity they can find there. Hence, countries must collaborate to detect and track suspect online behaviors.

As per the United Nations Resolution 1373,[28] member states need to afford one another the greatest measure of assistance in connection with criminal investigations or proceedings relating to the financing or support of terrorist acts: this includes assistance in obtaining evidence in their possession necessary for the proceedings, and underlines the importance of fulfilling this obligation with respect to such investigations or proceedings involving foreign terrorist fighters. Domestic, supranational and international levels of cooperation are vital for a good application of CTF measures and hence, protocols should be developed to promote better communication and exchanges among countries and jurisdictions. It is indeed hard to point out the appropriate competent authority when cases deal with plural jurisdictions, in such circumstances, protocols can offer guidelines for deconflicting measures.

---

27 U.N. SCOR, *Resolution 2178*, 24 September 2014, available from http://www.un.org/en/sc/ctc/docs/2015/SCR%202178_2014_EN.pdf.

28 U.S. Dep't. of State, *U.N. Security Council Resolution 1373*, 28 September 2001, available from https://2001-2009.state.gov/p/io/rls/othr/2001/5108.htm.

A complex issue to address is the threat posed by foreign fighters. Sponsoring terrorists' activities and their travel expenses allows money to cross the borders of several nations. The States neighboring zones of armed conflict should therefore welcome and encourage bilateral assistance to help with the tracing of terrorists and money linked to their activities. International cooperation very much depends on network, procedures, global or regional multilateral enforcement actions, exchange of best practices to harmonize and monitor information exchange among countries at the supranational level.

Cross-border cash is often hard to detect despite procedures in place within partner jurisdictions such as cash declarations and disclosure which must be overseen and exchanged daily through updated databases. Border security, intelligence and law enforcement should be working closely together, sharing expertise between countries to find and discourage terrorist financers and smugglers. The World Customs Organization (WCO) and related (regional) entities are also helpful partners for achieving such a complex task. Law enforcement organizations, such as INTERPOL, Europol and Eurojust share the difficult duty to facilitating financial crime deterrence and better cooperation among countries, including the arrest of suspect travelers carrying cash with the aim of financing illicit activities. The danger encountered by international law enforcement in cross-border activities is that customs have a very limited time to allow travelers to proceed and act upon suspicions, as well as apprehend individuals travelling across nations through regular port of entry including road, air or maritime means.

Preventive measures, such as proactive contact with law enforcement foreign counterparts to facilitate information exchange and detect ML/TF, as well as pre-interdiction operations and cross-checking to determine suspect behavior can greatly contribute to the deterrence and apprehension of individuals before they cross borders.[29] The scope and application of international cooperation between authorities could be enhanced by improving administrative structures, the speed with which information is obtained, and information exchange for investigative, supervisory and prosecutorial purposes. Better cooperation would also help countries in the tracing, freezing and confiscating of illegal monetary units or assets.

29 Financial Action Task Force (FATF), *International Best Practices: Detecting and Preventing the Illicit Cross-Border Transportation of Cash and Bearer Negotiable Instruments*, 19 February 2010, available from http://www.fatf-gafi.org/media/fatf/documents/recommendations/International%20BPP%20Detecting%20and%20Preventing%20illicit%20cross-border%20transportation%20SR%20IX%20%20COVER%202012.pdf.

D Political Pressure

The main obstacles at the international level that will be difficult to overcome are: the political pressure concerning international terrorism definitions, corruption, cross-border enforcement and privacy issues.

In this regard, as previously discussed in Chapter 1 B, it is hard to decide on a common definition of terrorism to give the Convention, in particular, because the word is highly sensitive on the international scale. Depending on the definition, one could point one's fingers at states for being terrorists themselves because of actions, decisions, political intimidation, or preventive/war campaigns they are involved in that are judged as being non-just by public opinion. A legal definition that remains too vague by including most terrorist-related activities, could represent a direct threat to certain powerful developed countries. Signing such a convention would provide other countries a tool, which could, in the end, play against certain of their international military decisions and operations.

Schemes involving financing terrorist groups (such as environmental groups, political groups, or the acquisition of WMDs for terrorist purpose, etc.) are often centred on influential international actors, who have the means to finance terrorist action and have a keen interest in the criminal act itself. Political actors are therefore frequently involved with TF, ML, corruption and other illegal activities they sponsor and do not wish to obey an international law that could imprison them for financing, initiating and/or participating in terrorist events worldwide. Diplomatic immunity is also an obstacle in certain cases, whereby funds can be easily brought out of a country and handed to terrorists by a person benefiting from immunity.

Money derived from corruption linked to domestic politicians is more widespread in some countries than others. These donations of money are legal and current ways of doing business in certain parts of the world, but huge amounts of money can be displaced in cash and potentially end up financing illicit activities. Hence, while PEPs can be involved with financing criminal activity, detection and investigation of terrorism-financing faces a big obstacle of corrupt money entering or exiting the financial system, being transferred into major banks in larger financial centers, or being cashed out elsewhere. A complicated task is to find the illegitimacy of the money related to the transaction, or the destination of the funds and the crimes it would finance.[30]

---

30 U.S. Dep't. of the Treasury, Financial Crimes Enforcement Network, *FATF-VIII Money-Laundering Typologies Exercise Public Report*, November 1996, available from http://www.fincen.gov/news_room/rp/files/fatf.pdf.

State sponsored terrorism is clearly a big issue. OFAC listed government officials are foreign PEPs whose actions and ideas are going against US morals, such as, for example: the North Korean cyberattacks, the Russian actions against Ukraine, or the Palestinian Authority figures working against Israel. Election interference, as was the case during the 2016 US political campaign is regarded as terrorism. On Feb 16th, 2018, the US department of Justice charged 13 Russians and three companies, who were part of the sophisticated politically themed ads scheme, of supporting, later to be President, Donald Trump's campaign.[31] They included several ML charges, for schemes used to finance the operation. Two of the Russian firms involved hold Russian government contracts.

Arab government officials have been indicted or at least targeted for supporting anti-Israel, anti-US or other organizations. In particular, Saudi Arabia is closely watched by the international community, as it is the biggest state to sponsor terrorism, and Wahhabism is the source of radical Islamic extremism. The United States estimated that nearly $100 million was sent annually to Deobandi and Ahl-e-Hadith clerics in these regions from "missionary" and "Islamic charitable" organizations in Saudi Arabia and the United Arab Emirates.[32] Saudi Arabia also finances extremist ideologies and activity in the UK, according to the British ambassador to Riyadh.[33] Qatar's is another Arab country, which has allegedly continued funding radical ideology and extremism. Its support for the Islamist Muslim Brotherhood, as well as its relationship with the Taliban and Al-Qaida affiliates along with Iran represents a great TF threat. Qatar agreed to increase cooperation on fighting TF and to announce sanctions on 13 individuals reportedly linked to Al-Qaida and Islamic State militants.[34] In April 2017, Qatar paid a ransom of $1 billion to an Al-Qaida affiliate in Syria and to Iran to free 26 royal family members and Shia fighters captured in Syria by

---

31 Matt Apuzzo & Sharon LaFraniere, *13 Russians Indicted as Mueller Reveals Effort to Aid Trump Campaign,* N.Y. Times, 16 February 2018, https://www.nytimes.com/2018/02/16/us/politics/russians-indicted-mueller-election-interference.html?ribbon-ad-idx=3&src=trending&module=ArrowsNav&contentCollection=Business%20Day&action=swipe&region=FixedRight&pgtype=article.

32 Adam Weinstein, *The Real Largest State Sponsor of Terrorism,* Huffington Post, 16 March 2017, available from https://www.huffingtonpost.com/entry/the-real-largest-state-sponsor-of-terrorism_us_58cafc26e4b00705db4da8aa.

33 Kenza Bryan, Home News, *Saudi Arabia Funding Linked to Terror in UK by Britain's Former Ambassador to Riyadh,* The Independent (14 July 2017), http://www.independent.co.uk/news/uk/home-news/saudi-arabia-terror-funding-uk-extremism-islamist-william-patey-former-ambassador-home-office-qatar-a7840406.html.

34 Eric Knecht, World News, *U.S., Qatar Agree to Further Curbs on Terrorist Financing,* Reuters, 30 October 2017, https://www.reuters.com/article/us-qatar-usa-security/u-s-qatar-agree-to-further-curbs-on-terrorist-financing-idUSKBN1CZ2I7.

Iranian-backed Iraqi Shia militiamen.[35] Such funds transfer represents a great risk, as it might directly be utilized to finance terrorism.

A new CTF Convention model will be hard to apply to nations that could consider its application to encroach on their state right of sovereignty. Countries might agree with information sharing for deterrence purposes, but would not accept boundary spanning investigative forces or Global Financial Unit Police coming into their territory. Unfortunately, only a multi-task, pluri-jurisdictional, fact-finding unit including investigators from different countries and with direct seizure and surrounding powers could be fast enough to act before financers vanish and hold enough expertise to avoid administrative and jurisdictional gaps.

The issue that remains unresolved and faces political blockages is the inclusion of provisions in a new CTF tool, which might violate citizens' privacy rights and breach civil liberties (such as the freedom of speech, or the freedom of association). Political pressure will therefore remain one of the most important obstacles to overcome before nations can reach a common agreement to standardize CTF policies at an international level. Agreeing on such terms, is a complex task as most countries already have their own laws on these matters that are often related to their Constitutional rights, or have already signed different conventions with other countries.

35 Tom Keatinge, Centre for Financial Crime and Security Studies, *Why Qatar is the Focus of Terrorism Claims,* BBC News, 13 June 2017, http://www.bbc.com/news/world-middle-east-40246734.

CHAPTER 5

The Ineffectiveness of the Current Enforcement System Mechanism

The aim of this chapter, is to discuss the ineffectiveness of the current enforcement system mechanism, by considering its main failures, so as to be able to build a more practicable CTF Convention.

Part A: discusses cross-border enforcement matters, including mutual legal assistance and cooperation between countries to implement sanctions.

Part B: Asset recovery legal tools are reviewed to demonstrate how assets linked to TF activities are located, frozen and recovered. Different types of recovery mechanisms at the international level are considered, in order to provide better understanding of what could be done to seize assets within the new Convention model.

A Cross-border Enforcement

Whilst various national, international and global industries and regulatory organizations keep an eye on TF activities and assist financial institutions by issuing recommendations and regulations to deter financial crimes, enforcement concerning TF remains a complex task. Geographical flexibility greatly facilitates TF and the movement of assets, or currencies across borders. The location of terrorist operations may change, if those perpetrating them are aware that law enforcement agencies are pursuing their financial activities. In such cases, terrorists may attempt to avoid detection by switching their scheme to the use of different commodities, industries or fundraising activities.[1] The main features of cross-border enforcement are mutual legal assistance in criminal proceedings, data sharing for investigation purposes, and extradition. A new legal CTF tool should consider it a priority to incorporate an obligation for states parties to extradite individuals under arrest warrants to countries that issued them per the well- known *Aut dedere aut judicare* principle. Extradition and mutual legal assistance may not be regarded for political offences, yet this

1 LexisNexis Risk Division, *Emerging Anti-Money-Laundering Risks to Financial Institutions*, 2007, available from http://www.scribd.com/doc/3941706/AntiMoney-Laundering-Risks-to-Financial-Institutions.

 | DOI:10.1163/9789004409675_009

justification cannot be invoked to avoid extradition for terrorists and their accomplices.[2]

General policy issues that have been identified regarding CTF include regulatory, law enforcement, and international policy coordination matters.[3] International cooperation is an effective prevention and detection tool in the fight against TF. Non-cooperative states are the closest accomplices of terrorists, whereby they allow criminals to pursue their illicit financial activities and to remain unpunished. Territories and jurisdictions that do not cooperate are an ongoing threat, and thus, a great concern and area of research for FATF members. In fact, these states represent a major hindrance to detecting, investigating and prosecuting CTF suspects successfully, since they refuse to provide information on the owners of foreign legal entities, offshore trusts, international business corporations and shell companies.[4] Mutual Legal Assistance Treaties (MLATS) generally allow for the exchange of evidence and information in criminal and related matters through the signature of treaties and agreements among countries. In AML/CTF and civil asset forfeiture cases, countries partners to such treaties can exchange financial and bank records. The use of Financial Information Exchange Agreements (FIEAS) can also facilitate the exchange of currency transaction information between governments' treasury departments and finance ministries. Regulatory issues, adaptation to new financial schemes, jurisdictional issues arising from borderless financial crimes, are at the heart of the criminalization of TF. International harmonization is therefore a top priority in this domain along with increased cooperation.

New types of service providers, transactions and instruments increase the need for definitions and regulations in this field. International and domestic practices, along with regulatory agencies constantly attempt to increase cooperation measures between countries. Nevertheless, they still need focus on developing procedures to ensure better reporting and information-sharing by financial institutions, banks and other relevant actors.[5] Enforcement also depends on specific cases, as well as: the motivations and *mens rea* of the suspects, the duration and frequency of the breach, and whether other

2 U.N. GAOR resolution 54/109 *International Convention for the Suppression of the Financing of Terrorism*, 9 December 1999, available from http://www.un.org/law/cod/finterr.htm.

3 Roger C. Molander et al., *Cyberpayments and Money-Laundering*, 1998, available from http://www.rand.org/content/dam/rand/pubs/monograph_reports/1998/MR965.sum.pdf.

4 Financial Action Task Force (FATF), *Typologies*, (last visited 5 July 2014), http://www.apgml.org/frameworks/docs/5/FATF%20Typologies%20rpt%201998-99.pdf.

5 Connie M. Friesen, *US and UK Anti-Money-Laundering Requirements Compared*, International Law Office, 5 September 2008, available from http://www.internationallawoffice.com/newsletters/detail.aspx?g=5e143642-6dd9-4b32-8d4e-cab33d724eea.

enforcement or remedial measures were previously envisaged. Enforcement measures taken on non-complying banks and financial institutions in the United States or the United Kingdom demonstrate that civil and criminal penalties can be applied in both jurisdictions. Sanctions include cancelling a bank's authorization or license to carry on business. The length of imprisonment faced and amount of fines imposed on institutions for failing to comply with the required security measures for TF varies amongst counties, for terrorism-financers, their accomplices, or employees participating in schemes.

B Assets Tracing, Freezing of Assets and Assets Recovery

The United Nations Resolution 2199 reaffirms its 2161 Resolution, which applies to financial and economic resources of every kind including, but not limited to, those used for the provision of Internet hosting or related services, that funds used to support Al-Qaida and other individuals, groups, undertakings or entities included on the Al-Qaida Sanctions List are a threat to the international community. Members of the United Nations should, therefore, work on enhancing their cooperation to locate terrorists and the persons financed to commit terrorist attacks. Pursuant to the provisions of the 1988 UN Drug Convention, foreign governments should cooperate in joint investigations of drug trafficking and ML, offering the inducement of sharing forfeited assets. The asset tracing context consists of locating, identifying and freezing stolen assets as well as tracing the transaction path from origin to destination. The Palermo, Merida, and Vienna Conventions are robust tools for achieving an international approach on assets' proceeds, property, and instrumentalities' confiscation, forfeiture and seizure.

Regarding asset recovery, TF and ML sharing similarities. Yet, banks should consider that the nature of the funding may vary depending on the type of terrorist organization. Banks should freeze the assets of designated persons and entities as per applicable local laws and regulations without delay and without prior notice. Recalling that transactions connected with TF can be conducted in very small amounts, tracing and freezing can be complicated. Since TF funds can come from both regular "legal" financial activities and criminal activities, they can easily be mistaken with general financial activities. Banks must have the capacity to identify funds and to enforce competent authorities' freezing decisions. The process for AML, anti-corruption, law enforcement, asset forfeiture in the context of asset recovery involves intelligence gathering, investigation, prosecution, and distribution. Three options are available to recover assets, these being the anticipated sale of assets, confiscation, and seizure. In order to recover these assets, law enforcement and competent authorities should identify, trace, freeze, confiscate and forfeit by gathering evidence, and work on the distribution of the collected proceeds especially in the case of multiple jurisdictions. The main challenges encountered are political will, capacity, conventions and agreements either multilateral or bilateral, as well as non-state actors.

The confiscation system procedure can be divided into three stages: investigative, judicial, and disposal. Regarding domestic law, confiscation procedures can differ.[6] In some countries financial investigation and asset confiscation actions will have to be completed simultaneously or even prior to the criminal prosecution, while in others it can be conducted separately, even after imprisonment. Mechanisms for the recovery of assets include criminal forfeiture, civil action, civil law suit, and non-conviction-based forfeiture. Civil forfeiture leads to imprisonment and/or a fine, the confiscation of people's proceeds and could also involve supplementary fines to repair the damage caused. There are five main types of assets that should be targeted for civil forfeiture: debarment, intermingled, transformed assets, instrumentalities, and value-based confiscation. The civil action is attached to, but independent from, and interrelated with civil action forfeiture. The civil action can continue even if the civil action led to an acquittal. A civil law suit is a completely independent action, while non-convention-based forfeiture is an action against the asset and not the person. Issues assimilated to asset recovery legal actions include: the lack of information and evidence, the amount of compensation chosen, the arbitration and bankruptcy processes, as well as the difficulty of meeting the burden of proof according to the standards of the country the procedure is initiated by (the standard of evidence *vs* reversed burden of proof).

Criminal forfeiture is deemed to be a much more powerful law enforcement tool than civil forfeiture, in that the former is part of the sentence of a criminal case. Criminal asset forfeiture is an *in personam* action against the defendant, whereas the civil forfeiture process is an *in rem* action against the specific property involved in the crime itself. The *in personam* nature of criminal forfeiture has important consequences owing to the volatility of assets, and to the fact that money used to finance terrorism can easily disappear, which means it cannot be forfeited if it is not found soon enough by law enforcement. In civil forfeiture cases when civil action *in rem* against the property is filed, law enforcement authorities should prove with clear evidence that the property at

6 Lexis PSL, *Anti-money-laundering and Counter-terrorist financing*, 2013, http://lexisweb.co.uk/sub-topics/anti-money-laundering-and-Counter-terrorist-financing.

stake was derived from a crime or was used to commit one. Examples of *in rem* legislation can be found in jurisdictions such as, those of the United States, the United Kingdom, Australia. Non-conviction-based asset forfeiture means the criminal forfeiture will occur with the guarantee that there will be no criminal conviction. This type of forfeiture undermines people's confidence in law enforcement and the efficiency of the criminal law system. Whilst criminal forfeiture requires a criminal trial and conviction, non-conviction-based asset forfeiture does not, and the procedures used to forfeit assets differ. Non-conviction-based asset forfeiture is therefore quite an effective asset recovery tool.

Considering the importance of information sharing and mutual legal assistance in the asset recovery process, the new Convention model should also include an International Information Gateways section, as provided by article 1 of the UK-Ireland-Canadian agreement:

Article 1- Informational Gateways and Mutual Legal Assistance Treaties

1. General provisions under this article pertain to the transference of information, evidence, and formal testimonies in reference to the pursuit, investigation, prosecution, forfeiture, recovery, and disposal of property comprised of those derived from or received in kind by means of monetary or any other tangible enrichment or benefit arising from the commission of any illicit act committed in concert with organized criminal enterprise transacting in a cross jurisdictional environment(s).
2. In the event of a formal investigation in the pursuit of a remedy by the requesting State an officially sanctioned Request for Mutual Legal Assistance must be ratified by the United Nations Governing Subcommittee, and the highest Criminal Court of each jurisdiction with a material interest in the recovery.
   (a.) The Subcommittee shall require that the requesting State's highest criminal court officially certify and sanction the intent and facts on the case on which the remedy and subsequent forfeiture is being sought.
   (b.) The value of the asset sought for forfeiture and remedy by the requesting State shall be officially certified by the jurisdiction of residence no later than the 60th day post certification of facts.
   (c.) The Subcommittee shall require that the requesting State post a bond to be held in trust by the United Nations in the amount of not less than 1/3 of the total declared value of the asset sought.
3. All parties involved in the exchange or engaging in the pursuit and of the forfeiture and recovery related activities are subject to the governing laws of the requesting State.

   (a.) All individuals participating in said matters in an evidentiary capacity are subject to formal certification as to fitness and character for participation in the action by their resident jurisdiction's highest court.
   (b.) The resident jurisdiction will further be required to certify the existence of any relevant conflicts of interest inherent to the parties that would bar participation in the Action.
   (c.) The resident jurisdiction shall be required to post a bond held in trust by an independent certified third party for each participating individual who intends to provide material evidence for the forfeiture proceedings in the amount to 1/3 of the total certified present value of the asset sought.
4. Should at any time during the pursuit either party deem that they are unduly burdened by their participation in the investigation and seizure they may appeal to the United Nations Governing Subcommittee for final determination of relief.
   (a.) Should the Governing body certify the existence of an undue burden the requesting Jurisdiction shall be offered a variance to allow for the appeal for certification of financial need. At such time that the certification is ratified the United Nations Subcommittee shall compel the International Monetary Fund to provide financial assistance related to participation in the form of a loan under customary present terms.
   (b.) Upon completion of the action and finalization of recovery and disposal all participating jurisdictions are required to submit an officially certified Request for Monetary Relief for expenses incurred during the course of the action.
   (c.) Upon recovery of the asset the requesting State shall be compelled to compensate all participating jurisdictions for incurred expenses not to exceed an amount totaling all jurisdictional payments of no greater than 75% of the forfeited items certified market value.

To be clear on definitions, a country receiving a request to follow orders of a forfeiture judgment against property within its border is a requested country, while one seeking to obtain a forfeiture judgment against property located beyond its borders is called a requesting country.[7] Dual criminality must exist between jurisdictions, as well as the predicate offence, which must be recognized by both the requesting and requested states in order to attain international

7 U.S. Dep't. of Justice, Offices of the United States Attorneys, *Asset Forfeiture*, 10 February 2016, available from http://www.justice.gov/usao/eousa/foia_reading_room/usab5506.pdf

enforcement. Enforceable confiscation orders and criminal convictions in the requesting state or the recipient state are vital to the international recovery process through MLAT, yet it is not easy to satisfy conditions of asset recovery with criminal convictions. Many countries are still reluctant to enforce a court order from another jurisdiction. The existence of MLAT treaties is often important for countries cooperating in enforcement matters. These are, nonetheless, bilateral measures generating complexity instead of providing standardisation, as they require a large number of agreements to be established to be fully effective. The conformance to a single standard for the exchange of information would, therefore, offer a worldwide process of recovery. Several international organizations are involved in this effort of regulating asset recovery at the international level. The UN Office on Drugs and Crime and the World Bank Group launched the Stolen Asset Recovery initiative, which recognizes the necessity to assist developing countries in recovering stolen assets. Moreover, the United Nations Convention against Corruption (UNCAC) has provided an international legal framework sustaining the initiative that came into force in 2005 after calls for international cooperation and assistance with regard to the recovery mechanisms of illicitly acquired assets in the tracing, freezing, seizing, forfeiture and return of assets. Part of the recovered assets are expected to provide funding for social programs and infrastructure. In cases in which no bilateral or multilateral arrangements are in place, UNCAC signatories may use the Convention itself as a legal basis for enforcing confiscation orders obtained in a foreign criminal court. Article 54 Section 1A of UNCAC provides that:

> Each State Party (will)... take such measures as may be necessary to permit its competent authorities to give effect to an order of confiscation issued by a court of another state party.[8]

Section 54. 2. A of UNCAC offers measures for the provisional freezing or seizing of property, where there are sufficient grounds for taking such actions in advance of a formal request being received. UNCAC also provides for adequate procedures to be followed by financial institutions. including suspicious activity involving the private banking accounts of prominent public officials, their family members and close associates, as well as procedures allowing State Parties to participate as private litigants in the courts of another State Party.

8 U.N. Office on Drugs and Crime, GAOR resolution 58/4, *Convention Against Corruption*, New York, 31 October 2003, available from http://www.unodc.org/documents/treaties/UNCAC/Publications/Convention/08-50026_E.pdf.

Concerning proceeds of crime or property confiscated, Article 14 of UNTOC states that:

1. Proceeds of crime or property confiscated by a State Party … shall be disposed of by that State Party in accordance with its domestic law and administrative procedures.
2. When acting on the request made by another State Party … States Parties shall, to the extent permitted by domestic law and if so requested, give priority consideration to returning the confiscated proceeds of crime or property to the requesting State Party so that it can give compensation to the victims of the crime or return such proceeds of crime or property to their legitimate owners.
3. When acting on the request made by another State Party … a State Party may give special consideration to concluding agreements or arrangements on:

> Contributing the value of such proceeds of crime or property or funds derived from the sale of such proceeds of crime or property or a part thereof to the account designated in accordance with article 30, paragraph 2 (c), of this Convention and to intergovernmental bodies specializing in the fight against organized crime;
>
> Sharing with other States Parties, on a regular or case-by-case basis, such proceeds of crime or property, or funds derived from the sale of such proceeds of crime or property, in accordance with its domestic law or administrative procedures.[9]

According to UNCAC Article 57.3, the requested State Party shall:

> In the case of embezzlement of public funds or of laundering of embezzled public funds … return the confiscated property to the requesting State Party;
>
> In the case of proceeds of any other offence covered by this Convention, … return the confiscated property to the requesting State Party, when the requesting State Party reasonably establishes its prior ownership of such confiscated property to the requested State Party or when

9 U.N. Office on Drugs and Crime, GAOR resolution 55/25, *Convention Against Transnational Organized Crime*, New York, 15 November 2000, available from https://www.unodc.org/documents/treaties/UNTOC/Publications/TOC%20Convention/TOCebook-e.pdf.

> the requested State Party recognizes damage to the requesting State Party as a basis for returning the confiscated property;
>
> In all other cases, give priority consideration to returning confiscated property to the requesting State Party, returning such property to its prior legitimate owners or compensating the victims of the crime.
>
> Where appropriate, unless States Parties decide otherwise, requested States Parties may deduct reasonable expenses incurred in investigations, prosecutions or judicial proceedings leading to the return or disposition of confiscated property pursuant to this article.
>
> Where appropriate, States Parties may also give special consideration to concluding agreements or mutually acceptable arrangements, on a case-by-case basis, for the final disposal of confiscated property.[10]

Within the content of UNCAC, adapting domestic law to create a legal basis for *in rem* recoveries is not demanded of State Parties.

Seizure should be part of the preventive part of the investigation, since apprehending the patrimony of the accused before judgment, which can take years, is the only way to make sure the money will not disappear. Permission of the Ministry of Finance is often necessary to recover as little as 1 euro from a frozen account to pay living expenses before an investigation is closed. Agencies for management and recovery of seized and confiscated assets can help unfreeze them for the payment of bills. Suspects might get compensation, if found not guilty and deprived of their assets over a period of time.

10 GAOR 58/4, *supra*.

CHAPTER 6

Potential Conflicts between a New CTF tool and Human Rights

This chapter discusses the concept of the right balance between the need for information and data collection, retention and sharing, and the right to financial privacy, as well as other inerrant human rights. This is a crucial matter to raise regarding the new proposed CTF Convention model.

Part A: describes the international regulatory scene for data protection and privacy laws.

Part B: recalls the human rights associated with CTF regulations, which might represent a blockage to the construction of an effective new tool incorporating strong data gathering and transfer mechanisms for the purpose of CTF deterrence and law enforcement.

A International Privacy Laws

The main legal issues faced by the international community regarding privacy and the effective implementation and use of CTF measures, include the right to be protected by law against unlawful or arbitrary interference with privacy. Article 17 of the International Covenant on Civil and Political Rights and art. 12 of the Universal Declaration of Human Rights provide an international standard concerning data collected, retained, transmitted and used which can apply in the field of CTF. Rights related to Privacy laws frequently include privacy, private life, personal information/data, identity, integrity, and autonomy. Financial Privacy laws are a great concern when dealing with the construction of a new convention model, as this topic currently leaves much of the international community sceptical about the end usage of the data collected for international law enforcement purposes. The transmission of personal data across national borders and beyond the jurisdiction of the country in which they were collected, along with the disclosure of personal data to third parties, are the biggest threats encountered at the international level regarding privacy. A key issue regarding data is that transferring them to anyone is quite easy and thus, it is almost impossible to know who will acquire information about an individual, whether lawfully or illegally.

 | DOI:10.1163/9789004409675_010

The right to privacy as a fundamental human right is a great concern for the international community, whereby this right might in many cases be infringed by law enforcement. There must be an appropriate balance between an individual's right to financial privacy and the need to collect and dispatch personal data for law enforcement purposes to discourage crimes, as well as to prevent and detect TF. Various international regulations concerning privacy are already in place. They block the effectiveness of potent data collection mechanisms and international cooperation for the purpose of data sharing. This challenge will remain, and will always exist unless nations decide to align and amend their prevailing tools to allow counties to share data with cooperating counterparts regarding TF and other related financial crimes. Even if national regulations differ with regard to individuals' rights in relation to their personal data, individuals should be protected by law against unlawful or arbitrary interference in their privacy, as well as against discrimination.[1] Accordingly, national laws should and do address the potential conflict between CTF obligations, on the one hand, and privacy and data protection laws, on the other. A few regulations and policies cover the right for privacy concerning data and information collected by law enforcement and financial institutions. The 1990 UN guidelines[2] on computerized personal data, provide the principles of lawfulness, non-discrimination, security, independent supervision, purpose specification, interested person access, trans-border data flows, and a limitation clause. Moreover, the Lisbon Treaty demands that State Parties should respect the right of privacy; however, there are no other international binding instruments concerning data protection.

Non-binding EU Human rights recommendations, EU Legal Sources and other EU instruments on Data protection, such as Directive 1995/46/EC, Directive 2002/58/EC and the retain Data Directive 2006/24/EC are useful tools regarding data collection, retention and transfer. Article 7 and 8 of the 2000 EU Charter of Fundamental Rights and Fundamental Freedom also provides EU regulations for the lawfulness and fairness of actions, as well as purpose specification, and a right of access and modification of personnal data, along with an independent supervision section, and criteria of the individual's consent.

1 U.N. Human Rights Council, *Annual Report of the United Nations High Commissioner for Human Rights and Reports of the Office of the High Commissioner and the Secretary General*, A/HRC/28/28 ¶ 53, 19 Dec. 2014, http://undocs.org/en/A/HRC/28/28.

2 U.N. GAOR 45/95, *Guidelines for the Regulation of Computerized Personal Data Files*, A/RES/45/95, 14 December 1990, available from http://www.un.org/documents/ga/res/45/a45r095.htm.

The necessity and proportionality of infringing privacy is a great concern when it comes to dealing with health, consumer, or financial information. EU resolutions from the Committee of Ministers and several recommendations on employment, social security, telecommunications deal with data collection, retention and transfer, but are not legally binding.

The Regulation (EU) 2016/679 of the European Parliament and of the Council of 27 April 2016 on the protection of natural persons with regard to the processing of personal data and on the free movement of such data, and repealing Directive 95/46/EC (General Data Protection Regulation)[3] introduces in its Section 3, the rights of rectification (article 16), and the right of erasure 'to be forgotten' (article 17). The Regulation entered into force on 24 May 2016 and applies since 25 May 2018. This Directive is an essential step to strengthen individuals' fundamental rights and facilitate business by clarifying rules on data protection.

While making rules on data protection, it remains complex to find the right balance between Privacy and data collection. In the fight against terrorism, the more information we can collect the better, whereas a private individual can perceive data collection policies as too invasive and violating its personal life. Specific concerns were also raised about the time period, as well as the access and use limitations for the retained data.

B Civil Liberties and Humanitarian Laws

The 2014 United Nations Resolution 2178[4] states that any measures taken by Member States to Counter-terrorism shall comply with international laws and Human Rights, therefore, measures that interfere with privacy should meet international obligations and commitments. The human rights dimension of information and communications technology issues should be addressed as a main issue regarding the construction of a new Convention along with principles of necessity, proportionality and legality, with appropriate safeguards to guarantee accountability and judicial redress. The principles related to criminal

3 The Regulation (EU) 2016/679 of the European Parliament and of the Council of 27 April 2016 on the protection of natural persons with regard to the processing of personal data and on the free movement of such data, and repealing Directive 95/46/EC (General Data Protection Regulation), 2016, https://eur-lex.europa.eu/eli/reg/2016/679/oj.

4 U.N. Meetings Coverage and Press Releases, *Security Council Unanimously Adopts Resolution Condemning Violent Extremism, Underscoring Need to Prevent Travel, Support for Foreign Terrorist Fighters*, SC 11580, 24 September 2014, available from http://www.un.org/press/en/2014/sc11580.doc.htm.

offences and penalties can be found in article 49 of the Charter of Fundamental Rights. Procedural safeguards and independent oversight should be in place to ensure non-discriminatory measures and the elimination of the abusive use of personal data. Intelligence and law enforcement measures taken by surveillance entities for digital communications might become an effective and essential tool to prevent the recruitment of terrorists through the internet.[5] Self-regulation by companies, as well as effective cooperation by private entities with intelligence and law enforcement agencies is crucial, if there is to be an effective use of surveillance policies.[6] The 2011 Human Rights Council Guiding Principles on Business and Human Rights[7] also provide guidelines to be considered by businesses and service providers when dealing with their users and customers. Private companies should identify, assess, prevent and mitigate their actions with human rights.

Automatic mass surveillance of the population and digital communications would affect fundamental human rights and freedoms.[8] The inherent internationally recognized right to respect private and family life might also be infringed by surveillance and intelligence initiatives.[9] The task for law enforcement while dealing with data collection to fight TF should always be to take into consideration the necessity to protect the rights and freedoms of others and meeting objectives of general interest. National security and terrorism-related objectives can be a reason for restricting fundamental rights, such as the freedom of expression,[10] movement, thought, conscience, and religion.[11] The freedom of expression of an individual can be incompatible with the general prohibition of discrimination on the grounds of: race, color, ethnic or social origin, genetic features, language, religion or belief, political or any other

5 U.N. Human Rights Council, *The Right to Privacy in the Digital Age*, A/HRC/27/37, ¶ 24, 30 June 2014, available from http://www.ohchr.org/EN/HRBodies/HRC/RegularSessions/Session27/Documents/A.HRC.27.37_en.pdf.

6 U.N. High Commissioner for Refugees (UNHCR), *Letter dated 2 September 2015 from the Chair of the Security Council Committee established pursuant to resolution 1373 (2001) concerning counter-terrorism addressed to the President of the Security Council*, S/2015/683, 2 September 2015, available from http://www.refworld.org/docid/5616128d4.html.

7 U.N. A/HRC/27/37, *supra*.

8 Martin Scheinin, U.N. GAOR, *Report of the Special Rapporteur on the Promotion and Protection of Human Rights and Fundamental Freedoms While Countering Terrorism*, A/HRC/13/37, ¶¶ 33–38, 28 December 2009, available from http://www2.ohchr.org/english/bodies/hrcouncil/docs/13session/A-HRC-13-37.pdf.

9 European Parliament, *The Charter of Fundamental Rights of the European Union*, October 2017, article 7, available from http://www.europarl.europa.eu/atyourservice/en/displayFtu.html?ftuId=FTU_4.1.2.html.

10 EP, *id.* article 11.

11 EP, *supra*, article 10.

opinion.[12] Prevention and removal of information communicated for terrorist purposes, including the financing phase, might therefore infringe the right of freedom of speech and opinion.

Charities being in the spotlight for the misuse of financing is becoming more frequent. Without any current international common agreement to detect and therefore enforce the misuse of these funds, legitimate organizations are used as a smokescreen to create funds to finance terrorism in the shade of law enforcement. Countries should firmly regulate Non-Profit Organizations, yet there is a risk of overstepping on the freedom of association and assembly of individuals.[13]

A new CTF Convention model should take into account fundamental rights, such as the right to life, to physical and mental integrity, to the effective remedy and a fair trial,[14] to the presumption of innocence and the right of defence,[15] to not be tried or punished twice in criminal proceedings for the same criminal offence (*ne bis in idem*),[16] and the right to property,[17] while confiscating assets from persons on trial, suspected, accused or convicted of terrorist offences and offences related to a terrorist group or terrorist activities. A new offence of travelling abroad for terrorist purposes can also restrict the freedom of movement and residence.[18] It also threatens the right to asylum and governmental protection in the event of removal, expulsion or extradition.[19] Other legal instruments dealing with human rights include: the European Union Convention for the Protection of Human Rights and Fundamental Freedoms, Case-law of the European Communities and of the European Court of Human Rights, and the Convention on the protection of Human Rights and Fundamental Freedom.

12 EP, *supra*, article 21.
13 EP, *supra*, article 12.
14 EP, *supra*, article 47.
15 EP, *supra*, article 48.
16 EP, *supra*, article 50.
17 EP, *supra*, article 17.
18 EP, *supra*, article 45.
19 EP, *supra*, article 18–19.

PART 3

Current Regulatory Instruments

Introduction to Part 3

In order to build a new convention model, past and present recommendations and policies from the United Nations, international organizations and countries around the world will be taken into consideration. Gaps among the current system acknowledged by specialists interviewed for the purpose of this analysis will be highlighted to understand what topics are important for a new convention model to cover.

Chapter 7 will provide a list and relevant extracts of Counter-terrorism. instruments concerning CTF, including International Counter-terrorism Regulations, agencies and financial institutions' recommendations, financial services best practice rules and countries' policies. These will be critically assessed to demonstrate the gaps in the current legal system and thus, illustrate the importance of a new convention model.

Chapter 8 will offer a criticism by the author to introduce the construction of a new convention model for monitoring TF worldwide. The successes and failures of existing counter-terrorism tools with regard to CTF will be discussed through interaction with experts of CTF's plurality of professions to determine where they believe problems arise or could be fixed at their level. A visual map will be constructed to show where a new model should intervene.

 | DOI:10.1163/9789004409675_011

CHAPTER 7

Analysis of Existing Counter-terrorism Tools with regard to Counter-terrorism Financing

The aim of this chapter is to analyse existing Counter-terrorism tools for implementing Counter-terrorism Financing. International Counter-terrorism regulations, agencies and financial institutions' recommendations, Financial Services Best Practices, and countries legislative contributions will be reviewed to determine what existing provisions should be included in a new model and what important recommendations must be incorporated in it to offer the most relevant CTF new Convention model to the international community. It is important to cover matters such as privacy, civil liberties, assets freezing, confiscation of assets and asset recovery tools, within a new convention model. Specific international cooperation and enforcement measures drawn and improved from current Counter-terrorism instruments will also be inserted in the new legal tool.

Sections of the secondary material contained within the three lists of advisory tools and regulations provided in Chapter 1, have been isolated methodically to be reviewed in this chapter. The relevant articles were selected and reviewed separately, according to their pertinence to building up the Convention set out in Chapter 10. The principal characteristics of each instrument have been extracted, and their particularities explained, as they represent a starting point to build up the new Convention. The extracts analysed were not automatically inserted into the puzzle Convention. They were either inserted into the new Convention, or replaced by other elements of the lists of legislative tools with similar impacts.

The aim of this exercise is to identify the important factors, which should belong to the new Convention, and to utilize the full potential of the secondary material studied in-depth in this chapter. This will provide the new tool with a full spectrum of what has been undertaken in this field. To this will be added the results of the gap analysis and personal recommendations found in Chapter 8. One can see with this analysis that the complexity of these instruments pertaining to terrorism has increased over the years, with articles being more and more focused on its financing.

 | DOI:10.1163/9789004409675_012

1 International Counter-terrorism Regulations

The United Nations has issued 14 Conventions related to terrorism. Even though several of these instruments appear to be irrelevant and do not mention the word "Terrorism" within the title of the legislative tool itself, they offer profound understanding of the evolution of the TF legal framework. That is, these International treaties offer a coherent legal framework for deterring and fighting terrorism, detecting perpetrators and limiting illicit access required by terrorists to pursue their actions, such as discrete financing. The Charter of the United Nations provides relevant protocols pertaining to human rights, refugee laws and international humanitarian law standards.[1]

The Security Council has also been active in CTF through terrorism related resolutions and by creating several subsidiary bodies.[2] The United Nations aim is:

> To refrain from organizing, instigating, facilitating, participating in, financing, encouraging or tolerating terrorist activities and to take appropriate practical measures to ensure that our respective territories are not used for terrorist installations or training camps, or for the preparation or organization of terrorist acts intended to be committed against other States or their citizens…
>
> …To cooperate fully in the fight against terrorism, in accordance with our obligations under international law, in order to find, deny safe haven and bring to justice, on the basis of the principle of extradite or prosecute, any person who supports, facilitates, participates or attempts to participate in the financing, planning, preparation or perpetration of terrorist acts or provides safe havens…
>
> …To encourage measures, including regular informal meetings, to enhance, as appropriate, more frequent exchanges of information on cooperation and technical assistance among Member States, United Nations bodies dealing with Counter-terrorism, relevant specialized agencies, relevant international, regional and sub-regional organizations, and the donor community, to develop States' capacities to implement relevant United Nations resolutions.[3]

---

1 U.N., *Counter-Terrorism Strategy*, United Nations, (last visited 5 July 2014), www.un.org/terrorism/strategy-counter-terrorism.shtml.

2 U.N., *United Nations*, available from http://www.un.org/terrorism/.

3 Counter-terrorism Strategy, *supra*.

The agreements of the United Nations do not make provisions for the material and mental elements of the crimes at stake and leave the critical task of defining terrorism to countries themselves, apart from the 1999 CTF Convention, which explicitly stands against TF by providing a clear definition of this crime.[4]

First, the list of International Counter-terrorism related Regulations offered by the United Nations and Security Council includes:

A. Convention on Offences and certain other acts committed on board aircraft[5] (No: 10106)

This Convention was signed in Tokyo on 14 September 1963 and came into force on 4 December 1969. It was the first UN instrument dealing with an offense related to terrorism and penalizing it. The Convention reads as such:

> CHAPTER I—SCOPE OF THE CONVENTION
> Article 1.
> 1.This Convention shall apply in respect of:
> (a) offences against penal law;
> (b) acts which, whether or not they are offences, may or do jeopardize the safety of the aircraft or of persons or property therein or which jeopardize good order and discipline on board.

Article 2 of this Convention provides that the offense had to be committed while an aircraft is in flight, and Article 4 specifies that the Convention shall not apply to aircraft used in the military, customs or police services.

B. Convention for the Suppression of Unlawful Seizure of Aircraft[6] (No: 12325)

The second Convention from the United Nations, which applied to terrorist acts, was signed at the Hague on 16 December 1970 and came into force on 14 October 1971. According to this legal international instrument:

4 U.N. GAOR resolution 54/109 *International Convention for the Suppression of the Financing of Terrorism,* 9 December 1999, available from http://www.un.org/law/cod/finterr.htm.

5 U.N. International Civil Aviation Organization, *Convention on Offences and Certain Other Acts Committed on Board Aircraft,* 14 September 1963, *U.N.T.S.*, No. 10106, available from http://treaties.un.org/doc/db/Terrorism/Conv1-english.pdf.

6 U.N., *Convention for the Suppression of Unlawful Seizure of Aircraft,* 16 December 1970, *U.N.T.S. 1973*, available from http://www.refworld.org/docid/3ddcaa774.html.

> ARTICLE 1. Any person who on board an aircraft in flight:
> (a) unlawfully, by force or threat, or by any other form of intimidation, seizes, or exercises control of, that aircraft, or attempts to perform any such act, or
> (b) is an accomplice of a person who performs in attempts to perform any such act.

Article 1 mentions the liability of an accomplice to the person performing an action considered unlawful pertaining to this Convention.

C. Convention for the Suppression of Unlawful Acts against the Safety of Civil Aviation[7] (No: 14118)

This Convention was concluded in Montreal on September 1971 and came into force on 26 January 1973. Article 1.1 defines an offence that shall be committed with intention and against the law. This Article states that:

> ARTICLE 1.1 Any person commits an offence if it unlawfully and intentionally:
> (a) performs an act of violence against a person on board an aircraft in flight if that act is likely to endanger the safety of that aircraft; or
> (b) destroys an aircraft in service or causes damage to such an aircraft which renders it incapable of flight or which is likely to endanger its safety in flight;
> (c) places or causes to be placed on aircraft in service, by any means whatsoever, a device or substance which is likely to destroy that aircraft, or to cause damage to it which renders it incapable of flight, or to cause damage to it which is likely to endanger its safety in flight; or
> (d) destroys or damages air navigation facilities or interferes with their operations if any such act is likely to endanger the safety of aircraft in flight; or
> (e) communicates information which he knows to be false, there by endangering the safety of an aircraft in flight.

7 U.N., *Convention for the Suppression of Unlawful Acts Against the Safety of Civil Aviation*, Montreal, 23 September 1971, *U.N.T.S.*, vol. 974, no. 1–14118, available from http://www.un.org/zh/terrorism/pdf/1971E.pdf.

The offence itself relates to "an act of violence," which "endangers" or "is likely to endanger" the safety of a person on board of an aircraft. The destruction of an aircraft in service, such as occurred in the United States on 9/11, would be encompassed within the specific wording of this article. Article 1.1 (e) discusses the impact of false communication, which could endanger the safety of an aircraft in flight and thus, mentions the clear intention to cause harm without weapons. Part (e) of Article 1.1 is a new level of *modus operandi* which is covered by this Convention.

Per Article 1.2 of this Convention:

> Any person also commits an offence if he:
> (a) attempts to commit any of the offences mentioned in paragraph 1 of this Article; or
> (b) is an accomplice of a person who commits or attempts to commit any such offence.

Part 1.2 specifies that attempting to commit an offence aforementioned or being an accomplice to the person who commits or attempts to commit the offence, makes the person in question guilty of an offence, according to this Convention.

Article 10.1 States that:

> Contracting States shall, in accordance with international and national law, endeavour to take all practicable measure for the purpose of preventing the offences mentioned in Article 1.

This Article proves the importance of including UN related instruments within national laws of States Parties.

The Protocol concluded on 24 February 1988, which came into force on 6 August 1989, in its Article II an additional paragraph 1 bis, which reads as such:

> Article II
> 1. In Article 1 of the Convention, the following shall be added as new paragraph 1 bis:
>
> 1 bis. Any person commits an offence if he unlawfully and intentionally, using any device, substance or weapon:
> (a) Performs an act of violence against a person at an airport serving international civil aviation which causes or is likely to cause services injury or death; or

(b) Destroys or seriously damages the facilities of an airport serving international civil aviation not in service located thereon or disrupts the services of the airport,

If such an act endangers or is likely to endanger safety at the airport.

This addition provides for the use of "any device, substance or weapon," which gets closer to the wording of WMDS, as biological or chemical substances are at stake, to endanger the safety at the airport and no longer solely during a flight. Endangering facilities or aviation personnel could also lead to human losses and a person with an intention to harm could have utilized these strategies as *modus operandi*. This Convention no longer discusses direct injury targeting persons on board, but all the surrounding factors, which could be part of an overall plan to intentionally harm.

D. Convention on the Prevention and Punishment of Crimes against Internationally Protected Persons[8] (Annexed to General Assembly resolution 3166 (XVIII))

This Convention was concluded on 14 December 1973 and entered into force on 20 February 1977. Within Article 1.2 of this Convention, the alleged offender means:

> a person as to whom there is sufficient evidence to determine prime facie that he has committed or participated in one or more of the crimes set forth in article 2.

The crimes corresponding to the offences of Article 2.1 pertaining to this Convention include:

The international commission of:

(a) A murder, kidnapping or other attack upon the person or liberty of an internationally protected person;

(b) A violent attack upon the official premises, the private accommodation or the means of transport of an internationally protected person likely to endanger his person or liberty;

(c) A threat to commit any such attack; and

8 U.N., *Convention on the Prevention and Punishment of Crimes against Internationally Protected Persons, U.N.T.S. 1973*, available from http://legal.un.org/ilc/texts/instruments/english/conventions/9_4_1973.pdf.

(d) An attempt to commit any such attack; and
(e) An act constituting participation as an accomplice in any such attack shall be made by each State Party a crime under its internal law.

This Convention might only apply to Internationally Protected Persons due to their importance in our economy and political frameworks, but this legal instrument is a first step towards the recognition of acts of terrors occurring on land. Murder, kidnapping or other attacks targeting Internationally Protected Persons, as well as, attempt, threats, or participation in an attack are therein condemned. The addition of the wording "violent attack" in Article 2.1 (b) explicitly condemns terrible acts of violence towards representatives of States and what they represent, which can be understood as a politically directed attack or towards what this person signifies for a country. Hence, this illustrates an attempt to threaten the safety of a whole population.

Article 4 of this Convention requires international cooperation and thus:

> States Parties shall co-operate in the prevention of the crimes set forth in article 2, particularly by:
> (a) taking all practicability measures to prevent preparations in their respective territories for the commission of those crimes within or outside their territories;
> (b) exchanging information and coordinating the taking of administrative and other measures as appropriate to prevent the commission of those crimes.

Prevention in the form of international information exchange and cooperation is therefore crucial, according to this Convention, to avoid what could be perceived as "intentional acts of terror" on Internationally Protected Persons.

E. United Nations Convention on the Law of the Sea[9] (resolution 2749 (XXV))

Piracy is conceived as the first international crime, representing the birth of international customary law and of international terrorism, whereby these

9 U.N. GAOR resolution 3067 (XXVIII), *Convention on the Law of the Sea*, 19 November 1973, available from http://www.un.org/depts/los/convention_agreements/texts/unclos/unclos_e.pdf.

acts were economically or politically motivated. The Convention of the Law of the Sea is therefore a milestone in the creation of a terrorism convention related to the financing part of this international issue. As per Article 101, piracy consists of any of the following acts:

> (a) Any illegal acts of violence or detention or any act of depredation, committed for private ends by the crew or the passengers of a private ship or a private aircraft, and directed:
> 1. On the high seas, against another ship or aircraft, or against persons or property on board such ship or aircraft;
> 2. Against a ship, aircraft, persons or property in a place outside the jurisdiction of any State;
>
> (b) Any act of voluntary participation in the operation of a ship or of an aircraft with knowledge of facts making it a pirate ship or aircraft;
>
> (c) Any act of inciting or of internationally facilitating an act described in subparagraph (a) or (b).

Whilst pirates are known to extort money from people, the stolen assets they collect could be used to finance and lead to the perpetration of further criminal activities, which most likely intentionally initiate terror. Piracy in this Article includes crimes on the high seas, against another ship or aircraft, or against persons or property on board this ship or aircraft in a place outside the jurisdiction of any State. International terrorists sometimes commit crimes outside the jurisdiction of any State, and hold plural or no citizenship. Participation, incitement and facilitating piracy must be voluntary and with knowledge for the purpose of this Convention.

Retention or loss of nationality of a pirate ship or aircraft is discussed within Article 104, such as:

> A ship or aircraft may retain its nationality although it has become a pirate ship or aircraft. The retention of loss of nationality is determined by the law of the State from which such nationality was derived.

The importance of mentioning this Article comes from the recent discussions about the nationality of terrorists perpetrating actions in one country, while carrying a dual-nationality. Many countries wish to prohibit certain terrorist fighters who went to fighting zones to come back to their territories, yet the idea of making these terrorists, or potential terrorists (if no crimes occurred so far), "stateless", is hard to sustain with international law, as these persons would be subject to apartheid, responding to no nations or laws. The Convention for the Law of Sea therefore becomes a starting point to building a specific article pertaining to loss or retention of nationality for terrorists and their dangerous accomplices.

F. International Convention against the Taking of Hostages[10] (No: 21931)

This Convention was concluded in New York on December 17th 1979 and came into force on June 3rd 1983.

Over the years, United Nations Conventions has come to focus more and more on the violence of acts committed intentionally. Taking hostages is a frequent parameter of terrorist actions. According to Article 1 of this Convention:

1. Any person who seizes or detains and threatens to kill, to injure or to continue to detain another person (hereinafter referred to as the 'hostage') in order to compel a third party, namely, a State, an international intergovernmental organization, a natural person or a group of persons, to do or abstain from doing any act as an explicit or implicit condition for the release of the hostage commits the offense of taking of hostages ('hostage-taking') within the meaning of the Convention.

2. Any person who:
   (a) Attempts to commit an act of hostage-taking, or
   (b) Participates as an accomplice of anyone who commits or attempts to commit an act of ('hostage-taking')

   likewise commits an offense for the purpose of this Convention.

Article 1.2 (b) describes the participation of an accomplice as "anyone who commits or attempts to commit an act of 'hostage-taking'" and in such a case, opens the definition of an accomplice in the sense that the person participating no longer requires to be on site or violent. This means the accomplice could indeed be a financer of hostage-taking related to terrorist actions.

Article 2 underlines the grave nature of hostage-taking and offences set forth in article 1, and demands that penalties shall be enforced upon offenders.

10 U.N., *International Convention against the Taking of Hostages*, New York, 17 December 1979, available from http://www.unodc.org/documents/treaties/Special/1979%20International%20Convention%20against%20the%20Taking%20of%20Hostages.pdf.

Per Article 4, States Parties shall cooperate in the prevention of offences set forth in article 1, particularly by:

> (a) Taking all practicable measures to prevent preparations in their respective territories for the commission of those offences within or outside their territories, including measures to prohibit their territories illegal activities of persons, groups and organizations that encourage, instigate, organize or engage in the perpetration of acts of taking of hostages;

Article 4 (a), therefore, recognizes the importance of intelligence and cooperation between countries to discourage persons from their territories, including groups and organizations that encourage, instigate, organize or engage in the perpetration of acts of taking of hostages. This is indeed pertinent to the context of terrorists taking hostages.

The loophole of this Convention is that, per Article 13, it only applies where:

> the offence is committed within a single State, the hostage and the alleged offender are nationals of that State and the alleged offender is found in the territory of that State.

G. Convention on the Physical Protection of Nuclear Material,[11] May 1980 (IAEA).

Nuclear Material is a clear source of financing for terrorists, which could lead to dramatic consequences, especially if they decided to utilize nuclear capacities to attain their objectives or spread terror. Non-state actors, such as terrorist groups, are known to be principal accomplices of states trying to obtain a nuclear capacity without breaking related Conventions they might be tight to.

The scope of the intentional commission is defined within article 7 of this present Convention and includes a variety of unlawful actions connected to nuclear material. This can be explained by the threat posed by the utilization of nuclear material, and the fear that it could end in the hand of persons with wrong intention. Therefore, discouraging the receipt, possession, use, transfer, alteration, disposal or dispersal of nuclear material, as well as its theft, is vital to

11 International Atomic Energy Agency, *Convention on the Physical Protection of Nuclear Material*, 26 October 1979, available from https://www.iaea.org/publications/documents/conventions/convention-physical-protection-nuclear-material.

prevent dramatic consequences according to this Convention. More explicitly, article 1 reads as:

> 1. (a) an act without lawful authority which constitutes the receipt, possession, use, transfer, alteration, disposal or dispersal of nuclear material and which causes or is likely to cause death or serious injury to any person or substantial damage to property;
> (b) a theft or robbery of nuclear material;
> (c) an embezzlement or fraudulent obtaining of nuclear material;
> (d) an act constituting a demand for nuclear material by threat or use of force or by any other form of intimidation;
> (e) a threat:
> (i) to use material to cause death or serious injury to any person or substantial property damage, or
> (ii) to commit an offence described in sub-paragraph (b) in order to compel a natural or legal person, international organization or State to do or to refrain from doing any act;
> (f) an attempt to commit any offence described in paragraph (a), (b) or (c); and
> (g) an act which constitutes participation in any offence described in paragraphs (a) to (f).

Participation in an offence described in Article 1 paragraphs (a) to (f) constitutes an offence as well, according to Article 1 (g). Financing the acquisition of nuclear material linked to terrorism can therefore constitute a crime within the scope of this Convention.

H. Protocol for the Suppression of Unlawful Acts of Violence at Airports Serving International Civil Aviation, supplementary to the Convention for the Suppression of Unlawful Acts against the Safety of Civil Aviation[12] Concluded in Montreal on 24 February 1988.

The Protocol within Article II proposes the inclusion of a new paragraph 1 bis, whereby:

12 U.N., *Protocol for the Suppression of Unlawful Acts of Violence at Airports Serving International Civil Aviation, supplementary to the Convention for the Suppression of Unlawful Acts against the Safety of Civil Aviation*, 24 February 1988, *U.N.T.S 1990*, available from http://www.refworld.org/docid/3ddcac634.html.

> Any person commits an offence if he unlawfully and intentionally, using any device, substance or weapon:
> a) performs an act of violence against a person at an airport serving international civil aviation which causes or is likely to cause seriously injury or death; or
> b) destroys or seriously damages the facilities of an airport serving international civil aviation or aircraft not in service located thereon or disrupts the services of the airport,
>
> if such an act endangers or is likely to endanger safety at the airport.

International crimes are no longer just targeting aircrafts, international waters, internationally protected persons, hostages or nuclear materials, but also airports themselves and their personnel.

Article III of the Protocol states that in Article 5 of the Convention, the following shall be added as paragraph 2 bis:

> 2 bis. Each Contracting State shall likewise take such measures as may be necessary to establish its jurisdiction over the offences mentioned in Article 1, paragraph 1 bis, and in Article 1, paragraph 2, in so far as that paragraph relates to those offences, in the case where the alleged offender is present in its territory and it does not extradite him pursuant to Article 8 to the State mentioned in paragraph 1(a) of this Article.

Extradition is now mentioned within a United Nations instrument and contracting states are urged to take appropriate measures to establish jurisdiction over offences mentioned in Article 1.

I. Convention for the Suppression of Unlawful Acts against the Safety of Maritime Navigation[13] (No: 29004) Concluded in Rome on 10 March 1988.

According to Article 3.1 of this Convention, which describes offences, any person who unlawfully and intentionally:

13 International Environmental Agreements (IEA) Database Project, *Convention for The Suppression of Unlawful Acts Against the Safety Of Maritime Navigation*, 10 March 1988, available from http://iea.uoregon.edu/treaty-text/1988-unlawfulactssafetymaritime navigationentxt.

(i) seizes or exercises control over a ship by force or threat thereof or any other form of intimidation; or
(ii) performs an act of violence against a person on board a ship if that act is likely to endanger the safe navigation of that ship; or
(iii) destroys a ship or causes damage to a ship or to its cargo which is likely to endanger the safe navigation of that ship; or
(iv) places or causes to be placed on a ship, by any means whatsoever, a device or substance which is likely to destroy that ship, or cause damage to that ship or its cargo which endangers or is likely to endanger the safe navigation of that ship; or
(v) destroys or seriously damages maritime navigational facilities or seriously interferes with their operation, if any such act is likely to endanger the safe navigation of a ship; or
(vi) communicates information which he knows to be false, thereby endangering the safe navigation of a ship; or
(vii) injures or kills any person, in connection with the commission or the attempted commission of any of the offences (a) to (f).

Per Article 3.2, any person commits an offence if that person:

(a) attempts to commit any of the offences set forth in paragraph 1; or
(b) abets the commission of any of the offences set forth in paragraph 1 perpetrated by any person or is otherwise an accomplice of a person who commits such an offence; or

The Convention condemns attempts to commit the offences previously mentioned as well as abetting a person to perpetrate them.

J. Protocol for the Suppression of Unlawful Acts against the Safety of Fixed Platforms located on the Continental Shelf[14] concluded in Rome on March 1988.

Article 2 provides that:

1. Any person commits an offence if that person unlawfully and intentionally:

---

14 Admiralty and Maritime Law Guide, International Conventions, *Protocol for the Suppression of Unlawful Acts against the Safety of Fixed Platforms Located on the Continental Shelf*, 10 March 1988, available from http://www.admiraltylawguide.com/conven/fixedplatforms1988.html.

(a) seizes or exercises control over a fixed platform by force or threat thereof or any other form of intimidation; or
(b) performs an act of violence against a person on board a fixed platforms an act is likely to endanger its safety; or
(c) destroys a fixed platform or cause damage to it which is likely to endanger its safety; or
(d) places or causes to be placed on a fixed platform, by any mean whatsoever, a device or substance which is likely to destroy that fixed platform or likely to endanger its safety; or
(e) injures or kills any person in connection with the commission or the attempt commission of any of the offences set forth in subparagraphs (a) to (d).

2. Any person also commits an offence if that person:
(a) attempts to commit any of the offences set forth in paragraph 1; or
(b) abets the commission of any such offences perpetrated by any person or is otherwise an accomplice of a person who commits such an offence; or
(c) threatens, with or without a condition, as is provided for under national law, aimed at compelling a physical or juridical person to do or refrain from doing any of the offences set forth in paragraph 1, subparagraph (b) and (c), if that threat is likely to endanger the safety of the fixed platform.

Within the UN Conventions cited above, the participation offence evolves progressively to non-direct support. Article 2.2 (b) condemns accomplices of offenders, who do not necessarily provide immediate help to the criminal, but might provide other sorts of technical support, such as financing.

K. The United Nations Convention Against Illicit Traffic in Narcotic Drugs and Psychotropic Substances[15]

This is the first International Convention that criminalizes Money-laundering.

Article 3 defines offences and sanctions related to Illicit Traffic in Narcotic Drugs and Psychotropic Substances as:

15 U.N. Commission on Narcotic Drugs and the Economic and Social Council, *United Nations Convention Against Illicit Traffic in Narcotic Drugs and Psychotropic Substances*, 25 May 1988, available from http://www.unodc.org/pdf/convention_1988_en.pdf.

1. a)
   i) The production, manufacture, extraction; preparation, offering, offering for sale, distribution sale, delivery on any terms whatsoever, brokerage, dispatch, dispatch in transit, transport, importation or exportation of any narcotic drug or any psychotropic substance contrary to the provisions of the 1961 Convention, the 1961 Convention as amended or the 1971 Convention;
   ii) The organization, management or financing of any of the offences enumerated in i), ii), iii) or iv) above;

Article 3.1. a) ii) explicitly cites the organization, management or financing of any of the offences as an offence. Furthermore, Article 3.1. b) describes property derived from the previously cited offences and the unlawfulness of its usage.

Article 3.1. b) provides that:

> i) The conversion or transfer of property, knowing that such property is derived from any offences established in accordance with subparagraph a) of this paragraph, or from an act of participation in such offence or offences, for the purpose of concealing or disguising the illicit origin of the property or of assisting any person who is involved in the commission of such an offence or offences to evade the legal consequences of his actions;
> ii) The concealment or disguise of the true nature, source, location, disposition, movement, rights with respect to, or ownership of property, knowing that such property is derived from an offence or offences established in accordance with subparagraph a) of this paragraph or from an act of participation in such an offence or offences;

Article 3.1. c) states that:

> Subject to its constitutional principles and the basic concepts of its legal system:
> i) Publicly inciting or inducing others, by any means, to commit any of the offences established in accordance with this article or to use narcotic drugs or psychotropic substances illicitly;

ii) Participation in, association or conspiracy to commit, attempts to commit and aiding, abetting, facilitating and counselling the commission of any of the offences established in accordance with this article.

Most importantly, Article 3.3 insists on the fact that:

3. Knowledge, intent or purpose required as an element of an offence set forth in paragraph 1 of this article may be inferred from objective factual circumstances.

L. Convention on the Marking of Plastic Explosives for the Purpose of Detection[16]

Terrorism is mentioned within the preamble as a threat to international security, which states that:

CONSCIOUS of the implications of acts of terrorism for international security;
EXPRESSING deep concern regarding terrorism acts aimed at destruction or aircraft, other means of transportation and other targets;
CONCERNED that plastic explosives have been used for such terrorist acts;

M. International Convention for the Suppression of Terrorist Bombings[17]

Per Article 2 of the Suppression of Terrorist Bombings Convention,

1. Any person commits an offence within the meaning of this Convention if that person unlawfully and intentionally delivers, places, discharges or detonates an explosive or other lethal device in, into or against a place of public use, a State or government facility, a public

16 U.N. International Explosives Technical Commission, *Convention on the Marking of Plastic Explosives for the Purpose of Detection,* 1 Mar. 1991, available from http://www.un.org/en/sc/ctc/docs/conventions/Conv10.pdf.

17 U.N. GAOR, *International Convention for the Suppression of Terrorist Bombings,* A/52/653, 25 November 1997, available from http://www.un.org/law/cod/terroris.htm.

transportation system or an infrastructure facility, a public transportation system or an infrastructure facility:
   (a) With the intent to cause death or serious bodily injury; or
   (b) With the intent to cause extensive destruction of such a place, facility or system, where such destruction results in or is likely to result in major economic loss.
2. Any person also commits an offence if that person attempts to commit an offence as set forth in paragraph 1.
3. Any person also commits an offence if that person:
   (a) Participates as an accomplice in an offence as set forth in paragraph 1 or 2; or
   (b) Organizes or directs others to commit an offence as set forth in paragraph 1 or 2; or
   (c) In any other way contributes to the commission of one or more offences as set forth in paragraph 1 or 2 by q group of persons acting with a common purpose; such contribution shall be intentional and either be made with the aim of furthering the general criminal activity or purpose of the group or be made in the knowledge of the intention of the group to commit the offences concerned.

Article 2.3 (a) and (b) relate to participation in criminal actions, which might include their financing. Article 2.3 (c), once again, insists on the requirement of acting with a common purpose; the knowledge and intentional element to commit the offence.

Article 15 demands that States Parties shall cooperate in the prevention of the offences set forth in article 2, particularly:

(a) By taking all practicable measures, including, if necessary, adapting their domestic legislation, to prevent and counter preparations in their territories for the commission of those offences within or outside their territories, including measures to prohibit in their territories illegal activities of persons, groups and organizations that encourage, instigate, organize, knowingly finance or engage in the perpetration of offences as set forth in article 2;
(b) By exchanging accurate and verified information in accordance with their national law, and coordinating administrative and other measures taken as appropriate to prevent the commission of offences as set forth in article 2;

N. International Convention for the Suppression of the Financing of Terrorism[18]

This Convention was adopted by the General Assembly of the United Nations in resolution 54/109 of 9 December 1999 and requires member states to take measures to protect their financial systems from being misused by persons planning or engaged in terrorist activities.

The International Convention for the Suppression of the Financing of Terrorism recalls within its preamble that in 1999:

> ...existing multilateral legal instruments do not expressly address such financing.

The 1999 Convention is the most relevant United Nations instrument regarding terrorism-financing. In its Article 2:

1. Any person commits an offence within the meaning of this Convention if that person by any means, directly or indirectly, unlawfully and wilfully, provides or collects funds with the intention that they should be used or in the knowledge that they are to be used, in full or in part, in order to carry out:
   (a) An act which constitutes an offence within the scope of and as defined in one of the treaties listed in the annex; or
   (b) Any other act intended to cause death or serious bodily injury to a civilian, or to any other person not taking an active part in the hostilities in a situation of armed conflict, when the purpose of such act, by its nature or context, is to intimidate a population, or to compel a government or an international organization to do or to abstain from doing any act.
2. (a) On depositing its instrument of ratification, acceptance, approval or accession, a State Party which is not a party to a treaty listed in the annex may declare that, in the application of this Convention to the State Party, the treaty shall be deemed not to be included in the annex referred to in paragraph 1, subparagraph (a). The declaration shall cease to have effect as soon as the treaty enters into force for the State Party, which shall notify the depositary of this fact;

18 U.N. GAOR resolution 54/109 *International Convention for the Suppression of the Financing of Terrorism,* 9 December 1999, available from http://www.un.org/law/cod/finterr.htm.

(b) When a State Party ceases to be a party to a treaty listed in the annex, it may make a declaration as provided for in this article, with respect to that treaty.

3. For an act to constitute an offence set forth in paragraph 1, it shall not be necessary that the funds were actually used to carry out an offence referred to in paragraph 1, subparagraphs (a) or (b).
4. Any person also commits an offence if that person attempts to commit an offence as set forth in paragraph 1 of this article.
5. Any person also commits an offence if that person:
   (a) Participates as an accomplice in an offence as set forth in paragraph 1 or 4 of this article;
   (b) Organizes or directs others to commit an offence as set forth in paragraph 1 or 4 of this article;
   (c) Contributes to the commission of one or more offences as set forth in paragraphs 1 or 4 of this article by a group of persons acting with a common purpose. Such contribution shall be intentional and shall either:
      (i) Be made with the aim of furthering the criminal activity or criminal purpose of the group, where such activity or purpose involves the commission of an offence as set forth in paragraph 1 of this article; or
      (ii) Be made in the knowledge of the intention of the group to commit an offence as set forth in paragraph 1 of this article.

This definition of the crime of financing illicit activities is a more complete version than the progressive attempt to define aiding terrorist activities, as explained within the previous UN instruments.

Article 3 of this Convention is interesting to consider for the purpose of this study, as it states that:

> This Convention shall not apply where the offence is committed within a single State, the alleged offender is a national of that State and is present in the territory of that State and no other State has a basis under article 7, paragraph 1, or article 7, paragraph 2, to exercise jurisdiction, except that the provisions of articles 12 to 18 shall, as appropriate, apply in those cases.

Therefore, this Convention would likely not apply to offences taking place within a single State, where the alleged offender is a national of that State. This is consequently, an important point to reconsider within the new proposed Convention model of this work, as nowadays, terrorists are frequently nationals or 2nd to 3rd generation of immigrants currently nationalized within the country where the crime occurred.

Jurisdiction over Terrorist Financers is established within Article 7, as:

1. Each State Party shall take such measures as may be necessary to establish its jurisdiction over the offences set forth in article 2 when:
   (a) The offence is committed in the territory of that State;
   (b) The offence is committed on board a vessel flying the flag of that State or an aircraft registered under the laws of that State at the time the offence is committed;
   (c) The offence is committed by a national of that State.
2. A State Party may also establish its jurisdiction over any such offence when:
   (a) The offence was directed towards or resulted in the carrying out of an offence referred to in article 2, paragraph 1, subparagraph (a) or (b), in the territory of or against a national of that State;
   (b) The offence was directed towards or resulted in the carrying out of an offence referred to in article 2, paragraph 1, subparagraph (a) or (b), against a State or government facility of that State abroad, including diplomatic or consular premises of that State;
   (c) The offence was directed towards or resulted in an offence referred to in article 2, paragraph 1, subparagraph (a) or (b), committed in an attempt to compel that State to do or abstain from doing any act;
   (d) The offence is committed by a stateless person who has his or her habitual residence in the territory of that State;
   (e) The offence is committed on board an aircraft which is operated by the Government of that State.
3. Upon ratifying, accepting, approving or acceding to this Convention, each State Party shall notify the Secretary-General of the United Nations of the jurisdiction it has established in accordance with paragraph 2. Should any change take place, the State Party concerned shall immediately notify the Secretary-General.
4. Each State Party shall likewise take such measures as may be necessary to establish its jurisdiction over the offences set forth in article 2 in cases where the alleged offender is present in its territory and it does not extradite that person to any of the States Parties that

have established their jurisdiction in accordance with paragraphs 1 or 2.

5. When more than one State Party claims jurisdiction over the offences set forth in article 2, the relevant States Parties shall strive to coordinate their actions appropriately, in particular concerning the conditions for prosecution and the modalities for mutual legal assistance.
6. Without prejudice to the norms of general international law, this Convention does not exclude the exercise of any criminal jurisdiction established by a State Party in accordance with its domestic law.

Article 8 focuses on identification, detection and freezing or seizure of any funds used or allocated for the purpose of committing the offences and states that:

1. Each State Party shall take appropriate measures, in accordance with its domestic legal principles, for the identification, detection and freezing or seizure of any funds used or allocated for the purpose of committing the offences set forth in article 2 as well as the proceeds derived from such offences, for purposes of possible forfeiture.
2. Each State Party shall take appropriate measures, in accordance with its domestic legal principles, for the forfeiture of funds used or allocated for the purpose of committing the offences set forth in article 2 and the proceeds derived from such offences.
3. Each State Party concerned may give consideration to concluding agreements on the sharing with other States Parties, on a regular or case-by-case basis, of the funds derived from the forfeitures referred to in this article.
4. Each State Party shall consider establishing mechanisms whereby the funds derived from the forfeitures referred to in this article are utilized to compensate the victims of offences referred to in article 2, paragraph 1, subparagraph (a) or (b), or their families.
5. The provisions of this article shall be implemented without prejudice to the rights of third parties acting in good faith.

Article 18 deals with cooperation. According to this Article:

1. States Parties shall cooperate in the prevention of the offences set forth in article 2 by taking all practicable measures, inter alia, by adapting their domestic legislation, if necessary, to prevent and

counter preparations in their respective territories for the commission of those offences within or outside their territories, including:

(a) Measures to prohibit in their territories illegal activities of persons and organizations that knowingly encourage, instigate, organize or engage in the commission of offences set forth in article 2;

(b) Measures requiring financial institutions and other professions involved in financial transactions to utilize the most efficient measures available for the identification of their usual or occasional customers, as well as customers in whose interest accounts are opened, and to pay special attention to unusual or suspicious transactions and report transactions suspected of stemming from a criminal activity. For this purpose, States Parties shall consider:

(i) Adopting regulations prohibiting the opening of accounts the holders or beneficiaries of which are unidentified or unidentifiable, and measures to ensure that such institutions verify the identity of the real owners of such transactions;

(ii) With respect to the identification of legal entities, requiring financial institutions, when necessary, to take measures to verify the legal existence and the structure of the customer by obtaining, either from a public register or from the customer or both, proof of incorporation, including information concerning the customer=s name, legal form, address, directors and provisions regulating the power to bind the entity;

(iii) Adopting regulations imposing on financial institutions the obligation to report promptly to the competent authorities all complex, unusual large transactions and unusual patterns of transactions, which have no apparent economic or obviously lawful purpose, without fear of assuming criminal or civil liability for breach of any restriction on disclosure of information if they report their suspicions in good faith;

(iv) Requiring financial institutions to maintain, for at least five years, all necessary records on transactions, both domestic or international.

2. States Parties shall further cooperate in the prevention of offences set forth in article 2 by considering:

(a) Measures for the supervision, including, for example, the licensing, of all money-transmission agencies;
(b) Feasible measures to detect or monitor the physical cross-border transportation of cash and bearer negotiable instruments, subject to strict safeguards to ensure proper use of information and without impeding in any way the freedom of capital movements.

3. States Parties shall further cooperate in the prevention of the offences set forth in article 2 by exchanging accurate and verified information in accordance with their domestic law and coordinating administrative and other measures taken, as appropriate, to prevent the commission of offences set forth in article 2, in particular by:
(a) Establishing and maintaining channels of communication between their competent agencies and services to facilitate the secure and rapid exchange of information concerning all aspects of offences set forth in article 2;
(b) Cooperating with one another in conducting inquiries, with respect to the offences set forth in article 2, concerning:
(i) The identity, whereabouts and activities of persons in respect of whom reasonable suspicion exists that they are involved in such offences;
(ii) The movement of funds relating to the commission of such offences.

4. States Parties may exchange information through the International Criminal Police Organization (INTERPOL).

International cooperation is key to the prevention of terrorism and the seizure of terrorist related assets.

O. United Nations' Model Legislation on Laundering, Confiscation and International Cooperation in Relation to the Proceeds of Crime[19]

This legislation model on laundering, confiscation and international cooperation in relation to the proceeds of crime offers interesting provisions related

19 International Money-Laundering Information Network, Global Programme Against Money-Laundering, *Model legislation on laundering, confiscation and international cooperation in relation to the proceeds of crime,* 1999, available from http://www.imolin.org/imolin/en/ml99eng.html.

to money-laundering, which therefore could relate to potential terrorist financing or laundering of proceeds of crimes schemes.

Title II relates to the prevention of money-laundering and provides within its Chapter 2 recommendations that could be inserted within a new convention model concerning transparency in financial transactions. Article 2.2.8 states that internal anti-laundering programs at credit and financial institutions shall:

> ...develop programmes for the prevention of money-laundering. Such programmes shall include the following:
> (a) Centralization of information on the identity of customers, principals, beneficiaries, proxies, authorized agents and beneficial owners, and on suspicious transactions;
> (b) Designation of compliance officers, at central management level, in each branch and at each agency or local office;
> (c) Ongoing training for officials or employees;
> (d) Internal audit arrangements to check compliance with and effectiveness of the measures taken to apply the present law.

As discussed in Chapter 2 B, casinos and gambling establishments are targets for financial criminals. Article 2.2.10 provides that casinos and gambling establishments shall be required:

> (a) Before commencing their operations, to submit a declaration of activity to ... [variants: the ministry of finance or the ministry of the interior or the central bank of the country or any other competent authority] for the purpose of obtaining a license to set up and operate a business, as provided for under the national legislation in force, and, in that declaration, to furnish proof of the lawful origin of the capital required to set up the establishment;
> (b) To keep regular accounts and maintain such accounts for at least ... years. The accounting principles laid down by the national legislation shall be applicable to casinos and gambling clubs;
> (c) To verify, by requiring the presentation of an official original document that is unexpired and bears a photograph, a copy of which shall be taken, the identity of gamblers who buy, bring or exchange chips or tokens for a sum greater than ... [amount to be fixed by the State];

(d) To record, in chronological order, all operations referred to in subparagraph (c) of this article, their nature and amount, indicating the gamblers' surnames and forenames, and the number of the document submitted, in a register numbered and initialled by the competent administrative authority, and to retain such register for at least … years [a period of not less than five years] after the last operation recorded;
(e) To record, in chronological order, all transfers of funds effected between such casinos and gambling clubs in a register numbered and initialled by the competent administrative authority, and to retain such register for at least … years [a period of not less than five years] after the last operation recorded.

If the gambling establishment is owned by a legal person possessing two or more subsidiaries, the chips shall show the identity of the subsidiary by which they are issued. In no circumstances may chips issued by one subsidiary be cashed at any other subsidiary, including subsidiaries abroad.

Regarding financial intelligence units, Title III on Detection of laundering, in its Chapter 1 in relation to its collaboration with anti-laundering authorities, states in its Section 1 Article 3.1.1 on general provisions concerning FIUs:

> A financial intelligence unit, organized under the terms laid down by decree, shall be responsible for receiving, analysing and processing reports required of the persons and organizations referred to in article 2.1.1. It shall also receive all relevant information, in particular that communicated by the judicial authorities. Its officials shall be required to keep confidential the information thus obtained, which may not be used for any purposes other than those provided for herein.
>
> The composition and powers of the intelligence unit, the measures to safeguard or strengthen its independence, and the content and methods of transmission of the reports submitted to it shall be fixed by decree.

Better access to information is depicted in Article 3.1.2 and reads:

> The intelligence unit may also, at its request, obtain from any public authority, or from any natural or legal person referred to in article 2.1.1, information and records, as specified in article 2.2.7, within the scope of investigations conducted following the report of a suspicion. It may further exchange information with the authorities responsible for imposing the disciplinary penalties provided for in article 4.2.4.

> Option: It shall, upon request, be granted access to databases of the public authorities. In all cases, the use of information thus obtained shall be strictly limited to the purposes pursued hereunder.

Article 3.1.3 discusses how to strengthen the relationships with FIUs abroad as below:

> The financial intelligence unit may, subject to a reciprocal arrangement, exchange information with foreign intelligence units responsible for receiving and processing reports of suspicions, provided that they are subject to similar requirements of confidentiality and irrespective of the nature of those units. It may, for that purpose, conclude cooperation agreements with such units.
>
> Upon receipt of a request for information or transmission from a counterpart foreign unit processing a report of a suspicion, it shall comply with that request within the scope of the powers hereby conferred upon it to deal with such reports.

Requirements to report suspicions are explicitly provided within Section 2 and offer variants:

> Section 2. Reporting of suspicions
>
> Article 3.1.4 Requirement to report suspicious transactions
>
> Any natural or legal person [option 1: referred to in articles 2.1.1, 2.2.9 and 2.2.10] [option 2: and [chartered accountants, inspectors, auditors, etc.] shall be required to report to the financial intelligence unit transactions referred to in article 2.1.1 involving money which appears to be derived from the perpetration of:
>
> 3 variants:
>
> variant (a): a crime.
>
> variant (b): an offence linked to organized crime.
>
> variant (c): one or more of the following offences: [list of offences].
>
> The persons referred to above shall be required to report the transactions carried out even if it was not feasible to defer their execution or if it became clear only after completion of a transaction that it involved suspect money.
>
> They shall also be required to report without delay any information that might confirm or invalidate the suspicion.

Financial institutions and other related entities shall report to their corresponding FIU and provide the specific details listed below:

Article 3.1.5 Reporting to the financial intelligence unit

Reports of suspicions shall be transmitted to the financial intelligence unit by facsimile or, failing which, by any other written means. Reports communicated by telephone shall be confirmed by facsimile or any other written means within the shortest possible time. Such reports shall, as appropriate, indicate:

(1) The reasons why the transaction has already been executed;
(2) The time-limit within which the suspect transaction is to be executed.

The intelligence unit shall acknowledge receipt of the report upon receipt thereof.

An international crime requires specific techniques of investigation and mutual legal assistance in an effort to cooperate to collect information related to the alleged misconduct. Chapter 3 focuses on evidence gathering and lists techniques that might be utilized for investigation matters:

Chapter 3. Investigative techniques

Article 3.3.1 Special investigative techniques

For the purpose of obtaining evidence of the predicate offence and evidence of offences provided for under the present law, the judicial authorities may order for a specific period:

(a) The monitoring of bank accounts and the like;
(b) Access to computer systems, networks and servers;
(c) The placing under surveillance or tapping of telephone lines, facsimile machines or electronic transmission or communication facilities;
(d) The audio or video recording of acts and behaviour or conversations;
(e) The communication of notarial and private deeds, or of bank, financial and commercial records.

The judicial authorities may also order the seizure of the aforementioned documents.

However, these operations shall be possible only when there are strong grounds for suspecting that such accounts, telephone lines, computer systems and networks or documents are or may be used by persons suspected of participating in offences referred to in the first paragraph of this article.

According to the following article, bank secrecy should not be invoked considering the gravity of the crime at stake and the duty to surrender terrorists and their accomplices quickly to avoid future actions. It reads:

> Chapter 4. Banking and professional secrecy
> Article 3.4.1 Disallowance of bank secrecy
> Banking or professional secrecy may not be invoked as a ground for refusal to provide information referred to in article 2.2.7 or required in connection with an investigation which relates to laundering and is ordered by, or carried out under the supervision of, a judicial authority.

Deciding on mutual punishment guidelines for the purpose of the Convention model is complicated, since most jurisdictions have their own punitive measures that can be completely opposite to one another. This Model offers applicable penalties to be inserted within local laws concerning money-laundering that can be useful for this analysis.

> TITLE IV: COERCIVE MEASURES
> Chapter 2: Punishment of offences
> Section 1. Penalties applicable
> Article 4.2.1 Money-laundering
> The penalty of imprisonment of … to … and a fine of … to … [option: and a fine of up to xxx times the amount of the laundered sums] shall be imposed on anyone who commits a laundering offence.
> An attempt to commit a laundering offence or aiding, abetting, facilitating or counselling the commission of any such offence shall be punishable as if the offence had been completed [variant: shall be punishable by a penalty reduced by [fraction] in relation to the main penalty].

It is not enough to prohibit terrorism-financing, for the new Convention model should also condemn association or conspiracy, as reflected in Article 4.2.2, which again focuses on money-laundering:

> Article 4.2.2 Association or conspiracy to commit money-laundering
> The same penalties shall apply to participation in an association or conspiracy to commit the offences referred to in article 4.2.1.

Corporate entities involved in schemes should face penalties to discourage their association with criminals, as companies might have access to financial means which could directly or indirectly be connected to terrorism-financing and represent a serious threat for law enforcement even though they can appear to be from lawful origins.

> Article 4.2.3 Penalties applicable to corporate entities
>
> Corporate entities, other than the State, on whose behalf or for whose benefit a subsequent offence has been committed by one of their agents or representatives shall be liable to a fine of an amount equal to five times the fines specified for natural persons, without prejudice to the conviction of those individuals as perpetrators of the offence or accessories to it.
>
> Corporate entities may additionally be:
>
> (a) Banned permanently or for a maximum period of five years from directly or indirectly carrying on certain business activities;
>
> (b) Ordered to close permanently or for a maximum period of five years their premises which were used for the commission of the offence;
>
> (c) Wound up if they had been established for the purpose of committing the offence in question;
>
> (d) Required to publicize the judgement in the press or by radio or television.

A credit or financial institution or any other natural or legal person shall also result in penalties following serious failure to exercise vigilance or a deficiency in the organization of internal anti-laundering procedures.

> Article 4.2.4. Penalties imposed by disciplinary or supervisory authorities
>
> Where, as a result of a serious failure to exercise vigilance or a deficiency in the organization of internal anti-laundering procedures, a credit or financial institution or any other natural or legal person referred to in article 2.1.1 commits a breach of any of the obligations devolving upon it under the present law, the disciplinary or supervisory authority may act ex officio in conformity with the internal or administrative regulations.

Confiscation is a complex issue at the international level, yet, the following articles show how it can occur, along with confiscation of property in the hands of criminal organizations. It also explains how the disposal of confiscated property should take place.

Section II. Confiscation
Article 4.2.9 Confiscation

In the event of a conviction for actual or attempted money-laundering, an order shall be issued for the confiscation:

1. Of the property forming the subject of the offence, including income and other benefits obtained therefrom, against any person to whom they may belong, unless their owner can establish that he acquired them by actually paying a fair price or in return for the provision of services corresponding to their value or on any other legitimate grounds and that he was unaware of their illicit origin;
2. Of property belonging directly or indirectly to a person convicted of a laundering offence [option: to his spouse, cohabitee or children], unless the parties concerned can establish the lawful origin thereof.

Moreover, if, in cases where an offence is established by the court, the perpetrator or perpetrators thereof cannot be convicted, the court may nevertheless order the confiscation of the property to which the offence related.

Article 4.2.11 Confiscation of property of criminal organizations

Property of which a criminal organization has power of disposal shall be confiscated …

variant (a): if there is a connection between that property and the offence.

variant (b): unless the lawful origin of the property is established.

Article 4.2.13 Disposal of confiscated property

Confiscated property and proceeds shall accrue to the State, which shall be empowered to allocate them to a fund for combating organized crime or drug trafficking. They shall remain encumbered, up to their value, by any rights in rem lawfully established in favour of third parties.

In cases where confiscation is ordered under a judgement by default, the confiscated property shall accrue to the State and be realized in accordance with the relevant procedures laid down. However, if the court, ruling on an application to set aside such judgement, acquits the person prosecuted, it shall order restitution to the value of the confiscated property by the State, unless it is established that such property is the proceeds of crime.

Double criminality is an important matter, which relates to international crimes with several jurisdictions and therefore:

> Article 5.3.2 Double criminality
>
> Under the present law, extradition shall be carried out only if the offence giving rise to extradition or a similar offence is provided for under the legislation of the requesting State and of ... [name of the country adopting the model law].

Asset seizure is explained by the following article on the surrender of property, which states that:

> Article 5.3.6 Surrender of property
>
> Within the limits authorized under the national legislation and subject to the rights of third parties, all property found in the territory of ... [name of the country adopting the model law] that has been acquired as a result of the offence committed or that may be required as evidence shall, if the requesting State so requests, be surrendered to the requesting State if extradition is granted.
>
> The property in question may, if the requesting State so requests, be surrendered to the requesting State even if the extradition agreed to cannot be carried out.
>
> Should that property be liable to seizure or confiscation in the territory of ... [name of the country adopting the model law], the State may temporarily retain it or hand it over.
>
> Where the national legislation or the rights of third parties so require, any property so surrendered shall be returned to ... [name of the country adopting the model law] free of charge, after the completion of the proceedings, if ... [name of the country adopting the model law] so requests.

The principal aim of this instrument model is to help countries' implementation of AML/CTF standards. It is, indeed, a lot of information to be considered for the purpose of the new CTF Convention model this study is involved in building. Many features of this juridical element will be found within the model.

P. UN Convention against Transnational Organized Crime[20]

This Convention declares that money-laundering offences should not only apply to the proceeds of illicit drug trafficking, for it should also cover the proceeds of all serious crimes.

Article 3. Scope of application

1. This Convention shall apply, except as otherwise stated herein, to the prevention, investigation and prosecution of:
   (a) The offences established in accordance with articles 5, 6, 8 and 23 of this Convention; and (b) Serious crime as defined in article 2 of this Convention; where the offence is transnational in nature and involves an organized criminal group.
2. For the purpose of paragraph 1 of this article, an offence is transnational in nature if:
   (a) It is committed in more than one State;
   (b) It is committed in one State but a substantial part of its preparation, planning, direction or control takes place in another State;
   (c) It is committed in one State but involves an organized criminal group that engages in criminal activities in more than one State; or
   (d) It is committed in one State but has substantial effects in another State.

The sovereignty of States is an important principle of law, which becomes a problem when attempting to deal with trans-national crime effectively. This Convention therefore discusses principles of non-intervention in domestic affairs, as well as exercise of jurisdiction, which remains the competency of the State in question. According to Article 4 on the Protection of Sovereignty:

1. States Parties shall carry out their obligations under this Convention in a manner consistent with the principles of sovereign equality and territorial integrity of States and that of non-intervention in the domestic affairs of other States.

---

20 U.N. GAOR 55/25, *Convention on Transnational Organized Crime and the Protocols Thereto*, Article 14, 15 Nov. 2000, available from https://www.unodc.org/documents/middleeast-andnorthafrica/organised-crime/united_nations_convention_against_transnational_organized_crime_and_the_protocols_thereto.pdf.

2. Nothing in this Convention entitles a State Party to undertake in the territory of another State the exercise of jurisdiction and performance of functions that are reserved exclusively for the authorities of that other State by its domestic law.

Whilst this Convention provides for the criminalization of participation in an organized criminal group, Article 6 also proscribes the laundering of the proceeds of crime. As per Article 6:

1. Each State Party shall adopt, in accordance with fundamental principles of its domestic law, such legislative and other measures as may be necessary to establish as criminal offences, when committed intentionally:
   (a)
      (i) The conversion or transfer of property, knowing that such property is the proceeds of crime, for the purpose of concealing or disguising the illicit origin of the property or of helping any person who is involved in the commission of the predicate offence to evade the legal consequences of his or her action;
      (ii) The concealment or disguise of the true nature, source, location, disposition, movement or ownership of or rights with respect to property, knowing that such property is the proceeds of crime;

Converting property linked to terrorism and its financing and taking advantage of the proceeds of crimes is considered unlawful according to this Article.

Confiscating and seizing assets related to terrorism is important to prevent crimes from occurring. Article 12 on Confiscation and seizure provides that:

1. States Parties shall adopt, to the greatest extent possible within their domestic legal systems, such measures as may be necessary to enable confiscation of:
   (a) Proceeds of crime derived from offences covered by this Convention or property the value of which corresponds to that of such proceeds;
   (b) Property, equipment or other instrumentalities used in or destined for use in offences covered by this Convention.
2. States Parties shall adopt such measures as may be necessary to enable the identification, tracing, freezing or seizure of any item

referred to in paragraph 1 of this article for the purpose of eventual confiscation.

3. If proceeds of crime have been transformed or converted, in part or in full, have been intermingled with property acquired from legitimate sources, Income or other benefits derived from proceeds of crime, from property into which proceeds of crime have been transformed or converted or from property

Article 13 also provides for international cooperation for the purposes of confiscation, as an international crime demands international assistance, here stated as:

1. A State Party that has received a request from another State Party having jurisdiction over an offence covered by this Convention for confiscation of proceeds of crime, property, equipment or other instrumentalities referred to in article 12, paragraph 1, of this Convention situated in its territory shall, to the greatest extent possible within its domestic legal system:
   (a) Submit the request to its competent authorities for the purpose of obtaining an order of confiscation and, if such an order is granted, give effect to it; or
   (b) Submit to its competent authorities, with a view to giving effect to it to the extent requested, an order of confiscation issued by a court in the territory of the requesting State Party in accordance with article 12, paragraph 1, of this Convention insofar as it relates to proceeds of crime, property, equipment or other instrumentalities referred to in article 12, paragraph 1, situated in the territory of the requested State Party.

The disposal of confiscated proceeds of crime or property is discussed within article 14 of this Convention and offers a provision on the sharing of confiscated assets with other parties on a case-by-case basis or the creation of a fund, such as:

3. When acting on the request made by another State Party in accordance with articles 12 and 13 of this Convention, a State Party may give special consideration to concluding agreements or arrangements on:
   (a) Contributing the value of such proceeds of crime or property or funds derived from the sale of such proceeds of crime or

property or a part thereof to the account designated in accordance with article 30, paragraph 2 (c), of this Convention and to intergovernmental bodies specializing in the fight against organized crime;

(b) Sharing with other States Parties, on a regular or case-by-case basis, such proceeds of crime or property, or funds derived from the sale of such proceeds of crime or property, in accordance with its domestic law or administrative procedures.

Article 18 on mutual legal assistance provides that:

> 2. Mutual legal assistance shall be afforded to the fullest extent possible under relevant laws, treaties, agreements and arrangements of the requested State Party with respect to investigations, prosecutions and judicial proceedings in relation to the offences for which a legal person may be held liable in accordance with article 10 of this Convention in the requesting State Party.

As per this Convention, detention of a person serving a sentence in the territory of one State Party whose presence in another State Party is requested:

> ...for purposes of identification, testimony or otherwise providing assistance in obtaining evidence for investigations, prosecutions or judicial proceedings in relation to offences covered by this Convention may be transferred if the following conditions are met:
> (a) The person freely gives his or her informed consent;
> (b) The competent authorities of both States Parties agree, subject to such conditions as those States Parties may deem appropriate.

The content of a request for mutual legal assistance is listed within this Convention. It may, indeed, be refused on several grounds listed in the Convention.

States Parties are asked to consider the possibility of concluding bilateral or multilateral agreements or arrangements, which would give practical effect to or enhance the provisions of this article.

States Parties can also, according to Article 21:

> ...consider the possibility of transferring to one another proceedings for the prosecution of an offence covered by this Convention in cases where

> such transfer is considered to be in the interests of the proper administration of justice, in particular in cases where several jurisdictions are involved, with a view to concentrating the prosecution.

The protection of witnesses from intimidation or retaliation in criminal proceedings, as well as when appropriate for their relatives and other persons close to them is a strong point raised in Article 24.1, which is not always taken with the same degree of seriousness by the country implementing such a measure. This is why, the assistance to and protection of victims is offered by Article 25 stating that:

> 1. Each State Party shall take appropriate measures within its means to provide assistance and protection to victims of offences covered by this Convention, in particular in cases of threat of retaliation or intimidation.
> 2. Each State Party shall establish appropriate procedures to provide access to compensation and restitution for victims of offences covered by this Convention.

Law enforcement cooperation, training and technical assistance are crucial for understanding the evolving threat of terrorism and its financing.

Per Article 27.1:

> States Parties shall cooperate closely with one another, consistent with their respective domestic legal and administrative systems, to enhance the effectiveness of law enforcement action to combat the offences covered by this Convention.

Article 29 explains the importance of training for all types of actors linked to CTF, stating that:

> 1. Each State Party shall, to the extent necessary, initiate, develop or improve specific training programmes for its law enforcement personnel, including prosecutors, investigating magistrates and customs personnel, and other personnel charged with the prevention, detection and control of the offences covered by this Convention.

In Article 11 on border measures, border controls are perceived as necessary to prevent and detect trafficking in persons. State Parties are also encouraged to adopt legislative or other appropriate measures to prevent, to the the greatest possible extent, means of transport operated by commercial carriers from being used in the commission of previously stated offences.

Joint investigations and special investigative techniques also play a key role in this Convention.

Q. The United Nations Convention Against Corruption[21]

The private sector plays a key role in detecting financial crimes, therefore, it should be regulated to prevent misbehavior. Article 12 provides that regarding the private sector:

> 1. Each State Party shall take measures, in accordance with the fundamental principles of its domestic law, to prevent corruption involving the private sector, enhance accounting and auditing standards in the private sector and, where appropriate, provide effective, proportionate and dissuasive civil, administrative or criminal penalties for failure to comply with such measures.

This Convention highlights the importance of the participation of society within its Article 13 and states that:

> 1. Each State Party shall take appropriate measures, within its means and in accordance with fundamental principles of its domestic law, to promote the active participation of individuals and groups outside the public sector, such as civil society, non-governmental organizations and community-based organizations, in the prevention of and the fight against corruption and to raise public awareness regarding the existence, causes and gravity of and the threat posed by corruption.

Regarding the laundering of proceeds of crime, each State Party shall adopt measures in accordance with fundamental principles of its domestic law, to establish as criminal offences, when committed intentionally:

> (a) (i) The conversion or transfer of property, knowing that such property is the proceeds of crime, for the purpose of concealing

21 U.N. Office on Drugs and Crime, GAOR 58/4, *Convention Against Corruption*, New York, 31 October 2003, available from https://www.unodc.org/documents/brussels/UN_Convention_Against_Corruption.pdf.

or disguising the illicit origin of the property or of helping any person who is involved in the commission of the predicate offence to evade the legal consequences of his or her action;

(ii) The concealment or disguise of the true nature, source, location, disposition, movement or ownership of or rights with respect to property, knowing that such property is the proceed of crime;

(b) Subject to the basic concepts of its legal system:

1. The acquisition, possession or use of property, knowing, at the time of receipt, that such property is the proceeds of crime;
2. Participation in, association with or conspiracy to commit, attempts to commit and aiding and abetting, facilitating and counselling the commission of any of the offences established in accordance with this article.

Per Article 24, the concealment or continued retention of property when the person involved knows that such property is the result of any of the offences established in accordance with this Convention is deemed to be an offence.

Embezzlement, misappropriation or other diversion of property by a public official, trading in influence, abuse of functions, bribery in the private sector, and embezzlement of property in the private sector are also condemned by this Convention. Participation or attempt, knowledge, intent and purpose, are required as elements of an offence, with this Convention and may be inferred from objective factual circumstances.

Per Article 31, regarding the freezing, seizure and confiscation of terrorist related assets:

1. Each State Party shall take, to the greatest extent possible within its domestic legal system, such measures as may be necessary to enable confiscation of:
   (a) Proceeds of crime derived from offences established in accordance with this Convention or property the value of which corresponds to that of such proceeds;
   (b) Property, equipment or other instrumentalities used in or destined for use in offences established in accordance with this Convention.
2. Each State Party shall take such measures as may be necessary to enable the identification, tracing, freezing or seizure of any item

referred to in paragraph 1 of this article for the purpose of eventual confiscation.

3. Each State Party shall adopt, in accordance with its domestic law, such legislative and other measures as may be necessary to regulate the administration by the competent authorities of frozen, seized or confiscated property covered in paragraphs 1 and 2 of this article.
4. If such proceeds of crime have been transformed or converted, in part or in full, into other property, such property shall be liable to the measures referred to in this article instead of the proceeds.
5. If such proceeds of crime have been intermingled with property acquired from legitimate sources, such property shall, without prejudice to any powers relating to freezing or seizure, be liable to confiscation up to the assessed value of the intermingled proceeds.
6. Income or other benefits derived from such proceeds of crime, from property into which such proceeds of crime have been transformed or converted or from property with which such proceeds of crime have been intermingled shall also be liable to the measures referred to in this article, in the same manner and to the same extent as proceeds of crime.

Cooperation between national authorities and the private sector may be necessary amongst prosecuting authorities and entities of the private sector, especially concerning financial institutions, or involving matters related to the commission of offences recognized in agreement with this Convention. Mutual legal assistance in investigations, prosecutions and judicial proceedings in relation to offences are all covered by this Convention. Article 53 mentions measures for direct recovery of property be implemented by each State Party in accordance with its domestic law. States should take such measures as necessary to permit:

(a) another State Party to initiate civil action in its courts to establish title to or ownership of property acquired through the commission of an offence established in accordance with this Convention;
(b) its courts to order those who have committed offences established in accordance with this Convention to pay compensation or damages to another State Party that has been harmed by such offences; and

Regarding mechanisms for the recovery of property through international cooperation in relation to confiscation, each State Party should take such measures as necessary to permit its competent authorities to freeze or seize property upon:

> (a) a freezing or seizure order issued by a court or competent authority of a requesting State Party that provides a reasonable basis for the requested State Party to believe that there are sufficient grounds for taking such actions and that the property would eventually be subject to an order of confiscation for purposes of paragraph 1 (a) of this article;
> (b) a request that provides a reasonable basis for the requested State Party to believe that there are sufficient grounds for taking such actions and that the property would eventually be subject to an order of confiscation for purposes of paragraph 1 (a) of this article; and

According to Article 60:

> ...training and assistance and the mutual exchange of relevant experience and specialized knowledge, which will facilitate international cooperation between States Parties in the areas of extradition and mutual legal assistance is important to fight terrorism-financing worldwide.

States Parties shall therefore consider:

> ...using subregional, regional and international conferences and seminars to promote cooperation and technical assistance and to stimulate discussion on problems of mutual concern, including the special problems and needs of developing countries and countries with economies in transition.

R. International Convention for the Suppression of Acts of Nuclear Terrorism,[22] 2005.

This Convention covers acts related to the acquisition of nuclear capacity by terrorists and criminalizes the intention to cause harm from this acquisition. The possession as well as the use of nuclear materials by terrorists are both regarded as serious offences for the purpose of this Convention.

22 U.N., *International Convention for The Suppression of Acts of Nuclear Terrorism*, (2005), available from https://treaties.un.org/doc/db/Terrorism/english-18-15.pdf.

Article 2

2. Any person commits an offence within the meaning of this Convention if that person unlawfully and intentionally:
   (a) Possesses radioactive material or makes or possesses a device:
      (i) With the intent to cause death or serious bodily injury; or
      (ii) With the intent to cause substantial damage to property or to the environment;
   (b) Uses in any way radioactive material or a device, or uses or damages a nuclear facility in a manner which releases or risks the release of radioactive material:
      (i) With the intent to cause death or serious bodily injury; or
      (ii) With the intent to cause substantial damage to property or to the environment; or
      (iii) With the intent to compel a natural or legal person, an international organization or a State to do or refrain from doing an act.

The threat to use nuclear force is deemed to be an offence as well. Participation, organizing directly or indirectly, or contributing to one or more of the offences, is also illegal per this convention:

3. Any person also commits an offence if that person:
   (a) Threatens under circumstances which indicate the credibility of the threat to commit an offence as set forth in paragraph 1 (b) of the present article; or
   (b) Demands unlawfully and intentionally radioactive material, a device or a nuclear facility by threat, under circumstances which indicate the credibility of the threat, or using force.
4. Any person also commits an offence if that person attempts to commit an offence as set forth in paragraph 1 of the present article.
5. Any person also commits an offence if that person:
   (a) Participates as an accomplice in an offence as set forth in paragraph 1,2 or 3 of the present article; or
   (b) Organizes or directs others to commit an offence as set forth in paragraph 1,2 or 3 of the present article; or
   (c) In any other way contributes to the commission of one or more offences as set forth in paragraph 1,2 or 3 of the present

article by a group of persons acting with a common purpose; such contribution shall be intentional and either be made with the aim of furthering the general criminal activity or purpose of the group or be made in the knowledge of the intention of the group to commit the offence or offences concerned.

S. Protocol of 2005 to the Convention for the Suppression of Unlawful CTs Against the Safety of Maritime Navigation[23]

This Convention mentions in its Article 3bis that:

1. Any person commits an offence within the meaning of this Convention if that person unlawfully and intentionally:
   (a) When the purpose of the act, by its nature or context, is to intimidate a population, or to compel a government or an international organization to do or to abstain from doing any act:

According to Article 3quarter, any person also commits an offence in the meaning of this Convention, if they:

(a) Unlawfully and intentionally injures or kills any person in connection with the commission of any of the offences set forth in article 3, paragraph 1, article 3bis, or article 3ter; or
(b) Participates as an accomplice in an offence set forth in article 3, article 3bis, article 3ter, or subparagraph (a) or (b) of this article; or
   (i) With the aim of furthering the criminal activity or criminal purpose of the group, where such activity or purpose involves the commission of an offence set forth in article 3, 3bis or 3ter; or
   (ii) In the knowledge of the intention of the group to commit an offence set forth in article 3, 3bis or 3ter.

Hence, participation is stated in Article 3quarter (c).

23 U.S. Dep't. of State, Bureau of International Security and Nonproliferation, *Protocol of 2005 to the Convention for the Suppression of Unlawful Acts Against the Safety of Maritime Navigation,* LEG/CONF.15/22, 1 November 2005, available from https://www.state.gov/t/isn/trty/81728.htm.

T. Convention on the Suppression of unlawful Acts relating to International Civil Aviation[24]

The last United Nation Convention, to date, that should be referred to is the "2010 BEIJING Convention" pertaining to unlawful acts related to international civil aviation. Within Article 1:

3. Any person also commits an offence if that person:
   (a) makes a threat to commit any of the offences in paragraphs (a), (b), (c), (d), (1), (g) and (h) of paragraph 1 or in paragraph 2; or
   (b) unlawfully and intentionally causes any person to receive such a threat, under circumstances which indicate that the threat is credible.
4. any person also commits an offence if that person:
   (c) attempts to commit any of the offences set forth in paragraph 1 or 2 of this Article; or
   (d) organizes or directs others to commit an offence set forth in paragraph 1,2,3 or 4(a) of this Article; or
   (e) participates as an accomplice in an offence. Set forth in paragraph 1,2,3 or 4(a) of this Article; or

Article 1.5 makes it clear that to "attempt to commit" a criminal action is just as illicit as succeeding in perpetrating this action. It reads:

5. Each State Party shall also establish as offences, when committed intentionally, whether or not any of the offences set forth in paragraph 1,2 or 3 of this Article is actually committed or attempted, either or both of the following:
   (a) agreeing with one or more other persons to commit an offence set forth in paragraph 1,2 or 3 of this Article and, where required by national law, involving an act undertaken by one of the participants in furtherance of the agreement; or
   (b) contributing in any other way to the commission of one or more offences set forth in paragraph 1,2 or 3 of this Article by

24 U.N., *Protocol Supplementary to the Convention for the Suppression of Unlawful Seizure of Aircraft*, Beijing, 10 September 2010, available from https://www.icao.int/secretariat/legal/Administrative%20Packages/Beijing_protocol_EN.pdf.

a group of persons acting with a common purpose, and such contribution shall either:

i. be made with the aim of furthering the general criminal activity or purpose of the group, where such activity or purpose involves the commission of an offence set forth in paragraph 1,2 or 3 of this Article; or
ii. be made in the knowledge of the intention of the group to commit an offence set forth in paragraph 1,2 or 3 of this Article.

This Convention includes most of the developments discovered within the UN instruments previously studied above.

It also is important to highlight the Security Council Resolutions pertinent to this study related to terrorism:

1. The United Nations Security Council Resolution 1373[25,26]

This Resolution was adopted by the Security Council at its 4385th meeting, on 28 September 2001. In Paragraph 1, the United Nations declares that all States shall:

(a) Prevent and suppress the financing of terrorist acts;
(b) Criminalize the wilful provision or collection, by any means, directly or indirectly, of funds by their nationals or in their territories with the intention that the funds should be used, or in the knowledge that they are to be used, in order to carry out terrorist acts;
(c) Freeze without delay funds and other financial assets or economic resources of persons who commit, or attempt to commit, terrorist acts or participate in or facilitate the commission of terrorist acts; of entities owned or controlled directly or indirectly by such persons; and of persons and entities acting on behalf of, or at the direction of such persons and entities, including funds derived or generated

25 U.N. SCOR, *Resolution 1373*, S/RES/1373, 28 September 2001, available from http://www.un.org/en/sc/ctc/specialmeetings/2012/docs/United%20Nations%20Security%20Council%20Resolution%201373%20(2001).pdf.
26 The Security Council Resolution 1373 (2001) was adopted under Chapter 7 of the Charter and provided for the implementation of a Counter-Terrorism Committee.

from property owned or controlled directly or indirectly by such persons and associated persons and entities;

(d) Prohibit their nationals or any persons and entities within their territories from making any funds, financial assets or economic resources or financial or other related services available, directly or indirectly, for the benefit of persons who commit or attempt to commit or facilitate or participate in the commission of terrorist acts, of entities owned or controlled, directly or indirectly, by such persons and of persons and entities acting on behalf of or at the direction of such persons.

In paragraph 2 of this Resolution, the United Nations also reminds that all States shall:

(a) Refrain from providing any form of support, active or passive, to entities or persons involved in terrorist acts, including by suppressing recruitment of members of terrorist groups and eliminating the supply of weapons to terrorists;
(b) Take the necessary steps to prevent the commission of terrorist acts, including by provision of early warning to other States by exchange of information;
(c) Deny safe haven to those who finance, plan, support, or commit terrorist acts, or provide safe havens;
(d) Prevent those who finance, plan, facilitate or commit terrorist acts from using their respective territories for those purposes against other States or their citizens;
(e) Ensure that any person who participates in the financing, planning, preparation or perpetration of terrorist acts or in supporting terrorist acts is brought to justice and ensure that, in addition to any other measures against them, such terrorist acts are established as serious criminal offences in domestic laws and regulations and that the punishment duly reflects the seriousness of such terrorist acts;
(f) Afford one another the greatest measure of assistance in connection with criminal investigations or criminal proceedings relating to the financing or support of terrorist acts, including assistance in obtaining evidence in their possession necessary for the proceedings;
(g) Prevent the movement of terrorists or terrorist groups by effective border controls and controls on issuance of identity papers and travel documents, and through measures for preventing

counterfeiting, forgery or fraudulent use of identity papers and travel documents.

The United Nations, with the third paragraph of this Resolution, calls upon all States to:

(a) Find ways of intensifying and accelerating the exchange of operational information, especially regarding actions or movements of terrorist persons or networks; forged or falsified travel documents; traffic in arms, explosives or sensitive materials; use of communications technologies by terrorist groups; and the threat posed by the possession of weapons of mass destruction by terrorist groups;
(b) Exchange information in accordance with international and domestic law and cooperate on administrative and judicial matters to prevent the commission of terrorist acts;
(c) Cooperate, particularly through bilateral and multilateral arrangements and agreements, to prevent and suppress terrorist attacks and take action against perpetrators of such acts;
(d) Become parties as soon as possible to the relevant international conventions and protocols relating to terrorism, including the International Convention for the Suppression of the Financing of Terrorism of 9 December 1999;
(e) Increase cooperation and fully implement the relevant international conventions and protocols relating to terrorism and Security Council resolutions 1269 (1999) and 1368 (2001);
(f) Take appropriate measures in conformity with the relevant provisions of national and international law, including international standards of human rights, before granting refugee status, for the purpose of ensuring that the asylum-seeker has not planned, facilitated or participated in the commission of terrorist acts;
(g) Ensure, in conformity with international law, that refugee status is not abused by the perpetrators, organizers or facilitators of terrorist acts, and that claims of political motivation are not recognized as grounds for refusing requests for the extradition of alleged terrorists.

The United Nations:

notes in paragraph 4 with concern the close connection between international terrorism and transnational organized crime, illicit drugs, money-laundering, illegal arms trafficking, and illegal movement of nuclear,

> chemical, biological and other potentially deadly materials, and in this regard emphasizes the need to enhance coordination of efforts on national, subregional, regional and international levels in order to strengthen a global response to this serious challenge and threat to international security.

In paragraph 5, the UN claims that:

> acts, methods, and practices of terrorism are contrary to the purposes and principles of the United Nations and that knowingly financing, planning and inciting terrorist acts are also contrary to the purposes and principles of the United Nations;

The importance of financing and knowledge is becoming a crucial element for the United Nations, according to the wording of its last Conventions.

The United Nations Security Council, Letter dated 18 February 2015 from the Chair of the Security Council Committee established pursuant to resolution 1373 (2001), concerning Counter-terrorism, addressed to the President of the Security Council, specifically refers to financial leads and investigating financial crimes committed before the departure of terrorist fighters. Paragraph 31 mentions that:

> Financial investigations, including the investigation of financial crimes, can significantly assist in exposing individuals' intentions. In some cases, the cost of travel may be equivalent to a few months' salary and many would-be foreign terrorist fighters do not have the money to travel themselves. Vulnerable persons of low income and without a steady job may obtain money from others, and that money may originate from financiers abroad. Such funding can be tracked. In several cases, prosecutors have been able, through financial investigations, to identify the sources of such monies. In other cases, individuals commit crimes such as fraud, theft, tax evasion and money-laundering as they prepare to travel. Prosecuting authorities can and have exposed the falsehood of suspects' stated purpose to travel for tourism by proving that they have sold all family property before attempting to leave the country. The sudden sales of property for lower than the market value of those assets in such cases could provide corroborating evidence of the intent to travel abroad for a different purpose, such as to join a terrorist organization.

This statement confirms the fact that financing has recently taken a new dimension since terrorists are a very new type of isolated individuals without the means necessary to finance a strong attack and rely on multiple well-known factors and individuals to carry-out their plans. Preventing the financing and travel of terrorists is crucial to stopping terrorism from occurring. Persons or organizations that finance, fund or facilitate the travel of foreign terrorist fighters are mentioned within paragraph 32 as:

> It seems clear that departures are now much more organized and are often backed by financial networks. One participant discussed the possibility of applying lessons learned from successful prosecutions of organized crime to those of terrorism and foreign terrorist fighters. Some countries already use participation in an organized criminal group as the offence to prosecute terrorists. In one State, much attention is given to links and similarities in *modus operandi* between foreign terrorist fighters and organized crime. In some instances, travel is facilitated by networks of criminals who arrange fraudulent passports and border crossings. Similarities in the financing of travel may mean similarities in moving money. Therefore, financial investigations may expose the existence of offshore accounts, professional money managers, frontmen and mediators. That creates investigative and prosecutorial opportunities. As with other financial investigations, the involvement of the relevant tax authorities, customs authorities and the financial intelligence unit at an early stage may assist in identifying links and methods of work.

2. United Nations Security Council Resolution 1566[27,28]

This Resolution was adopted by the Security Council at its 5053rd meeting, on 8 October 2004 and:

> Calls upon States to cooperate fully in the fight against terrorism, especially with those States where or against whose citizens terrorist acts are committed, in accordance with their obligations under international law, in order to find, deny safe haven and bring to justice, on the basis of the

27 U.N. SCOR, *Resolution 1566,* S/RES/1566, 8 October 2004, available from https://www.scribd.com/document/63963034/UNSCR-1566-2004.

28 The Security Council Resolution 1566 (2004) offers a potential description of "terrorism".

> principle to extradite or prosecute, any person who supports, facilitates, participates or attempts to participate in the financing, planning, preparation or commission of terrorist acts or provides safe havens;

This Resolution reaffirms the need to deny safe havens and to bring terrorists and anyone involved in any way with an offence to justice by prosecution or through extradition.

3. United Nations Security Council Resolution 2170[29,30]

Adopted by the Security Council at its 7242nd meeting, on 15 August 2014.

Per Resolution 2170:

> …all States shall prohibit their nationals or any persons and entities within their territories from making any funds, financial assets or economic resources or financial or other related services available, directly or indirectly, for the benefit of persons who commit or attempt to commit or facilitate or participate in the commission of terrorist acts, or for the benefit of entities owned or controlled, directly or indirectly, by such persons and of persons and entities acting on behalf of or at the direction of such persons.

Listing and delisting is a controversial topic, as when to delist is ambiguous for many. According to this Resolution, one should:

> …consider listing individuals, groups, undertakings and entities providing support to ISIL or to ANF, including those who are financing, arming, planning or recruiting for ISIL or ANF and all other individuals, groups, undertakings and entities associated with Al-Qaida through information and communications technologies including the internet and social media or through any other means;

---

29 U.N. Meetings Coverage and Press Releases, *Security Council Adopts Resolution 2170 (2014) Condemning Gross, Widespread Abuse of Human Rights by Extremist Groups in Iraq, Syria*, SC 11520, 15 August 2014, available from http://www.un.org/press/en/2014/sc11520.doc.htm.

30 United Nations Security Council Resolution 2170 imposes the asset freeze, travel ban and arms embargo on six individuals associated with Al-Qaida, Islamic State in Iraq and the Levant.

4. United Nations Security Council Resolution 2178[31,32]

Resolution 2178 was adopted by the Security Council at its 7272nd meeting, on 24 September 2014. According to this Resolution, States shall ensure that their domestic laws and regulations establish serious criminal offences sufficient to provide the ability to prosecute and penalize in a manner duly reflecting the seriousness of the offence:

(a) their nationals who travel or attempt to travel to a State other than their States of residence or nationality, and other individuals who travel or attempt to travel from their territories to a State other than their States of residence or nationality, for the purpose of the perpetration, planning, or preparation of, or participation in, terrorist acts, or the providing or receiving of terrorist training;

(b) the wilful provision or collection, by any means, directly or indirectly, of funds by their nationals or in their territories with the intention that the funds should be used, or in the knowledge that they are to be used, in order to finance the travel of individuals who travel to a State other than their States of residence or nationality for the purpose of the perpetration, planning, or preparation of, or participation in, terrorist acts or the providing or receiving of terrorist training; and,

(c) the wilful organization, or other facilitation, including acts of recruitment, by their nationals or in their territories, of the travel of individuals who travel to a State other than their States of residence or nationality for the purpose of the perpetration, planning, or preparation of, or participation in, terrorist acts or the providing or receiving of terrorist training.

Pursuant to this Resolution, states should also consider listing individuals, groups, undertakings and entities associated with Al-Qaida, who are financing, arming, planning, or recruiting for them, or otherwise supporting their acts or activities, including through information and communications technologies, such as the internet, social media, or any other means.

---

31 U.N. SCOR, *Resolution 2178*, 24 September 2014, available from http://www.un.org/en/sc/ctc/docs/2015/SCR%202178_2014_EN.pdf.

32 United Nations Security Council Resolution 2178 deals with States affected by foreign Terrorist Fighters: including preventing inter-States travel ban by foreign terrorist fighters, law enforcement, terrorism-financing, regional and international cooperation and countering violent extremism, including social media.

5. United Nations Security Council Resolution 2195[33,34]

Resolution 2195 was adopted by the Security Council at its 7351st meeting, on 19 December 2014.

This Resolution reaffirms:

> ...the need to prevent and suppress the financing of terrorist acts, Expressing concern that terrorists benefit from transnational organized crime in some regions, including from the trafficking of arms, persons, drugs, and artefacts and from the illicit trade in natural resources including gold and other precious metals and stones, minerals, wildlife, charcoal and oil, as well as from kidnapping for ransom and other crimes including extortion and bank robbery.

All member states are also urged to:

> ...participate actively in maintaining and updating the list created pursuant to resolutions 1267 (1999), 1333 (2000) and 1989 (2011) ('the Al-Qaida Sanctions List') by contributing additional information pertinent to current listings, submitting delisting requests when appropriate, and by identifying and nominating for listing additional individuals, groups, undertakings and entities which should be subject to the measures referred to in paragraph 1 of resolution 2161 (2014).

6. United Nations Security Council Resolution 2199[35,36]

Resolution 2199 was adopted by the Security Council at its 7379th meeting, on 12 February 2015.

Strong concerns are raised in this Resolution about the use of technology by terrorists and their supporters to facilitate terrorist acts, as well as its use to

33 U.N. Meetings Coverage and Press Releases, *Adopting Resolution 2195 (2014), Urges International Action to Break Links between Terrorists, Transnational Organized Crime*, S/2015/683, 2 September 2015, available from http://www.un.org/press/en/2014/sc11717.doc.htm.

34 United Nations Security Council Resolution 2195 urges International action to break links between Terrorists, Transnational Organized Crime.

35 U.N. Meetings Coverage and Press Releases, *Unanimously Adopting Resolution 2199 (2015), Security Council Condemns Trade with Al-Qaida Associated Groups, Threatens Further Targeted Sanctions*, SC 11775, 12 February 2015, available from http://www.un.org/press/en/2015/sc11775.doc.htm.

36 United Nations Security Council Resolution 2199 on threats to the International Peace and Security caused by acts of Al-Quaida.

incite, recruit, fund or plan terrorist acts. The United Nations in this Resolution strongly condemns any engagement in direct or indirect trade of oil and oil products, and modular refineries and related material as well as any funds or negotiable benefit arising from such economic resources and reiterates the importance of asset freezes as:

> ...vehicles, including aircraft, cars and trucks and oil tankers, departing from or going to areas of Syria and Iraq where ISIL, ANF or any other groups, undertakings and entities associated with Al-Qaida operate, could be used to transfer oil and oil products, modular refineries and related material, cash, and other valuable items including natural resources such as precious metals and minerals like gold, silver, copper and diamonds, as well as grain, livestock, machinery, electronics, and cigarettes by or on behalf of such entities for sale on international markets, for barter for arms, or for use in other ways that would result in violations of the asset freeze or arms embargo.

Cultural property is an issue that is not as often mentioned as other modes of financing. ISIL, ANF and all other individuals, groups, undertakings and entities associated with Al-Qaida for ongoing and multiple criminal terrorist acts destroy property, cultural and religious sites, whilst also stealing some of these items and selling them to generate income. Engaging directly or indirectly in the pillaging and smuggling of cultural heritage items from archaeological sites, museums, libraries, archives, and other sites in Iraq and Syria should require, therefore, travel bans, asset freezes and arms embargos to combat such trends. Moreover, this Resolution condemns the destruction of cultural heritage in Iraq and Syria, particularly by ISIL and ANF, whether such destruction is incidental or deliberate, including targeted destruction of religious sites and objects. Member States shall, therefore, take appropriate steps to prevent the trade in Iraqi and Syrian cultural property and other items of archaeological, historical, cultural, rare scientific, and religious importance illegally removed, including prohibiting cross-border trade in such items, thereby allowing for their eventual safe return to the Iraqi and Syrian people.

Kidnapping for ransom and external donations are also discussed within this Resolution, whereby it calls upon:

> ...all Member States to encourage private sector partners to adopt or to follow relevant guidelines and good practices for preventing and responding to terrorist kidnappings without paying ransom.

Hostage taking and kidnapping associated with terrorist groups aimed at raising funds or gaining political concessions should be strictly regulated, as ransoms can also be used to finance terrorist activities.

This Resolution urges Member States to take steps to safeguard that banking systems within their territory prevent ISIL, ANF or other individuals, groups, undertakings or entities associated with Al-Qaida from accessing the international financial system.

2 Agencies and Financial Institutions Recommendations

Several agencies and financial institutions recommendations exist and provide a comprehensive source of information, which is sometimes missing from international CTF legal standards and countries' legislative efforts and thus, should be incorporated within the new Model. The Financial Action Task Force is a crucial actor to recognize as a precursor concerning CTF/AML and various financial crimes linked to financing terrorism and hence, vital for the purpose of the proposed Convention. The FATF is an international government organization with great expertise in the global fight of CTF, which brings legal, financial and law enforcement experts into the policy-making process.[37]

The FATF, established in 1989 in Paris by the G-7 Summit, works closely with other organizations, such as the IMF, the World Bank, the United Nations and FATF-style regional bodies. Its aim is to offer a set of standards intended to identify and describe current money-laundering methods and terrorism-financing trends, emerging vulnerabilities, and potential counter-measures to deny terrorists and their supporters' access to the international financial system, as well as helping countries and financial institutions to track down and intercept terrorist assets. These standards, initially set in 1990, have been revised many times, according to the sector's need, including in 1996, 2003, and 2012 to strengthen global safeguards and protect the integrity of the financial system as well as to reflect changes in ML/TF trends and techniques. The FATF has offered an additional much needed supplement to the first 40 recommendations issued regarding ML/TF, which are internationally accepted as a global standard. The special recommendations emphasis is about ensuring that terrorist-financing be specifically listed as a criminal offence in a country's legislation; the seizure of terrorist assets; the reporting of suspect financial transactions linked to terrorism; international co-operation; and measures to

37 Jonathan Winer, *Combating Money-Laundering*, 11 June 1998, available from http://www.fas.org/irp/congress/1998_hr/980611_winer_launder.htm.

prevent the misuse of wire transfers and other remittance systems. The recourse to non-profit organizations used as a source of funding is also prescribed within FATF's work. Resolutions have been expanded to deal with new categories of financing menaces, such as the financing of the proliferation of weapons of mass destruction, transparency and corruption. These have also strengthened the requirements for high risk cases and encourage risk based approaches.[38]

The United Nations even recognizes the importance of the implementation of the FATF recommendations within the UN Security Council Resolution 1617 and the annexed plan of action of resolution 60/288, which insists on the relevance of the 40 Recommendations from FATF and the nine special TF recommendations. It reads as:

> ...Strongly urges all Member States to implement the comprehensive, international standards embodied in the Financial Action Task Force's (FATF) Forty Recommendations on Money-laundering and the FATF Nine Special Recommendations on Terrorist Financing;

Second, the list of actual advisory tools provided by agencies and financial institutions related to organized crime, corruption, and terrorism-financing pertinent to this analysis incorporates:

A. The FATF 40 Recommendations[39]

According to FATF:

5. Each country should consider extending the offense of drug money-laundering to any other crimes for which there is a link to narcotics; an alternative approach is to criminalize money-laundering based on all serious offenses, and/or on all offenses that generate a significant amount of proceeds, or on certain serious offenses.

Concerning provisional measures and confiscation, countries are asked to adopt measures comparable to those from the Vienna Convention and should

38 Financial Action Task Force (FATF), *FATF steps up the fight against money-laundering and terrorist financing*, 2012, available from http://www.fatf-gafi.org/topics/fatfrecommendations/documents/fatfstepsupthefightagainstmoneylaunderingandterroristfinancing.html.

39 Financial Action Task Force (FATF) on Money-Laundering, *The Forty Recommendations*, (1990), available from http://www.fatf-gafi.org/media/fatf/documents/recommendations/pdfs/FATF%20Recommendations%201990.pdf.

enable their competent authorities to confiscate property laundered, proceeds from, instrumentalities used in or intended for use in the commission of any money-laundering offence, and/or property of corresponding value, even by enabling legislative measures, if needed.

> Such measures should include the authority to:
> 1) identify, trace and evaluate property which is subject to confiscation;
> 2) carry out provisional measures, such as freezing and seizing, to prevent any dealing, transfer or disposal of such property;
> 3) and take any appropriate investigative measures.
>
> In addition to confiscation and criminal sanctions, countries also should consider monetary and civil penalties, and/or proceedings including civil proceedings, to void contracts entered by parties, where parties knew or should have known that as a result of the contract, the State would be prejudiced in its ability to recover financial claims, e.g. through confiscation or collection of fines and penalties.

Customer identification and record-keeping rules are also set by FATF so:

> 12. Financial institutions should not keep anonymous accounts or accounts in obviously fictitious names: they should be required (by law, by regulations, by agreements between supervisory authorities and financial institutions or by self-regulatory agreements among financial institutions) to identify, on the basis of an official or other reliable identifying document, and record the identity of their clients, either occasional or usual, when establishing business relations or conducting transactions (in particular opening of accounts or passbooks, entering into fiduciary transactions, renting of safe deposit boxes, performing large cash transactions).

Financial institutions should also:

> ...take reasonable measures to obtain information about the true identity of the persons on whose behalf an account is opened or a transaction conducted if there are any doubts as to whether these clients or customers are not acting on their own behalf, in particular, in the case of domiciliary companies (i.e. institutions, corporations, foundations, trusts, etc.

that do not conduct any commercial or manufacturing business or any other form of commercial operation in the country where their registered office is located).

... maintain, for at least five years, all necessary records on transactions, both domestic or international, to enable them to comply swiftly with information requests from the competent authorities.

Such records must be sufficient to permit reconstruction of individual transactions (including the amounts and types of currency involved if any) so as to provide, if necessary, evidence for prosecution of criminal behaviour.

... keep records on customer identification (e.g. copies or records of official identification documents like passports, identity cards, driving licenses or similar documents), account files and business correspondence for at least five years after the account is closed. These documents should be available to domestic competent authorities in the context of relevant criminal prosecutions and investigations.

... develop programs against money-laundering. These programs should include, as a minimum:

(a) the development of internal policies, procedures and controls, including the designation of compliance officers at management level, and adequate screening procedures to ensure high standards when hiring employees;

(b) an ongoing employee training programme;

(c) an audit function to test the system.

The importance of record keeping is underlined in this Article, as money-laundering or Counter-terrorism financing crimes can be detected through this process and only good record keeping can provide relevant information to authorities and explain actions and behaviors in a timely manner, sometimes before a crime has occurred.

The implementation, and role of regulatory and other administrative authorities are:

...supervising banks or other financial institutions or intermediaries, or other competent authorities, should ensure that the supervised institutions have adequate programs to guard against money-laundering. These authorities should cooperate and lend expertise spontaneously or on request with other domestic judicial or law enforcement authorities in money-laundering investigations and prosecutions.

> ...designated to ensure an effective implementation of all these Recommendations, through administrative supervision and regulation, in other professions dealing with cash as defined by each country.
>
> ...establish guidelines which will assist financial institutions in detecting suspicious patterns of behaviour by their customers. It is understood that such guidelines must develop over time, and will never be exhaustive. It is further understood that such guidelines will primarily serve as an educational tool for financial institutions' personnel.
>
> ...regulating or supervising financial institutions should take the necessary legal or regulatory measures to guard against control or acquisition of a significant participation in financial institutions by criminals or their confederates.

B. Convention on Combating Bribery of Foreign Officials in International Business Transactions (OECD)[40,41]

Article 1 of this Convention recognizes the offence of bribery of foreign public officials, whereby each party shall take such measures as may be necessary to establish that:

> ...it is a criminal offence under its law for any person intentionally to offer, promise or give any undue pecuniary or other advantage, whether directly or through intermediaries, to a foreign public official, for that official or for a third party, in order that the official act or refrain from acting in relation to the performance of official duties, in order to obtain or retain business or other improper advantage in the conduct of international business.
>
> ...complicity in, including incitement, aiding and abetting, or authorisation of an act of bribery of a foreign public official shall be a criminal offence. Attempt and conspiracy to bribe a foreign public official shall be criminal offences to the same extent as attempt and conspiracy to bribe a public official of that Party.

---

40 Organisation for Economic Co-Operation and Development (OECD), *OECD Convention on Combating Bribery of Foreign Public Officials in International Business Transactions*, 17 December 1997, available from http://www.oecd.org/corruption/oecdantibriberyconvention.htm.

41 And related Documents (into force since 1999), revised recommendations were adopted in 2009.

The responsibility of legal persons for the bribery of a foreign public official shall be established by each party as may be necessary, in accordance with its legal principles. In Article 7, the "bribery of its own public official" is to be established as a predicate offence for money-laundering legislation, whether a Party has made either active or passive bribery. If a party has made passive bribery a predicate offence for money-laundering purposes, the laundering of the bribe payment is subject to money-laundering legislation. Public officials are subject to corruption or abuse of powers pertaining to their functions, which can lead them to finance crime more discreetly in certain cases.

c. Basel Committee on Banking Supervision, Customer Due Diligence[42]

The implementation of KYC standards in a cross-border context means information collected by banks and other financial service providers, as well as compliance standards should be higher to face the international threat of abuse of financial circuits. In this regard:

> V. 63. Supervisors around the world should seek, to the best of their efforts, to develop and implement their national KYC standards fully in line with international standards so as to avoid potential regulatory arbitrage and safeguard the integrity of domestic and international banking systems.

Complying with international standards can be burdensome for financial service providers and diverse from their current national regulations. The internationalization of money and value service businesses demands that institutions comply with different sets of standards, which can be difficult while dealing with parent companies and subsidiaries. Per the Basel Committee:

> Parent banks must communicate their policies and procedures to their overseas branches and subsidiaries, including non-banking entities such as trust companies, and have a routine for testing compliance against both home and host country KYC standards in order for their programmes to operate effectively globally.
>
> Where the minimum KYC standards of the home and host countries differ, branches and subsidiaries in the host jurisdictions should apply

42 Bank for International Settlements, *Customer Due diligence for banks—final document*, October 2001, available from http://www.bis.org/publ/bcbs85.htm.

> the higher standard of the two. In general, there should be no impediment to prevent a bank from adopting standards that are higher than the minima required locally. If, however, local laws and regulations (especially secrecy provisions) prohibit the implementation of home country KYC standards, where the latter are more stringent, host country supervisors should use their best endeavours to have the law and regulations changed.

Nonetheless, overseas branches and subsidiaries are still required to comply with their host country's standards and ascertain that their supervisor at home and the head office of their parent bank are aware of the difference in standards. Jurisdictional matters should also be considered as criminal elements and might be drawn toward jurisdictions with such impediments, hence:

> ...banks should be aware of the high reputational risk of conducting business in these jurisdictions. Parent banks should have a procedure for reviewing the vulnerability of the individual operating units and implement additional safeguards where appropriate. In extreme cases, supervisors should consider placing additional controls on banks operating in those jurisdictions and ultimately perhaps encouraging their withdrawal.

Home country supervisors and auditors face on-site inspections, and therefore, should verify compliance with KYC policies and procedures, and decide in the case of conflict between these two and those of the parent office abroad, what is permitted and to what extent.

D. Basel Committee on Banking Supervision, Sharing of financial records between jurisdictions in connection with the fight against terrorist financing[43]

Per the summary of a meeting of representatives of Supervisors and Legal Experts of G10 Central Banks and Supervisory Authorities on 14 December 2001 in Basel, Switzerland, MLAT and official gateways are matters which shall be highlighted in this legal instrument.

Concerning official gateways for cross-border information, three official ones for sharing information between national jurisdictions are considered within this study. The first gateway commonly deals with formal procedures,

43 Bank for International Settlements, *Sharing of Financial Records Between Jurisdictions in Connection with the Fight Against Terrorist Financing* (April 2002), http://www.bis.org/publ/bcbs89.htm.

but is not customarily used for supervisory or regulatory matters, whilst the second, involves communication between Financial Intelligence Unit (FIUs) or other bodies set up to fight financial crime and thus, to track terrorist funds and follow up reports of potential terrorist accounts. The third is the supervisory channel gateway regarding banking activities, designed to monitor the soundness of the banking group.

According to this report:

> While each of these gateways is used to communicate financial information across a national border, the information received through each respective gateway serves a different purpose. Of course, these purposes may also complement one another with respect to an overall objective like fighting terrorism. If a prosecutor needs information to prosecute a criminal case of terrorism, the prosecutor will ordinarily use a MLAT. If a FIU in a host country learns information suggesting that a branch or subsidiary of a banking group has an account for a known terrorist organization, the FIU may pass that intelligence information to the FIU in the home country for the group.

MLAT and gateways should be strongly underlined within the new Convention model this study will provide, as they are crucial cooperation and information elements.

E. Wolfsberg AML Principles for Correspondent Banking[44]

The Wolfsberg Principles provide relevant information on correspondent banking relationships an institution establishes or maintains for another correspondent banking client. According to Wolfsberg:

> Correspondent Banking is the provision on current or other liability account and related services to another institution used to meet its cash clearing, liquidity management and short-term borrowing or investment needs. Institutions may decide to extend these Principles to all relationships that they maintain with financial institutions.

44 Wolfsberg, *Anti-Money-Laundering Principles for Correspondent Banking*, (last visited 5 July 2014), http://www.wolfsberg-principles.com/pdf/standards/Wolfsberg-Correspondent-Banking-Principles-2014.pdf.

AML/CTF should, therefore, look into correspondent banking as a potential threat. This topic should be included within the new Convention model and given close consideration.

The Principles offer recommendation for an international registry which:

> …encourages the development and regulatory endorsement of an international registry for financial institutions. Upon registering financial institutions would submit information useful for conducing due diligence as outlined in these Principles. Financial institutions would rely on this information in adhering to these Principles.

F. FATF Recommendations[45]

The 2003 FATF Recommendations discuss an important matter, which is the offence itself. Money-laundering is asked to be linked as a predicate offence to all serious wrongdoings and to include a wider range of predicate offences:

> Where countries apply a threshold approach, predicate offences should at a minimum comprise all offences that fall within the category of serious offences under their national law or should include offences which are punishable by a maximum penalty of more than one year's imprisonment or for those countries that have a minimum threshold for offences in their legal system, predicate offences should comprise all offences, which are punished by a minimum penalty of more than six months imprisonment.

Bearing in mind the international dimension of money-laundering, a predicate offence for it should apply to conduct abroad, which constitutes an offence in that country, and would have been a predicate offence if the crime had been committed domestically.

Concerning customer due diligence and record-keeping, financial institutions should not keep anonymous accounts in obviously fictitious names, as per FATF. They should also undertake customer due diligence measures, including identifying and verifying the identity of their customers, when:

---

45 Financial Action Task Force (FATF) on Money-Laundering, *The Forty Recommendations*, 20 June 2003, available from http://www.fatf-gafi.org/media/fatf/documents/recommendations/pdfs/FATF%20Recommendations%202003.pdf.

establishing business relations; carrying out occasional transactions:
(i) above the applicable designated threshold;
(ii) or that are wire transfers in the circumstances covered by the Interpretative Note to Special Recommendation VII; there is a suspicion of money-laundering or terrorist financing; or the financial institution has doubts about the veracity or adequacy of previously obtained customer identification data.

Recommended Customer Due Diligence (CDD) measures to be implemented as follows:

a) Identifying the customer and verifying that customer's identity using reliable, independent source documents, data or information.
b) Identifying the beneficial owner, and taking reasonable measures to verify the identity of the beneficial owner such that the financial institution is satisfied that it knows who the beneficial owner is. For legal persons and arrangements this should include financial institutions taking reasonable measures to understand the ownership and control structure of the customer.
c) Obtaining information on the purpose and intended nature of the business relationship.
d) Conducting ongoing due diligence on the business relationship and scrutiny of transactions undertaken throughout the course of that relationship to ensure that the transactions being conducted are consistent with the institution's knowledge of the customer, their business and risk profile, including, where necessary, the source of funds.

Enhanced due diligence is asked for, with accounts involving PEPs and financial institutions should therefore:

a) Have appropriate risk management systems to determine whether the customer is a politically exposed person.
b) Obtain senior management approval for establishing business relationships with such customers.
Reliable, independent source documents, data or information will hereafter be referred to as "identification data." Recommendations marked with an asterisk should be read in conjunction with their Interpretative Note.

c) Take reasonable measures to establish the source of wealth and source of funds.
d) Conduct enhanced ongoing monitoring of the business relationship.

For cross-border correspondent banking and other similar relationships, financial institutions should also perform Enhanced due diligence measures as follows:

a) Gather sufficient information about a respondent institution to understand fully the nature of the respondent's business and to determine from publicly available information the reputation of the institution and the quality of supervision, including whether it has been subject to a money-laundering or terrorist-financing investigation or regulatory action.
b) Assess the respondent institution's anti-money-laundering and terrorist financing controls.
c) Obtain approval from senior management before establishing new correspondent relationships.
d) Document the respective responsibilities of each institution.
e) With respect to "payable-through accounts," be satisfied that the respondent bank has verified the identity of and performed ongoing due diligence on the customers having direct access to accounts of the correspondent and that it is able to provide relevant customer identification data upon request to the correspondent bank.

New or developing technologies are serious ML/TF threats for financial service providers, as they favour anonymity. Financial institutions should thus have policies and procedures in place to address any specific risks associated with nonface to face business relationships or transactions. They should also be aware of the risk associated with NPM and keep records on the identification data obtained through customer due diligence and transaction records, which should be available to domestic competent authorities, such as copies or records of official identification documents like passports, identity cards, driving licenses or similar documents. This needs to include account files and business correspondence kept for at least five years after the business relationship is ended.

Another red flag is related to unusual activities. Financial institutions should check unusual large transactions, and all unusual patterns of transactions with no apparent economic or visible lawful purpose. Customer due diligence and record-keeping requirements apply to designated non-financial businesses and professions in the following situations:

a) Casinos—when customers engage in financial transactions equal to or above the applicable designated threshold.
b) Real estate agents—when they are involved in transactions for their client concerning the buying and selling of real estate.
c) Dealers in precious metals and dealers in precious stones—when they engage in any cash transaction with a customer equal to or above the applicable designated threshold.
d) Lawyers, notaries, other independent legal professionals and accountants when they prepare for or carry out transactions for their client concerning the following activities:
buying and selling of real estate; managing of client money, securities or other assets; management of bank, savings or securities accounts; organization of contributions for the creation, operation or management of companies; creation, operation or management of legal persons or arrangements, and buying and selling of business entities.
e) Trust and company service providers when they prepare for or carry out transactions for a client concerning the activities listed in the definition in the Glossary.

Designated non-financial businesses and professions should be subject to regulatory and supervisory measures as follows:

a) Casinos should be subject to a comprehensive regulatory and supervisory regime that ensures that they have effectively implemented the necessary anti-money-laundering and terrorist-financing measures. At a minimum:
casinos should be licensed; competent authorities should take the necessary legal or regulatory measures to prevent criminals or their associates from holding or being the beneficial owner of a significant or controlling interest, holding a management function in, or being an operator of a casino competent authorities should ensure that casinos are effectively supervised for compliance with requirements to combat money-laundering and terrorist-financing.
b) Countries should ensure that the other categories of designated non-financial businesses and professions are subject to effective

> systems for monitoring and ensuring their compliance with requirements to combat money-laundering and terrorist financing. This should be performed on a risk-sensitive basis. This may be performed by a government authority or by an appropriate self-regulatory organization, provided that such an organization can ensure that its members comply with their obligations to combat money-laundering and terrorist-financing.

Guidelines should be established by competent authorities regarding the detection and reporting of suspect transactions concerning ML and TF. Financial institutions and designated non-financial businesses and professions should be assisted in applying national measures by countries providing feedback.

According to Recommendation 14 on customer due diligence and tipping-off, financial institutions, their directors, officers and employees are prohibited from disclosing the fact that an STR or related information is being reported to the FIU. Per Recommendation 14, lawyers, notaries, other independent legal professionals and accountants acting as independent legal professionals are not tipping-off when they seek to dissuade a client form engaging in illegal activity. The CDD process in relation to legal persons or arrangements, financial institutions should be performed to:

a) Verify that any person purporting to act on behalf of the customer is so authorised, and identify that person.
b) Identify the customer and verify its identity—the types of measures that would be normally needed to satisfactorily perform this function would require obtaining proof of incorporation or similar evidence of the legal status of the legal person or arrangement, as well as information concerning the customer's name, the names of trustees, legal form, address, directors, and provisions regulating the power to bind the legal person or arrangement.
c) Identify the beneficial owners, including forming an understanding of the ownership and control structure, and take reasonable measures to verify the identity of such persons. The types of measures that would be normally needed to satisfactorily perform this function would require identifying the natural persons with a controlling interest and identifying the natural persons who comprise the mind and management of the legal person or arrangement. Where

> the customer or the owner of the controlling interest is a public company that is subject to regulatory disclosure requirements, it is not necessary to seek to identify and verify the identity of any shareholder of that company.

Regarding Recommendation 19 dealing with cross-border activities:

> If a country discovers an unusual international shipment of currency, monetary instruments, precious metals, or gems, etc., it should consider notifying, as appropriate, the Customs Service or other competent authorities of the countries from which the shipment originated and/or to which it is destined, and should co-operate with a view toward establishing the source, destination, and purpose of such shipment and toward the taking of appropriate action.

G. Basel Committee on Banking Supervision, Consolidated KYC Risk Management[46]

Bank secrecy, data protection, and privacy are discussed within this legal instrument, as some countries might include protection laws which prevent, or can be interpreted as preventing the transfer of information related to banking and financial activities. While gateways are in place in most jurisdictions to enable banks to share information with their head offices for risk management purposes, problems regarding the transfer of customer information sharing with overseas offices might arise and might conflict with the consolidated KYC objective.

BCBS therefore believes that:

> ...there is no justifiable reason why local legislation should impede the passage of customer information from a bank branch or subsidiary to its head office or parent bank for risk management purposes. If the law restricts disclosure of information to 'third parties' it is essential that the head office or parent bank is clearly excluded from the definition of a third party.

46 Bank for International Settlements, *Consolidated KYC Risk Management—Consultative Document*, August 2003, available from http://www.bis.org/publ/bcbs101.htm.

H. IMF Model Legislation on Money-laundering and Financing of Terrorism[47]

Wire transfers are an important point to discuss since they represent a strong risk of TF/ML and growing concerns have been raised by the international community regarding this method of funding.

According to Article 2.2.7:

(1) Financial institutions whose activities include wire transfers shall obtain and verify the full name, account number, and address, or in the absence of address the national identity number or date and place of birth, including, when necessary, the name of the financial institution, of the originator of such transfers. The information shall be included in the message or payment form accompanying the transfer. If there is no account number, a unique reference number shall accompany the transfer.

(2) The institutions referred to in paragraph (1) shall maintain all such information and transmit it when they act as intermediaries in a chain of payments.

(3) The [competent authority] may issue regulations regarding cross-border transfers executed as batch transfers and domestic transfers.

(4) Paragraphs (1) and (2) shall not apply to transfers executed as a result of credit card or debit card transactions, provided that the credit card or debit card number accompanies the transfer resulting from the transaction, nor shall they apply to transfers between financial institutions where both the originator and the beneficiary are financial institutions acting on their own behalf.

(5) If the institutions referred to in paragraph (1) receive wire transfers that do not contain the complete originator information they shall take measures to obtain and verify the missing information from the ordering institution or the beneficiary. Should they not obtain the missing information they shall Variant 1: refuse acceptance of the transfer. Variant 2: refuse acceptance of the transfer and report it to the financial intelligence unit.

47 U.N. Office on Drugs and Crime, *Model Legislation on Money-Laundering and Financing of Terrorism*, 1 December 2005, available from http://www.imf.org/external/np/leg/amlcft/eng/pdf/amlml05.pdf.

Article 4.1.1 lays down investigative techniques for the purpose of obtaining evidence in connection with ML and TF as well as tracing proceeds of crime. Pertaining to this Article, the judicial authorities may order for a specific period:

a) the monitoring of bank accounts and other similar accounts;
b) access to computer systems, networks and servers;
c) the placing under surveillance or interception of communication;
d) the audio or video recording or photographing of acts and behaviour or conversations;
e) the interception and seizure of correspondence.

Non-profit organizations are often accomplices to or abusers of a corrupted system leading to financing illicit activities. This Article aims to help countries implement the best guidelines regarding non-profit organizations. According to this Recommendation:

> Any non-profit organization [Option: that collects, receives, grants or transfers funds as part of its charitable activity] shall be subject to appropriate oversight by the [competent authority in the country]. [The Minister, competent authority] may prescribe regulations to ensure that non-profit organizations are not misused for the purpose of the financing of terrorism. [Option: Prior to recognition as a non-profit organization, the [competent authority in the country] [shall/may] require registration with [competent court/authority in the country] and stipulate by [regulation/decree] minimum conditions of operation, such as regular auditing of the non-profit organization's budget and accounting system.]

Article 4.1.2 dealing with undercover operations and controlled delivery provides that no punishment may be imposed on:

> … officials competent to investigate money-laundering and financing of terrorism who, for the purpose of obtaining evidence relating to these offences or the tracing of proceeds of crime, perform acts which might be construed as elements of money-laundering and financing of terrorism in connection with carrying out an undercover operation or a controlled delivery. The designated official shall not induce the suspect to commit any offences.

The criminal offence of financing terrorism is depicted by Article 5.2.2, such that a person commits a crime if:

(1) For the purposes of this law, financing of terrorism shall be defined as follows: An act by any person who by any means, directly or indirectly, wilfully, provides or collects funds, or attempts to do so, with the intention that they should be used or in the knowledge that they are to be used in full or in part: a) to carry out a terrorist act, or b) by a terrorist, or c) by a terrorist organization.

(2) The offence is committed irrespective of any occurrence of a terrorist act referred to in paragraph (1), or whether the funds have actually been used to commit such act.

(3) It shall also be an offence to:
   a) participate as an accomplice in an offence within the meaning of paragraph (1) of this Article;
   b) organize or direct others to commit an offence within the meaning of paragraph (1) of this Article.

(4) Financing of terrorism shall be punishable by a fine of ... to ... or imprisonment of ... to ... or either of these penalties.

(5) An attempt to commit the offence of financing of terrorism or aiding, abetting, facilitating or counselling the commission of any such offence shall be punished as if the offence had been completed. [Option: is punished by a penalty reduced by [fraction] in relation to the main penalty.]

Association or conspiracy to commit money-laundering or the financing of terrorism, participation in, association with or conspiracy to commit one of these actions, shall be punishable by the same penalties.

I. The Wolfsberg Group on PEPs[48]

The Wolfsberg Group on PEPs provides an answer to the question of reporting regarding them. For the Wolfsberg Group, financial institutions should apply global standards:

> Wherever possible, standards of identification and control should be applied globally. Nevertheless, in certain jurisdictions, local regulatory requirements may require, for example, the application of a broader PEP definition, specific control requirements, or guidance with respect to decategorisation as a PEP. In such cases local regulatory requirements will

48 Wolfsberg, *Frequently Asked Questions* ("FAQ's"), (last visited 5 July 2014), available from http://www.wolfsberg-principles.com/pdf/Wolfsberg_PEP_FAQs_(2008).pdf.

need to augment or replace global satndards in respect of that jurisdiction.

J. IMF Model Provisions on Money-laundering, Terrorist-Financing, Preventive Measures and Proceeds of Crime[49]

Annex I provides a model [decree, regulation] on the FIU issued for purposes of application within national laws. It can be inserted in 5 sections as follows:

> Section 1: The financial intelligence unit established under Section of the [insert name of law] shall have [Option: autonomy over the use of its budget and] independent decision-making authority over matters within its responsibility.
>
> Section 2: The financial intelligence unit shall be composed of suitably qualified staff [Option: with expertise particularly in the fields of finance, banking, law, information processing, customs or police investigations] and may be made available by Government agencies. It may also comprise liaison officers responsible for cooperation with the other administrations.
>
> Section 3: The head, experts, liaison officers and other staff of the financial intelligence unit may not concurrently hold a position in any of the financial institutions or designated non-financial businesses and professions referred to [insert name of law]. They shall not hold any kind of office, or undertake an assignment or perform an activity that might affect the independence of their position. [Option: Law enforcement officers appointed to posts in the financial intelligence unit shall cease to exercise any investigatory powers held by them in their former employment.]
>
> Section 4: The reports required of the financial institutions and designated non-financial businesses and professions shall be sent to the financial intelligence unit by any rapid means of communication. They shall, where applicable, be confirmed in writing and contain the identity and address of the reporting party, the customer or the beneficial owner and, where applicable, the beneficiary of the transaction and other persons involved in the transaction or events, and shall indicate the nature and description of the transaction or events/activity and, in the case of a transaction, the amount, transaction date and time, the account numbers

49 U.N. Office on Drugs and Crime, *Model Provisions on Money-Laundering, Terrorist-Financing, Preventative Measures and Proceeds of Crime,* April 2009, available from http://www.imolin.org/pdf/imolin/Model_Provisions_Final.pdf.

and any other financial institutions and designated non-financial businesses and professions involved, [Option: if applicable add: the time within which the operation is to be carried out or the reason why its execution cannot be deferred.]

Section 5: The financial intelligence unit shall, in conformity with the laws and regulations on the protection of privacy and on computerized databases, operate a database containing all relevant information concerning suspicious transaction reports and other information as provided for under the aforementioned law and by this [decree, regulation], the transactions carried out and the persons undertaking the operations, whether directly or through intermediaries.

K. IMF Compliance with the AML/CTF International Standard: Lessons from a cross country analysis[50]

The AML/CFT Compliance Index (AML/CFT CI) provided by this study is very interesting to look at within the context of this work, as it comprises seven components that serve to capture seven groupings of recommendations including legal measures, institutional measures, preventive measures for financial institutions, preventive measures for DNBFPs, preventive measures for the informal sector, entity transparency, and international cooperation. It reads:

> To yield the aggregate AML/CFT International Standards Compliance Index for an individual country, the seven components are summed up as follows:
>
> The Compliance Index = Legal+ Institutional+ Financial Institutions Prevention + DNBFPs Prevention+ Informal Sector Prevention+ Entity Transparency +International Cooperation.

L. FATF Recommendations[51]

Higher-risk countries' type of enhanced due diligence measures applied to business relationships and transactions with natural and legal persons as well as financial institutions should be effective and proportionate to the risks. As

50 Verdugo-Yepes, Concepcion, Compliance with the AML/CFT International Standard: Lessons from a Cross-Country Analysis, International Monetary Fund, July 2011, available from http://www.imf.org/external/pubs/ft/wp/2011/wp11177.pdf.

51 Financial Action Task Force (FATF), *International Standards on Combating Money-Laundering and the Financing of Terrorism & Proliferation,* February 2012, http://www.fatf-gafi.org/media/fatf/documents/recommendations/pdfs/FATF_Recommendations.pdf.

per FATF, regarding cash couriers, countries should have measures in place to detect the physical cross-border transportation of currency and bearer negotiable instruments, including through a declaration system and/or disclosure system.

According to FATF, terrorist financing offences should extend to any person who:

> ...wilfully provides or collects funds or other assets by any means, directly or indirectly, with the unlawful intention that they should be used, or in the knowledge that they are to be used, in full or in part:
> (a) to carry out a terrorist act(s);
> (b) by a terrorist organization;
> or (c) by an individual terrorist.

Terrorist financing should also include:

> ...the financing the travel of individuals who travel to a State other than their States of residence or nationality for the purpose of the perpetration, planning, or preparation of, or participation in, terrorist acts or the providing or receiving of terrorist training.

Criminalising TF solely on the basis of aiding and abetting, attempting, or conspiracy is not sufficient to comply with this Recommendation, offences should be extended to any funds or other assets, whether from a legitimate or illegitimate source not requiring that the funds or other assets:

(a) were actually used to carry out or attempt a terrorist act(s); or (b) be linked to a specific terrorist act(s).

It should also be an offence to attempt to undertake terrorist financing, and/or to engage in any of the following types of conduct:

(a) Participating as an accomplice in an offence, as set forth in paragraphs 2 or 9 of this Interpretive Note;
(b) Organising or directing others to commit an offence, as set forth in paragraphs 2 or 9 of this Interpretive Note;
(c) Contributing to the commission of one or more offence(s), as set forth in paragraphs 2 or 9 of this Interpretive Note, by a group of persons acting with a common purpose. Such contribution shall be intentional and shall either:

(i) be made with the aim of furthering the criminal activity or criminal purpose of the group, where such activity or purpose involves the commission of a terrorist financing offence; or
(ii) be made in the knowledge of the intention of the group to commit a terrorist financing offence.

Terrorist financing offences should apply:

> ...regardless of whether the person alleged to have committed the offence(s) is in the same country or a different country from the one in which the terrorist(s)/terrorist organization(s) is located or the terrorist act(s) occurred/will occur.

M. Revised Wolfsberg Principles[52]

Concerning follow-up on unusual or suspicious activities, the private banker, management and/or the control function should:

> carry out an analysis of the background of any unusual or suspicious activity, as there is no plausible explanation a decision involving the control function will be made to:
> - Continue the business relationship with increased monitoring
> - Cancel the business relationship
> - Report the business relationship to the Authorities.

Assets may be blocked and transactions may be subject to approval by the control function pertaining to local laws and regulations after a report to authorities has been made by the control function and senior management has been notified. Senior management may include the Senior Compliance Officer, CEO, Chief Auditor or General Counsel.

The "No Inappropriate Assistance" provision is crucial as:

> Neither the private banker, nor any other bank employee, will provide clients with any assistance with the knowledge that such assistance will be used to deceive Authorities, including Tax Authorities.

52 Wolfsberg, *Anti-Money-Laundering Principles for Private Banking*, (last visited 5 July 2014), available from http://www.wolfsberg-principles.com/pdf/Wolfsberg-Private-Banking-Prinicples-May-2012.pdf.

N. FATF International Best Practices[53,54]

The Best Practices highlight the importance of an effective freezing regime and refer to this as a critical preventive tool to combat TF. It is also an effective freezing regime by:

a) Deterring non-designated persons or entities who might otherwise be willing to finance terrorist activity.
b) Exposing terrorist financing "money trails" that may generate leads to previously unknown terrorist cells and financiers.
c) Dismantling terrorist financing networks by encouraging designated persons or entities to disassociate themselves from terrorist activity and renounce their affiliation with terrorist groups.
d) Terminating terrorist cash flows by shutting down the pipelines used to move terrorist related funds or other assets.
e) Forcing terrorists to use more costly and higher risk means of financing their activities, which makes them more susceptible to detection and disruption.
f) Fostering international co-operation and compliance with obligations under the AlQaida/Taliban sanctions regimes, and resolution 1373(2001).

Regarding this legal instrument, identifying targets for designation should focus on recognizing those persons and entities that represent key elements of terrorist support networks in order to obtain maximum impact in preventing and suppressing acts of terrorism.

Concerning due process, including review, delisting and unfreezing, all reasonable efforts should be made by the designating country and (where appropriate or practicable) the country of residence, as soon as possible after the designation has taken effect. To inform designated persons and entities directly of:

53 Financial Action Task Force (FATF), *International Best Practices: Targeted Financial Sanctions Related to Terrorism and Terrorist Financing* (*Recommendation 6*), 2012, available from http://www.fatf-gafi.org/publications/fatfrecommendations/documents/bpp-fin-sanctions-tf-r6.html.

54 Targeted Financial Sanctions Related to Terrorism and Terrorist Financing (Recommendation 6).

a) The designation and its implications, in order to prevent any unintentional breaches on the part of themselves or related third parties.
b) The review procedure and information on the de-listing process, including a contact point within the government to address any questions regarding the process.
c) Publicly-releasable information concerning the reasons for designation.
d) Procedures to allow licensed access to funds or other assets, as set out in resolution 1452(2002) and other relevant UNSCR(s), for basic and extraordinary expenses as soon as possible.

Pursuant to the United Nations Resolution 1373, countries should have appropriate legal authorities and procedures or mechanisms to delist and unfreeze the funds or other assets of persons and entities that no longer meet the criteria for designation. Procedures should also be in place to allow for review of the designation decision before a court of another independent competent authority. For persons and entities designated under resolution 1373(2001):

> ...countries should have appropriate legal authorities and procedures or mechanisms to delist, unfreeze the funds or other assets of, and remove the terms of sanctions against those parties that have for example credibly disassociated with the conditions and circumstances leading to their designation and/or no longer meet the criteria for designation.

With respect to the Al-Qaida/Taliban sanctions regimes, paragraph 17 of resolution 1822(2008) demands that:

> Member States receiving notification [of designation]...take, in accordance with their domestic laws and practices, all possible measures to notify or inform in a timely manner the listed individual or entity of the designation and to include with this notification a copy of the publicly releasable portion of the statement of case, any information on reasons for listing available on the [1267 or 1988] Committee's website, a description of the effects of designation, as provided in the relevant resolutions, the Committee's procedures for considering delisting requests, and the provisions of resolution 1452 (2002) regarding available exemptions.

Freezing funds or other assets should take place "without delay" on designation, yet, publication of the action should not take place until the freeze is in effect, and this irrespective of whether the designation was made by a country on its own motion or upon acceptance of a designation request from another country.

o. Methodology for assessing Compliance with the FATF Recommendations and the Effectiveness of AML/CTF Systems[55]

The methodology for assessing Compliance with the FATF Recommendations and the effectiveness of AML/CTF Systems demands that:

> A country properly identifies, assesses and understands its money-laundering and terrorist financing risks, and co-ordinates domestically to put in place actions to mitigate these risks. This includes the involvement of competent authorities and other relevant authorities; using a wide range of reliable information sources; using the assessment(s) of risks as a basis for developing and prioritising AML/CFT policies and activities; and communicating and implementing those policies and activities in a co-ordinated way across appropriate channels. The relevant competent authorities also cooperate, and co-ordinate policies and activities to combat the financing of proliferation.

To mitigate and monitor ML/TF risks, the supervisor should focus on:

1. preventing criminals and their associates from holding, or being the beneficial owner of, a significant or controlling interest or a management function in financial institutions or DNFBPs; and
2. promptly identifying, remedying, and sanctioning, where appropriate, violations of AML/CFT requirements or failings in money-laundering and terrorist financing risk management.

Important questions to consider according to this methodology are:

1. How well do financial institutions and DNFBPs apply the enhanced or specific measures for:
   (a) PEPs,
   (b) correspondent banking,
   (c) new technologies,

55 Financial Action Task Force (FATF), *Methodology for Assessing Technical Compliance with the FATF Recommendations and the Effectiveness of AML/CFT Systems,* November 2017, available from http://www.fatf-gafi.org/media/fatf/documents/methodology/FATF%20Methodology%2022%20Feb%202013.pdf.

(d) wire transfers rules,
(e) targeted financial sanctions relating to TF,
and (f) higher-risk countries identified by the FATF?

2. Do internal policies and controls of the financial institutions and groups, and DNFBPs enable timely review of:
(i) complex or unusual transactions,
(ii) potential STRs for reporting to the FIU,
and (iii) potential false-positives? To what extent do the STRs reported contain complete, accurate and adequate information relating to the suspicious transaction?

Measures in place deemed to have the characteristics of an effective system are to:

a. prevent legal persons and arrangements from being used for criminal purposes;
b. make legal persons and arrangements sufficiently transparent; and
c. ensure that accurate and up-to-date basic and beneficial ownership information is available on a timely basis.

> Legal persons and arrangements are prevented from misuse for money-laundering or terrorist financing, and information on their beneficial ownership is available to competent authorities without impediments.

P. Basel Committee on Banking Supervision, Sound Management of Risks related to Money-Laundering and Financing Terrorism[56]

This document comprises the guidelines issued in January 2014, and remained unchanged except for the addition in February 2016 of Annex IV-General Guide to Account Opening.

Essential elements of sound ML/FT risk management include various features such as:

> Training needs will vary depending on staff functions and job responsibilities and length of service with the bank. Training course organization and materials should be tailored to an employee's specific responsibility

56 Bank for International Settlements, *Sound Management of Risks Related to Money-Laundering and Financing of Terrorism* (January 2014), http://www.bis.org/publ/bcbs275.htm.

or function to ensure that the employee has sufficient knowledge and information to effectively implement the bank's AML/CFT policies and procedures. New employees should be required to attend training as soon as possible after being hired, for the same reasons.

Refresher training should be provided to ensure that staff are reminded of their obligations and their knowledge and expertise are kept up to date. The scope and frequency of such training should be tailored to the risk factors to which employees are exposed due to their responsibilities and the level and nature of risk present in the bank.

Internal audit, ..., plays an important role in independently evaluating the risk management and controls, and discharges its responsibility to the audit committee of the board of directors or a similar oversight body through periodic evaluations of the effectiveness of compliance with AML/CFT policies and procedures.

A bank should establish policies for conducting audits of:

(i) the adequacy of the bank's AML/CFT policies and procedures in addressing identified risks;
(ii) the effectiveness of bank staff in implementing the bank's policies and procedures;
(iii) the effectiveness of compliance oversight and quality control including parameters of criteria for automatic alerts; and
(iv) the effectiveness of the bank's training of relevant personnel.

A bank with the capacity to do so should effectively document and integrate the local and centralized transaction/account monitoring functions to ensure that it has the opportunity to monitor for patterns of potential suspicious activity across the group for more effective management or efficiency purposes.

Q. FATF Report on Financing of the Terrorist Organization Islamic State in Iraq and the Levant (ISIL)[57]

To deprive ISIL of its resources, Member States should develop additional listings proposals under the Al-Qaida sanctions regime of key individuals and

57 Financial Action Task Force (FATF), *Report on Financing of the Terrorist Organization Islamic State in Iraq and the Levant* (ISIL), (2015), available from http://www.fatf-gafi.org/media/fatf/documents/reports/Financing-of-the-terrorist-organisation-ISIL.pdf.

entities, including facilitators and those most vulnerable to the impact of being sanctioned. Relevant candidates for listing requests can be:

1. facilitators of FTF recruitment networks based outside of territory where ISIL operates;
2. key individuals involved in providing logistical support associated with ISIL and ANF who may travel and be vulnerable to the travel ban;
3. financiers whose involvement in terrorist funding to ISIL has been established by Member States;
4. companies and smuggling networks that trade in commodities that derive from ISIL, thereby supporting ISIL financially;
5. other parties, including terrorist groups that facilitate or give assistance to ISIL; and/or
6. non-profit organizations involved in providing funding or other material support to ISIL.

ISIL is known to abuse diverse sectors, such as humanitarian assistance to vulnerable populations, new payment technologies, as well as the selling of tainted antiquities. It should be noted that the distinction between legitimate and illegitimate money is often challenging.

R. FATF Report on Emerging Terrorist Financing Risks[58]

Emerging risk is found of relevance within this report, which represents a growing TF vulnerability in relation to social media, new payment products and services as well as the exploitation of natural resources. Fundraising through social media with online payments such as virtual currencies like bitcoin, or crowdfunding websites, can allow people to set up a fundraising page easily and collect donations to spread their terrorist propaganda. Moreover, they can reach out globally to sympathizers. In fact, the anonymity of the internet has been exploited by terrorist groups to raise funds from sympathetic individuals globally. Prepaid cards represent an elevated TF risk, as these can be loaded via cash or non-reportable electronic methods and carried offshore unnoticeably with no requirement to declare their movement across the border.

58 Financial Action Task Force (FATF), *Emerging Terrorist Financing Risks*, October 2015, available from http://www.fatf-gafi.org/media/fatf/documents/reports/Emerging-Terrorist-Financing-Risks.pdf.

Moreover, some prepaid cards provide the possibility of person-to-person transfers.

Companies can provide data similar to credit cards or debit records to competent authorities through obligatory measures, such as a court orders. Data about the card itself can include:

1. activation date,
2. card holder information such as phone and e-mail address,
3. transaction activity,
4. transaction time and location, and
5. IP addresses used when logging in.

In countries where the government lacks effective control of territory and its resources, the natural resource sector may be vulnerable to exploitation for TF as these sectors represent a profitable source of revenue and are appealing to terrorists owing to their weak regulations and policies. The use of natural resources by terrorists to raise funds by controlling or exploiting a wide variety of vulnerable resources such as, gas, oil, timber, diamonds, gold and other precious metals, wildlife and charcoal is an important concern. For, countries carry a big responsibility in regulating and controlling the licit use of resources and deterring corruption as well as other underlining crimes related to the theft of valuable resources.

Concerning the oil and gas sector:

> The FATF ISIL report notes that ISIL seeks to operate local oil infrastructure, to extract and refine oil for its own use, and for onward sale or swap to local and regional markets, at a lower market price. ISIL benefits mostly from using the petroleum and petroleum products it controls or by earning revenue from sales of these resources to local customers. The remaining portion of ISIL's oil revenue stems from sales routed through middlemen and smugglers who trade and transport the illicit petroleum and petroleum products for sale to end-users. According to press reports, ISIL is paid mostly in cash for the oil it sells, making the transactions underlying its oil trade difficult to track and disrupt.

The mining sector is especially at risk as well since:

> Mining companies often operate in areas that are ungoverned or under the control of corrupt officials. Sometimes, these same areas have a

> significant presence of terrorist groups. Operators of mining operations may be sympathisers of terrorist organizations and may seek to contribute financially to the cause of terrorist organizations. There is a risk that the donations from legal and illegal mining operators could be sent directly or indirectly to terrorist groups.

The investigation and prosecution of crimes associated with the natural resources sector represent a big challenge, as it is difficult to identify the entire criminal network and specific actors (including facilitators), who are committing these crimes.

S. IMF Working Paper on Islamic Finance and Anti-money-laundering and Combatting the Financing of Terrorism[59]

In Part 4, the question of whether the current FATF standards are applicable and adequate for Islamic finance arises. The specificities of the FATF standards, which do not seem to consider the features of Islamic finance comprehensively, are the concept of a "customer" and the definition of a financial institution."

Concerning the definition of a "customer":

> A key element of an effective AML/CFT framework is the identification of the 'customer.' The concept of 'customer' is not defined in the standards and its meaning is not entirely clear. In particular, it is not clear whether it applies to the types of partner-based relationship (rather than an 'institution to customer' relationship) that are a key feature of Islamic finance. To the extent that such parties are not considered to be 'customers,' they would fall outside of the provisions of the standards requiring countries to have in place robust regimes for customer identification and due diligence.

Therefore, it would be useful to make it explicit that the FATF standards CDD measures apply to the other party in the contractual relationship, including the partner in the type of "partnerships" found in Islamic finance.

59 Nadim Kyriakos-Saad et al., *Islamic Finance and Anti-Money-Laundering and Combating the Financing of Terrorism* (*AML/CFT*), 2016, available from https://www.imf.org/external/pubs/ft/wp/2016/wp1642.pdf.

T. FATF Guidance on the Criminalization of Terrorist Financing[60]

Recommendation 5 provides guidance on the criminalization of TF and insists on the fact that:

> In the context of financing terrorist organizations and individual terrorists, the person providing or collecting the funds or other assets (the terrorist financier) must have the unlawful intention or knowledge that those funds or other assets were being collected for or provided to a terrorist organization or individual terrorist.

This requirement to criminalize the financing of terrorist organizations and individual terrorists, "for any purpose," has already triggered some confusion as to what explicit level of knowledge is required for the offence and what sort of unlawful intention/purpose must be proven. In more specific wording:

(a) the terrorist financier must be acting with the knowledge that the funds or other assets are to be provided or collected for a terrorist organization or individual terrorist; and
(b) it is only the terrorist financier's unlawful intention/purpose which is relevant, and that unlawful intention/purpose must be to provide or collect funds or other assets for a terrorist organization or individual terrorist.

Terrorist financing offences should not require that the funds or other assets: (a) were actually used to carry out or attempt a terrorist act(s); or (b) be linked to a specific terrorist act, since within this legal instrument, the TF offence should not be restricted to cases where the funds or other assets were used to carry out or attempt to carry a terrorist attack. Moreover, they should not require prosecutors to link the funds or other assets to a specific terrorist act.

3 Countries Legislative Contribution

As most international elements concerning CTF are either recommendations or UN legislative efforts, the best way to create sanctions is within national laws themselves. To have an impact on people, CTF related efforts must be included

60 Financial Action Task Force (FATF), *Criminalising Terrorist Financing* (*Recommendation 5*), October 2016, available from http://www.fatf-gafi.org/media/fatf/documents/reports/Guidance-Criminalising-Terrorist-Financing.pdf.

within national regulations to be enforceable. By reviewing the regulations and policies provided by common or civil law nations worldwide, best practices to be included within the new CTF Convention model will become evident.

Third, the list of countries' legislative most significant contributions related to terrorism and TF, including the European Union, consists of:

A. Council of Europe's Convention on Laundering, Search, Seizure and Confiscation of the Proceeds from Crime[61]

Article 8 provides an obligation to assist and makes clear that:

> upon request, the widest possible measure of assistance in the identification and tracing of instrumentalities, proceeds and other property liable to confiscation. Such assistance shall include any measure providing and securing evidence as to the existence, location or movement, nature, legal status or value of the aforementioned property.

Spontaneous information is also discussed within Article 10, which provides that:

> a Party may without prior request forward to another Party information on instrumentalities and proceeds, when it considers that the disclosure of such information might assist the receiving Party in initiating or carrying out investigations or proceedings or might lead to a request by that Party.

An obligation to take provisional measures is also part of this policy, which states that:

> a Party shall take the necessary provisional measures, such as freezing or seizing, to prevent any dealing in, transfer or disposal of property which, at a later stage, may be the subject of a request for confiscation or which might be such as to satisfy the request.

61 Council of Europe, Treaty Office, *Convention on Laundering, Search, Seizure and Confiscation of the Proceeds from Crime*, http://www.coe.int/web/conventions/full-list/-/conventions/treaty/141.

Within Section 4 on Confiscation, Article 13 obligates Parties to confiscate as:

> 1. A Party, which has received a request made by another Party for confiscation concerning instrumentalities or proceeds, situated in its territory, shall:
>   a. enforce a confiscation order made by a court of a requesting Party in relation to such instrumentalities or proceeds; or
>   b. submit the request to its competent authorities for the purpose of obtaining an order of confiscation and, if such order is granted, enforce it.

Additionally, per Article 15:

> Any property confiscated by the requested Party shall be disposed of by that Party in accordance with its domestic law, unless otherwise agreed by the Parties concerned.

It should also be highlighted that this legal instrument offers a right of enforcement and maximum amount of confiscation within the following article 16. Per article 17, The requested Party shall not impose imprisonment in default or any other measure restricting the liberty, if the requesting Party has so specified.

B. Commonwealth Model Law for the Prohibition of Money-laundering & Supporting Documentation[62]

Part 2 of this Model law discusses Anti-Money-laundering supervision, and states that:

> 5. The Money-laundering Authority or law enforcement agency upon application to a Magistrate and satisfying him that there are reasonable grounds for believing 'that a person is committing. has committed or is about to commit a money-laundering offence may obtain an order:
>
> (1) That any document relevant to:
>   1. Identifying, locating or quantifying any property; or

62 *Commonwealth Model Law for the Prohibition of Money-Laundering*, 1996, http://www.imolin.org/pdf/imolin/Comsecml.pdf.

2. Identifying or locating any document necessary for the transfer of any property.

belonging to, or in the possession or under the control of that person be delivered forthwith to the Money-laundering Authority or law enforcement agency.

C. The Financial Transactions Reporting Act (New Zealand)[63]

Article 17 on the Protection of persons reporting suspicious transactions provides that:

(1) If any person—
 (a) discloses or supplies any information in any suspicious transaction report made under Section 15; or
 (b) supplies any information in connection with such a report, whether at the time the report is made or afterwards,—that person has immunity from civil, criminal, and disciplinary proceedings in accordance with subsection (1A).

(1A) No civil, criminal, and disciplinary proceedings lie against a person to whom subsection (1) applies—
 (a) in respect of the disclosure or supply, or the manner of the disclosure or supply, by that person, of the information referred to in that subsection; or
 (b) for any consequences that follow from the disclosure or supply of that information,—unless the information was disclosed or supplied in bad faith.

(2) Where any information is disclosed or supplied, pursuant to Section16, to any constable by any person, no civil, criminal, or disciplinary proceedings shall lie against that person—
 (a) in respect of the disclosure or supply, or the manner of the disclosure or supply, of that information by that person; or
 (b) for any consequences that follow from the disclosure or supply of that information,—unless the information was disclosed or supplied in bad faith.

---

63 Parliamentary Counsel Office, New Zealand Legislation, *Financial Transactions Reporting Act 1996, No 9*, 1 April 2017, available from http://www.legislation.govt.nz/act/public/1996/0009/latest/DLM373804.html.

Disclosure provision is an important point to include within the new convention model in order to determine appropriate penalties.

In Article 18, immunity from liability for disclosure of information related to money-laundering transactions is explained as:

> (c) that person discloses, to any constable, any information relating to a money-laundering transaction (within the meaning of Section 243(4) of that Act), being a money-laundering transaction that constitutes (in whole or in part),or is connected with or related to, the act referred to in paragraph (a) of this section; and
>
> (d) that information is so disclosed, in good faith, for the purpose for in connection with the enforcement or intended enforcement of any enactment or provision referred to in Section 244(a) of the Crimes Act 1961; and
>
> (e) that person is otherwise under any obligation.

D. Organization of African Unity combating Terrorism[64]

Article 1 of the General of the Organization of African Unity defines what constitutes a terrorist act, and includes an interesting reference to "calculated or intended" disruption of any public service, or of essential service to the public, as well as to the creation of a public emergency, or general insurrection in a State. Several of these actions have been seen in the past and not encompassed by other CTF legislative tools and recommendation. It reads:

> 3. 'Terrorist act' means:
>
> (a) any act which is a violation of the criminal laws of a State Party and which may endanger the life, physical integrity or freedom of, or cause serious injury or death to, any person, any number or group of persons or causes or may cause damage to public or private property, natural resources, environmental or cultural heritage and is calculated or intended to:
>
> (i) intimidate, put in fear, force, coerce or induce any government, body, institution, the general public or any segment thereof, to do or abstain from doing any act, or to

64 Organization of African Unity, *Convention on the Prevention and Combating of Terrorism,* (*1999*), 14 July 199, available from http://treaties.un.org/doc/db/Terrorism/OAU-english.pdf.

adopt or abandon a particular standpoint, or to act according to certain principles; or

(ii) disrupt any public service, the delivery of any essential service to the public or to create a public emergency; or

(iii) create general insurrection in a State;

(b) any promotion, sponsoring, contribution to, command, aid, incitement, encouragement, attempt, threat, conspiracy, organizing, or procurement of any person, with the intent to commit any act referred to in paragraph (a) (i) to (iii).

According to Article 3,

1. Notwithstanding the provisions of Article 1, the struggle waged by peoples in accordance with the principles of international law for their liberation or self-determination, including armed struggle against colonialism, occupation, aggression and domination by foreign forces shall not be considered as terrorist acts.
2. Political, philosophical, ideological, racial, ethnic, religious or other motives shall not be a justifiable defence against a terrorist act.

This Article is particularly important, as terrorist acts are perpetrated in various contexts which are not necessarily invoked in similar conventions.

E. Convention of the Islamic Conference on Combating International Terrorism[65]

Article 2 of this Convention provides details as to what is a terrorist act; it reads:

a) Peoples struggle including armed struggle against foreign occupation, aggression, colonialism, and hegemony, aimed at liberation and self-determination in accordance with the principles of international law shall not be considered a terrorist crime.
b) None of the terrorist crimes mentioned in the previous article shall be considered political crimes.

65 Convention of the Islamic Conference on Combatting International Terrorism, available from www.oic-cdpu.org/en/getdoc/?dID=13.

c) In the implementation of the provisions of this Convention the following crimes shall not be considered political crimes even when politically motivated:
   1. Aggression against kings and heads of state of Contracting States or against their spouses, their ascendants or descendants.
   2. Aggression against crown princes or vice-presidents or deputy heads of government or ministers in any of the Contracting States.
   3. Aggression against persons enjoying international immunity including Ambassadors and diplomats in Contracting States or in countries of accreditation.
   4. Murder or robbery by force against individuals or authorities or means of transport and communications.
   5. Acts of sabotage and destruction of public properties and properties geared for public services, even if belonging to another Contracting State.
   6. Crimes of manufacturing, smuggling or possessing arms and ammunition or explosives or other materials prepared for committing terrorist crimes.

d) All forms of international crimes, including illegal trafficking in narcotics and human beings money-laundering aimed at financing terrorist objectives shall be considered terrorist crimes.

For the Purpose of this Regulation, "Terrorist act" shall mean:

(a) any act which is a violation of the criminal laws of a State Party and which may endanger the life, physical integrity or freedom of, or cause serious injury or death to, any person, any number or group of persons or causes or may cause damage to public or private property, natural resources, environmental or cultural heritage and is calculated or intended to:
   (i) intimidate, put in fear, force, coerce or induce any government, body, institution, the general public or any segment thereof, to do or abstain from doing any act, or to adopt or abandon a particular standpoint, or to act according to certain principles; or
   (ii) disrupt any public service, the delivery of any essential service to the public or to create a public emergency; or
   (iii) create general insurrection in a State;

(b) any promotion, sponsoring, contribution to, command, aid, incitement, encouragement, attempt, threat, conspiracy, organizing, or procurement of any person, with the intent to commit any act referred to in paragraph (a) (i) to (iii).

F. UK Terrorism Act[66]

In this Act "terrorist property" means:

(a) money or other property which is likely to be used for the purposes of terrorism (including any resources of a proscribed organization),
(b) proceeds of the commission of acts of terrorism, and
(c) proceeds of acts carried out for the purposes of terrorism.
(2) In subsection (1)—
  (a) a reference to proceeds of an act includes a reference to any property which wholly or partly, and directly or indirectly, represents the proceeds of the act (including payments or other rewards in connection with its commission), and
  (b) the reference to an organization's resources includes a reference to any money or other property which is applied or made available, or is to be applied or made available, for use by the organization.

Such a definition incorporates the idea that proceeds are just as important as regular property and terrorist assets.

Per this Act, offences are committed when:

(1) A person commits an offence if he—Fund-raising.
  (a) invites another to provide money or other property, and
  (b) intends that it should be used, or has reasonable cause to suspect that it may be used, for the purposes of terrorism.
(2) A person commits an offence if he—(a) receives money or other property, and (b) intends that it should be used, or has reasonable cause to suspect that it may be used, for the purposes of terrorism.

66 Terrorism Act 2000, available from http://www.legislation.gov.uk/ukpga/2000/11/contents.

(3) A person commits an offence if he—(a) provides money or other property, and (b) knows or has reasonable cause to suspect that it will or may be used for the purposes of terrorism.

(4) In this section a reference to the provision of money or other property is a reference to its being given, lent or otherwise made available, whether or not for consideration.

16.—

(1) A person commits an offence if he uses money or other Use and possession. property for the purposes of terrorism.

(2) A person commits an offence if he—

(a) possesses money or other property, and

(b) intends that it should be used, or has reasonable cause to suspect that it may be used, for the purposes of terrorism.

17. A person commits an offence if—Funding arrangements.

(a) he enters into or becomes concerned in an arrangement as a result of which money or other property is made available or is to be made available to another, and

(b) he knows or has reasonable cause to suspect that it will or may be used for the purposes of terrorism.

18.—

(1) A person commits an offence if he enters into or becomes Money-laundering. Concerned in an arrangement which facilitates the retention or control by or on behalf of another person of terrorist property—

(a) by concealment,

(b) by removal from the jurisdiction,

(c) by transfer to nominees, or

(d) in any other way.

(2) It is a defence for a person charged with an offence under subsection(1)to prove that he did not know and had no reasonable cause to suspect that the arrangement related to terrorist property.

“Entering into arrangements to fund terrorists” is an important contribution in this Act, whereby an intention from the part of the suspect is clearly underlined. Retention or control of terrorist assets or money-laundering do count as an offence pertaining to this Act.

In Part 5, Counter-Terrorist Powers Regarding Suspected Terrorists:

(4) A person guilty of an offence under this section shall be liable—
  (a) on conviction on indictment, to imprisonment for a term not exceeding 10 years, to a fine or to both, or
  (b) on summary conviction, to imprisonment for a term not exceeding six months, to a fine not exceeding the statutory maximum or to both.

G. Anti-terrorism, Crime and Security Act[67]

Regarding Terrorist Property, Part 1 discusses the forfeiture of cash as:

(1) Schedule 1 (which makes provision for enabling cash which-
  1. is intended to be used for the purposes of terrorism,
  2. consists of resources of an organization which is a proscribed organization, or
  3. is, or represents, property obtained through terrorism,

  To be forfeited in civil proceedings before a magistrates' court or (in Scotland) the sheriff) is to have effect.

(2) The powers conferred by Schedule 1 are exercisable in relation to any cash whether or not any proceedings have been brought for an offence in connection with the cash.

Disclosure of information, extension of existing disclosure powers, restriction on disclosure of information for overseas purposes, and disclosure of information held by revenue departments, are also part of this legal instrument and relevant for the purpose of this study. So too, are the immigration and asylum provisions for suspected international terrorist, which include certification, deportation, removal, detention, and bail provisions. Police powers within this policy also include the power to stop and search in anticipation of violence, and retention of communication data.

H. USA Patriot Act[68]

SEC. 217. regulates the interception of computer trespasser communications and reads as follows:

---

67 Anti-terrorism, Crime and Security Act, 2001, c. 24, http://www.legislation.gov.uk/ukpga/2001/24/pdfs/ukpga_20010024_en.pdf.

68 Financial Crimes Enforcement Network, *USA Patriot Act*, FinCEN.gov, (last visited 5 July 2014), https://www.fincen.gov/resources/statutes-regulations/usa-patriot-act.

> (A) means a person who accesses a protected computer without authorization and thus has no reasonable expectation of privacy in any communication transmitted to, through, or from the protected computer; and (B) does not include a person known by the owner or operator of the protected computer to have an existing contractual relationship with the owner or operator of the protected computer for access to all or part of the protected computer.
>
> ...by inserting at the end the following: (i) It shall not be unlawful under this chapter for a person acting under color of law to intercept the wire or electronic communications of a computer trespasser transmitted to, through, or from the protected computer, if—(I) the owner or operator of the protected computer authorizes the interception of the computer trespasser's communications on the protected computer; (II) the person acting under color of law is lawfully engaged in an investigation; (III) the person acting under color of law has reasonable grounds to believe that the contents of the computer trespasser's communications will be relevant to the investigation; and (IV) such interception does not acquire communications other than those transmitted to or from the computer trespasser.

This Act mentions immunity for compliance with FISA wiretap in that Section 105 of the Foreign Intelligence Surveillance Act of 1978 (50 U.S.C. 1805) is amended by inserting after subsection (g) the following:

18 USC 2510 note.

> (h) No cause of action shall lie in any court against any provider of a wire or electronic communication service, landlord, custodian, or other person (including any officer, employee, agent, or other specified person thereof) that furnishes any information, facilities, or technical assistance in accordance with a court order or request for emergency assistance under this Act.

Concerning jurisdiction over foreign persons, and long-arm jurisdiction over foreign money-launderers:

> For purposes of adjudicating an action filed or enforcing a penalty ordered under this section, the district courts shall have jurisdiction over any foreign person, including any financial institution authorized under the laws of a foreign country, against whom the action is brought, if

> service of process upon the foreign person is made under the Federal Rules of Civil Procedure or the laws of the country in which the foreign person is found, and—
>
> (A) the foreign person commits an offense under subsection (a) involving a financial transaction that occurs in whole or in part in the United States;
>
> (B) the foreign person converts, to his or her own use, property in which the United States has an ownership interest by virtue of the entry of an order of forfeiture by a court of the United States;
>
> or (C) the foreign person is a financial institution that maintains a bank account at a financial institution in the United States.

Per SEC. 320 on the proceeds of foreign crimes, Section 981(a)(1)(B) of title 18, United States Code, is amended to read as follows:

> (B) Any property, real or personal, within the jurisdiction of the United States, constituting, derived from, or traceable to, any proceeds obtained directly or indirectly from an offense against a foreign nation, or any property used to facilitate such an offense, if the offense—
>
> (i) involves the manufacture, importation, sale, or distribution of a controlled substance (as that term is defined for purposes of the Controlled Substances Act), or any other conduct described in section 1956(c)(7)(B);
>
> (ii) would be punishable within the jurisdiction of the foreign nation by death or imprisonment for a term exceeding 1 year; and
>
> (iii) would be punishable under the laws of the United States by imprisonment for a term exceeding 1 year, if the act or activity constituting the offense had occurred within the jurisdiction of the United States.

Thus, the United States describes proceeds of foreign crimes by defining it.

I. Inter-American Convention against Terrorism[69]

Cooperation on border controls, is once again, a concern in this Convention, which states that:

69 U.N. GAOR, *Inter-American Convention Against Terrorism*, AG/RES 1840, 3 June 2002, available from http://www.oas.org/xxxiiga/english/docs_en/docs_items/AGres1840_02.htm.

1. The states parties, consistent with their respective domestic legal and administrative regimes, shall promote cooperation and the exchange of information in order to improve border and customs control measures to detect and prevent the international movement of terrorists and trafficking in arms or other materials intended to support terrorist activities.
2. In this context, they shall promote cooperation and the exchange of information to improve their controls on the issuance of travel and identity documents and to prevent their counterfeiting, forgery, or fraudulent use.
3. Such measures shall be carried out without prejudice to applicable international commitments in relation to the free movement of people and the facilitation of commerce.

Making money-laundering a predicate offence is also part of this Convention's framework.

J. UK Proceeds of Crime Act[70]

Criminal lifestyle, conduct and benefit, tainted gifts, gifts and their recipients, the basic rule of value, the value of property obtained from conduct and the value of tainted gifts are interesting points raised in this Act.

Property obtained through unlawful conduct is described as:

(1) A person obtains property through unlawful conduct (whether his own conduct or another's) if he obtained property by or in return for the conduct.
(2) In deciding whether any property was obtained through unlawful conduct-
    (a) It is immaterial whether or not any money, goods or services were provided in order to put the person in question in a position to carry out the conduct,
    (b) It is not necessary to show that the conduct was of a particular kind if it is shown that the property was obtained through

70 Proceeds of Crime Act 2002, available from http://www.legislation.gov.uk/ukpga/2002/29/contents.

conduct of one of a number of kinds, each of which would have been unlawful conduct.

Associated property means:

property of any of the following descriptions (including property held by the respondent) which is not itself the recoverable property-
(a) any interest in the recoverable property,
(b) any other interest in the property in which the recoverable property subsists.

The grounds for the seizure of cash are explained as:

1. A customs officer or constable may seize any cash if he has reasonable grounds for suspecting that it is-
   1. Recoverable property, or
   2. Intended by any person for the use in unlawful conduct.
2. A customs officer or constable may also seize cash part of which he has reasonable grounds for suspecting to be-
   1. Recoverable property, or
   2. Intended by any person for the use in unlawful conduct,

   If it is not reasonably practicable to seize only that part.
3. This section does not authorise the seizure of an amount of cash if it or, as the case may be, the part to which his suspicions relates, is less than the minimum amount.

Tipping-off, failure to disclose, disclosure powers, and concealing information are important points mentioned by this Act.

Arrangements are per this Act:

(1) A person commits an offence if he enters into or becomes concerned in an arrangement which he knows or suspects facilitates (by whatever means) the acquisition, retention, use or control of criminal property by or on behalf of another person.

This Article is of great importance, as it would be complicated to charge most criminals that committed terrorism-financing, if the act did not occur. The financing was still planned or happened and therefore, it still needs to be regulated.

K. Terrorism Suppression Act (New Zealand)[71]

In this legislation, the act of financing terrorism is defined as:

(1) A person commits an offence who, directly or indirectly, wilfully and without lawful justification or reasonable excuse, provides or collects funds intending that they be used, or knowing that they are to be used, in full or in part, in order to carry out 1 or more acts of a kind that, if they were carried out, would be 1 or more terrorist acts.

(2) [Repealed] (2A) A person commits an offence who, directly or indirectly, wilfully and without lawful justification or reasonable excuse, provides or collects funds intending that they benefit, or knowing that they will benefit, an entity that the person knows is an entity that carries out, or participates in the carrying out of, 1 or more terrorist acts.

(3) In a prosecution for financing of terrorism, it is not necessary for the prosecutor to prove that the funds collected or provided were actually used, in full or in part, to carry out a terrorist act.

(4) A person who commits financing of terrorism is liable on conviction on indictment to imprisonment for a term not exceeding 14 years.

The fact that the prosecutor does not need to prove the funds collected or provided were used to carry out the terrorist act opens up the definition of terrorism-financing, making it much wider than other definitions in order to charge a greater number of suspects.

This Act also offers prohibition on dealing with property of, or derived or generated from property of, a designated terrorist entity and reads as follows:

(1) A person commits an offence who, without lawful justification or reasonable excuse, deals with any property knowing that the property is—(a) property owned or controlled, directly or indirectly, by a designated terrorist entity; or (b) property derived or generated from any property of the kind specified in paragraph (a).

71 Terrorism Suppression Act 2002, No 34, 1 March 2017, available from http://www.legislation.govt.nz/act/public/2002/0034/latest/DLM151491.html.

(2) For the purposes of subsection (1), examples of a reasonable excuse for dealing with property referred to in those provisions are—(a) where the dealing with the property comprises an act that does no more than satisfy essential human needs of (or of a dependant of) an individual designated under this Act: (b) where a financial institution acts to freeze assets of a designated terrorist entity.

Participating in terrorist groups is for the purpose of the Act defined as:

(1) A person commits an offence who participates in a group or organization for the purpose stated in subsection.
(2) Knowing that or being reckless as to whether the group or organization is—(a) a designated terrorist entity; or (b) an entity that carries out, or participates in the carrying out of, 1 or more terrorist acts. (2) The purpose referred to in subsection (1) is to enhance the ability of any entity (being an entity of the kind referred to in subsection(1)(a)or(b)) to carry out, or to participate in the carrying out of, 1 or more terrorist acts.
(3) A person who commits an offence against subsection (1) is liable on conviction on indictment to imprisonment for a term not exceeding 14 years.

L. Council of Europe Convention on Laundering, Search, Seizure, and Confiscation of the Proceeds from Crime and on the Financing of Terrorism[72]

For the purpose of this Convention, "Requests for information on bank accounts" can be made via Article 17, such that:

1. 1. Each Party shall, under the conditions set out in this article, take the measures necessary to determine, in answer to a request sent by another Party, whether a natural or legal person that is the subject of a criminal investigation holds or controls one or more accounts, of whatever nature, in any bank located in its territory and, if so, provide the particulars of the identified accounts.

---

72 Council of Europe Treaty Office *Council of Europe Convention on Laundering, Search, Seizure, and Confiscation of the Proceeds of Crime and on the Financing of Terrorism*, 15 May 2005, available from http://conventions.coe.int/Treaty/en/Treaties/Html/198.htm.

2. The obligation set out in this article shall apply only to the extent that the information is in the possession of the bank keeping the account.
3. In addition to the requirements of Article 37, the requesting party shall, in the request:
   a. state why it considers that the requested information is likely to be of substantial value for the purpose of the criminal investigation into the offence;
   b. state on what grounds it presumes that banks in the requested Party hold the account and specify, to the widest extent possible, which banks and/or accounts may be involved; and
   c. include any additional information available which may facilitate the execution of the request.
4. The requested Party may make the execution of such a request dependant on the same conditions as it applies in respect of requests for search and seizure.
5. Each State or the European Community may, at the time of signature or when depositing its instrument of ratification, acceptance, approval or accession, by a declaration addressed to the Secretary General of the Council of Europe, declare that this article applies only to the categories of offences specified in the list contained in the appendix to this Convention.
6. Parties may extend this provision to accounts held in non-bank financial institutions. Such extension may be made subject to the principle of reciprocity.

Article 18 and 19 respectively offer a mechanism for requests for information on banking transactions, and for the monitoring of them.

Article 26 deals with the right of enforcement and maximum amount of confiscation, stating that:

> Nothing in this Convention shall be so interpreted as to permit the total value of the confiscation to exceed the amount of the sum of money specified in the confiscation order. If a Party finds that this might occur, the Parties concerned shall enter into consultations to avoid such an effect.

This provision is particularly relevant to the new Convention model, as confiscating more than specified in the confiscation order could easily occur and be unfair.

M. Serious Organised Crime and Police Act[73]

Disclosures to identify persons and property related to Money-laundering is part of this Police Act. Hence, for Section 330(4) to (6) (the required disclosure) substitute:

> (3A) The third condition is—(a) that he can identify the other person mentioned in subsection (2) or the whereabouts of any of the laundered property, or (b) that he believes, or it is reasonable to expect him to believe, that the information or other matter mentioned in subsection (3) will or may assist in identifying that other person or the whereabouts of any of the laundered property.
>
> (4) The fourth condition is that he does not make the required disclosure to—(a) a nominated officer, or (b) a person authorised for the purposes of this Part by the Director General of the Serious Organised Crime Agency, as soon as is practicable after the information or other matter mentioned in subsection (3) comes to him.
>
> (5) The required disclosure is a disclosure of—(a) the identity of the other person mentioned in subsection (2), if he knows it, (b) the whereabouts of the laundered property, so far as he knows it, and (c) the information or other matter mentioned in subsection (3).
>
> (5A) The laundered property is the property forming the subject-matter of the money-laundering that he knows or suspects, or has reasonable grounds for knowing or suspecting, that other person to be engaged in.
>
> (6) But he does not commit an offence under this section if—(a) he has a reasonable excuse for not making the required disclosure, (b) he is a professional legal adviser and—(i) if he knows either of the things mentioned in subsection (5)(a) and (b), he knows the thing because of information or other matter that came to him in privileged circumstances, or (ii) the information or other matter mentioned in subsection (3) came to him in privileged circumstances, or (c) subsection (7) applies to him.

In the Proceeds of Crime Act 2002 (c. 29), Part 7 (money-laundering) Section 330(1) (regulated sector: failure to disclose: offence committed if three conditions satisfied), for "each of the following three conditions is satisfied" substitute "the conditions in subsections (2) to (4) are satisfied."

73 Serious Organised Crime and Police Act 2005, available from http://www.legislation.gov.uk/ukpga/2005/15/pdfs/ukpga_20050015_en.pdf.

N. Third EU Directive[74]

The term "beneficial owner" means:

> the natural person(s) who ultimately owns or controls the customer and/or the natural person on whose behalf a transaction or activity is being conducted. The beneficial owner shall at least include:
> (a) in the case of corporate entities:
> (i) the natural person(s) who ultimately owns or controls a legal entity through direct or indirect ownership or control over a sufficient percentage of the shares or voting rights in that legal entity, including through bearer share holdings, other than a company listed on a regulated market that is subject to disclosure requirements consistent with Community legislation or subject to equivalent international standards; a percentage of 25 % plus one share shall be deemed sufficient to meet this criterion;
> (ii) the natural person(s) who otherwise exercises control over the management of a legal entity.
> (b) in the case of legal entities, such as foundations, and legal arrangements, such as trusts, which administer and distribute funds:
> (i) where the future beneficiaries have already been determined, the natural person(s) who is the beneficiary of 25 % or more of the property of a legal arrangement or entity;
> (ii) where the individuals that benefit from the legal arrangement or entity have yet to be determined, the class of persons in whose main interest the legal arrangement or entity is set up or operates;
> (iii) the natural person(s) who exercises control over 25 % or more of the property of a legal arrangement or entity.

This definition is a key term in this Directive, as it might be used within the Convention to criminalize and penalize certain actions of actors. It is therefore crucial to know who is part of this definition.

---

74 European Union, *Directive 2005/60/EC of the European Parliament and of the Council of 26 October 2005 on the prevention of the use of the financial system for the purpose of money-laundering and terrorist financing,* 26 October 2005, available from http://eur-lex.europa.eu/legal-content/EN/TXT/?uri=CELEX%3A32005L0060.

Article 10 mentions Casinos CDD requirements:

1. Member States shall require that all casino customers be identified and their identity verified if they purchase or exchange gambling chips with a value of EUR 2000 or more.
2. Casinos subject to State supervision shall be deemed in any event to have satisfied the customer due diligence requirements if they register, identify and verify the identity of their customers immediately on or before entry, regardless of the amount of gambling chips purchased.

As casinos are frequent schemes for ML/FT, it is important to set a maximum amount at which verification should occur to establish the customer's identity.

Enhanced customer due diligence is required in certain cases and must follow specific guidelines as provided by this Directive:

> Where the customer has not been physically present for identification purposes, Member States shall require those institutions and persons to take specific and adequate measures to compensate for the higher risk, for example by applying one or more of the following measures:
> (a) ensuring that the customer's identity is established by additional documents, data or information;
> (b) supplementary measures to verify or certify the documents supplied, or requiring confirmatory certification by a credit or financial institution covered by this Directive;
> (c) ensuring that the first payment of the operations is carried out through an account opened in the customer's name with a credit institution.
>
> In respect of cross-frontier correspondent banking relationships with respondent institutions from third countries, Member States shall require their credit institutions to:
> (a) gather sufficient information about a respondent institution to understand fully the nature of the respondent's business and to determine from publicly available information the reputation of the institution and the quality of supervision;
> (b) assess the respondent institution's anti-money-laundering and anti-terrorist financing controls;
> (c) obtain approval from senior management before establishing new correspondent banking relationships;

> (d) document the respective responsibilities of each institution;
> (e) with respect to payable-through accounts, be satisfied that the respondent credit institution has verified the identity of and performed ongoing due diligence on the customers having direct access to accounts of the correspondent and that it is able to provide relevant customer due diligence data to the correspondent institution, upon request.
>
> 4. In respect of transactions or business relationships with politically exposed persons residing in another Member State or in a third country, Member States shall require those institutions and persons covered by this Directive to:
> (a) have appropriate risk-based procedures to determine whether the customer is a politically exposed person;
> (b) have senior management approval for establishing business relationships with such customers;
> (c) take adequate measures to establish the source of wealth and source of funds that are involved in the business relationship or transaction;
> (d) conduct enhanced ongoing monitoring of the business relationship.
>
> 5. Member States shall prohibit credit institutions from entering into or continuing a correspondent banking relationship with a shell bank and shall require that credit institutions take appropriate measures to ensure that they do not engage in or continue correspondent banking relationships with a bank that is known to permit its accounts to be used by a shell bank.
>
> 6. Member States shall ensure that the institutions and persons covered by this Directive pay special attention to any money-laundering or terrorist financing threat that may arise from products or transactions that might favour anonymity, and take measures, if needed, to prevent their use for money-laundering or terrorist financing purposes.

Concerning suspicious transaction reporting, Article 27 states that:

> Member States shall take all appropriate measures in order to protect employees of the institutions or persons covered by this Directive who report suspicions of money-laundering or terrorist-financing either internally or to the FIU from being exposed to threats or hostile action.

Yet, it should be reminded that there are different FIU types, which means that reporting directly to that incorporated into the Country's Department of

Finance would be problematic in case of State corruption linked to TF. In such case, the existence of a Global FIU would make sense and offer more transparent and safe reporting mechanism.

o. United Kingdom Terrorism Act[75]

Per this Act, the requirements to commit an offence of encouragement of terrorism are met when:

> (2) A person commits an offence if—(a) he publishes a statement to which this section applies or causes another to publish such a statement; and (b) at the time he publishes it or causes it to be published, he—(i) intends members of the public to be directly or indirectly encouraged or otherwise induced by the statement to commit, prepare or instigate acts of terrorism or Convention offences; or (ii) is reckless as to whether members of the public will be directly or indirectly encouraged or otherwise induced by the statement to commit, prepare or instigate such acts or offences.

Regarding the preparation of terrorist acts:

> (1) A person commits an offence if, with the intention of—(a) committing acts of terrorism, or (b) assisting another to commit such acts, he engages in any conduct in preparation for giving effect to his intention.
> (2) It is irrelevant for the purposes of subsection (1) whether the intention and preparations relate to one or more particular acts of terrorism, acts of terrorism of a particular description or acts of terrorism generally.
> (3) A person guilty of an offence under this section shall be liable, on conviction on indictment, to imprisonment for life.

It is interesting to note that imprisonment for life is mentioned within this article as punishment for the offence listed above.

75 Terrorism Act 2006, available from http://www.legislation.gov.uk/ukpga/2006/11/section/1.

P. Anti-money-laundering and Counter-terrorism Financing Act (2006)[76]

Part 1- Section 8 of the Act discusses multiple-institution person-to-person electronic funds transfer instruction, same-institution person-to-person electronic funds transfer instruction, same-person electronic funds transfer instructions, multiple-institution same-person electronic funds transfer instruction, and same-institution same-person electronic funds transfer instruction. These methods are difficult to detect as they demand strict surveillance and attention to detail on the part of financial institutions and law enforcement.

For the purpose of this Act, a shell banks is:

(1) …a corporation that:
- (a) is incorporated in a foreign country; and
- (b) is authorised to carry on banking business in its country of incorporation; and
- (c) does not have a physical presence in its country of incorporation; and
- (d) is not an affiliate of another corporation that:
  - (i) is incorporated in a particular country; and
  - (ii) is authorised to carry on banking business in its country of incorporation; and
  - (iii) has a physical presence in its country of incorporation.

A corporation has a physical presence in a country if, and only if:

(2)
- (a) the corporation carries on banking business at a place in that country; and
- (b) at least one full-time employee of the corporation performs banking-related duties at that place.

To determine what is a shell bank, a corporation is affiliated with another corporation if, and only if:

76 Australian Government Federal Register of Legislation, *Anti-Money-Laundering and Counter-Terrorism Financing Act 2006 No. 169*, 2006, available from https://www.legislation.gov.au/Details/C2006A00169.

(3) (a) the corporation is a subsidiary of the other corporation; or
(b) at least one individual passes the control test in relation to both corporations; or
(c) under the regulations, both corporations are taken to be under common control.

For the purpose of this Act, a ML/TF risk assessment program is an assessment by a reporting entity of:

(a) the risk the reporting entity may reasonably face that the provision by the reporting entity of designated services at or through a permanent establishment of the reporting entity in Australia might (whether inadvertently or otherwise) involve or facilitate:
 (i) money-laundering; or
 (ii) financing of terrorism; and
(b) what the reporting entity will need to do, or continue to do, to:
 (i) identify; and
 (ii) mitigate; and
 (iii) manage".

Q. Australia, Anti-money-laundering and Counter-terrorism Financing Rules Instrument 2007 (No. 1)[77]

Chapter 3, Part 3, deals with correspondent banking due diligence, and states that:

a financial institution (the first financial institution) must carry out an assessment of the following matters, where and to the extent warranted by the risk identified in accordance with subsection 97(1):
 (1) the nature of the other financial institution's business, including its product and customer base;
 (2) the domicile of the other financial institution;
 (3) the domicile of any parent company of the other financial institution;
 (4) the existence and quality of any anti-money-laundering and Counter-terrorism financing regulation in the other financial institution's country of domicile;

77 Australian Government Federal Register of Legislation, *Anti-Money-Laundering and Counter-terrorism Financing Rules Instrument 2007 (No. 1)*, 10 April 2007, available from https://www.legislation.gov.au/Details/F2007L01000/Html/Text.

(5) the existence and quality of any anti-money-laundering and Counter-terrorism financing regulation in the country of domicile of any parent company of the other financial institution—where the parent company has group-wide controls and where the other financial institution operates within the requirements of those controls;
(6) the adequacy of the other financial institution's controls and internal compliance practices in relation to anti-money-laundering and Counter-terrorism financing;
(7) the ownership, control and management structures of the other financial institution and any parent company, including whether a politically exposed person has ownership or control of the other financial institution or any parent company;
(8) the other financial institution's financial position;
(9) the reputation and history of the other financial institution;
(10) the reputation and history of any parent company of the other financial institution.

These factors are important for deciding upon the risks posed by a financial institution.

The risk-based approach and ML/TF risk implies:

> determining and putting in place appropriate risk-based systems or controls, the reporting entity must have regard to the nature, size and complexity of its business and the type of ML/TF risk that it might reasonably face.

Therefore, in identifying its ML/TF risk, a reporting entity must consider the risk posed by the following factors:

(1) its customer types, including any politically exposed persons;
(2) the types of designated services it provides;
(3) the methods by which it delivers designated services; and
(4) the foreign jurisdictions with which it deals.

Employee due diligence programs also play a significant role for employees to understand how to detect and report the right transactions, as well as the punishment they would encounter for non-compliance. For this purpose:

> 8.3.2 The employee due diligence program must put in place appropriate risk-based systems and controls for the reporting entity to determine

whether to, and in what manner to, screen any prospective employee who, if employed, may be in a position to facilitate the commission of a money-laundering or financing of terrorism offence in connection with the provision of a designated service by the reporting entity.

8.3.3 The employee due diligence program must include appropriate risk-based systems and controls for the reporting entity to determine whether to, and in what manner to, re-screen an employee where the employee is transferred or promoted and may be in a position to facilitate the commission of a money-laundering or financing of terrorism offence in connection with the provision of a designated service by the reporting entity.

8.3.4 The employee due diligence program must establish and maintain a system for the reporting entity to manage any employee who fails, without reasonable excuse, to comply with any system, control or procedure established in accordance with Part A or Part B.

R. UK Counter-terrorism Act[78]

Part 5 makes provision conferring powers on the Treasury to act against terrorist financing, money-laundering and certain other activities. For the purposes of this Act an offence has a terrorist connection if the offence:

(a) is, or takes place in the course of, an act of terrorism, or
(b) is committed for the purposes of terrorism.

The meaning of "ancillary offence" is:

(1) In this Act 'ancillary offence,' in relation to an offence, means any of the following—
  (a) aiding, abetting, counselling or procuring the commission of the offence (or, in Scotland, being art and part in the commission of the offence);
  (b) an offence under Part 2 of the Serious Crime Act 2007 (c.27) (encouraging or assisting crime) in relation to the offence (or, in Scotland, inciting a person to commit the offence);
  (c) attempting or conspiring to commit the offence.

78 Counter-Terrorism Act 2008, c. 28, available from http://www.legislation.gov.uk/ukpga/2008/28/pdfs/ukpga_20080028_en.pdf.

The separate mention of "ancillary offence" makes any type of assistance, attempt or conspiracy to the commission of the offence singular and dislocated from the definition of the crime itself. In most of the legal instruments previously mentioned, this was an integral part of the offence definition.

S. Fourth EU Directive[79]

Article 2, paragraph 3, on "Financial activity on an occasional or very limited basis" of the Fourth European Directive defines engagement in financial activities:

> 3. Member States may decide that persons that engage in a financial activity on an occasional or very limited basis where there is little risk of money-laundering or terrorist financing do not fall within the scope of this Directive, provided that all of the following criteria are met:
> (a) the financial activity is limited in absolute terms;
> (b) the financial activity is limited on a transaction basis;
> (c) the financial activity is not the main activity of such persons;
> (d) the financial activity is ancillary and directly related to the main activity of such persons;
> (e) the main activity of such persons is not an activity referred to in points (a) to (d) or point (f) of paragraph 1(3);
> (f) the financial activity is provided only to the customers of the main activity of such persons and is not generally offered to the public.
>
> The first subparagraph shall not apply to persons engaged in the activity of money remittance as defined in point (13) of Article 4 of Directive 2007/64/EC of the European Parliament and of the Council (1)."

Paragraphs 4 to 7 of Article 2 precise Article 2.3:

> 4. For the purposes of point (a) of paragraph 3, Member States shall require that the total turnover of the financial activity does not exceed a threshold which must be sufficiently low. That threshold

79 European Union, *Directive (EU) 2015/849 of the European Parliament and of the Council of 20 May 2015 on the prevention of the use of the financial system for the purposes of money-laundering or terrorist financing, amending Regulation (EU) No 648/2012 of the European Parliament and of the Council, and repealing Directive 2005/60/EC of the European Parliament and of the Council and Commission Directive 2006/70/EC*, 20 May 2015, available from http://eur-lex.europa.eu/legal-content/EN/TXT/?uri=CELEX%3A32015L0849.

shall be established at national level, depending on the type of financial activity.

5. For the purposes of point (b) of paragraph 3, Member States shall apply a maximum threshold per customer and per single transaction, whether the transaction is carried out in a single operation or in several operations which appear to be linked. That maximum threshold shall be established at national level, depending on the type of financial activity. It shall be sufficiently low in order to ensure that the types of transactions in question are an impractical and inefficient method for money-laundering or terrorist-financing, and shall not exceed EUR 1 000.
6. For the purposes of point (c) of paragraph 3, Member States shall require that the turnover of the financial activity does not exceed 5 % of the total turnover of the natural or legal person concerned.
7. In assessing the risk of money-laundering or terrorist financing for the purposes of this Article, Member States shall pay particular attention to any financial activity which is considered to be particularly likely, by its nature, to be used or abused for the purposes of money-laundering or terrorist financing.

This Article is very useful to the purpose of this study, as this definition is not necessarily provided in each legal instrument.

The Fourth Directive provides for due diligence and reporting limitations for payments, as well as sanctions.

Concerning large cash payments:

> (6) The use of large cash payments is highly vulnerable to money-laundering and terrorist financing. In order to increase vigilance and mitigate the risks posed by such cash payments, persons trading in goods should be covered by this Directive to the extent that they make or receive cash payments of EUR 10 000 or more. Member States should be able to adopt lower thresholds, additional general limitations to the use of cash and further stricter provisions.

The Directive also provides transaction limits for the gambling industry regarding reporting and states that:

> (21) The use of gambling sector services to launder the proceeds of criminal activity is of concern. In order to mitigate the risks relating to

> gambling services, this Directive should provide for an obligation for providers of gambling services posing higher risks to apply customer due diligence measures for single transactions amounting to EUR 2 000 or more.

Per Article 11, Member States shall ensure that obliged entities apply customer due diligence measures under the following circumstances:

> (a) when establishing a business relationship;
> (b) when carrying out an occasional transaction that:
>   (i) amounts to EUR 15 000 or more, whether that transaction is carried out in a single operation or in several operations which appear to be linked; or
>   (ii) constitutes a transfer of funds, as defined in point (9) of Article 3 of Regulation (EU) 2015/847 of the European Parliament and of the Council (1), exceeding EUR 1 000;
> (c) in the case of persons trading in goods, when carrying out occasional transactions in cash amounting to EUR 10 000 or more, whether the transaction is carried out in a single operation or in several operations which appear to be linked;
> (d) for providers of gambling services, upon the collection of winnings, the wagering of a stake, or both, when carrying out transactions amounting to EUR 2 000 or more, whether the transaction is carried out in a single operation or in several operations which appear to be linked;
> (e) when there is a suspicion of money-laundering or terrorist financing, regardless of any derogation, exemption or threshold;
> (f) when there are doubts about the veracity or adequacy of previously obtained customer identification data.

Section 4 provides sanctions within Article 59- 2. It reads as:

> Member States shall ensure that in the cases referred to in paragraph 1, the administrative sanctions and measures that can be applied include at least the following:
> (a) a public statement which identifies the natural or legal person and the nature of the breach;
> (b) an order requiring the natural or legal person to cease the conduct and to desist from repetition of that conduct;
> (c) where an obliged entity is subject to an authorisation, withdrawal or suspension of the authorisation;

(d) a temporary ban against any person discharging managerial responsibilities in an obliged entity, or any other natural person, held responsible for the breach, from exercising managerial functions in obliged entities;
(e) maximum administrative pecuniary sanctions of at least twice the amount of the benefit derived from the breach where that benefit can be determined, or at least EUR 1 000 000.

Member States shall ensure that, by way of derogation from paragraph 2(e), where the obliged entity concerned is a credit institution or financial institution, the following sanctions can also be applied:
(a) in the case of a legal person, maximum administrative pecuniary sanctions of at least EUR 5 000 000 or 10 % of the total annual turnover according to the latest available accounts approved by the management body; where the obliged entity is a parent undertaking or a subsidiary of a parent undertaking which is required to prepare consolidated financial accounts in accordance with Article 22 of Directive 2013/34/EU, the relevant total annual turnover shall be the total annual turnover or the corresponding type of income in accordance with the relevant accounting Directives according to the last available consolidated accounts approved by the management body of the ultimate parent undertaking;
(b) in the case of a natural person, maximum administrative pecuniary sanctions of at least EUR 5 000 000, or in the Member States whose currency is not the euro, the corresponding value in the national currency on 25 June 2015.

Concerning reporting mechanisms, Article 61 also states that Member States shall:

1. ensure that competent authorities establish effective and reliable mechanisms to encourage the reporting to competent authorities of potential or actual breaches of the national provisions transposing this Directive.
2. The mechanisms referred to in paragraph 1 shall include at least:
   (a) specific procedures for the receipt of reports on breaches and their follow-up;
   (b) appropriate protection for employees or persons in a comparable position, of obliged entities who report breaches committed within the obliged entity;

(c) appropriate protection for the accused person;
(d) protection of personal data concerning both the person who reports the breaches and the natural person who is allegedly responsible for a breach, in compliance with the principles laid down in Directive 95/46/EC;
(e) clear rules that ensure that confidentiality is guaranteed in all cases in relation to the person who reports the breaches committed within the obliged entity, unless disclosure is required by national law in the context of further investigations or subsequent judicial proceedings.

3. Member States shall require obliged entities to have in place appropriate procedures for their employees, or persons in a comparable position, to report breaches internally through a specific, independent and anonymous channel, proportionate to the nature and size of the obliged entity concerned.

Reporting and sanctions are important as they are the only incentive to push the private sector for better cooperation with authorities to detect suspect activities.

T. EU Directive on Combating Terrorism[80]

TITLE III of the 2017 Directive details new and interesting Offences Related to Terrorist Activities such as:

Article 5: Public provocation to commit a terrorist offence,
Article 6: Recruitment for terrorism,
Article 7: Providing training for terrorism,
Article 8: Receiving training for terrorism,
Article 9: Travelling for the purpose of terrorism,
Article 10: Organising or otherwise facilitating travelling for the purpose of terrorism.

80 European Union, Directive (EU) *2017/541 of the European Parliament and of the Council of 15 March 2017 on combating terrorism and replacing Council Framework Decision 2002/475/JHA and amending Council Decision 2005/671/JHA*, 15 March 2017, available from https://eur-lex.europa.eu/legal-content/EN/TXT/PDF/?uri=CELEX:32017L0541&from=EN.

Article 11 on Terrorist Financing provides that:

1. Member States shall take the necessary measures to ensure that providing or collecting funds, by any means, directly or indirectly, with the intention that they be used, or in the knowledge that they are to be used, in full or in part, to commit, or to contribute to the commission of, any of the offences referred to in Articles 3 to 10 is punishable as a criminal offence when committed intentionally.
2. Where the terrorist financing referred to in paragraph 1 of this Article concerns any of the offences laid down in Articles 3, 4 and 9, it shall not be necessary that the funds be in fact used, in full or in part, to commit, or to contribute to the commission of, any of those offences, nor shall it be required that the offender knows for which specific offence or offences the funds are to be used.

This Directive also offers various measures of assistance to victims, penalties for natural persons, as well as measures against public provocation online.

U. The Parliament of the Commonwealth of Australia Anti-money-laundering and Counter-terrorism Financing Amendment Bill (2017)[81]

This Amendment Bill displays the importance of regulating e-currencies to enhance CTF measures. Under which:

"digital currency" means:
(a) a digital representation of value that:
  (i) functions as a medium of exchange, a store of economic value, or a unit of account; and
  (ii) is not issued by or under the authority of a government body; and
  (iii) is interchangeable with money (including through the crediting of an account) and may be used as consideration for the supply of goods or services; and

81 Anti-Money-Laundering and Counter-Terrorism Financing Amendment Bill 2017, available from http://parlinfo.aph.gov.au/parlInfo/download/legislation/bills/r5952_aspassed/toc_pdf/17177b01.pdf;fileType=application%2Fpdf.

(iv) is generally available to members of the public without any restriction on its use as consideration; or

(b) a means of exchange or digital process or crediting declared to be digital currency by the AML/CTF Rules; but does not include any right or thing that, under the AML/CTF Rules, is taken not to be digital currency for the purposes of this Act.

This Amendment Bill provides for a system of registration for providers of digital currency exchange services. It sets out offences and civil penalties in relation to the provision of registrable digital currency exchange services by persons who are not registered, and also requires the AUSTRAC CEO to maintain the Digital Currency Exchange Register as well as setting out the process of applying for registration.

Per 76G, Registration may be subject to conditions:

(1) The AUSTRAC CEO may, in writing, impose conditions to which the registration of a person under this Part is subject.

Note: A decision to impose a condition is reviewable (see Part 17A).

(2) Without limiting the conditions that the AUSTRAC CEO may impose under subsection (1), the conditions may relate to the following:

(a) the value of digital currency or money exchanged;

(b) the volume of digital currency exchanged (whether by reference to a particular period, a particular kind of digital currency, or otherwise);

(c) the kinds of digital currencies exchanged;

(d) requiring notification of the exchange of particular kinds of digital currency, changes in circumstances, or other specified events.

Note: Section 76P imposes a general obligation in relation to notification of changes in circumstances.

General modifications to the original document are particularly useful to the construction of the new CTF tool proposed in this book, as they adjust the whole legislation to include digital currencies. The term "other serious crime" was added to the money-laundering and terrorist financing offenses. Similarly, gambling was also inserted as a core topic of this legislation, where gaming chips or tokens, or betting instruments are now part of the Bill. Vostro accounts are also included in this amendment. By adapting its National Law to the threat of new technologies, Australia has differentiated between physical currency and virtual, giving both similar importance, and therefore, has become a pioneer country in regulating these matters.

V. Fifth EU Directive[82]

Article 1 provides amendments to the Directive (EU) 2015/849, whereby to (1) in point (3) of Article 2(1), the following points (g) and (h) are added:

(g) providers engaged primarily and professionally in exchange services between virtual currencies and fiat currencies;
(h) wallet providers offering custodial services of credentials necessary to access virtual currencies.;

Article 3 is amended as follows:

the following point is added: '"virtual currencies" means a digital representation of value that is neither issued by a central bank or a public authority, nor necessarily attached to a fiat currency, but is accepted by natural or legal persons as a means of payment and can be transferred, stored or traded electronically.'

Article 12 sets limits to online payments and is amended as follows:

paragraph 1 is amended as follows:
(i) in the first subparagraph, points (a) and (b) are replaced by the following: (a) the payment instrument is not reloadable, or has a maximum monthly payment transactions limit of eur 150 which can be used only in that Member State; (b) the maximum amount stored electronically does not exceed eur 150;
(ii) the second subparagraph is deleted.

paragraph 2 is replaced by the following: 'Member States shall ensure that the derogation provided for in paragraph 1 is not applicable in the

82 European Union, *Directive (EU) 2018/843 of the European Parliament and of the Council of 30 May 2018 amending Directive (EU) 2015/849 on the prevention of the use of the financial system for the purposes of money-laundering or terrorist financing, and amending Directives 2009/138/EC and 2013/36/EU*, 30 May 2018, available from https://eur-lex.europa.eu/legal-content/EN/TXT/PDF/?uri=CELEX:32018L0843&from=EN.

> case either of online payment or of redemption in cash or cash withdrawal of the monetary value of the electronic money where the amount redeemed exceeds eur 50.';

Article 47, paragraph 1 is also replaced by the following:

> Member States shall ensure that providers of exchanging services between virtual currencies and fiat currencies, custodian wallet providers, currency exchange and cheque cashing offices, and trust or company service providers are licensed or registered, and that providers of gambling services are regulated.

Virtual currencies are now added to the scope of the Directive, as the European Union has come to understand the importance of such inclusion.

The Fifth EU Directive offers a new Article 4 on Transposition. It reads:

> 1. Member States shall bring into force the laws, regulations and administrative provisions necessary to comply with this Directive by 10 January 2020. They shall immediately communicate the text of those provisions to the Commission.
>
>   When Member States adopt those measures, they shall contain a reference to this Directive or be accompanied by such a reference on the occasion of their official publication.
> 2. Member States shall communicate to the Commission the text of the main provisions of national law which they adopt in the field covered by this Directive.

EU members States therefore have 18 months to implement the Fifth AML/CTF Directive into their National Law. The Directive also furthermore discusses high-value goods, prepaid cards and cryptocurrencies.

CHAPTER 8

Current Counter-terrorism Tools and Regulations Successes and Failures

This chapter will review current regulations successes and failures to provide a comprehensive New Counter-terrorism Financing model. Conclusions will be drawn from previous chapters' findings as well as based on interviews and surveys conducted with international CTF actors.

Part A provides a critique of Counter-terrorism financing tools and regulations, thereby highlighting the importance of a new CTF framework to monitor TF worldwide.

Part B reviews results of surveys on CTF regulations distributed to experts and offers original gap analysis by means of a visual map to define where a new model should intervene.

Part C reports on where problems are perceived at their level by interviewed experts from different CTF professions and how these could be surmounted by inserting new provisions into the new model CTF tool.

A Critique of Current Counter-terrorism Financing Tools and Regulations

This part includes a criticism of the weaknesses found in Chapter 1–6. It should be made clear that the key words in CTF remain: DETECT, PREVENT, ENFORCE, RE-REGULATE. Re-regulating is important, because terrorists and financial evaders will always find creative new ways to bypass the system; one moment you watch them and define their *modus operandi*, the next, they have found another way to abuse the financial world. To strengthen world detection, prevention and enforcement at the domestic and international level, collaborating with the private sector is becoming vital for deterring TF. Governments need laws and regulations that establish corporate criminal liability for bank and non-bank financial institutions for ML violations, which should apply to all financial transactions.

The main risks to be acknowledged from Chapters 3 and 4 include: anonymity, the evolution of technology, with a special focus on new payment technologies, online gaming, internet frauds, cross-border activities, third-party

 | DOI:10.1163/9789004409675_013

reliance, employee participations in the schemes, misuses, as well as slow processes when dealing with paperwork and procedures. Further risk factors include non-face to face relationships and anonymity, geographic reach, the variety of methods of funding, easy access to cash, and the segmentation of services. Other risk factors comprise the complexity of reporting, the challenging use of software for TF (since it is on a case by case basis), the lack of transparency, and employees' participation in CT schemes.

The blockages faced by the international community raised here are: political pressure, the lack of an international definition of terrorism, weak international cooperation, miscommunication (or lack of communication) between the main actors related to CTF, privacy rights, civil liberties, disclosure of association funds, tracing, freezing and recovery of assets presumably linked to TF. Other blockages include: prioritizing over incoming TF cases and the gravity of terrorist incidents, the cost of investigation/ compared to the cost of retrieved assets (is it worth it?), investigations in multiple jurisdictions, Courts and enforcement by actors, and the need for International cooperation. Steps forward should include risk mitigation such as Customer Due Diligence (CDD), geographic limits with specific enhanced monitoring, identifying sources of funding, robust record keeping, transaction monitoring and more effective reporting. Controls are not associated to the risk assessments within most common AML/CTF programs. They should be implemented to provide feedbacks and solutions to Banks and Institutions.

To strengthen world detection, prevention and enforcement at the domestic and international levels, collaborating with the private sector is becoming vital to deter TF. Collaboration with the Private Sector, Actors' Involvement and Cooperation at the Domestic and International Levels, Global Financial Intelligence Units Development are of great importance to deter Terrorism financing. They promote effective international cooperation including exchange of information between relevant authorities, conduct of joint investigations, and tracing, freezing and confiscation of illegal assets. Law enforcement and FIUs require better operational tools and a wider range of techniques and powers to investigate and prosecute ML/TF.[1]

1 Financial Action Task Force (FATF), *FATF steps up the fight against money laundering and terrorist financing*, 2012, available from http://www.fatf-gafi.org/topics/fatfrecommendations/documents/fatfstepsupthefightagainstmoneylaunderingandterroristfinancing.html.

Terrorism financing measures and reporting should be extended to the scope of all serious international crimes, including tax crimes and not solely drug trafficking. This would ultimately make the proceeds of tax crimes within the scope of the powers and authorities used to investigate ML for TF purposes, as well as criminalize investments in legitimate industry, if the investment proceeds were derived from illegal acts. Smuggling should also be established as an offence linked to TF within the jurisdiction of the new Convention model. Financial and corporate ownership information disclosure should also be shared with law enforcement agencies and judicial authorities, being part of the new disclosure requirement prescribed by the new Convention model.

B Counter-terrorism Financing Regulations' Gap Analysis

In order to offer a Gap Analysis of current CTF regulations' current successes and failures, based on a visual map of experts' opinions, a questionnaire was provided to several CTF specialists. It was distributed to 120 CTF actors in multiple institutions and at various levels. The role of the questionnaire was to discover the relationships and administrative issues perceived amongst specialized agencies. The results demonstrate which problems need to be at least acknowledged, if not fixed, to build the new CTF regulatory tool. The questionnaire, which can be found in Annex 3, is divided into eight sections. It was delivered to six categories of actors. The eight sections of questions put to the participants included: background information, current regulatory tools efficiency, privacy issues, reporting procedures, cooperation and links with other agencies, financial intelligence units' work and connections, cross-border enforcement, and cost-benefit of monitoring TF. The actors involved with this questionnaire are: government agencies, military/police, members of tribunals, international organizations, consulting agencies and banks.

The questions were written in a way that they could be addressed both by experts and lower level professionals as a cross sectorial study. In this way, depending on the agency represented, the professional could provide further elements that would deepen the understanding of the various problems encountered at their levels to demonstrate where the gaps in CTF detection, prevention and enforcement were to be found.

The first section of the questionnaire was for gathering information about the participant's job title, hierarchy level and the CTF actor's category, which could include government, military, police, FIU, international organization, tribunal/law firm, consultant, bank, insurance and financial institution. The second section was focused on current CTF/AML tools and regulations concerning the way that these were used daily and how they were perceived by participants. These tools and regulations might include the company's internal rules, consulting guidelines, recommendations provided by international organizations, EU directives, applicable national law, United Nations Conventions, etc. The participants were asked if they found the existing regulatory and advisory tools efficient and appropriate for CTF monitoring. They were also asked whether they perceived any usefulness or breach in the regular usage of these tools. Such factors are critical, and should be considered while creating a new regulatory model that would benefit all CTF sectors.

The third section of questions asked whether or not the participants felt the need for a privacy related clause. The fourth section covered the procedures applied by the participants at work, such as customer due diligence, enhanced due diligence, currency transaction reports, suspicious activity reports, national security letters, etc. They asked which CTF preventive and reporting procedures they were familiar with and used at work if any, as well as how close the participant's work was to other reporting entities. CTF actors were asked if they found the procedures too burdensome, slow, misused, useless or inappropriate and whether they could recall any procedural/paperwork problems their unit frequently encountered. They were also asked if they trusted that people working in CTF had received adequate training.

The fifth section was about to international cooperation between CTF agencies and actors. Participants were asked about their links with other CTF players and frequency of exchanges to discover whether there are existing communication issues between them. Collaboration with the private sector has been mentioned by FATF. Participants were asked to give their opinion on this possible collaboration to determine if it can benefit CTF monitoring. The sixth section was about gathering information on the efficiency of FIUs' work, blockages in the effectiveness of this work and ideas as to how FIUs could be improved. The seventh section covered cross-border enforcement. The aim of this section was to discover how enforcement worldwide could be improved. The eighth section focused on the cost of monitoring and attempts to determine if the price of confiscated TF assets exceeds the cost of investigation. This section was based on experts' knowledge and evidence they might have encountered during their work. This question was important as it could provide key information on the potential obstacles encountered in CTF.

As a result of the questionnaire, the following conclusions can be drawn:

TABLE 1 Counter-terrorism financing review of experts opinions and supporting data, 2017

Expert opinions	Supporting data
CTF existing regulatory and advisory tools are efficient	Based on the analysis of the questionnaire, 80% of respondents that work in banks found that CTF tools in relation to their daily work are useful.
A new CTF monitoring tool that would benefit all sectors	97% of respondents reported that there is a need for a more appropriate CTF monitoring tool that would benefit all sectors.
Privacy and Data Protection is an important factor to incorporate in a new tool	92% of respondents believed that privacy and data protection were important issues in CTF.
There is a general lack of familiarity and understanding with CTF preventive and reporting procedures	Based on the analysis of the questionnaire, 76% of the respondents did not know all the CTF tools available apart from the one they worked with daily.
There is no close connection between all reporting entities	68% of the respondents agreed that there is a lack of knowledge of other CTF actors and their works.
The most current CTF related procedural/ paperwork problems respondents or their co-workers encountered is identification/proving the crime of TF	Based on the analysis of the questionnaire, 100% of respondents that worked in financial institutions had found that the main blockage in their procedure was the identification of a TF red flag versus ML or other financial crime. 85% of the respondents that worked in FIUs and law enforcement reported that proving the crime was a core procedural issue.
Current CTF procedures are useless or inappropriate	92% of respondents reported that CTF procedures are too burdensome and lack uniformity. 95% of respondents answered that CTF procedures are too slow.
CTF procedures are misused	75% of the respondents contended that CTF actors have inadequate training for ensuring appropriate usage of procedures and producing significant results.

Expert opinions	Supporting data
CTF actors most often encounter cooperation problems with banks	66% of the respondents believed that the CTF actor that is most often reluctant to cooperate is banks.
Believe collaboration with the private sector is crucial in CTF	Based on the analysis of the questionnaire, 90% of respondents believed there should be better collaboration with the private sector.
The work of FIUs is efficient	73% of the respondents believed in the effectiveness of FIUs' work. 15% of the respondents from financial institutions admitted reporting to the local police directly and had little communication with their FIU.
Communication between key players must be enhanced	72% of the respondents thought that communication between key CTF players should be improved.
Full cross-border enforcement is deemed impossible by CTF actors	97% of the respondents believed full cross-border enforcement is not possible due to the internet. 76% of the respondents claimed that full cross-border enforcement is not possible because of different legislations worldwide.
A centralized effort for asset recovery would improve enforcement worldwide	65% of the respondents answered that there is a need for a centralization of assets recovery at the international level.
Strongly believe that the price of confiscated assets for TF might exceed the cost of investigation	88% of the respondents believed the cost of CFT work is higher than the money collected from confiscated assets.
No professional encountered evidence during their work that investigation in fact costs more than the confiscated assets on a yearly basis.	0% of the respondents could provide supporting evidence that investigation in fact costs more than the confiscated assets on a yearly basis. Moreover, 62% of them felt that their job was inefficient.

The following visual map provides a gap analysis of the current Counter-terrorism tools and regulations' successes and failures, according to the Counter-terrorism Financing Review of Experts Opinions and Supporting Data provided in Table 1.

TABLE 2 Counter-terrorism financing gap analysis visual map, 2017

Actors	Governmental agencies	Military & police	Tribunals	International organizations	Consulting agencies	Banks
Actual regulatory tools efficiency	End of the chain/relying on other actors' data for efficiency	– Time issues – Means lacking – Cooperation problems (due to other actors)	N/A	– Middle man – Risk of lack of/or misinformation	N/A	Too many gaps linked with human interaction
Privacy issues & Civil Liberties	Often inappropriate to the threat and preventing appropriate data collection	Often inappropriate to the threat and preventing appropriate data collection	Often inappropriate to the threat and preventing appropriate data collection	Not reviewed enough	Not reviewed enough	– High-risk of employees providing information without enough verification – Not enough training
Reporting Procedures	N/A (collection)	– Depending on banks cooperation – Too long to fill paperwork and collect data from banks	Burdensome (when applicable)	Timely (to collect from other actors)	Well reviewed	– Too burdensome – Rather not do it each time – Not reporting to the right agency

Actors	Governmental agencies	Military & police	Tribunals	International organizations	Consulting agencies	Banks
Cooperation and links to other Agencies	– Well done – Risk of retaining information as governments are involved	– Depending on banks cooperation – Too long to fill paperwork and collect data from banks	– Well done (when applicable) – Specific cells	– Well done – Specific cells	Not reviewed enough	Not in their favor for big accounts = big losses + name affiliated to fraud
Financial Intelligence Units	Efficiency depends on type of FIUS	Efficiency depends on type of FIUS	Well connected (depends on the type of FIU)	Well recognized	Well recognized	Some Directors did not know what it was
Cross-border Enforcement & Assets Confiscation	– Need for International standard for more efficiency in enforcement proceedings – N/A (more applicable to police)	Hard to prove « Terrorism » threshold (or else ML/tax evasion charges)	– Problem with Terrorism definition – Issue: Requirement to prove « terrorism »	N/A	Not reviewed enough	Well processed/ comply with law enforcement when asked
Cost-Benefit of Monitoring TF	Not enough return to judge	– Long period of investigation – Hard to prove « Terrorism » = release of frozen assets	N/A	– High – Not enough return	N/A	– Reputation benefit of a « clean » bank – Costly (trainings/ procedures)

First, government agencies are perceived by participants as the end of the chains/relying on other actors' data for efficiency, which means if the information from other actors is incorrect, they will not function effectively. The military and police actors who answered the questionnaire claimed to lack means, and experienced time issues, as well as cooperation problems mainly due to other actors' work. International organizations are seen as the "middle man" and hence, there is the risk of a lack of information or even misinformation. Banks see many gaps linked with human interaction, such as negligence or complicity in schemes.

Second, privacy issues and civil liberties are often seen as being a hindrance to data collection for tribunals, governmental agencies as well as the military and the police. International organizations and consulting agencies do not review these privacy and civil liberties issues enough, while banks do not provide enough training to their employees at every level in this regard. Banks also face a high-risk of employees providing information without enough verification.

Third, reporting procedures need alignment for greater effectiveness. At present, the military and the police take too long filling paperwork and collecting data from banks, for which they depend on their cooperation. Reporting procedures are perceived as too time consuming when it comes to the collection of data from other actors for international organizations, and burdensome (when applicable) for tribunals. Banks play a critical role in reporting and experience burdensome procedures, sometimes not knowing how to report to the right agency. Consulting Agencies' work includes well reviewed reporting procedures.

Fourth, cooperation and links with other agencies is implemented well by government agencies. Yet, the risk of retaining information is high as governments are involved. International organizations (when applicable) experience successful cooperation with their specific cells. Consulting agencies do not review links with other agencies or cooperate in an in-depth manner.

The work of military and police linked to TF depends on banks' cooperation. These actors deal with paperwork often too long to fill in when they collect data from banks. Too much cooperation in investigating big clients is not at all favorable for banks, because if they have to report them, they would lose big accounts and have their banks' names associated with fraud. For this reason, banks do weigh the appropriateness of the cost of reporting their clients versus the risk of prison or fines for their administration when dealing with big accounts.

Fifth, FIUs require a standard to remain sufficiently independent from governments' interaction, especially in countries with a culture accepting corruption. Sometimes assets connected to TF belong to politicians. Hence, CTF work will be ineffective in countries with FIUs inside ministries. For, political actors can block important data and information collected before they are sent to another FIU in a different country. Efficiency depends on the type of FIUs for government agencies, the military and police, and courts. In the case of banks, a few Compliance and Security Directors did not know about FIUs and their work and so, would directly called local authorities.

Six, regarding cross-border enforcement and assets confiscation, governmental agencies need an international standard for more efficiency in enforcement proceedings. The military and police find it hard to prove the terrorism threshold. Courts also have a problem with its definition and with the requirement to prove terrorism as opposed to other crimes. Banks comply with law enforcement when asked, consulting agencies do not review this topic enough. Jurisdiction, extradition and the release and selling of TF-related assets require more unification to be understood and applied easily by all players.

Seven, the cost-benefit of Monitoring TF is unknown. Although there is no return of data to judge the cost-benefit of monitoring for government agencies, and international organizations, it seems to be a high cost for limited benefits due to the timeframe of investigations and the collection of money, according to professionals involved. The military and the police require long periods of investigation and have a hard time proving terrorism before the crime even occurred. This can trigger the release of frozen assets, if the individual does not get charged with another crime, such as ML/tax evasion. Banks' reputation relies on monitoring despite costly training and procedures, which are sometimes seen inadequate by the actors concerned.

C Constructive Criticism and Advice by International Experts for Building a New Model

This part draws on interview data gather from professionals working in CTF. 36 participants of the survey distributed among CTF actors to build the gap analysis, agreed to provide additional information about their experience through an interview. Participants shall remain anonymous for the purpose of this study. The interviewees came from government, the military, Police, FIU, international organization, tribunal/law firm, consulting company, bank, insurance and financial institution backgrounds at various hierarchical levels. These interviews were conducted to provide additional details on topics approached in the questionnaire that they found important to discuss and wanted to offer valuable input on.

The absence of active legislation for criminal offences that result in property profits seems to be a great concern for most of the professionals interviewed. The problems differentiating AML from CTF for many respondents and for the general public demands a better explanation from a new convention model to ensure better understanding of the problem at stake. As per experts' opinion, *CTF detection problems arise when trying to distinguish clean licit money or legitimate investors in illegal businesses from money derived from business operations, which are not connected to criminal acts.* The original classification that the reporting infrastructure allows, influences subsequent investigations. MLROs have no idea whether to report on ML/TF in a SAR, as plenty of indictors are overlapping between them.

Countries are not perceived as willing to fight TF in a veritable manner due to political pressure and national political agendas. Tax havens are often located in countries where law enforcement is non-cooperative and local regulations in favor of anonymity. According to professionals, despite the G20 putting together a convention to destabilize tax havens, *many countries ignore such voluntary actions and there is a failure to punish their voluntary non-cooperation. Moreover, enforcement powers at the national and international level are very specific and do not allow some actors to investigate and apprehend financers of illicit activities easily.*

Government agencies need to understand the drawbacks of the system and actors' interests in order to codify CTF. Actors claimed that t*here is a need for more inside knowledge from the private sector to regulate effectively*. Government agencies also claim to suffer from the lack of a far-reaching jurisdiction. *FIUs, which are part of governments, represent opportunities and threats, which should be discussed and well-reviewed. They would benefit from a standardization at the international level which could happen through the implementation of the GFIU initiative.* International organizations rely on others for accurate data, and information regarding TF. therefore, they would need to work with a centralized organization with more power. Blacklisting was discussed by most interviewees and recognized as a main concern for CTF professionals as this preventive measure represents a dilemma. The listing decision criteria and delisting processes still appear to be a vague notion to some concerned professionals, who demand more comprehensive guidelines.

Delays in judicial procedures and investigation were cited by professionals as critical to finding terrorist financers. Another problem comes from the AML/CTF burden of proof, or inversion of burden of proof, which demands that potential financers should provide evidence of non-guilt in CT cases. Participation in TF can take place through regular business activities, such as purchasing oil from states willing to finance terrorist activities. Interviewees agreed that *when it is a complicated task to apprehend terrorist financers, law enforcement's only chance is to find another count possible for external actions, such as fiscal fraud/ tax avoidance,* to apprehend potential criminals which fall with the current legislative gaps. Tribunals are required to have "sufficient reasons to believe in terrorist perpetration". They also have found it hard to produce evidence of the means utilized and to seize assets. *Moreover, interviewees pointed that it is hard demonstrate terrorism and to prove how a crime took place, if it has not happened yet.*

Per CTF actors interviewed, *banks face insider threat and lack of training.* These issues stood out as the biggest obstacles to overcome for them. According to the interviewees, there *are not enough trained professionals working in specialized units owing to lack of budget.* Banks' interests appear to come first and compliance officers are therefore, left with the dilemma of trying to keep their job and the probability of getting caught for keeping big accounts deemed "high-risk" or non-compliant. Several Compliance Officers agreed that *FI may therefore be attributing* TF *risk scores arbitrarily to keep important accounts.* Unfortunately, this easy approach for them may have significant side-effects as individuals and transactions can evade the system. *Banks need more training and adequate sanctions to discourage non-compliant entities.*

Consulting agencies are viewed by financial institutions' employees as *compromised by* FIs' *hierarchy, which want to receive reports in their favor.* Their work is also perceived as *having little involvement afterwards and being very costly.* Consulting companies might benefit from a stronger connection with government to leverage these issues. *More transparent training is required by banks and financial institutions, which they could assist in delivering* according to interviewees. A proposed solution could be to involve police inside regulators to audit and monitor financial institutions, but unfortunately, this would be deemed abusive.

Multiple underground "hundi," "hawala," and "chop" remittance systems, are indispensable to countries' economic lives in the Middle East, South and East Asia, whilst also being utilized in the western financial community. They are used by drug traffickers, such as the "cambios" in Latin America, and non-bank institutions. According to professionals' opinion: *Finding a way to regulate these remittance systems is going to be one of the hardest challenges in* CTF.

The key solution suggested is *to solve the problems encountered internationally at first by judicial agreements and know how.* There is also *a need for a moderator to be the bridge between countries involved in fighting* TF, *which needs to happen in a transparent manner.*

PART 4

New Counter-terrorism Financing Convention Model and Recommendations

Introduction to Part 4

This study will provide a significant contribution to the area of International Legal Compliance by identifying risks that have not been acknowledged in previous legislations, and by offering the international community a new tool to fight TF. Part 4 explains the importance of a new Counter-terrorism Financing Convention model and proposes a new CTF tool to be used by international actors. This part will also offer a range of recommendations, which will include those found within existing legislations and policies as well as concepts derived from the analysis in Chapter 7.

Chapter 9 will discuss the importance of a new CTF framework and the way to create a context in which this legal tool will have the best chances of being implemented.

Chapter 10 will provide a new CTF Model, which will include specific topics that were found to be crucial in Chapter 7.

Chapter 11 will offer recommendations of ways to strengthen worldwide detection, prevention and enforcement. It will propose the inclusion of specific areas of concerns, including actors' involvement and cooperation at the domestic and international levels, collaboration with the private sector and global financial units' development.

 | DOI:10.1163/9789004409675_014

CHAPTER 9

The Importance of a New CTF Framework

The salience of a new model comes from the increasing terrorist threat. Many conventions, recommendations and national laws offer a whole host of options as ways to tackle the TF threat, which is undeniably an issue at the international level. Harmonization through a new tool, including all best practices would allow for better deterrence worldwide. Accordingly, Chapter 10 will provide a toolbox of existing tools, specifically adapted to deal with the obstacles observed throughout this work. The new model provided in the next chapter has to be contextualised regarding its implementation. To justify its legal ratification, it needs to have a concrete foundation. Hence, the idea of a new international coalition is proposed as solid ground for the Convention so as to become legally binding.

From the jurisdictional angle, there needs to be consideration as to which countries would agree to sign such new CTF Model Agreement: independent states, unions of countries and/or states under a treaty mandating them to incorporate the new model? How about Continents? Whilst the idea would appear ambitious, picturing a united world in the fight against terrorism, where continents act as one, provides the right image as to what should be achieved with this new model. Naming the new model is a complex task since the title of the tool should incorporate space and the internet, which remain intangible components.

For the purpose of this study, the proposed structure will be called: "The Alliance for the Safety of our People" and the new legal tool: "The Intercontinental CTF Initiative," namely ASOPICI.

To pursue a common goal of CTF deterrence, the concept of membership will be an integral part of the Convention. However, there could be some reluctance towards the establishment of yet another international association of countries working side by side against the undefined "International Crime of Terrorism" and its financing. The proposed structure will provide new and more comprehensive guidelines that will thus lead to better international cooperation, stronger enforcement and enhance extradition procedures. The New Convention model will incorporate every characteristic reviewed in Chapters 1 to 8 and recall prior Conventions and Recommendations Best Practices. The new tool will propose solutions to defining "Terrorism," its scope and jurisdiction, as well as punishment guidelines for non-compliance, arrest warrant

 | DOI:10.1163/9789004409675_015

provisions, and will define the role of Global Financial Intelligence Units and the Police, who would coordinate cases and their outcomes.

The preamble must begin in a way similar that seen in United Nations and EU Directives, which is to say by recalling the importance of fighting this specific crime. To be coherent, the new Convention model should begin with the use of terms such as international terrorism, funds, designated categories of offences, and financial institutions. By including different types of digital or physical currencies, and incorporating many services providers into the core definitions, the entire Convention will automatically apply to these critical issues, which are for the most part ignored by international binding instruments. The scope of the Convention, the definition of the offences, and the jurisdiction requirement parts will describe the context in which this Convention is applicable and what constitutes a crime pertaining to it. The novelty of this Convention is the creation of a group of nations named the "Alliance for The Safety of Our People," which will be necessary to provide signatories and enforcement of this Convention. This association will offer mediation and punitive guidelines, as well as administrative support being proposed for countries willing to participate.

Knowledge, intent, and "arrangements" to fund TF should be included in the new Convention. Moreover, ML should be made a predicate crime, while TF ought to become a stand-alone offence. Indirect contribution and encouraging terrorist actions with knowledge of participation must be an equally serious crime. This new Convention Model will consider methods of financing, which will encounter legislating issues. such as wire transfers, new payment technologies, precious commodities, casino laundering, private donations and charities. Regarding this matter, houses of remittance and gambling institutions will be required to register and report threshold amounts. Non-designated financial institutions will also be part of the definitions of this Convention.

As previously recognized in Chapter 7, Islamic finances cannot realistically correspond to the actual definitions of "customer" and "financial institution." This matter should therefore be resolved by implementing a definition countries will be bound to. The definitions of "funds" and "financial institution," shall also include e-currencies and its providers, as new payment technologies are one of the major threats in our century and the only way to apply this entire convention to such issue is to include it directly into the core definition. Beneficial ownership, as seen in European Directives, is a term that demands to be defined more clearly to ensure that legal persons, including companies, hold adequate, accurate, and updated information on their own beneficial ownership. They should make this information readily available to both competent authorities and obliged entities on request. Trustees should also be required to disclose their status to obliged entities.

As pointed out in Chapter 3, PEPs and their entourage must also be defined more clearly to find funds they might dissimulate and recognize the right individuals as PEPs before and a few years after their mandates end. Bribery of foreign officials and abuse of public officials' functions are a worldwide reality, which leave space for criminals to collect money that was once in government hands. This Convention will make provisions to encompass these relevant issues. Preventive measures and reporting requirements will be highlighted, as well as the dangerousness of tipping-off. The protection of victims and reporting persons should also be mentioned within a new legal tool, as well as immunity from liability for disclosure of information. Employee's participation will always remain a risk. Strong measures should therefore be implemented to discourage individuals willing to cooperate with criminals. The non-face to face nature of financial institutions nowadays remains hard to regulate. Hence, collaboration with the private sector should indeed be envisioned in the Convention, along with the proposition of the creation of a task force and training system for actors involved in CTF. A procedure change for financial institutions is required internally to make change possible as, it would be hard to force financial institutions to report "without delay," or "with the shortest possible time," any information related to TF, and even more complex to help them perceive the difference between ML and TF factors.

Each Party shall ensure that it can search, trace, identify, freeze, seize and confiscate property, of a licit or illicit origin, used or alleged to be used by any means, in whole or in part, for the financing of terrorism, or the proceeds of this offence, and to provide co-operation to this end to the widest possible extent. Forfeiture of terrorist property and its profit requires strong border control cooperation, which shall be regulated under the new Model Convention. Under certain conditions, the restitution of a minimum amount to live on once assets are seized should become a possibility, while clarifying the listing, delisting process should become a priority.

A major mission of this model is to define privacy and civil liberties rights and obligations at the international level. International cooperation and coordination is also a key point to incorporate in this tool to strengthen information exchange worldwide and prevent crimes, while exchanging information on assets that could be recovered at some point by one state. A complex task for this Convention is to include extradition provision that would allow countries to prosecute those who attempted to finance or financed terrorist activities. An international regulation pertaining to terrorism shall include a mechanism to recover money derived from seized assets and build a common fund to compensate victims of terrorist acts.

This Convention shall lead to the appointment a centralized agency and competent authority, which will deliver realistic penalties, technical assistance, the creation of procedures, guidelines and training to standardize the CTF system. On a more technical level, this Convention includes articles from the lists of tools offered in Chapter 1, specifically customized for this new legal instrument, as well as articles related to the gap analysis. Required definitions, dates and sanctions envisioned for the new Convention must provide adequate answers and fill the gaps in this field, identified in the previous chapters. Three key provisions will also be inserted into the new Convention, namely, participation of society as seen previously in UNCAC, the creation of a fund to compensate victims, and the denial of refugee status. The lattermost will aim at refusing access to a country's territory to a person with strong links to terrorism, who would be a potential threat and might commit an attack or aid another terrorist with similar ideals.

The matters that it will be difficult to find answers to are the strong link between the definition of terrorism and state sponsored terrorism, the differentiation between TF and other serious financial crimes by professionals, and the complexity of harmonizing procedures. It will take time for internal procedures to become uniform, have less delays and be less burdensome. Recalling that these were some of the salient issues highlighted in Chapter 8.

CHAPTER 10

Building a New Counter-terrorism Financing Model

The International Convention for the Prevention, Detection, Reporting and Enforcement of the Grave Crime against the International Community of Terrorism Financing

•••

The Alliance for the Safety of our People: "Intercontinental CTF Initiative" (ASOPICI)
October 2019

•
•
•

The States Parties to this Convention,[1]

CONSCIOUS of the implications of acts of terrorism for international security;
BELIEVING that the commission of such crimes is a matter of grave concern to the international community and calls for the use of modern and effective methods on an international scale;
CONSIDERING that unlawful acts of Terrorism and their Financing jeopardize the safety of persons and property, seriously affects the security and undermine the confidence of the people of the world in the safety of Nations;
CONSIDERING FURTHERMORE that the occurrence of such acts is a matter of group concern to the international community as a whole;
CONVINCED that, for the purpose of deterring such acts, there is an urgent need to provide appropriate measures for punishment of offenders;
AFFIRMING that matters not regulated by this Convention continue to be governed by the rules and principles of general law;

1 Based on the introductory statements of the United Nations, the European Union, and other International Institutions Counter-Terrorism legal and advisory tools.

 | DOI:10.1163/9789004409675_016

HAVING IN MIND the purposes and principles of the Charter of the United Nations concerning the maintenance of international peace and security and the promotion of good-neighborliness and friendly relations and co-operation among States;
RECOGNIZING in particular that everyone has the right to life, liberty and security of person, as set out in the Universal Declaration of Human Rights and the International Covenant on Civil and Political Rights;
DEEPLY CONCERNED about the world-wide escalation of acts of terrorism in all its forms, which endanger or take innocent human lives, jeopardize fundamental freedoms and seriously impair the dignity of human beings;
CONSIDERING resolution 58/187 of the United Nations General Assembly, which reaffirmed that States must ensure that any measures taken to combat terrorism complies with their obligations under international law, in particular international human rights, refugee and humanitarian law;
REITERATES it call upon all States to adopt further measures in accordance with the relevant provisions of international law, including international standards of human rights, to prevent terrorism and to strengthen international cooperation in combatting terrorism and, to that end, to consider, in particular, the adoption of the measures set out in paragraphs 3 (a) to (f) if the United Nations Resolution 51/210;
RECALLING resolution 40/61 of the General Assembly of the United Nations of 9 December 1985 which, inter alia, "*urges all States unilaterally and in co-operation with other States, as well as relevant United Nations organs, to contribute to the progressive elimination of causes underlying international terrorism and to pay special attention to all situations, including colonialism, racism and situations involving mass and flagrant violations of human rights and fundamental freedoms and those involving alien occupation, that may give rise to international terrorism and may endanger international peace and security*";
BEING CONVINCED of the urgent need to develop international co-operation between States in devising and adopting effective and practical measures for the prevention of such acts of terrorism, and the prosecution and punishment of their perpetrators;
AWARE OF THE NEED FOR international cooperation to establish, in conformity with National law of each State Party and with this Convention, effective measures for the protection of people of the world;
RECOGNIZING the urgency of strengthening and establishing new forms of regional cooperation against terrorism with a view to its eradication;
AWARE of the growing links between terrorism and organized crime, including the illicit traffic of arms, drugs and money-laundering;
NOTING that the number and seriousness of acts of international terrorism depend on the financing that terrorists may obtain;

BELIEVING that one of these methods consists in depriving criminals of the proceeds from crime;
CONVINCED that terrorism constitutes a serious violation of human rights and, in particular, the rights to physical integrity, life, freedom and security, and impedes socio-economic development through destabilization of States;
CONVINCED FURTHER that terrorism cannot be justified under any circumstances and, consequently, should be combated in all its forms and manifestations, including those in which States are involved directly or indirectly, without regard to its origin, causes and objectives;
BELIEVING that there is an urgent need to adopt appropriate and effective measures for the prevention and punishment of such crimes;
CONVINCED that the adoption, ratification, and effective implementation of the ASOP CTF Convention contribute to the progressive development and the codification of international law;
REAFFIRMING the commitment of the states to prevent, combat, punish, and eliminate terrorism;
CONVINCED that this Convention should facilitate the international safety;
AFFIRMING FURTHER that matters not regulated by this Convention continue to be governed by the rules and principles of general international law;
DETERMINED to eliminate terrorism in all its forms and manifestations;
RECALLING the United Nations Resolutions 1368 (2001) and 1373 (2001) of the United Nations Security Council, which reflect international will to combat terrorism in all its forms and manifestations, and which assigned tasks and responsibilities to States, and taking into account the continued threat from terrorist attacks;
NOTING that the activities of military forces of States are governed by rules of international law outside of the framework of this Convention and that the exclusion of certain actions from the coverage of this Convention does not condone or make lawful otherwise unlawful acts, or preclude prosecution under other laws.

The States Parties to this Convention have agreed as follows:

Table of Contents

Article 36: Prohibition of Tipping-off
Article 37: Action Taken on Suspicious Activity Reports
Article 38: Anonymous Testimony and Witness Protection
Article 39: Enhanced Customer Due Diligence
Article 40: Increased Diligence of Financial Institutions
Article 41: Implementation, and Role of Regulatory and Other Administrative Authorities
Article 42: Implementation of KYC Standards in a Cross-border Context
Article 43: Privacy and Civil Liberty
Article 44: Notification of Documents
Article 45: Private Sector Collaboration
Article 46: Cooperation Between National Authorities and the Private Sector
Article 47: AML/CTF Compliance Officer
Article 48: Internal Procedures, Training and Feedback
Article 49: Anti-money-laundering and Counter-terrorism Financing Program
Article 50: Supervision
Article 51: Bank Secrecy
Article 52: Protection of Identity of Persons Making Reports
Article 53: Bribery in the Private Sector
Article 54: Embezzlement of Property in the Private Sector
Article 55: Participation of Society
Article 56: Collection, Exchange and Analysis of Information on the Nature of Organized Crime
Article 57: Exchange of Information
Article 58: Protection Measures
Article 59: Training and Technical Assistance
Article 60: Information Exchange and Training
Article 61: International Cooperation and Coordination
Article 62: Co-operation Between FIUS
Article 63: Access to Information
Article 64: Confidentiality
Article 65: Relations with Foreign Counterpart Agency
Article 66: International Co-operation for Postponement of Suspicious Transactions
Article 67: Content of Request
Article 68: Requests for Information on Banking Transactions
Article 69: Requests for the Monitoring of Banking Transactions
Article 70: Plurality of Requests
Article 71: Mutual Legal Assistance

Article 72: Border Measures

Article 73: Investigations

Article 74: Joint Investigations

Article 75: Special Investigative Powers and Techniques

Article 76: Prevention and Detection of Transfers of Proceeds of Crime

Article 77: Asset Freezing, Seizure, Confiscation & Recovery

Article 78: Seizure of Cash

Article 79: Obligation to Take Provisional Measures

Article 80: Execution of Provisional Measures

Article 81: Freezing of Funds Associated with Financing of Terrorism

Article 82: Obligation to Confiscate

Article 83: Confiscation Measures

Article 84: Provisional Measures and Confiscation

Article 85: Confiscation and Seizure

Article 86: Confiscation of Property of Criminal Organizations

Article 87: Execution of Confiscation

Article 88: Confiscated Property

Article 89: Right of Enforcement and Maximum Amount of Confiscation

Article 90: Surrender of Property

Article 91: Forfeiture of Terrorist Cash

Article 92: Disposal of Confiscated Proceeds of Crime or Property

Article 93: Management of Seized Funds and Property

Article 94: Proceeds of Foreign Crimes.

Article 95: Return of Cash Necessary to Satisfy Essential Human Needs

Article 96: Review of Designation, Delisting and Unfreezing

Article 97: Establishment of a Central Authority for Seizure and Confiscation

Article 98: Transfer of Criminal Proceedings

Article 99: International Cooperation for Purposes of Confiscation

Article 100: Informational Gateways and Mutual Legal Assistance Treaties

Article 101: Funds to Compensate Victims

Article 102: Establishment of Criminal Record

Article 103: Denial of Refugee Status

Article 104: Enforcement

Article 105: Penalties

Article 106: Association or Conspiracy to Commit Terrorist-Financing

Article 107: Penalties Applicable to Legal Persons

Article 108: Penalties Applicable to Corporate Entities

Article 109: Penalties Imposed by Disciplinary or Supervisory Authorities

Article 110: Statute of Limitations

Article 111: Central Authority

Article 1: Use of Terms[2]

Except where otherwise expressly indicated or where the context otherwise requires, the following definitions shall apply throughout this Convention:

a) "Alliance for the Safety of Our People (ASOP)" as recognized by State Parties to the Alliance, refers to a group of States that agrees to collaborate in the prevention, detection, reporting and enforcement of international crimes, to surrender distractors of peace to the international community;

b) "Associated property" means property of any of the following descriptions (including property held by the respondent) which is not itself the recoverable property-
   (a) any interest in the recoverable physical or digital property,
   (b) any other interest in the physical or digital property in which the recoverable property subsists;

c) "Beneficial owner" means the natural person(s) who ultimately owns or controls the customer and/or the natural person on whose behalf a transaction or activity is being conducted. It also incorporates those persons who exercise ultimate effective control over a legal person or arrangement. The beneficial owner shall at least include:
   (a) in the case of corporate entities:
      (i) the natural person(s) who ultimately owns or controls a legal entity through direct or indirect ownership or control over a sufficient percentage of the shares or voting rights in that legal entity, including through bearer share holdings, other than a company listed on a regulated market that is subject to disclosure requirements consistent with Community legislation or subject to equivalent international standards; a percentage of 25 % plus one share shall be deemed sufficient to meet this criterion;
      (ii) the natural person(s) who otherwise exercises control over the management of a legal entity:
   (b) in the case of legal entities, such as foundations, and legal arrangements, such as trusts, which administer and distribute funds:

2 Based on terms provided by the International Conventions, National Policies and Recommendations analyzed in Chapter 7.

(i) where the future beneficiaries have already been determined, the natural person(s) who is the beneficiary of 25 % or more of the property of a legal arrangement or entity;
(ii) where the individuals that benefit from the legal arrangement or entity have yet to be determined, the class of persons in whose main interest the legal arrangement or entity is set up or operates;
(iii) the natural person(s) who exercises control over 25 % or more of the property of a legal arrangement or entity;

d) "Betting instrument" means a thing (whether real or virtual):
(a) that represents monetary value or digital currency value; and
(b) that is designed to be used for the purpose of, or for purposes which include:
(i) placing or making a bet; or
(ii) paying out winnings in respect of a bet;
but does not include:
(i) a gaming chip or token; or
(ii) a thing that, under international AML/CTF Rules, is taken not to be a betting instrument;

e) "Business relationship" means a business, professional or commercial relationship which is connected with the professional activities of an obliged entity and which is expected, at the time when the contact is established, to have an element of duration;

f) "Competent authority" refers to all administrative and law enforcement authorities concerned with combating money-laundering and terrorist financing, including the FIU, GFIU, and supervisors;

g) "Confiscation", which includes forfeiture where applicable, means a penalty or a measure, ordered by a court following proceedings in relation to a criminal offence or criminal offences resulting in the final deprivation of physical or digital property;

h) "Correspondent relationship" means:
(a) the provision of banking services by one bank as the correspondent to another bank as the respondent, including providing a current or other liability account and related services, such as cash management, international funds transfers, check clearing, payable-through accounts and foreign exchange services;
(b) the relationships between and among credit institutions and financial institutions including where similar services are provided by a correspondent institution to a respondent institution, and including relationships established for securities transactions or funds transfers;

i) "Designated non-financial businesses and professions"[3] means:
   (a) Casinos (which also includes internet casinos).
   (b) Real estate agents.
   (c) Dealers in precious metals.
   (d) Dealers in precious stones.
   (e) Lawyers, notaries, other independent legal professionals and accountants—this refers to sole practitioners, partners or employed professionals within professional firms. It is not meant to refer to "internal" professionals that are employees of other types of businesses, nor to professionals working for government agencies, who may already be subject to measures that would combat money-laundering;

j) "Designated categories of offences"[4] refers to: the participation in an organized criminal group and racketeering; terrorism, including terrorist financing; trafficking in human beings and migrant smuggling; sexual exploitation, including sexual exploitation of children; illicit trafficking in narcotic drugs and psychotropic substances; illicit arms trafficking; illicit trafficking in stolen and other goods; corruption and bribery; fraud; counterfeiting currency; counterfeiting and piracy of products; environmental crime; murder, grievous bodily injury; kidnapping, illegal restraint and hostage-taking; robbery or theft; smuggling; extortion; forgery; piracy; and insider trading and market manipulation;

k) "Digital currency" means:
   (a) a digital representation of value that:
      (i) functions as a medium of exchange, a store of economic value, or a unit of account; and
      (ii) is not issued by or under the authority of a government
      (iii) body; and
      (iv) is interchangeable with money (including through the crediting of an account) and may be used as consideration for the supply of goods or services; and
      (v) is generally available to members of the public without any restriction on its use as consideration; or
   (b) a means of exchange or digital process or crediting declared to be digital currency by international AML/CTF Rules;

3 Financial Action Task Force (FATF), *International Standards On Combating Money-Laundering and the Financing of Terrorism & Proliferation,* February 2012, http://www.fatf-gafi.org/media/fatf/documents/recommendations/pdfs/FATF_Recommendations.pdf.

4 U.N. Office on Drugs and Crime, *Model Provisions on Money-Laundering, Terrorist Financing, Preventative Measures and Proceeds of Crime,* April 2009, available from http://www.imolin.org/pdf/imolin/Model_Provisions_Final.pdf.

l) "Financial institution" means any person or entity who conducts as a business one or more of the following activities or operations for or on behalf of a customer:
   (a) Acceptance of deposits and other repayable funds from the public;
   (b) Lending;
   (c) Financial leasing;
   (d) The transfer of money or value;
   (e) Issuing and managing means of payment (e.g. credit and debit cards, checks, traveler's checks, money orders and bankers' drafts, electronic money);
   (f) Financial guarantees and commitments;
   (g) Trading in;
      (i) money market instruments (checks, bills, CDs, derivatives etc.);
      (ii) foreign exchange;
      (iii) exchange, interest rate and index instruments;
      (iv) transferable securities;
      (v) commodity futures trading;
   (h) Participation in securities issues and the provision of financial services related to such issues;
   (i) Individual and collective portfolio management;
   (j) Safekeeping and administration of cash or liquid securities on behalf of other persons;
   (k) Otherwise investing, administering or managing funds or money on behalf of other persons;
   (l) Underwriting and placement of life insurance and other investment related insurance;
   (m) Money and currency changing;

This also captures private banking.

This includes inter alia: consumer credit; mortgage credit; factoring, with or without recourse; and finance of commercial transactions (including forfaiting).

This does not extend to financial leasing arrangements in relation to consumer products.

This applies to financial activity in both the formal or informal sector e.g. alternative remittance activity.

This applies both to insurance undertakings and to insurance intermediaries (agents and brokers).

Islamic Finance is comprised in the definition of Financial institution. This allows the ASOPICI Convention to apply to its customers;

m) "Financial Intelligence Unit" (hereinafter referred to as "FIU") means a central, national agency responsible for receiving (and, as permitted, requesting), analyzing and disseminating to the competent authorities, disclosures of financial information:
   (a) concerning suspected proceeds and potential financing of terrorism, or
   (b) required by national legislation or regulation, in order to combat money-laundering and financing of terrorism;

n) "Freezing" or "Seizure" means temporarily prohibiting the transfer, conversion, disposition or movement of property or temporarily assuming custody or control of property on the basis of an order issued by a court or other competent authority;

o) "Funds" means assets of every kind, whether tangible or intangible, movable or immovable, however acquired, and legal documents or instruments in any form, including electronic or digital, evidencing title to, or interest in, such assets, including bank credits, traveler's checks, bank checks, money orders, shares, securities, bonds, drafts and letters of credit without such enumeration being exhaustive;

p) "Gambling services" means a service which involves wagering a stake with monetary value in games of chance, including those with an element of skill such as lotteries, casino games, poker games and betting transactions that are provided at a physical location, or by any means at a distance, by electronic means or any other technology for facilitating communication, and at the individual request of a recipient of services;

q) "Global Financial Intelligence Unit (GFIU)" shares the same attributions than an FIU, yet operates as a stand-alone FIU to gather information from actors and fight TF at the worldwide level;

r) "Grave Crime of International Terrorism (GCIT)" as recognized by Nations as a threat against the International Community and the freedom, safety, integrity and values of its people, shall consists of a group or individual, (apart from a State or institution orders), endangering humans, structures, the environment, using indiscriminate killing and/or taking hostages to attain a goal or spread Terror among a population;

s) "Instrumentalities" means any property used or intended to be used, in any manner, wholly or in part, to commit a criminal offence or criminal offences;

t) "Intercontinental CTF Initiative" from the Alliance for the Safety of our People: (ASOP) as recognized by this Convention, means the Counter-terrorism Financing task force set by ASOP to fight TF at the Intercontinental level;

u) "Legal persons" refers to bodies corporate, foundations, partnerships, or associations, or any similar bodies that can establish a permanent customer relationship with a financial institution or otherwise own property;

v) "Payable-through accounts" refers to correspondent accounts that are used directly by third parties to transact business on their own behalf;

w) "Politically Exposed Person" (PEP) means a natural person who is or who has been entrusted with prominent public functions and includes the following:

(a) Politically Exposed Persons:
   (i) heads of State, heads of government, ministers and deputy or
   (ii) assistant ministers;
   (iii) members of parliament or of similar legislative bodies;
   (iv) members of the governing bodies of political parties;
   (v) members of supreme courts, of constitutional courts or of other high-level judicial bodies, the decisions of which are not subject to further appeal, except in exceptional circumstances;
   (vi) members of courts of auditors or of the boards of central banks;
   (vii) ambassadors, chargés d'affaires and high-ranking officers in the armed forces;
   (viii) members of the administrative, management or supervisory bodies of State-owned enterprises;
   (ix) directors, deputy directors and members of the board or equivalent function of an international organization.

No public function referred to in points (i) to (ix) shall be understood as covering middle-ranking or more junior officials;

Business relationships with family members or close associates of PEPs involve reputational risks similar to those with PEPs themselves. The definition is not intended to cover middle ranking or more junior individuals in the foregoing categories.

(b) Family members includes the following:
   (i) the spouse, or a person considered to be equivalent to a spouse, of a politically exposed person;

(ii) the children and their spouses, or persons considered to be equivalent to a spouse, of a politically exposed person;
(iii) the parents of a politically exposed person;
(c) Persons known to be close associates' means:
(i) natural persons who are known to have joint beneficial ownership of legal entities or legal arrangements, or any other close business relations, with a politically exposed person;
(ii) natural persons who have sole beneficial ownership of a legal entity or legal arrangement which is known to have been set up for the de facto benefit of a politically exposed person;

x) "Proceed of Crime" means any property, derived from or obtained, directly or indirectly, through the commission of an offence;

y) "Property" means assets of any kind, whether corporeal or incorporeal, movable or immovable, tangible or intangible, and legal documents or instruments in any form including electronic or digital, evidencing title to or an interest in such assets;

z) "Property obtained by unlawful conduct"
(a) A person obtains property through unlawful conduct (whether his own conduct or another's) if he obtained property by or in return for the conduct;
(b) In deciding whether any property was obtained through unlawful conduct;
(c) It is immaterial whether or not any money, digital currency, goods or services were provided in order to put the person in question in a position to carry out the conduct;
(d) It is not necessary to show that the conduct was of a particular kind if it is shown that the property was obtained through conduct of one of a number of kinds, each of which would have been unlawful conduct;

aa) "Suspicious Activity Report" (SAR) or "Suspicious Transaction Report" (STR), are filed by Financial Institutions or, by a concerned citizen to the local Financial Intelligence Unit if they have reasonable grounds to believe that a transaction is related to criminal activity;

bb) "Senior management" means an officer or employee with sufficient knowledge of the institution's money-laundering and terrorist financing risk exposure and sufficient seniority to take decisions affecting its risk exposure, and need not, in all cases, be a member of the board of directors;

cc) "Shell bank" means a bank, or a credit institution or financial institution, or an institution that carries out activities equivalent to those carried out by credit institutions and financial institutions, incorporated in a jurisdiction in which it has no physical presence, and which is unaffiliated with a regulated financial group;

dd) "States Parties" means States which have consented to be bound by this Convention and for which this Convention is in force;

ee) "Stored value card means a thing" (whether real or virtual):
   (a) that stores monetary value in a form other than physical currency; or
   (b) that gives access to monetary value stored in a form other than physical currency; or
   (c) that is declared to be a stored value card by the general AML/CTF Rules; but does not include:
   (d) a debit card or a credit card (whether real or virtual) linked to an account provided by a financial institution; or
   (e) unless declared under paragraph (c):
      (i) a thing that is intended to give access to monetary value in a debit card or credit card account provided by a financial institution; or
      (ii) a gaming chip or token, or a betting instrument; or
      (iii) a thing that stores, or gives access to, digital currency; or
   (f) a thing that, is taken not to be a stored value card;

ff) "Supervisors" refers to the designated competent authorities responsible for ensuring compliance by financial institutions with requirements to combat money-laundering and terrorist financing;

gg) "Terrorist" shall mean any natural person who:
   (a) commits, or attempts to commit, terrorist acts by any means, directly or indirectly, unlawfully and willfully;
   (b) participates as an accomplice in terrorist acts;
   (c) organizes or directs others to commit terrorist acts; or (d)
   (d) contributes to the commission of terrorist acts by a group of persons acting with a common purpose where the contribution is made intentionally and with the aim of furthering the terrorist act or with the knowledge of the intention of the group to commit a terrorist act;

hh) "Terrorist act" shall mean:

any act which is a violation of the criminal laws of a State Party and which may endanger the life, physical integrity or freedom of, or cause serious injury or death to, any person, any number or group of persons or causes or may cause damage to public or private property, natural resources, environmental or cultural heritage and is calculated or intended to:

(a) intimidate, put in fear, force, coerce or induce any government, body, institution, the general public or any segment thereof, to do or abstain from doing any act, or to adopt or abandon a particular standpoint, or to act according to certain principles; or
(b) disrupt any public service, the delivery of any essential service to the public or to create a public emergency; or
(c) create general insurrection in a State;

ii) "Terrorism Financing" means the acts set out in Article 2 of the International Convention for the Suppression of the Financing of Terrorism, cited above;

jj) "Trust or company service provider" means any person that, by way of its business, provides any of the following services to third parties:
(a) the formation of companies or other legal persons;
(b) acting as, or arranging for another person to act as, a director or secretary of a company, a partner of a partnership, or a similar position in relation to other legal persons;
(c) providing a registered office, business address, correspondence or administrative address and other related services for a company, a partnership or any other legal person or arrangement;
(d) acting as, or arranging for another person to act as, a trustee of an express trust or a similar legal arrangement;
(e) acting as, or arranging for another person to act as, a nominee shareholder for another person other than a company listed on a regulated market that is subject to disclosure requirements in accordance with National law or subject to equivalent international standards;

Article 2: Scope of the Convention[5,6,7]

1. The purpose of this Convention is to prevent, punish, and eliminate terrorism, and apprehend individuals or groups, with proven knowledge of direct or indirect financial contribution to the GCIT, indiscriminately of

5 Organization of African Unity, *Convention on the Prevention and Combating of Terrorism, (1999)*, 14 July 199, available from http://treaties.un.org/doc/db/Terrorism/OAU-english.pdf.

6 U.N. Office on Drugs and Crime, GAOR resolution 58/4, *Convention Against Corruption*, New York, 31 October 2003, available from http://www.unodc.org/documents/treaties/UNCAC/Publications/Convention/08-50026_E.pdf.

7 U.N. GAOR, *International Convention for the Suppression of Terrorist Bombings*, A/52/653, 25 November 1997, available from http://www.un.org/law/cod/terroris.htm.

the type of aid provided to the commission or attempt to perpetrate a crime.

2. To that end, the States Parties agree to adopt the necessary measures and strengthen cooperation among them, in accordance with the terms of this Convention.
3. This Convention shall promote co-operation among the Parties so that they may address more effectively the various aspects of Terrorism Financing having an international dimension. In carrying out their obligations under the Convention, the Parties shall take necessary measures, including legislative and administrative measures, in conformity with the fundamental provisions of their respective domestic legislative systems.
4. The Parties shall carry out their obligations under this Convention in a manner consistent with the principles of sovereign and territorial integrity of States and that of non-intervention in the domestic affairs of other States.
5. The activities of armed forces during an armed conflict, as those terms are understood under international humanitarian law, which are governed by that law are not governed by this Convention, and the activities undertaken by military forces of a State in the exercise of their official duties, inasmuch as they are governed by other rules of international law, are not governed by this Convention.

Article 3: Offences[8,9,10,11]

1. Any person commits an offence within the meaning of this Convention if that person by any means, directly or indirectly, unlawfully and willfully, provides or collects funds with the intention and knowledge that they are to be used, in full or in part, in order to carry out:

---

8 OAU (1999), *supra.*

9 Proceeds of Crime Act 2002, available from http://www.legislation.gov.uk/ukpga/2002/29/contents. Short Form Citation: PCA (2002), *supra.*

10 U.N. Office on Drugs and Crime, GAOR resolution 55/25, *Convention Against Transnational Organized Crime,* New York, 15 November 2000, available from https://www.unodc.org/documents/treaties/UNTOC/Publications/TOC%20Convention/TOCebook-e.pdf.

11 U.N. GAOR resolution 54/109 *International Convention for the Suppression of the Financing of Terrorism,* 9 December 1999, available from http://www.un.org/law/cod/finterr.htm.

(a) terrorist acts.
(b) designated categories of offences.
(c) any other act intended to cause death or serious bodily injury to a civilian, or to any other person not taking an active part in the hostilities in a situation of armed conflict, when the purpose of such act, by its nature or context, is to intimidate a population, or to compel a government or an international organization to do or to abstain from doing any act.

2. For an act to constitute an offence set forth in paragraph 1, it shall not be necessary that the funds were actually used to carry out an offence referred to in paragraph 1, subparagraphs (a), (b) or (c).
3. Any person also commits an offence if that person attempts to commit an offence as set forth in paragraph 1 of this article.
4. Any person also commits an offence if that person:
   (a) Participates as an accomplice in an offence as set forth in paragraph 1, subparagraphs (a), (b) or (c) of this article;
   (b) Organizes, encourages or directs others to commit an offence as set forth in paragraph 1, subparagraphs (a), (b) or (c) of this article.
5. The laundering of the proceeds of crime shall be criminalized:
   (a) Proceeds of crime shall include:
      (i) The conversion or transfer of property, knowing that such property is the proceeds of crime, for the purpose of concealing or disguising the illicit origin of the property or of helping any person who is involved in the commission of the predicate offence to evade the legal consequences of his or her action;
      (ii) The concealment or disguise of the true nature, source, location, disposition, movement or ownership of or rights with respect to property, knowing that such property is the proceeds of crime.
   (b) Subject to the basic concepts of its legal system:
      (i) The acquisition, possession or use of property, knowing, at the time of receipt, that such property is the proceeds of crime;
      (ii) Participation in, association with or conspiracy to commit, attempts to commit and aiding, abetting, facilitating and counselling the commission of any of the offences established in accordance with this article.
6. A person commits an offence if he enters into or becomes concerned in an arrangement which he knows, or suspects facilitates (by whatever means) the acquisition, retention, use or control of criminal property by or on behalf of another person.

7. Notwithstanding the provisions of Article 1, the struggle waged by peoples in accordance with the principles of international law for their liberation or self-determination, including armed struggle against colonialism, occupation, aggression and domination by foreign forces shall not be considered as terrorist acts.

Article 4: Participation and Attempt[12]

1. Each State Party shall adopt such legislative and other measures as may be necessary to establish as a criminal offence, in accordance with its domestic law, participation in any capacity such as an accomplice, assistant or instigator in an offence established in accordance with this Convention.
2. Each State Party may adopt such legislative and other measures as may be necessary to establish as a criminal offence, in accordance with its domestic law, any attempt to commit an offence established in accordance with this Convention.
3. Each State Party may adopt such legislative and other measures as may be necessary to establish as a criminal offence, in accordance with its domestic law, the preparation for an offence established in accordance with this Convention.

Article 5: Knowledge, Intent and Purpose as Elements of an Offence[13]

Knowledge, intent or purpose required as an element of an offence established in accordance with this Convention may be inferred from objective factual circumstances.

Article 6: Concealment[14]

Each State Party shall consider adopting such legislative and other measures as may be necessary to establish as a criminal offence, when committed

12 U.N. Office on Drugs and Crime, GAOR resolution 58/4, *Convention Against Corruption*, New York, 31 October 2003, available from http://www.unodc.org/documents/treaties/UNCAC/Publications/Convention/08-50026_E.pdf.

13 GAOR 55/25, *supra*.

14 GAOR 58/4, *supra*.

intentionally after the commission of any of the offences established in accordance with this Convention without having participated in such offences, the concealment or continued retention of property when the person involved knows that such property is the result of any of the offences established in accordance with this Convention.

Article 7: Embezzlement, Misappropriation or Other Diversion of Property by a Public Official[15,16]

1. Each State Party shall adopt such legislative and other measures as may be necessary to establish as criminal offences, when committed intentionally, the embezzlement, misappropriation or other diversion by a public official for his or her benefit or for the benefit of another person or entity, of any property, public or private funds or securities or any other thing of value entrusted to the public official by virtue of his or her position.
2. "Bribery of its own public official" shall be made a predicate offence for money-laundering and terrorism-financing legislation on the same terms, when a Party has made either active or passive bribery of its own public official such an offence. When a Party has made only passive bribery of its own public officials a predicate offence for money-laundering or terrorism-financing purposes, this article requires that the laundering of the bribe payment be subject to money-laundering legislation.
3. In order to combat bribery of foreign public officials effectively, each Party shall take such measures as may be necessary, within the framework of its laws and regulations regarding the maintenance of books and records, financial statement disclosures, and accounting and auditing standards, to prohibit the establishment of off-the-books accounts, the making of off-the-books or inadequately identified transactions, the recording of non-existent expenditures, the entry of liabilities with incorrect identification of their object, as well as the use of false documents, by companies subject to those laws and regulations, for the purpose of bribing foreign public officials or of hiding such bribery.
4. Each Party shall provide effective, proportionate and dissuasive civil, administrative or criminal penalties for such omissions and falsifications in

15 GAOR 58/4, *supra*.

16 Organisation for Economic Co-Operation and Development (OECD), *OECD Convention on Combating Bribery of Foreign Public Officials in International Business Transactions*, 17 December 1997, available from http://www.oecd.org/corruption/oecdantibriberyconvention.htm.

respect of the books, records, accounts and financial statements of such companies.

Article 8: Abuse of Functions[17]

Each State Party shall consider adopting such legislative and other measures as may be necessary to establish as a criminal offence, when committed intentionally, the abuse of functions or position, that is, the performance of or failure to perform an act, in violation of laws, by a public official in the discharge of his or her functions, for the purpose of obtaining an undue advantage for himself or herself or for another person or entity.

Article 9: Jurisdiction[18,19,20]

1. This Convention shall not apply where the offence is committed within a single State, the victims and the alleged offender are nationals of that State and the alleged offender is found in the territory of that State.
2. For the purpose of paragraph 1 of this article, Each State Party shall take such measures as may be necessary to establish its jurisdiction over the offences set forth in article 3 in the following cases:
   (a) an offence is transnational in nature if:
      (i) It is committed in more than one State;
      (ii) It is committed in one State but a substantial part of its preparation, planning, direction or control takes place in another State;
      (iii) It is committed in one State but involves an organized criminal group that engages in criminal activities in more than one State; or
      (iv) It is committed in one State but has substantial effects in another State.
   (b) when the offence is committed in the territory of that State or on board a ship or aircraft registered in that State;

17 GAOR 58/4, *supra*.

18 U.S. Dep't. of State, Bureau of International Security and Nonproliferation, *Protocol of 2005 to the Convention for the Suppression of Unlawful Acts Against the Safety of Maritime Navigation*, LEG/CONF.15/22, 1 November 2005, available from https://www.state.gov/t/isn/trty/81728.htm.

19 GAOR 55/25, *supra*.

20 GAOR 54/109, *supra*.

(c) when the alleged offender is a national of that State or, if that State considers it appropriate, by those stateless persons who have their habitual residence in its territory;

3. A State Party may also establish its jurisdiction over any such offence when:
   (a) It is committed by a stateless person whose habitual residence is that State; or
   (b) During its commission a national of that State is seized, threatened, injured or killed; or against a State or government facility of that State abroad, including diplomatic or consular premises of that State;
   (c) It is committed in an attempt to compel that State to do or abstain from doing any act.
4. Each State Party shall likewise take such measures as may be necessary to establish its jurisdiction over these offences in cases where the alleged offender is present in its territory and it does not extradite him.
5. Upon ratifying, accepting, approving or acceding to this Convention, each State Party shall notify the Secretary of the Alliance of the jurisdiction it has established in accordance with paragraph 2. Should any change take place, the State Party concerned shall immediately notify the Secretary of the Alliance.
6. When more than one State Party claims jurisdiction over the offences set forth in article 3, the relevant States Parties shall strive to coordinate their actions appropriately, in particular concerning the conditions for prosecution and the modalities for mutual legal assistance.
7. Without prejudice to the norms of general international law, this Convention does not exclude the exercise of any criminal jurisdiction established by a State Party in accordance with its domestic law.
8. Nothing in this Convention shall be constructed as justifying the violation of the territorial integrity of political independence of a State in contravention of the Charter of the United Nations and the Alliance principles.

Article 10: Protection of Sovereignty[21]

1. States Parties shall carry out their obligations under this Convention in a manner consistent with the principles of sovereign equality and territorial integrity of States and that of non-intervention in the domestic affairs of other States.

21 GAOR 55/25, *supra*.

2. Nothing in this Convention entitles a State Party to undertake in the territory of another State the exercise of jurisdiction and performance of functions that are reserved exclusively for the authorities of that other State by its domestic law.

Article 11: Prevention[22,23,24]

1. States Parties shall endeavor to develop and evaluate national projects and to establish and promote best practices and policies aimed at the prevention of transnational organized crime.
2. States Parties shall endeavor, in accordance with fundamental principles of their domestic law, to reduce existing or future opportunities for organized criminal groups to participate in lawful markets with proceeds of crime, through appropriate legislative, administrative or other measures. These measures should focus on:
   - (a) The strengthening of cooperation between law enforcement agencies or prosecutors and relevant private entities, including industry;
   - (b) The promotion of the development of standards and procedures designed to safeguard the integrity of public and relevant private entities, as well as codes of conduct for relevant professions, in particular lawyers, notaries public, tax consultants and accountants;
   - (c) The prevention of the misuse by organized criminal groups of tender procedures conducted by public authorities and of subsidies and licenses granted by public authorities for commercial activity;
   - (d) The prevention of the misuse of legal persons by organized criminal groups; such measures could include:
     - (i) The establishment of public records on legal and natural persons involved in the establishment, management and funding of legal persons;
     - (ii) The introduction of the possibility of disqualifying by court order or any appropriate means for a reasonable period of time persons convicted of offences covered by this Convention

---

22 Financial Action Task Force (FATF) on Money-Laundering, *The Forty Recommendations*, (1990), available from http://www.fatf-gafi.org/media/fatf/documents/recommendations/pdfs/FATF%20Recommendations%201990.pdf

23 GAOR 55/25, *supra*.

24 GAOR 58/4, *supra*.

from acting as directors of legal persons incorporated within their jurisdiction;

(iii) The establishment of national records of persons disqualified from acting as directors of legal persons;

(iv) and (iv) The exchange of information contained in the records referred to in subparagraphs (d) (i) and (iii) of this paragraph with the competent authorities of other States Parties.

3. States Parties shall endeavor to promote the reintegration into society of persons convicted of offences covered by this Convention.
4. States Parties shall endeavor to evaluate periodically existing relevant legal instruments and administrative practices with a view to detecting their vulnerability to misuse by organized criminal groups.
5. States Parties shall endeavor to promote public awareness regarding the existence, causes and gravity of and the threat posed by transnational organized crime. Information may be disseminated where appropriate through the mass media and shall include measures to promote public participation in preventing and combating such crime.
6. Each State Party shall inform the Secretary of the Alliance of the name and address of the authority or authorities that can assist other States Parties in developing measures to prevent transnational organized crime.

Article 12: Preventive Measures[25,26]

1. States Parties shall, as appropriate, collaborate with each other and relevant international and regional organizations in promoting and developing the measures referred to in this article. This includes participation in international projects aimed at the prevention of transnational organized crime, for example by alleviating the circumstances that render socially marginalized groups vulnerable to the action of transnational organized crime.
2. Member States shall take all appropriate measures in order to protect employees of the institutions or persons covered by this Convention who

---

25 FATF (1990), *supra.*

26 European Union, *Directive 2005/60/EC of the European Parliament and of the Council of 26 October 2005 on the prevention of the use of the financial system for the purpose of money-laundering and terrorist financing,* 26 October 2005, available from http://eur-lex.europa.eu/legal-content/EN/TXT/?uri=CELEX%3A32005L0060.

report suspicions of money-laundering or terrorist financing either internally or to the FIU from being exposed to threats or hostile action.

3. Member States shall require the institutions and persons covered by this Convention to keep the following documents and information for use in any investigation into, or analysis of, possible money-laundering or terrorist financing by the FIU or by other competent authorities in accordance with national law:
   (a) in the case of the customer due diligence, a copy or the references of the evidence required, for a period of at least five years after the business relationship with their customer has ended;
   (b) in the case of business relationships and transactions, the supporting evidence and records, consisting of the original documents or copies admissible in court proceedings under the applicable national legislation for a period of at least five years following the carrying-out of the transactions or the end of the business relationship.
4. Countries should establish a FIU that serves as a national center for the receiving (and, as permitted, requesting), analysis and dissemination of STR and other information regarding potential money-laundering or terrorist financing. The FIU should have access, directly or indirectly, on a timely basis to the financial, administrative and law enforcement information that it requires to properly undertake its functions, including the analysis of STR.
5. Countries should ensure that designated law enforcement authorities have responsibility for money-laundering and terrorist financing investigations. Countries are encouraged to support and develop, as far as possible, special investigative techniques suitable for the investigation of money-laundering, such as controlled delivery, undercover operations and other relevant techniques. Countries are also encouraged to use other effective mechanisms such as the use of permanent or temporary groups specialized in asset investigation, and co-operative investigations with appropriate competent authorities in other countries.
6. When conducting investigations of money-laundering and underlying predicate offences, competent authorities should be able to obtain documents and information for use in those investigations, and in prosecutions and related actions. This should include powers to use compulsory measures for the production of records held by financial institutions and other persons, for the search of persons and premises, and for the seizure and obtaining of evidence.

7. Supervisors should have adequate powers to monitor and ensure compliance by financial institutions with requirements to combat money-laundering and terrorist financing, including the authority to conduct inspections. They should be authorized to compel production of any information from financial institutions that is relevant to monitoring such compliance, and to impose adequate administrative sanctions for failure to comply with such requirements.
8. Countries should provide their competent authorities involved in combating money-laundering and terrorist financing with adequate financial, human and technical resources. Countries should have in place processes to ensure that the staff of those authorities are of high integrity.
9. Countries should ensure that policy makers, the FIU, law enforcement and supervisors have effective mechanisms in place which enable them to co-operate, and where appropriate coordinate domestically with each other concerning the development and implementation of policies and activities to combat money-laundering and terrorist financing.
10. Countries should ensure that their competent authorities can review the effectiveness of their systems to combat money-laundering and terrorist financing systems by maintaining comprehensive statistics on matters relevant to the effectiveness and efficiency of such systems. This should include statistics on the STR received and disseminated; on money-laundering and terrorist financing investigations, prosecutions and convictions; on property frozen, seized and confiscated; and on mutual legal assistance or other international requests for co-operation.

Article 13: Transparency of Legal Persons and Arrangements[27]

1. Countries should take measures to prevent the unlawful use of legal persons by money-launderers. Countries should ensure that there is adequate, accurate and timely information on the beneficial ownership and control of legal persons that can be obtained or accessed in a timely fashion by competent authorities. In particular, countries that have legal persons that are able to issue bearer shares should take appropriate measures to ensure that they are not misused for money-laundering and be

27 FATF (1990), *supra*.

able to demonstrate the adequacy of those measures. Countries could consider measures to facilitate access to beneficial ownership and control information to financial institutions.

2. Countries should take measures to prevent the unlawful use of legal arrangements by money-launderers. In particular, countries should ensure that there is adequate, accurate and timely information on express trusts, including information on the settlor, trustee and beneficiaries, that can be obtained or accessed in a timely fashion by competent authorities. Countries could consider measures to facilitate access to beneficial ownership and control information to financial institutions.

Article 14: Transposition[28,29]

1. Member States shall ensure that competent authorities establish effective and reliable mechanisms to encourage the reporting to competent authorities of potential or actual breaches of the national provisions transposing this Convention.
2. The mechanisms referred to in paragraph 1 shall include at least:
   (a) specific procedures for the receipt of reports on breaches and their follow-up;
   (b) appropriate protection for employees or persons in a comparable position, of obliged entities who report breaches committed within the obliged entity;
   (c) appropriate protection for the accused person;
   (d) protection of personal data concerning both the person who reports the breaches and the natural person who is allegedly responsible for a breach;
   (e) clear rules that ensure that confidentiality is guaranteed in all cases in relation to the person who reports the breaches committed within the obliged entity, unless disclosure is required by national law in the context of further investigations or subsequent judicial proceedings.

28 EU (2005), *supra.*

29 European Union, *Directive (EU) 2018/843 of the European Parliament and of the Council of 30 May 2018 amending Directive (EU) 2015/849 on the prevention of the use of the financial system for the purposes of money-laundering or terrorist financing, and amending Directives 2009/138/EC and 2013/36/EU*, 30 May 2018, available from https://eur-lex.europa.eu/legal-content/EN/TXT/PDF/?uri=CELEX:32018L0843& from=EN.

3. Member States shall require obliged entities to have in place appropriate procedures for their employees, or persons in a comparable position, to report breaches internally through a specific, independent and anonymous channel, proportionate to the nature and size of the obliged entity concerned.

Article 15: Reports of Suspicious Matters[30,31,32]

1. A suspicious matter reporting obligation arises for a reporting entity in relation to a person (the first person) if, at a particular time (the relevant time):
   (a) the reporting entity commences to provide, or proposes to provide, a designated service to the first person; or
   (b) both:
      (i) the first person requests the reporting entity to provide a designated service to the first person; and
      (ii) the designated service is of a kind ordinarily provided by the reporting entity; or
   (c) both:
      (i) the first person inquires of the reporting entity whether the reporting entity would be willing or prepared to provide a designated service to the first person; and
      (ii) the designated service is of a kind ordinarily provided by the reporting entity; and any of the following conditions is satisfied.
   (d) at the relevant time or a later time, the reporting entity suspects on reasonable grounds that the first person is not the person the first person claims to be;
   (e) at the relevant time or a later time, the reporting entity suspects on reasonable grounds that an agent of the first person who deals with the reporting entity in relation to the provision or prospective

30 Australian Government Federal Register of Legislation, *Anti-Money-Laundering and Counter-Terrorism Financing Act 2006 No. 169*, 2006, available from https://www.legislation.gov.au/Details/C2006A00169.

31 EU (2005), *supra*.

32 Australian Government Federal Register of Legislation, *Anti-Money-Laundering and Counter-Terrorism Financing Rules Instrument 2007 (No. 1)*, 10 April 2007, available from https://www.legislation.gov.au/Details/F2007L01000/Html/Text.

provision of the designated service is not the person the agent claims to be;

(f) at the relevant time or a later time, the reporting entity suspects on reasonable grounds that information that the reporting entity has concerning the provision, or prospective provision, of the service:
   (i) may be relevant to investigation of, or prosecution of a person for, an evasion, or an attempted evasion, of a taxation law; or
   (ii) may be relevant to investigation of, or prosecution of a person for, an evasion, or an attempted evasion, of a law of a State or Territory that deals with taxation; or
   (iii) may be relevant to investigation of, or prosecution of a person for, an offence against International Customary law or of a State or Territory of the Alliance; or
   (iv) may be of assistance in the enforcement Proceeds of Crimes; or
   (v) may be of assistance in the enforcement of a law of a State of the Alliance;

(g) at the relevant time or a later time, the reporting entity suspects on reasonable grounds that the provision, or prospective provision, of the service is preparatory to the commission of an offence covered article 3;

(h) at the relevant time or a later time, the reporting entity suspects on reasonable grounds that information that the reporting entity has concerning the provision, or prospective provision, of the service may be relevant to the investigation of, or prosecution of a person for, an offence covered article 3;

(i) at the relevant time or a later time, the reporting entity suspects on reasonable grounds that the provision, or prospective provision, of the service is preparatory to the commission of an offence covered by paragraph the definition of money-laundering;

(j) at the relevant time or a later time, the reporting entity suspects on reasonable grounds that information that the reporting entity has concerning the provision, or prospective provision, of the service may be relevant to the investigation of, or prosecution of a person for, an offence covered by the definition of money-laundering.

2. Member States shall require that all casino customers be identified, and their identity verified if they purchase or exchange gambling chips with a value of $2000 or more.

3. Casinos subject to State supervision shall be deemed in any event to have satisfied the customer due diligence requirements if they register, identify and verify the identity of their customers immediately on or before entry, regardless of the amount of gambling chips purchased.

Article 16: Reporting of Suspicions[33]

1. Applicable customer identification procedure with respect to individuals:
   (a) In so far as a reporting entity has any customer who is an individual, must comply with the requirements specified in this Convention.
   (b) Must include appropriate risk-based systems and controls that are designed to enable the reporting entity to be reasonably satisfied, where a customer is an individual, that the customer is the individual that he or she claims to be.
2. Collection of information:
   (a) Must include a procedure for the reporting entity to collect, at a minimum, the following KYC information from an individual (other than an individual who notifies the reporting entity that he or she is a customer of the reporting entity in his or her capacity as a sole trader):
      (i) the customer's full name;
      (ii) the customer's date of birth; and
      (iii) the customer's residential address.
   (b) Must include a procedure for the reporting entity to collect, at a minimum, the following KYC information from a customer who notifies the reporting entity that he or she is a customer of the reporting entity in his or her capacity as a sole trader:
      (i) the customer's full name;
      (ii) the customer's date of birth;
      (iii) the full business name (if any) under which the customer carries on his or her business;
      (iv) the full address of the customer's principal place of business (if any) or the customer's residential address; and
      (v) any ABN issued to the customer.
   (c) Must include appropriate risk-based systems and controls for the reporting entity to determine whether, in addition to the KYC

33 AMLCTFRI (2007), *supra*.

information, any other KYC information will be collected from a customer.

Note: Reporting entities should consider their obligations under other legislation, when deciding what information is required to be collected to fulfil their obligations under these Rules.

3. Verification of information:
   (a) Must include a procedure for the reporting entity to verify, at a minimum, the following KYC information about a customer:
      (1) the customer's full name; and
      (2) either:
         (i) the customer's date of birth; or
         (ii) the customer's residential address.
   (b) Must require that the verification of information collected about a customer be based on:
      (1) reliable and independent documentation;
      (2) reliable and independent electronic data; or
      (3) a combination of (1) and (2) above.
   (c) Must include appropriate risk-based systems and controls for the reporting entity to determine whether, in addition to the KYC information, any other KYC information collected from the customer should be verified from reliable and independent documentation, reliable and independent electronic data or a combination of the two.

Article 17: Reporting of Suspicious Transactions and Compliance[34]

1. If a financial institution suspects or has reasonable grounds to suspect that funds are the proceeds of a criminal activity, or are related to terrorist financing, it should be required, directly by law or regulation, to report promptly its suspicions to the Financial Intelligence Unit (FIU).
2. Financial institutions, their directors, officers and employees should be:
   (a) Protected by legal provisions from criminal and civil liability for breach of any restriction on disclosure of information imposed by contract or by any legislative, regulatory or administrative provision, if they report their suspicions in good faith to the FIU, even if they did not know precisely what the underlying criminal activity was, and regardless of whether illegal activity actually occurred.

34 FATF (1990), *supra*.

(b) Prohibited by law from disclosing the fact that a Suspicious Transaction Report (STR) or related information is being reported to the FIU.

3. Financial institutions should develop programs against money-laundering and terrorist financing. These programs should include:
   (a) The development of internal policies, procedures and controls, including appropriate compliance management arrangements, and adequate screening procedures to ensure high standards when hiring employees.
   (b) An ongoing employee training program.
   (c) An audit function to test the system.
4. The abovementioned requirements apply to all designated nonfinancial businesses and professions, subject to the following qualifications:
   (a) Lawyers, notaries, other independent legal professionals and accountants should be required to report suspicious transactions when, on behalf of or for a client, they engage in a financial transaction deemed suspicious by the content of this Convention. Countries are strongly encouraged to extend the reporting requirement to the rest of the professional activities of accountants, including auditing.
   (b) Dealers in precious metals and dealers in precious stones should be required to report suspicious transactions when they engage in any cash transaction with a customer equal to or above the applicable designated threshold.
   (c) Trust and company service providers should be required to report suspicious transactions for a client when, on behalf of or for a client, deemed suspicious by the content of this Convention.
5. Lawyers, notaries, other independent legal professionals, and accountants acting as independent legal professionals, are not required to report their suspicions if the relevant information was obtained in circumstances where they are subject to professional secrecy or legal professional privilege.

Article 18: Reporting Requirements[35,36]

1. This Convention shall apply to:

---

35 EU (2005), *supra.*

36 *European Union, Directive (EU) 2015/849 of the European Parliament and of the Council of 20 May 2015 on the prevention of the use of the financial system for the*

(1) credit institutions;
(2) financial institutions;
(3) the following legal or natural persons acting in the exercise of their professional activities:
    (a) auditors, external accountants and tax advisors;
    (b) notaries and other independent legal professionals, when they participate, whether by acting on behalf of and for their client in any financial or real estate transaction, or by assisting in the planning or execution of transactions for their client concerning the:
        (i) buying and selling of real property or business entities;
        (ii) managing of client money, securities or other assets;
        (iii) opening or management of bank, savings or securities accounts;
        (iv) organization of contributions necessary for the creation, operation or management of companies;
        (v) creation, operation or management of trusts, companies or similar structures;
    (c) trust or company service providers not already covered under points (a) or (b);
    (d) real estate agents;
    (e) other natural or legal persons trading in goods, only to the extent that payments are made in cash in an amount of $15,000 or more, whether the transaction is executed in a single operation or in several operations which appear to be linked;
    (f) casinos.

2. Member States may decide that legal and natural persons who engage in a financial activity on an occasional or very limited basis and where there is little risk of money-laundering or terrorist financing occurring do not fall within the scope of Article 3.
3. With the exception of casinos, and following an appropriate risk assessment, Member States may decide to exempt, in full or in part, providers

purposes of money-laundering or terrorist financing, amending Regulation (EU) No 648/2012 of the European Parliament and of the Council, and repealing Directive 2005/60/EC of the European Parliament and of the Council and Commission Directive 2006/70/EC, 20 May 2015, available from http://eur-lex.europa.eu/legal-content/EN/TXT/?uri=CELEX%3A32015L0849.

of certain gambling services from national provisions transposing this Convention on the basis of the proven low risk posed by the nature and, where appropriate, the scale of operations of such services.

4. Member States shall require the institutions and persons covered by this Convention to keep the following documents and information for use in any investigation into, or analysis of, possible money-laundering or terrorist financing by the FIU or by other competent authorities in accordance with national law:
   (a) in the case of the customer due diligence, a copy or the references of the evidence required, for a period of at least five years after the business relationship with their customer has ended;
   (b) in the case of business relationships and transactions, the supporting evidence and records, consisting of the original documents or copies admissible in court proceedings under the applicable national legislation for a period of at least five years following the carrying-out of the transactions or the end of the business relationship.
5. The institutions and persons covered by this Convention shall apply customer due diligence measures in the following cases:
   (a) when establishing a business relationship;
   (b) when carrying out occasional transactions amounting to $15,000 or more, whether the transaction is carried out in a single operation or in several operations which appear to be linked;
   (c) when there is a suspicion of money-laundering or terrorist financing, regardless of any derogation, exemption or threshold;
   (d) when there are doubts about the veracity or adequacy of previously obtained customer identification data.
6. This Convention should also apply to activities of obliged entities which are performed on the internet.
7. New technologies provide time-effective and cost-effective solutions to businesses and to customers and should therefore be taken into account when evaluating risk. The competent authorities and obliged entities should be proactive in combating new and innovative ways of money-laundering.
8. The use of gambling sector services to launder the proceeds of criminal activity is of concern. In order to mitigate the risks relating to gambling services, this Convention should provide for an obligation for providers of gambling services posing higher risks to apply customer due diligence measures for single transactions amounting to $2,000 or more.

Article 19: Customer Due Diligence[37]

1. Member States shall prohibit their credit institutions and financial institutions from keeping anonymous accounts or anonymous passbooks. Member States shall, in any event, require that the owners and beneficiaries of existing anonymous accounts or anonymous passbooks be subject to customer due diligence measures as soon as possible and in any event before such accounts or passbooks are used in any way.
2. Member States shall take measures to prevent misuse of bearer shares and bearer share warrants.
3. Member States shall ensure that obliged entities apply customer due diligence measures in the following circumstances:
   (a) when establishing a business relationship;
   (b) when carrying out an occasional transaction that:
      (i) amounts to $15,000 or more, whether that transaction is carried out in a single operation or in several operations which appear to be linked; or
      (ii) constitutes a transfer of funds, exceeding $1,000;
   (c) in the case of persons trading in goods, when carrying out occasional transactions in cash amounting to $10,000 or more, whether the transaction is carried out in a single operation or in several operations which appear to be linked;
   (d) for providers of gambling services, upon the collection of winnings, the wagering of a stake, or both, when carrying out transactions amounting to $2,000 or more, whether the transaction is carried out in a single operation or in several operations which appear to be linked;
   (e) when there is a suspicion of money-laundering or terrorist financing, regardless of any derogation, exemption or threshold;
   (f) when there are doubts about the veracity or adequacy of previously obtained customer identification data.

Article 20: Customer Due Diligence Measures Requirements[38,39]

1 The institutions and persons covered by this Convention shall apply each of the customer due diligence requirements, but may determine the

37 EU (2015), *supra*.
38 FATF (1990), *supra*.
39 EU (2015), *supra*.

extent of such measures on a risk-sensitive basis depending on the type of customer, business relationship, product or transaction.

2 Customer Due Diligence measures requirements shall include:

(a) identifying the customer and verifying the customer's identity on the basis of documents, data or information obtained from a reliable and independent source;

(b) identifying, where applicable, the beneficial owner and taking risk-based and adequate measures to verify his identity so that the institution or person covered by this Convention is satisfied that it knows who the beneficial owner is, including, as regards legal persons, trusts and similar legal arrangements, taking risk-based and adequate measures to understand the ownership and control structure of the customer;

(c) obtaining information on the purpose and intended nature of the business relationship;

(d) conducting ongoing monitoring of the business relationship including scrutiny of transactions undertaken throughout the course of that relationship to ensure that the transactions being conducted are consistent with the institution's or person's knowledge of the customer, the business and risk profile, including, where necessary, the source of funds and ensuring that the documents, data or information held are kept up-to-date.

3 The institutions and persons covered by this Convention shall be able to demonstrate to the competent authorities, including self-regulatory bodies, that the extent of the measures is appropriate in view of the risks of money-laundering and terrorist financing.

Article 21: Customer Due Diligence and Tipping-off[40]

1. If, during the establishment or course of the customer relationship, or when conducting occasional transactions, a financial institution suspects that transactions relate to money-laundering or terrorist financing, then the institution should:

(a) Normally seek to identify and verify the identity of the customer and the beneficial owner, whether permanent or occasional, and irrespective of any exemption or any designated threshold that might otherwise apply;

(b) Make a STR to the FIU.

40 FATF (1990), *supra.*

2. Financial institutions, their directors, officers and employees shall be prohibited from disclosing the fact that an STR or related information is being reported to the FIU. A risk exists that customers could be unintentionally tipped off when the financial institution is seeking to perform its Customer Due Diligence (CDD) obligations in these circumstances. The customer's awareness of a possible STR or investigation could compromise future efforts to investigate the suspected money-laundering or terrorist financing operation.
3. Therefore, if financial institutions form a suspicion that transactions relate to money-laundering or terrorist financing, they should take into account the risk of tipping-off when performing the customer due diligence process. If the institution reasonably believes that performing the CDD process will tip-off the customer or potential customer, it may choose not to pursue that process, and should file an STR. Institutions should ensure that their employees are aware of and sensitive to these issues when conducting CDD.

Article 22: Customer Due Diligence and Record-Keeping[41,42]

1. Financial institutions should not keep anonymous accounts or accounts in obviously fictitious names. Financial institutions should undertake customer due diligence measures, including identifying and verifying the identity of their customers, when:
   establishing business relations; carrying out occasional transactions:
   (a) above the applicable designated threshold;
   (b) or that are wire transfers in the circumstances there is a suspicion of money-laundering or terrorist financing; or the financial institution has doubts about the veracity or adequacy of previously obtained customer identification data.
2. The Customer Due Diligence (CDD) measures to be taken are as follows:
   (a) Identifying the customer and verifying that customer's identity using reliable, independent source documents, data or information;
   (b) Identifying the beneficial owner, and taking reasonable measures to verify the identity of the beneficial owner such that the financial

41 FATF (1990), *supra.*

42 Financial Action Task Force (FATF), *International Standards On Combating Money-Laundering and the Financing of Terrorism & Proliferation,* February 2012, http://www.fatf-gafi.org/media/fatf/documents/recommendations/pdfs/FATF_Recommendations.pdf.

institution is satisfied that it knows who the beneficial owner is. For legal persons and arrangements this should include financial institutions taking reasonable measures to understand the ownership and control structure of the customer;

(c) Obtaining information on the purpose and intended nature of the business relationship;

(d) Conducting ongoing due diligence on the business relationship and scrutiny of transactions undertaken throughout the course of that relationship to ensure that the transactions being conducted are consistent with the institution's knowledge of the customer, their business and risk profile, including, where necessary, the source of funds.

3. Financial institutions should apply each of the CDD measures under (a) to (d) above, but may determine the extent of such measures on a risk sensitive basis depending on the type of customer, business relationship or transaction. The measures that are taken should be consistent with any guidelines issued by competent authorities. For higher risk categories, financial institutions should perform enhanced due diligence. In certain circumstances, where there are low risks, countries may decide that financial institutions can apply reduced or simplified measures.

4. Financial institutions should verify the identity of the customer and beneficial owner before or during the course of establishing a business relationship or conducting transactions for occasional customers. Countries may permit financial institutions to complete the verification as soon as reasonably practicable following the establishment of the relationship, where the money-laundering risks are effectively managed and where this is essential not to interrupt the normal conduct of business.

5. Where the financial institution is unable to comply with paragraphs (a) to (c) above, it should not open the account, commence business relations or perform the transaction; or should terminate the business relationship; and should consider making a suspicious transactions report in relation to the customer.

6. These requirements should apply to all new customers, though financial institutions should also apply this Recommendation to existing customers on the basis of materiality and risk, and should conduct due diligence on such existing relationships at appropriate times.

7. Financial institutions should, in relation to politically exposed persons, in addition to performing normal due diligence measures:

(a) Have appropriate risk management systems to determine whether the customer is a politically exposed person.

(b) Obtain senior management approval for establishing business relationships with such customers.
(c) Take reasonable measures to establish the source of wealth and source of funds.
(d) Conduct enhanced ongoing monitoring of the business relationship.

8. Financial institutions should, in relation to cross-border correspondent banking and other similar relationships, in addition to performing normal due diligence measures:
(a) Gather sufficient information about a respondent institution to understand fully the nature of the respondent's business and to determine from publicly available information the reputation of the institution and the quality of supervision, including whether it has been subject to a money-laundering or terrorist financing investigation or regulatory action.
(b) Assess the respondent institution's anti-money-laundering and terrorist financing controls.
(c) Obtain approval from senior management before establishing new correspondent relationships.
(d) Document the respective responsibilities of each institution.
(e) With respect to "payable-through accounts", be satisfied that the respondent bank has verified the identity of and performed on-going due diligence on the customers having direct access to accounts of the correspondent and that it is able to provide relevant customer identification data upon request to the correspondent bank.

9. Financial institutions should pay special attention to any money-laundering threats that may arise from new or developing technologies that might favor anonymity, and take measures, if needed, to prevent their use in money-laundering schemes. In particular, financial institutions should have policies and procedures in place to address any specific risks associated with nonface to face business relationships or transactions.

10. Countries may permit financial institutions to rely on intermediaries or other third parties to perform elements (a)—(c) of the CDD process or to introduce business, provided that the criteria set out below are met. Where such reliance is permitted, the ultimate responsibility for customer identification and verification remains with the financial institution relying on the third party. The criteria that should be met are as follows:

(a) A financial institution relying upon a third party should immediately obtain the necessary information concerning elements (a)—(c) of the CDD process. Financial institutions should take adequate steps to satisfy themselves that copies of identification data and other relevant documentation relating to the CDD requirements will be made available from the third party upon request without delay.

(b) The financial institution should satisfy itself that the third party is regulated and supervised for, and has measures in place to comply with CDD.

11. It is left to each country to determine in which countries the third party that meets the conditions can be based, having regard to information available on countries that do not or do not adequately apply the FATF Recommendations.
12. Financial institutions should maintain, for at least five years, all necessary records on transactions, both domestic or international, to enable them to comply swiftly with information requests from the competent authorities.
13. Such records must be sufficient to permit reconstruction of individual transactions (including the amounts and types of currency involved if any) so as to provide, if necessary, evidence for prosecution of criminal activity.
14. Financial institutions should keep records on the identification data obtained through the customer due diligence process (e.g. copies or records of official identification documents like passports, identity cards, driving licenses or similar documents), account files and business correspondence for at least five years after the business relationship is ended.
15. The identification data and transaction records should be available to domestic competent authorities upon appropriate authority.
16. Financial institutions should pay special attention to all complex, unusual large transactions, and all unusual patterns of transactions, which have no apparent economic or visible lawful purpose. The background and purpose of such transactions should, as far as possible, be examined, the findings established in writing, and be available to help competent authorities and auditors.
17. The customer due diligence and record-keeping requirements apply to designated non-financial businesses and professions in the following situations:

(a) Casinos—when customers engage in financial transactions equal to or above the applicable designated threshold.
(b) Real estate agents—when they are involved in transactions for their client concerning the buying and selling of real estate.
(c) Dealers in precious metals and dealers in precious stones—when they engage in any cash transaction with a customer equal to or above the applicable designated threshold.
(d) Lawyers, notaries, other independent legal professionals and accountants when they prepare for or carry out transactions for their client concerning the following activities: buying and selling of real estate; managing of client money, securities or other assets; management of bank, savings or securities accounts; organization of contributions for the creation, operation or management of companies; creation, operation or management of legal persons or arrangements, and buying and selling of business entities.
(e) Trust and company service providers when they prepare for or carry out transactions for a client concerning the activities listed in the definition in the Terms.

Article 23: CDD for Legal Persons and Arrangements[43]

When performing elements of the CDD process in relation to legal persons or arrangements, financial institutions should:
(a) Verify that any person purporting to act on behalf of the customer is so authorized, and identify that person.
(b) Identify the customer and verify its identity—the types of measures that would be normally needed to satisfactorily perform this function would require obtaining proof of incorporation or similar evidence of the legal status of the legal person or arrangement, as well as information concerning the customer's name, the names of trustees, legal form, address, directors, and provisions regulating the power to bind the legal person or arrangement.
(c) Identify the beneficial owners, including forming an understanding of the ownership and control structure, and take reasonable measures to verify the identity of such persons. The types of measures that would be normally needed to satisfactorily perform this function would require identifying the natural persons with a controlling interest and identifying the natural persons who comprise the

43 FATF (1990), *supra*.

mind and management of the legal person or arrangement. Where the customer or the owner of the controlling interest is a public company that is subject to regulatory disclosure requirements, it is not necessary to seek to identify and verify the identity of any shareholder of that company.

The relevant information or data may be obtained from a public register, from the customer or from other reliable sources.

Article 24: Simplified Customer Due Diligence[44,45,46,47,48]

1. Where a Member State or an obliged entity identifies areas of lower risk, that Member State may allow obliged entities to apply simplified customer due diligence measures.
2. Before applying simplified customer due diligence measures, obliged entities shall ascertain that the business relationship or the transaction presents a lower degree of risk.
3. Member States shall ensure that obliged entities carry out sufficient monitoring of the transactions and business relationships to enable the detection of unusual or suspicious transactions.
4. With respect to cross-border correspondent relationships with a third-country respondent institution, Member States shall, in addition to the customer due diligence measures require their credit institutions and financial institutions to:
   (a) gather sufficient information about the respondent institution to understand fully the nature of the respondent's business and to

44 EU (2015), *supra.*

45 FATF (1990), *supra.*

46 Financial Action Task Force (FATF), *International Best Practices: Targeted Financial Sanctions Related to Terrorism and Terrorist Financing (Recommendation 6)*, 2012, available from http://www.fatf-gafi.org/publications/fatfrecommendations/documents/bpp-fin sanctions-tf-r6.html.

47 European Union, Directive (EU) *2017/541 of the European Parliament and of the Council of 15 March 2017 on combating terrorism and replacing Council Framework Decision 2002/475/JHA* and amending Council Decision 2005/671/JHA, 15 March 2017, available from https://eur-lex.europa.eu/legal-content/EN/TXT/PDF/?uri=CELEX:32017L0541&from=EN.

48 European Union, Directive (EU) 2018/843 of the European Parliament and of the Council of 30 May 2018 amending *Directive (EU) 2015/849 on the prevention of the use of the financial system for the purposes of money-laundering or terrorist financing, and amending Directives 2009/138/EC and 2013/36/EU,* 30 May 2018, available from https://eur-lex.europa.eu/legal-content/EN/TXT/PDF/?uri=CELEX:32018L0843& from=EN.

determine from publicly available information the reputation of the institution and the quality of supervision;
(b) assess the respondent institution's AML/CFT controls;
(c) obtain approval from senior management before establishing new correspondent relationships;
(d) document the respective responsibilities of each institution;
(e) with respect to payable-through accounts, be satisfied that the respondent institution has verified the identity of, and performed ongoing due diligence on, the customers having direct access to accounts of the correspondent institution, and that it is able to provide relevant customer due diligence data to the correspondent institution, upon request.

5. With respect to transactions or business relationships with politically exposed persons, Member States shall, in addition to the customer due diligence measures require obliged entities to:
(a) have in place appropriate risk management systems, including risk-based procedures, to determine whether the customer or the beneficial owner of the customer is a politically exposed person;
(b) apply the following measures in cases of business relationships with politically exposed persons:
(i) obtain senior management approval for establishing or continuing business relationships with such persons;
(ii) take adequate measures to establish the source of wealth and source of funds that are involved in business relationships or transactions with such persons;
(iii) conduct enhanced, ongoing monitoring of those business relationships.

6. Member States shall require obliged entities to take reasonable measures to determine whether the beneficiaries of a life or other investment-related insurance policy and/or, where required, the beneficial owner of the beneficiary are politically exposed persons. Those measures shall be taken no later than at the time of the payout or at the time of the assignment, in whole or in part, of the policy. Where there are higher risks identified, in addition to applying the customer due diligence measures, Member States shall require obliged entities to:
(a) inform senior management before payout of policy proceeds;
(b) conduct enhanced scrutiny of the entire business relationship with the policyholder.

7. Where a politically exposed person is no longer entrusted with a prominent public function by a Member State or a third country, or with a prominent public function by an international organization, obliged

entities shall, for at least 12 months, be required to take into account the continuing risk posed by that person and to apply appropriate and risk sensitive measures until such time as that person is deemed to pose no further risk specific to politically exposed persons.

8. Member States shall prohibit credit institutions and financial institutions from entering into, or continuing, a correspondent relationship with a shell bank. They shall require that those institutions take appropriate measures to ensure that they do not engage in or continue correspondent relationships with a credit institution or financial institution that is known to allow its accounts to be used by a shell bank.
9. Member States may permit obliged entities to rely on third parties to meet the customer due diligence requirements. However, the ultimate responsibility for meeting those requirements shall remain with the obliged entity which relies on the third party.
10. For the purposes of this Section, "third parties" means obliged entities, the member organizations or federations of those obliged entities, or other institutions or persons situated in a Member State or third country that:
    (a) apply customer due diligence requirements and record-keeping requirements that are consistent with those laid down in this Convention; and
    (b) have their compliance with the requirements of this Convention supervised in a manner consistent with this Convention and the Alliance's requirements.
11. Member States shall prohibit obliged entities from relying on third parties established in high-risk third countries. Member States may exempt branches and majority-owned subsidiaries of obliged entities established in the Union from that prohibition where those branches and majority-owned subsidiaries fully comply with the group-wide policies and procedures.
12. Member States shall ensure that obliged entities obtain from the third party relied upon the necessary information concerning the customer due diligence requirements.
13. Member States shall ensure that obliged entities to which the customer is referred take adequate steps to ensure that the third party provides, immediately, upon request, relevant copies of identification and verification data and other relevant documentation on the identity of the customer or the beneficial owner.
14. Institutions and persons covered by this Convention shall not be subject to the requirements provided for in those Articles where the customer is a credit or financial institution covered by this Convention, or a credit or

financial institution situated in a third country which imposes requirements equivalent to those laid down in this Convention and supervised for compliance with those requirements.

15. Member States may allow the institutions and persons covered by this Convention not to apply customer due diligence in respect of:
    (a) listed companies whose securities are admitted to trading on a regulated market in one or more Member States and listed companies from third countries which are subject to disclosure requirements consistent with National legislation;
    (b) beneficial owners of pooled accounts held by notaries and other independent legal professionals from the Member States, or from third countries provided that they are subject to requirements to combat money-laundering or terrorist financing consistent with international standards and are supervised for compliance with those requirements and provided that the information on the identity of the beneficial owner is available, on request, to the institutions that act as depository institutions for the pooled accounts;
    (c) domestic public authorities, or in respect of any other customer representing a low risk of money-laundering or terrorist financing.
16. Institutions and persons covered by this Convention shall in any case gather sufficient information to establish if the customer qualifies for an exemption as mentioned in these paragraphs.
17. The Member States shall inform each other and the Commission of cases where they consider that a third country meets the conditions laid down in paragraphs 1 or 2.
18. Member States may allow the institutions and persons covered by this Convention not to apply customer due diligence in respect of:
    (a) life insurance policies where the annual premium is no more than $1,000 or the single premium is no more than $2,500;
    (b) insurance policies for pension schemes if there is no surrender clause and the policy cannot be used as collateral;
    (c) a pension, superannuation or similar scheme that provides retirement benefits to employees, where contributions are made by way of deduction from wages and the scheme rules do not permit the assignment of a member's interest under the scheme;
    (d) electronic money, where, if the device cannot be recharged, the maximum amount stored in the device is no more than $150, or where, if the device can be recharged, a limit of $2,500 is imposed on the total amount transacted in a calendar year, except when an amount of $1,000 or more is redeemed in that same calendar year by

the bearer, or in respect of any other product or transaction representing a low risk of money-laundering or terrorist financing.

19. Member States may, subject to paragraph 4 of this Article, consider customers who are public authorities or public bodies and who fulfil all the following criteria as customers representing a low risk of money-laundering or terrorist financing:
    (a) the customer has been entrusted with public functions;
    (b) the customer's identity is publicly available, transparent and certain;
    (c) the activities of the customer, as well as its accounting practices, are transparent;
    (d) either the customer is accountable to a Community institution or to the authorities of a Member State, or appropriate check and balance procedures exist ensuring control of the customer's activity.

20. States may, subject to paragraph 4 of this Article, consider customers who are legal entities which do not enjoy the status of public authority or public body but which fulfil all the following criteria as customers representing a low risk of money-laundering or terrorist financing:
    (a) the customer is an entity that undertakes financial activities;
    (b) the identity of the customer is publicly available, transparent and certain;
    (c) the customer is subject to a mandatory licensing requirement under national law for the undertaking of financial activities and licensing may be refused if the competent authorities are not satisfied that the persons who effectively direct or will direct the business of such an entity, or its beneficial owner, are fit and proper persons;
    (d) the customer is subject to supervision by competent authorities as regards compliance with the national legislation transposing that Convention and, where applicable, additional obligations under national legislation;
    (e) failure by the customer to comply with the obligations referred to in point (a) is subject to effective, proportionate and dissuasive sanctions including the possibility of appropriate administrative measures or the imposition of administrative sanctions.

21. For the purposes of point (c) of the first subparagraph, the activity conducted by the customer shall be supervised by competent authorities. Supervision is to be understood in this context as meaning the type of supervisory activity with the highest supervisory powers, including the possibility of conducting on-site inspections. Such inspections shall

include the review of policies, procedures, books and records, and shall extend to sample testing.

22. States may, subject to paragraph 4 of this Article, allow the institutions and persons covered by that Convention to consider products which fulfil all the following criteria, or transactions related to such products, as representing a low risk of money-laundering or terrorist financing:
   (a) the product has a written contractual base;
   (b) the related transactions are carried out through an account of the customer with a credit institution or a credit institution situated in a third country which imposes requirements equivalent to those laid down in that Convention;
   (c) the product or related transactions are not anonymous;
   (d) the product is subject to a predetermined maximum threshold;
   (e) the benefits of the product or related transactions cannot be realized for the benefit of third parties, except in the case of death, disablement, survival to a predetermined advanced age, or similar events;
   (f) in the case of products or related transactions allowing for the investment of funds in financial assets or claims, including insurance or other kind of contingent claims:
      (i) the benefits of the product or related transactions are only realizable in the long term;
      (ii) the product or related transactions cannot be used as collateral;
      (iii) during the contractual relationship, no accelerated payments are made, no surrender clauses are used and no early termination takes place.

23. For the purposes of point (d) of the first subparagraph, the thresholds shall apply in the case of insurance policies or savings products of similar nature. Without prejudice to the third subparagraph, in the other cases the maximum threshold shall be $15,000. Member States may derogate from that threshold in the case of products which are related to the financing of physical or virtual assets and where the legal and beneficial title of the assets is not transferred to the customer until termination of the contractual relationship, provided that the threshold established by the Member State for the transactions related to this type of product, whether the transaction is carried out in a single operation or in several operations which appear to be linked, does not exceed $15,000 per year.

24. Member States may derogate from the criteria set out in points (e) and (f) of the first subparagraph in the case of products the characteristics

of which are determined by their relevant domestic public authorities for purposes of general interest, which benefit from specific advantages from the State in the form of direct grants or tax rebates, and the use of which is subject to control by those authorities, provided that the benefits of the product are realizable only in the long term and that the threshold established for the purposes of point (d) of the first subparagraph is sufficiently low. Where appropriate, that threshold may be set as a maximum annual amount.

25. In assessing whether the customers or products and transactions referred to in paragraphs 1, 2 and 3 represent a low risk of money-laundering or terrorist financing, Member States shall pay special attention to any activity of those customers or to any type of product or transaction which may be regarded as particularly likely, by its nature, to be used or abused for money-laundering or terrorist financing purposes.
26. Member States shall not consider that customers or products and transactions referred to in paragraphs 1, 2 and 3 represent a low risk of money-laundering or terrorist financing if there is information available to suggest that the risk of money-laundering or terrorist financing may not be low.

Article 25: Ongoing Customer Due Diligence[49]

A reporting entity must:

1. monitor the reporting entity's customers in relation to the provision by the reporting entity of designated services at or through a permanent establishment of the reporting entity in a Member State, with a view to:
   (a) identifying; and
   (b) mitigating; and
   (c) managing; the risk the reporting entity may reasonably face that the provision by the reporting entity of a designated service at or through a permanent establishment of the reporting entity in a Member State might (whether inadvertently or otherwise) involve or facilitate:
      i. money-laundering; or
      ii. financing of terrorism; and
2. do so in accordance with the AML/CTF Rules.

49 AMLCTFRI (2007), *supra*

Article 26: Reliance on Identification and Verification Already Performed[50]

The CDD measures do not imply that financial institutions have to repeatedly identify and verify the identity of each customer every time that a customer conducts a transaction. An institution is entitled to rely on the identification and verification steps that it has already undertaken unless it has doubts about the veracity of that information. Examples of situations that might lead an institution to have such doubts could be where there is a suspicion of money-laundering in relation to that customer, or where there is a material change in the way that the customer's account is operated which is not consistent with the customer's business profile.

Article 27: Timing of Verification[51]

1. Examples of the types of circumstances where it would be permissible for verification to be completed after the establishment of the business relationship, because it would be essential not to interrupt the normal conduct of business include:
   (a) Non face-to-face business;
   (b) Securities transactions. In the securities industry, companies and intermediaries may be required to perform transactions very rapidly, according to the market conditions at the time the customer is contacting them, and the performance of the transaction may be required before verification of identity is completed;
   (c) Life insurance business. In relation to life insurance business, countries may permit the identification and verification of the beneficiary under the policy to take place after having established the business relationship with the policyholder.

   However, in all such cases, identification and verification should occur at or before the time of payout or the time where the beneficiary intends to exercise vested rights under the policy.
2. Financial institutions will also need to adopt risk management procedures with respect to the conditions under which a customer may utilize the business relationship prior to verification. These procedures should include a set of measures such as a limitation of the number,

50 FATF (1990), *supra*.
51 FATF (1990), *supra*.

types and/or amount of transactions that can be performed and the monitoring of large or complex transactions being carried out outside of expected norms for that type of relationship. Financial institutions should refer to the Basel CDD paper10 (Section 2.2.6.) for specific guidance on examples of risk management measures for non-face to face business.

Article 28: Requirement to Identify Existing Customers[52]

The principles set out in the Basel CDD paper concerning the identification of existing customers should serve as guidance when applying customer due diligence processes to institutions engaged in banking activity, and could apply to other financial institutions where relevant.

Article 29: Customer Identification and Record-Keeping Rules[53]

1. Financial institutions should not keep anonymous accounts or accounts in obviously fictitious names: they should be required (by law, by regulations, by agreements between supervisory authorities and financial institutions or by self-regulatory agreements among financial institutions) to identify, on the basis of an official or other reliable identifying document, and record the identity of their clients, either occasional or usual, when establishing business relations or conducting transactions (in particular opening of accounts or passbooks, entering into fiduciary transactions, renting of safe deposit boxes, performing large cash transactions).
2. Financial institutions should take reasonable measures to obtain information about the true identity of the persons on whose behalf an account is opened or a transaction conducted if there are any doubts as to whether these clients or customers are not acting on their own behalf, in particular, in the case of domiciliary companies (i.e. institutions, corporations, foundations, trusts, etc. that do not conduct any commercial or manufacturing business or any other form of commercial operation in the country where their registered office is located).

52 FATF (1990), *supra.*

53 Bank for International Settlements, *Customer Due diligence for banks—final document*, October 2001, available from http://www.bis.org/publ/bcbs85.htm.

3. Financial institutions should maintain, for at least five years, all necessary records on transactions, both domestic or international, to enable them to comply swiftly with information requests from the competent authorities. Such records must be sufficient to permit reconstruction of individual transactions (including the amounts and types of currency involved if any) so as to provide, if necessary, evidence for prosecution of criminal behavior.
4. Financial institutions should keep records on customer identification (e.g. copies or records of official identification documents like passports, identity cards, driving licenses or similar documents), account files and business correspondence for at least five years after the account is closed.
5. These documents should be available to domestic competent authorities in the context of relevant criminal prosecutions and investigations.

Article 30: Applicable Customer Identification Procedure with Respect to Companies[54]

In so far as a reporting entity has any customer who is a domestic or a foreign company, must comply with the requirements which must include appropriate risk-based systems and controls that are designed to enable the reporting entity to be reasonably satisfied, where a customer is a company, that:
1. the company exists; and
2. in respect of certain companies, the name and address of any beneficial owner of the company has been provided.

Article 31: Existence of the Company—Collection of Minimum Information[55]

1. Companies shall adopt a procedure for the reporting entity to collect, at a minimum, the following KYC information from a company:
   (1) in the case of a domestic company:
      (a) the full name of the company;
      (b) the full address of the company's registered office;
      (c) the full address of the company's principal place of business, if any;

54 AMLCTFRI (2007), *supra.*
55 AMLCTFRI (2007), *supra*

(d) the registration number issued to the company;
(e) whether the company is registered as a proprietary or public company; and
(f) if the company is registered as a proprietary company, the name of each director of the company;

(2) in the case of a registered foreign company:
(a) the full name of the company;
(b) the full address of the company's registered office;
(c) the full address of the company's principal place of business or the full name and address of the company's local agent, if any;
(d) the registration number issued to the company;
(e) the country in which the company was formed, incorporated or registered;
(f) whether the company is registered by the relevant foreign registration body and if so whether it is registered as a private or public company or some other type of company; and
(g) if the company is registered as a private company by the relevant foreign registration body—the name of each director of the company;

(3) in the case of an unregistered foreign company:
(a) the full name of the company;
(b) the country in which the company was formed, incorporated or registered;
(c) whether the company is registered by the relevant foreign registration body and if so:
(i) any identification number issued to the company by the relevant foreign registration body upon the company's formation, incorporation or registration;
(ii) the full address of the company in its country of formation, incorporation or registration as registered by the relevant foreign registration body; and
(iii) whether it is registered as a private or public company or some other type of company by the relevant foreign registration body;
(d) if the company is registered as a private company by the relevant foreign registration body—the name of each director of the company; and
(e) if the company is not registered by the relevant foreign registration body, the full address of the principal place of business of the company in its country of formation or incorporation.

2. Companies must include appropriate risk-based systems and controls for the reporting entity to determine whether, in addition to the KYC information, any other KYC information relating to the company's existence will be collected in respect of a company.
3. Companies must include a procedure for the reporting entity to verify, at a minimum, the following information about a company:
   (1) in the case of a domestic company:
      (a) the full name of the company;
      (b) whether the company is registered as a proprietary or public company; and
      (c) the registration number issued to the company;
   (2) in the case of a registered foreign company:
      (a) the full name of the company;
      (b) whether the company is registered by the relevant foreign registration body and if so whether it is registered as a private or public company; and
      (c) the registration number issued to the company;
   (3) in the case of an unregistered foreign company:
      (a) the full name of the company; and
      (b) whether the company is registered by the relevant foreign registration body and if so:
         (i) any identification number issued to the company by the relevant foreign registration body upon the company's formation, incorporation or registration; and
         (ii) whether the company is registered as a private or public company.

Article 32: Requirement to Report Suspicious Transactions[56]

1. Any natural or legal person shall be required to report to the financial intelligence unit transactions involving money which appears to be derived from the perpetration of: a crime, an offence linked to organized crime, one or more of the following designated categories of offences.

56 International Money-Laundering Information Network, Global Programme Against Money-Laundering, *Model legislation on laundering, confiscation and international cooperation in relation to the proceeds of crime,* 1999, available from http://www.imolin.org/imolin/en/ml99eng.html.

2. The persons referred to above shall be required to report the transactions carried out even if it was not feasible to defer their execution or if it became clear only after completion of a transaction that it involved suspect money.
3. They shall also be required to report without delay any information that might confirm or invalidate the suspicion.

Article 33: Reporting to the Financial Intelligence Unit[57]

Reports of suspicions shall be transmitted to the financial intelligence unit by facsimile or, failing which, by any other written means. Reports communicated by telephone shall be confirmed by facsimile or any other written means within the shortest possible time. Such reports shall, as appropriate, indicate:

(a) The reasons why the transaction has already been executed;
(b) The time-limit within which the suspect transaction is to be executed.

The intelligence unit shall acknowledge receipt of the report upon receipt thereof.

Article 34: Obligation to Report Suspicious Activities[58]

1. Financial institutions and designated non-financial businesses and professions, that suspect or have reasonable grounds to suspect that funds or property are the proceeds of crime, or are related or linked to, or are to be used for the financing of terrorism, or that have knowledge of a fact or an activity that may be an indication of money-laundering or financing of terrorism, are required to submit promptly a report setting forth its suspicions to the financial intelligence unit. This obligation shall also apply to attempted transactions.

---

57 International Money-Laundering Information Network, Global Programme Against Money-Laundering, *Model legislation on laundering, confiscation and international cooperation in relation to the proceeds of crime*, 1999, available from http://www.imolin.org/imolin/en/ml99eng.html.

58 U.N. Office on Drugs and Crime, *Model Legislation on Money-Laundering and Financing of Terrorism*, 1 December 2005, available from http://www.imf.org/external/np/leg/amlcft/eng/pdf/amlml05.pdf.

2. Lawyers, notaries and other independent legal professionals, auditors, accountants and tax advisers may submit reports of suspicions to the FIU through their respective self-regulatory organizations. Self-regulatory organizations shall pass on the information to the financial intelligence unit whenever the report.
3. Lawyers, notaries and other independent legal professionals accountants, auditors and tax advisers have no obligation to report information they receive from or obtain on a client, in the course of determining the legal position for their client or performing their task of defending or representing that client in, or concerning judicial proceeding, including advice on instituting or avoiding proceedings, whether such information is received or obtained before, during or after such proceedings.
4. Dealers in precious metals and dealers in precious stones and other dealers in high value goods shall report suspicious transactions to the financial intelligence unit when they engage in any cash transaction equal or above $15,000.
5. Real estate agents shall report suspicious transactions to the financial intelligence unit when involved in transactions for their client concerning the buying or selling of real estate.
6. The financial intelligence unit, competent authority shall issue regulation on the procedures and form in which the reports shall be submitted.
7. Cash transaction reporting Financial institutions and designated non-financial businesses and professions shall report to the financial intelligence unit cash transactions in an amount equal to or above $15,000, whether conducted as a single transaction or several transactions that appear to be linked.

Article 35: Postponing of Transactions[59]

1. Financial institutions and designated non-financial businesses and professions shall refrain from carrying out transactions which they suspect to be related to money-laundering or financing of terrorism until they have reported their suspicion to the financial intelligence unit.

59 IMF (2005), *supra*.

2. This option is valid only when these professions represent a client before a court.
3. If, by reason of the seriousness or urgency of the case, the financial intelligence unit considers it necessary, it may order, or seek the suspension of a transaction for a period not to exceed 3 business days.
4. Where refraining from the carrying out transaction it is impossible or is likely to frustrate the efforts to investigate a suspected transaction, the financial institutions and designated non-financial businesses and professions can execute the transaction and shall report their suspicion to the financial intelligence unit immediately afterwards.

Article 36: Prohibition of Tipping-off[60]

Under no circumstance shall financial institutions and designated non-financial businesses and professions, their directors, officers and employees disclose to their customer or a third party that information was provided to the financial intelligence unit or that a report concerning suspected money-laundering or financing of terrorism will be, is being or has been submitted to the financial intelligence unit or that a money-laundering or financing of terrorism investigation is being or has been carried out.

This shall not preclude disclosures or communications regarding suspicious money-laundering or financing of terrorism between and among directors, officers and employees of the financial institutions and designated non-financial businesses and professions, legal counsel and appropriate competent authorities.

Article 37: Action Taken on Suspicious Activity Reports[61]

Whenever the financial intelligence unit has reasonable grounds to suspect serious indications of money-laundering or financing of terrorism, it shall forward the relevant information, to prosecutor, investigative authority, judicial authority, etc., which shall decide upon further action.

60 IMF (2005), *supra.*
61 IMF (2005), *supra.*

Article 38: Anonymous Testimony and Witness Protection[62]

1. Either at its own initiative or at the request of a witness, defendant or aggrieved private party, a competent judicial authority may determine that:
   (a) certain identifying information shall not be included in the hearing transcript if there is a reasonable presumption that the witness could suffer serious injury following the disclosure of certain information;
   (b) a witness's identity is kept secret if the competent authority concludes that the witness, a member of his family or one of his associates could reasonably be endangered by reason of the testimony.
2. The witness's identity shall be kept secret only if the investigation of the offence so requires and other investigative methods appear inadequate to uncover the truth. The witness whose identity is kept secret shall not be summoned to testify at a hearing without his consent. Anonymous testimony shall not serve as the sole basis for or a determining factor in any conviction.

Article 39: Enhanced Customer Due Diligence[63,64]

1. Member States shall require the institutions and persons covered by this Convention to apply, on a risk-sensitive basis, enhanced customer due diligence measures, in situations which by their nature can present a higher risk of money-laundering or terrorist financing, in situations representing a high risk of money-laundering or terrorist financing.
2. Where the customer has not been physically present for identification purposes, Member States shall require those institutions and persons to take specific and adequate measures to compensate for the higher risk, for example by applying one or more of the following measures:
   (a) ensuring that the customer's identity is established by additional documents, data or information;
   (b) supplementary measures to verify or certify the documents supplied, or requiring confirmatory certification by a credit or financial institution covered by this Convention;

62 IMF (2005), *supra.*
63 EU (2005), *supra.*
64 FATF (2012c), *supra.*

(c) ensuring that the first payment of the operations is carried out through an account opened in the customer's name with a credit institution.

3. In respect of cross-frontier correspondent banking relationships with respondent institutions from third countries, Member States shall require their credit institutions to:
   (a) gather sufficient information about a respondent institution to understand fully the nature of the respondent's business and to determine from publicly available information the reputation of the institution and the quality of supervision;
   (b) assess the respondent institution's anti-money-laundering and anti-terrorist financing controls;
   (c) obtain approval from senior management before establishing new correspondent banking relationships;
   (d) document the respective responsibilities of each institution;
   (e) with respect to payable-through accounts, be satisfied that the respondent credit institution has verified the identity of and performed ongoing due diligence on the customers having direct access to accounts of the correspondent and that it is able to provide relevant customer due diligence data to the correspondent institution, upon request.
4. In respect of transactions or business relationships with politically exposed persons residing in another Member State or in a third country, Member States shall require those institutions and persons covered by this Convention to:
   (a) have appropriate risk-based procedures to determine whether the customer is a politically exposed person;
   (b) have senior management approval for establishing business relationships with such customers;
   (c) take adequate measures to establish the source of wealth and source of funds that are involved in the business relationship or transaction;
   (d) conduct enhanced ongoing monitoring of the business relationship.
5. Member States shall prohibit credit institutions from entering into or continuing a correspondent banking relationship with a shell bank and shall require that credit institutions take appropriate measures to ensure that they do not engage in or continue correspondent banking relationships with a bank that is known to permit its accounts to be used by a shell bank.

6. Member States shall ensure that the institutions and persons covered by this Convention pay special attention to any money-laundering or terrorist financing threat that may arise from products or transactions that might favor anonymity, and take measures, if needed, to prevent their use for money-laundering or terrorist financing purposes.

Article 40: Increased Diligence of Financial Institutions[65]

1. Financial institutions should pay special attention to all complex, unusual large transactions, and all unusual patterns of transactions, which have no apparent economic or visible lawful purpose. The background and purpose of such transactions should, as far as possible, be examined, the findings established in writing, and be available to help supervisors, auditors and law enforcement agencies.
2. If financial institutions suspect that funds stem from a criminal activity, they should be permitted or required to report promptly their suspicions to the competent authorities. Accordingly, there should be legal provisions to protect financial institutions and their employees from criminal or civil liability for breach of any restriction on disclosure of information imposed by contract or by any legislative, regulatory or administrative provision, if they report in good faith, in disclosing suspected criminal activity to the competent authorities, even if they did not know precisely what the underlying criminal activity was, and regardless of whether illegal activity actually occurred.
3. Financial institutions, their directors and employees, should not, or, where appropriate, should not be allowed to, warn their customers when information relating to them is being reported to the competent authorities.
4. In the case of a mandatory reporting system, or in the case of a voluntary reporting system where appropriate, financial institutions reporting their suspicions should comply with instructions from the competent authorities.
5. When a financial institution develops suspicions about the operations of a customer, and when no obligation of reporting these suspicious exists, makes no report to the competent authorities, it should deny assistance to this customer, sever relations with him and close his accounts.

65 FATF (1990), *supra*.

6. Financial institutions should develop programs against money-laundering. These programs should include, as a minimum:
   (a) the development of internal policies, procedures and controls, including the designation of compliance officers at management level, and adequate screening procedures to ensure high standards when hiring employees;
   (b) an ongoing employee training program;
   (c) an audit function to test the system.
7. The feasibility of measures to detect or monitor cash at the border should be studied, subject to strict safeguards to ensure proper use of information and without impeding in any way the freedom of capital movements.
8. Countries should consider the feasibility and utility of a system where banks and other financial institutions and intermediaries would report all domestic and international currency transactions above a fixed amount, to a national central agency with a computerized data base, available to competent authorities for use in money-laundering cases, subject to strict safeguards to ensure proper use of the information.
9. Countries should further encourage in general the development of modern and secure techniques of money management, including increased use of checks, payment cards, direct deposit of salary checks, and book entry recording of securities, as a means to encourage the replacement of cash transfers.

Article 41: Implementation, and Role of Regulatory and Other Administrative Authorities[66]

1. The competent authorities supervising banks or other financial institutions or intermediaries, or other competent authorities, should ensure that the supervised institutions have adequate programs to guard against money-laundering. These authorities should cooperate and lend expertise spontaneously or on request with other domestic judicial or law enforcement authorities in money-laundering investigations and prosecutions.
2. Competent authorities should be designated to ensure an effective implementation of all these Recommendations, through administrative

66 FATF (1990), *supra*.

supervision and regulation, in other professions dealing with cash as defined by each country.

3. The competent authorities should establish guidelines which will assist financial institutions in detecting suspicious patterns of behavior by their customers. It is understood that such guidelines must develop over time, and will never be exhaustive. It is further understood that such guidelines will primarily serve as an educational tool for financial institutions' personnel.
4. The competent authorities regulating or supervising financial institutions should take the necessary legal or regulatory measures to guard against control or acquisition of a significant participation in financial institutions by criminals or their confederates.

Article 42: Implementation of KYC Standards in a Cross-border Context[67]

1. Supervisors around the world should seek, to the best of their efforts, to develop and implement their national KYC standards fully in line with international standards so as to avoid potential regulatory arbitrage and safeguard the integrity of domestic and international banking systems. The implementation and assessment of such standards put to the test the willingness of supervisors to cooperate with each other in a very practical way, as well as the ability of banks to control risks on a groupwide basis. This is a challenging task for banks and supervisors alike.
2. Supervisors expect banking groups to apply an accepted minimum standard of KYC policies and procedures to both their local and overseas operations. The supervision of international banking can only be effectively carried out on a consolidated basis, and reputational risk as well as other banking risks are not limited to national boundaries. Parent banks must communicate their policies and procedures to their overseas branches and subsidiaries, including non-banking entities such as trust companies, and have a routine for testing compliance against both home and host country KYC standards in order for their programs to operate effectively globally. Such compliance tests will also

67 Due Diligence (2001), *supra*.

be tested by external auditors and supervisors. Therefore, it is important that KYC documentation is properly filed and available for their inspection. As far as compliance checks are concerned, supervisors and external auditors should in most cases examine systems and controls and look at customer accounts and transactions monitoring as part of a sampling process.

3. However small an overseas establishment is, a senior officer should be designated to be directly responsible for ensuring that all relevant staff are trained in, and observe, KYC procedures that meet both home and host standards. While this officer will bear primary responsibility, he should be supported by internal auditors and compliance officers from both local and head offices as appropriate.
4. Where the minimum KYC standards of the home and host countries differ, branches and subsidiaries in the host jurisdictions should apply the higher standard of the two. In general, there should be no impediment to prevent a bank from adopting standards that are higher than the minima required locally. If, however, local laws and regulations (especially secrecy provisions) prohibit the implementation of home country KYC standards, where the latter are more stringent, host country supervisors should use their best endeavors to have the law and regulations changed. In the meantime, overseas branches and subsidiaries would have to comply with host country standards, but they should make sure the head office or parent bank and its home country supervisor are fully informed of the nature of the difference.
5. Criminal elements are likely to be drawn toward jurisdictions with such impediments. Hence, banks should be aware of the high reputational risk of conducting business in these jurisdictions. Parent banks should have a procedure for reviewing the vulnerability of the individual operating units and implement additional safeguards where appropriate. In extreme cases, supervisors should consider placing additional controls on banks operating in those jurisdictions and ultimately perhaps encouraging their withdrawal.
6. During on-site inspections, home country supervisors or auditors should face no impediments in verifying the unit's compliance with KYC policies and procedures. This will require a review of customer files and some random sampling of accounts. Home country supervisors should have access to information on sampled individual customer accounts to the extent necessary to enable a proper evaluation of the application of KYC standards and an assessment of risk management practices, and should

not be impeded by local bank secrecy laws. Where the home country supervisor requires consolidated reporting of deposit or borrower concentrations or notification of funds under management, there should be no impediments. In addition, with a view to monitoring deposit concentrations or the funding risk of the deposit being withdrawn, home supervisors may apply materiality tests and establish some thresholds so that if a customer's deposit exceeds a certain percentage of the balance sheet, banks should report it to the home supervisor. However, safeguards are needed to ensure that information regarding individual accounts is used exclusively for lawful supervisory purposes, and can be protected by the recipient in a satisfactory manner. A statement of mutual cooperation to facilitate information sharing between the two supervisors would be helpful in this regard.

7. In certain cases, there may be a serious conflict between the KYC policies of a parent bank imposed by its home authority and what is permitted in a cross-border office. There may, for example, be local laws that prevent inspections by the parent banks' compliance officers, internal auditors or home country supervisors, or that enable bank customers to use fictitious names or to hide behind agents or intermediaries that are forbidden from revealing who their clients are. In such cases, the home supervisor should communicate with the host supervisor in order to confirm whether there are indeed genuine legal impediments and whether they apply extraterritorially. If they prove to be insurmountable, and there are no satisfactory alternative arrangements, the home supervisor should make it clear to the host that the bank may decide for itself, or be required by its home supervisor, to close down the operation in question. In the final analysis, any arrangements underpinning such on-site examinations should provide a mechanism that permits an assessment that is satisfactory to the home supervisor. Statements of cooperation or memoranda of understanding setting out the mechanics of the arrangements may be helpful. Access to information by home country supervisors should be as unrestricted as possible, and at a minimum they should have free access to the banks' general policies and procedures for customer due diligence and for dealing with suspicions.

Article 43: Privacy and Civil Liberty[68]

1. The measures carried out by the states parties under this Convention shall take place with full respect for the rule of law.

68 GAOR 54/109, *supra*.

2. Nothing in this Convention shall be interpreted as affected other rights and obligations of states and individuals under international law, in particular the Charter of the United Nations, the Alliance initiative, international humanitarian law, international human rights law, and international refugee law.
3. Any person who is taken into custody or regarding whom any other measures are taken or proceedings are carried out pursuant to this Convention shall be guaranteed fair treatment, including the enjoyment of all rights and guaranteed in conformity with the law of the state in the territory of which that person is present and applicable provisions of international law.

Article 44: Notification of Documents[69]

1. The Parties shall afford each other the widest measure of mutual assistance in the serving of judicial documents to persons affected by provisional measures and confiscation.
2. Nothing in this article is intended to interfere with:
   (a) the possibility of sending judicial documents, by postal channels, directly to persons abroad;
   (b) the possibility for judicial officers, officials or other competent authorities of the Party of origin to effect service of judicial documents directly through the consular authorities of that Party or through judicial officers, officials or other competent authorities of the Party of destination, unless the Party of destination makes a declaration to the contrary to the Secretary General of the Alliance at the time of signature or when depositing its instrument of ratification, acceptance, approval or accession.
3. When serving judicial documents to persons abroad affected by provisional measures or confiscation orders issued in the sending Party, this Party shall indicate what legal remedies are available under its law to such persons.

69 Council of Europe, Treaty Office, *Convention on Laundering, Search, Seizure and Confiscation of the Proceeds from Crime*, http://www.coe.int/web/conventions/full-list/-/conventions/treaty/141.

Article 45: Private Sector Collaboration[70]

The states parties shall also promote, where appropriate, technical cooperation and training programs with other regional and international organizations conducing activities related to the purposes of this Convention.

AML/CTF training assists committed countries to:

1. implement the Financial Action Task Force (FATF) standards, which mainly address:
   (a) the types of AML/CTF laws and regulations a country should have;
   (b) the agencies a country should establish (Financial Intelligence Units (FIUs), regulatory agencies, specialized law enforcement and prosecutorial authorities);
   (c) the reporting regime and the entities within and outside of the financial sector that should be obliged to file reports (e.g., banks, money remitters, exchange houses, securities brokers, mutual funds, insurance companies, casinos, lawyers, accountants, realtors, art dealers, etc); and
   (d) the sharing of non-evidentiary information via the FIU and evidentiary information via MLATs and MLAAs to generate cooperation with other countries to ensure conviction of launderers;
2. Provide Law Enforcement With Financial Investigative Skills;
3. Obtain Training For Prosecutors To Develop Money-laundering Cases;
4. Obtain Training For Those In The Regulatory And Supervisory Authorities, Such As Bank Supervisors;
5. Train Judges In specific elements of money-laundering and terrorist financing crimes. AML/CTF programs shall also provide support on issues related to access to financial intelligence reports (suspicious transaction reports, cash transaction reports, reports on the cross-border transportation of currency or monetary instruments, and reports on cross-border wire transfers); obligated reporting entities (both financial and non-financial institutions); interagency and international information exchange; and broad asset seizure, forfeiture and management capabilities.
6. Each State Party shall take measures, in accordance with the fundamental principles of its domestic law, to prevent corruption involving the private sector, enhance accounting and auditing standards in the private sector and, where appropriate, provide effective, proportionate and dissuasive civil, administrative or criminal penalties for failure to comply with such measures.

70 GAOR 58/4, *supra*.

7. Measures to achieve these ends may include, inter alia:
   (a) Promoting cooperation between law enforcement agencies and relevant private entities;
   (b) Promoting the development of standards and procedures designed to safeguard the integrity of relevant private entities, including codes of conduct for the correct, honorable and proper performance of the activities of business and all relevant professions and the prevention of conflicts of interest, and for the promotion of the use of good commercial practices among businesses and in the contractual relations of businesses with the State;
   (c) Promoting transparency among private entities, including, where appropriate, measures regarding the identity of legal and natural persons involved in the establishment and management of corporate entities;
   (d) Preventing the misuse of procedures regulating private entities, including procedures regarding subsidies and licenses granted by public authorities for commercial activities;
   (e) Preventing conflicts of interest by imposing restrictions, as appropriate and for a reasonable period of time, on the professional activities of former public officials or on the employment of public officials by the private sector after their resignation or retirement, where such activities or employment relate directly to the functions held or supervised by those public officials during their tenure;
   (f) Ensuring that private enterprises, taking into account their structure and size, have sufficient internal auditing controls to assist in preventing and detecting acts of corruption and that the accounts and required financial statements of such private enterprises are subject to appropriate auditing and certification procedures.
8. In order to prevent corruption, each State Party shall take such measures as may be necessary, in accordance with its domestic laws and regulations regarding the maintenance of books and records, financial statement disclosures and accounting and auditing standards, to prohibit the following acts carried out for the purpose of committing any of the offences established in accordance with this Convention:
   (a) The establishment of off-the-books accounts;
   (b) The making of off-the-books or inadequately identified transactions;
   (c) The recording of non-existent expenditure;
   (d) The entry of liabilities with incorrect identification of their objects;
   (e) The use of false documents;

and (f) The intentional destruction of bookkeeping documents earlier than foreseen by the law.

9. Each State Party shall disallow the tax deductibility of expenses that constitute bribes, the latter being one of the constituent elements of the offences, where appropriate, other expenses incurred in furtherance of corrupt conduct.

Article 46: Cooperation between National Authorities and the Private Sector[71]

Each State Party shall take such measures as may be necessary to encourage, in accordance with its domestic law, cooperation between national investigating and prosecuting authorities and entities of the private sector, in particular financial institutions, relating to matters involving the commission of offences established in accordance with this Convention.

Article 47: AML/CTF Compliance Officer[72]

A program must provide for the designated business group to designate a person as the "AML/CTF Compliance Officer" at the management level. The AML/CTF Compliance Officer may have other duties.

Article 48: Internal Procedures, Training and Feedback[73]

1. Member States shall require that the institutions and persons covered by this Convention establish adequate and appropriate policies and procedures of customer due diligence, reporting, record keeping, internal control, risk assessment, risk management, compliance management and communication in order to forestall and prevent operations related to money-laundering or terrorist financing.
2. Member States shall require that credit and financial institutions covered by this Convention communicate relevant policies and procedures where applicable to branches and majority-owned subsidiaries in third countries.

---

71 GAOR 58/4, *supra.*

72 AMLCTFRI (2007), *supra.*

73 EU (205), *supra.*

3. Member States shall require that the institutions and persons covered by this Convention take appropriate measures so that their relevant employees are aware of the provisions in force on the basis of this Convention.
4. These measures shall include participation of their relevant employees in special ongoing training programs to help them recognize operations which may be related to money-laundering or terrorist financing and to instruct them as to how to proceed in such cases.
5. Where a natural person, falling within any of the categories, performs his professional activities as an employee of a legal person, the obligations in this Section shall apply to that legal person rather than to the natural person.
6. Member States shall ensure that the institutions and persons covered by this Convention have access to up-to-date information on the practices of money launderers and terrorist financers and on indications leading to the recognition of suspicious transactions.
7. Member States shall ensure that, wherever practicable, timely feedback on the effectiveness of and follow-up to reports of suspected money-laundering or terrorist financing is provided.

Article 49: Anti-money-laundering and Counter-terrorism Financing Program[74]

1. A standard anti-money-laundering and Counter-terrorism financing program is a written program that:
   (a) applies to a particular reporting entity; and
   (b) is divided into the following parts:
      (i) Part A (general);
      (ii) Part B (customer identification).

Note: A standard anti-money-laundering and Counter-terrorism financing program does not bind the reporting entity unless the reporting entity adopts the program.

2. Part A of a standard anti-money-laundering and Counter-terrorism financing program is a part:
   (a) the primary purpose of which is to:
      (i) identify; and
      (ii) mitigate; and

74 AMLCTF (2006), *supra.*

(iii) manage; the risk the reporting entity may reasonably face that the provision by the reporting entity of designated services at or through a permanent establishment of the reporting entity in a Member State might (whether inadvertently or otherwise) involve or facilitate:
(iv) money-laundering; or
(v) financing of terrorism; and

(b) if the reporting entity provides designated services at or through a permanent establishment of the reporting entity in a foreign country—another purpose of which is to ensure that the reporting entity takes such action (if any) as is specified in the AML/CTF Rules in relation to the provision by the reporting entity of designated services at or through a permanent establishment of the reporting entity in a foreign country; and

(c) that complies with such requirements (if any) as are specified in the AML/CTF Rules.

3. For the purposes of this Convention, a money-laundering and terrorism-financing risk assessment is an assessment by a reporting entity of:

(a) the risk the reporting entity may reasonably face that the provision by the reporting entity of designated services at or through a permanent establishment of the reporting entity in a Member State might (whether inadvertently or otherwise) involve or facilitate:
(i) money-laundering; or
(ii) financing of terrorism; and

(b) what the reporting entity will need to do, or continue to do, to:
(i) identify; and
(ii) mitigate; and
(iii) manage; the risk the reporting entity may reasonably face that the provision by the reporting entity of designated services at or through a permanent establishment of the reporting entity in a Member State might (whether inadvertently or otherwise) involve or facilitate:
(iv) money-laundering; or
(v) financing of terrorism.

4. For the purposes of these Rules, in identifying its ML/TF risk a reporting entity must consider the risk posed by the following factors:

(1) its customer types, including any politically exposed persons;
(2) the types of designated services it provides;
(3) the methods by which it delivers designated services; and
(4) the foreign jurisdictions with which it deals.

Article 50: Supervision[75]

1. Member States shall provide that currency exchange offices, trust and company service providers shall be licensed or registered and casinos be licensed in order to operate their business legally. Member States shall provide that money transmission or remittance offices shall be licensed or registered in order to operate their business legally.
2. Member States shall require competent authorities to refuse licensing or registration of the entities referred to in paragraph 1 if they are not satisfied that the persons who effectively direct or will direct the business of such entities or the beneficial owners of such entities are fit and proper persons.

Article 51: Bank Secrecy[76]

1. Each State Party shall ensure that, in the case of domestic criminal investigations of offences established in accordance with this Convention, there are appropriate mechanisms available within its domestic legal system to overcome obstacles that may arise out of the application of bank secrecy laws.
2. Banking or professional secrecy may not be invoked as a ground for refusal to provide information or required in connection with an investigation which relates to laundering and is ordered by, or carried out under the supervision of, a judicial authority.
3. Professional secrecy or privilege shall not be invoked as a ground not to comply with the obligations under this law when the information is requested, or the production of a related document is ordered in accordance with this law.

Article 52: Protection of Identity of Persons Making Reports[77]

This section applies in respect of the following information:

(a) any report;
(b) any information the disclosure of which will identify, or is reasonably likely to identify, any person:

75 EU (2005), *supra*.
76 GAOR 58/4, *supra*.
77 AMLCTFAB (2017), *supra*.

(i) as a person who, in his or her capacity as an officer, employee, or agent of a financial institution or reporting entity, has handled or identified property that was the subject of a report;
(ii) as a person who has prepared a report;
(iii) or (iii) as a person who has made a report;

(c) any information that discloses or is reasonably likely to disclose the existence of a report.

Article 53: Bribery in the Private Sector[78]

Each State Party shall consider adopting such legislative and other measures as may be necessary to establish as criminal offences, when committed intentionally in the course of economic, financial or commercial activities:

1. The promise, offering or giving, directly or indirectly, of an undue advantage to any person who directs or works, in any capacity, for a private sector entity, for the person himself or herself or for another person, in order that he or she, in breach of his or her duties, act or refrain from acting;
2. The solicitation or acceptance, directly or indirectly, of an undue advantage by any person who directs or works, in any capacity, for a private sector entity, for the person himself or herself or for another person, in order that he or she, in breach of his or her duties, act or refrain from acting.

Article 54: Embezzlement of Property in the Private Sector[79]

Each State Party shall consider adopting such legislative and other measures as may be necessary to establish as a criminal offence, when committed intentionally in the course of economic, financial or commercial activities, embezzlement by a person who directs or works, in any capacity, in a private sector entity of any property, private funds or securities or any other thing of value entrusted to him or her by virtue of his or her position.

---

78 GAOR 58/4, *supra.*
79 GAOR 58/4, *supra.*

Article 55: Participation of Society[80]

1. Each State Party shall take appropriate measures, within its means and in accordance with fundamental principles of its domestic law, to promote the active participation of individuals and groups outside the public sector, such as civil society, non-governmental organizations and community-based organizations, in the prevention of and the fight against corruption and to raise public awareness regarding the existence, causes and gravity of and the threat posed by corruption. This participation should be strengthened by such measures as:
   (a) Enhancing the transparency of and promoting the contribution of the public to decision-making processes;
   (b) Ensuring that the public has effective access to information;
   (c) Undertaking public information activities that contribute to non-tolerance of corruption, as well as public education programs, including school and university curricula;
   (d) Respecting, promoting and protecting the freedom to seek, receive, publish and disseminate information concerning corruption. That freedom may be subject to certain restrictions, but these shall only be such as are provided for by law and are necessary:
      (i) For respect of the rights or reputations of others;
      (ii) For the protection of national security or *ordre public* or of public health or morals.
2. Each State Party shall take appropriate measures to ensure that the relevant anti-corruption bodies referred to in this Convention are known to the public and shall provide access to such bodies, where appropriate, for the reporting, including anonymously, of any incidents that may be considered to constitute an offence established in accordance with this Convention.

Article 56: Collection, Exchange and Analysis of Information on the Nature of Organized Crime[81]

1. Each State Party shall consider analyzing, in consultation with the scientific and academic communities, trends in organized crime in its

80 GAOR 58/4, *supra*.
81 GAOR 55/25, *supra*.

territory, the circumstances in which organized crime operates, as well as the professional groups and technologies involved.

2. States Parties shall consider developing and sharing analytical expertise concerning organized criminal activities with each other and through international and regional organizations. For that purpose, common definitions, standards and methodologies should be developed and applied as appropriate.
3. Each State Party shall consider monitoring its policies and actual measures to combat organized crime and making assessments of their effectiveness and efficiency.

Article 57: Exchange of Information[82,83]

Contracting Parties shall, in accordance with international and national law, endeavor to take all practicable measure in:

1. Developing and strengthening systems related to surveillance procedures, securing borders, and land, sea and air passages in order to prevent infiltration through them.
2. Strengthening systems for ensuring the safety and protection of personalities, vital installations and means of public transport.
3. Re-enforcing protection, security and safety of diplomatic and consular persons and missions; and regional and international organizations accredited in the Contracting State in accordance with the conventions and rules of international law which govern this subject.
4. Promoting security intelligence activities and coordinating them with the intelligence activities of each Contracting State pursuant to their respective intelligence policies, aimed at exposing the objectives of terrorist groups and organizations, thwarting their designs and revealing the extent of their danger to security and stability.
5. Parties in a bid to enhance public awareness of the scourge of terrorist acts and the need to combat such acts, by providing guarantees and incentives that will encourage the population to give information on terrorist acts or other acts which may help to uncover such acts and arrest their perpetrators.

---

82 Organization of African Unity, *Convention on the Prevention and Combating of Terrorism, (1999)*, 14 July 199, available from http://treaties.un.org/doc/db/Terrorism/OAU-english.pdf.

83 Convention of the Islamic Conference on Combatting International Terrorism, available from www.oic-cdpu.org/en/getdoc/?dID=13

6. Establishing a data base by each Contracting State to collect and analyze data on terrorist elements, groups, movements and organizations and monitor developments of the phenomenon of terrorism and successful experiences in combating it. Moreover, the Contracting State shall update this information and exchange them with competent authorities in other Contracting States within the limits of the laws and regulations in every State.
7. Develop and strengthen methods of controlling and monitoring land, sea and air borders and customs and immigration checkpoints in order to pre-empt any infiltration by individuals or groups involved in the planning, organization and execution of terrorist acts;
8. To take all necessary measures to eliminate and prevent the establishment of webs supporting all kinds of terrorist crimes and support networks in any form whatsoever.
9. To ascertain, when granting asylum, that the asylum seeker is not involved in any terrorist act.

States Parties shall co-operate among themselves in preventing and combating terrorist acts in conformity with national legislation and procedures of each State in the following areas:

1. States Parties undertake to strengthen the exchange of information among them regarding:
   (a) acts and crimes committed by terrorist groups, their leaders and elements, their headquarters and training camps, their means and sources of funding and acquisition of arms, the types of arms, ammunition and explosives used, and other means in their possession;
   (b) the communication and propaganda methods and techniques used by the terrorists groups, the behavior of these groups, the movement of their leaders and elements, as well as their travel documents.
2. States Parties undertake to exchange any information that leads to:
   (a) the arrest of any person charged with a terrorist act against the interests of a State Party or against its nationals, or attempted to commit such an act or participated in it as an accomplice, instigator, or financer, being implicated in such acts either by assistance, collusion, instigation, or financing.
   (b) the seizure and confiscation of any type of arms, ammunition, explosives, devices or funds or other instrumentalities of crime used to commit a terrorist act or intended for that purpose.

3. Secured network
   (a) States Parties shall take appropriate measures consistent with their national law to protect the confidentiality of any information which they receive in confidence by virtue of the provisions of this Convention from another State Party or through the participation in an activity carried out for the implementation of this Convention. If States Parties provide information to international organizations in confidence, steps shall be taken to ensure that the confidentiality of such information is protected.
   (b) States Parties shall not be required by this Convention to provide any information which they are not permitted to communicate pursuant to national law or which would jeopardize the security of the State concerned or the physical protection of individuals.
   (c) Each State Party shall, in accordance with its national law, provide to the Alliance, as promptly as possible, any relevant information in their possession concerning:
   (d) The circumstances of the offences;
      (i) The action taken pursuant to
      (ii) The measures taken in relation to the offender or the alleged offender and, in particular, the results of any extradition proceedings or other legal proceedings.
4. States Parties undertake to respect the confidentiality of the information exchanged among them and not to provide such information to another State that is not party to this Convention, or to a third State Party, without the prior consent of the State from where such information originated.
5. Contracting States shall exchange information with the other Parties to combat terrorist crimes and to inform the Contracting State or other States of all available information or data that could prevent terrorist crimes within its territory or against its nationals or residents or interests.
6. Contracting States shall expeditiously inform any other Contracting State regarding available information about any terrorist crime perpetrated in its territory aimed at undermining the interests of that State or its nationals and to state the facts surrounding the crime in terms of its circumstances, criminals involved, victims, losses, devices and methods utilized to carry out the crime, without prejudicing investigation and inquiry requisites.
7. States Parties undertake to promote co-operation among themselves and to help each other with regard to procedures relating to the investigation

and arrest of persons suspected of, charged with or convicted of terrorist acts, in conformity with the national law of each State.

8. States Parties shall co-operate among themselves in conducting and exchanging studies and researches on how to combat terrorist acts and to exchange expertise relating to control of terrorist acts.
9. States Parties shall co-operate among themselves, where possible, in providing any available technical assistance in drawing up programs or organizing, where necessary and for the benefit of their personnel, joint training courses involving one or several States Parties in the area of control of terrorist acts, in order to improve their scientific, technical and operational capacities to prevent and combat such acts.

Article 58: Protection Measures[84,85]

Contracting Parties shall, in accordance with international and national law, endeavor to take all practicable measure for the purpose of preventing the offences mentioned in Article 3.

1. States Parties shall cooperate in the prevention of the crimes set forth in article 3, particularly by:
   (a) Taking all practicable measures, including, if necessary, adapting their domestic legislation, to prevent and counter preparations in their respective territories for the commission of those crimes within or outside their territories, including measures to prohibit in their territories illegal activities of persons, groups and organizations that encourage, instigate, organize, knowingly finance or engage in the perpetration of offences as set forth in article 3;
   (b) Exchanging accurate and verified information in accordance with their national law, and coordinating the taking of administrative and other measures as appropriate to prevent the commission of those crimes. promote the exchange of information and expertise on terrorist acts and establish data bases for the collection and analysis of information and data on terrorist elements, groups, movements and organizations;
   (c) Where appropriate, through research and development regarding methods of detection of explosives and other harmful substances

84 U.N., *Convention for the Suppression of Unlawful Seizure of Aircraft*, 16 December 1970, *U.N.T.S.* 1973, available from http://www.refworld.org/docid/3ddcaa774.html.

85 CICCIT (1999), *supra*.

that can cause death or bodily injury, consultations on the development of standards for...in order to identify the origin of the funds, investigations, exchange of information on preventive measures, cooperation and transfer of technology, equipment and related materials;

(d) In respect of the offences set forth in article 3, as well as preparations to commit such offences about which has learned, and also to inform, where appropriate, international organizations. If States Parties provide information to international organizations in confidence, steps shall be taken to ensure that the confidentiality of such information is protected;

(e) In the absence of a treaty, consider facilitating the extradition of persons suspected of having committed terrorist acts.

2. States Parties undertake to refrain from any acts aimed at organizing, supporting, financing, committing or inciting to commit terrorist acts, or providing havens for terrorists, directly or indirectly, including the provision of weapons and their stockpiling in their countries and the issuing of visas and travel documents.

3. States Parties shall adopt any legitimate measures aimed at preventing and combating terrorist acts in accordance with the provisions of this Convention and their respective national legislation, in particular, they shall do the following:

(a) Arresting perpetrators of terrorist's crimes and prosecuting them according to the national law or extraditing them in accordance with the provisions of this Convention or existing Conventions between the requesting and requested States.

(b) Barring their territories from being used as an arena for planning, organizing, executing terrorist crimes or initiating or participating in these crimes in any form; including preventing the infiltration of terrorist elements or their gaining refuge or residence therein individually or collectively, or receiving hosting, training, arming, financing or extending any facilities to them.

(c) Cooperating and coordinating with the rest of the Contracting States, particularly neighboring countries which suffer from similar or common terrorist crimes.

(d) Establish effective co-operation between relevant domestic security officials and services and the citizens of the States.

(e) Developing and strengthening systems relating to detecting transportation, importing, exporting stockpiling, and using of weapons, ammunition and explosives as well as other means of aggression, killing and destruction in addition to strengthening trans-border and custom controls in order to intercept their transfer from one Contracting State to another or to other States unless they are intended for specific legitimate purposes.

(f) Ensuring effective protection of persons working in the field of criminal justice as well as to witnesses and investigators.

(g) Ensuring effective protection of information sources and witnesses on terrorist crimes.

(h) Extending necessary assistance to victims of terrorism.

(i) Establishing effective cooperation between the concerned organs in the contracting States and the citizens for combating terrorism including extending appropriate guarantees and appropriate incentives to encourage informing on terrorist acts and submitting information to help uncover them and cooperating in arresting the perpetrators.

Article 59: Training and Technical Assistance[86,87]

1. Each State Party shall, to the extent necessary, initiate, develop or improve specific training programs for its law enforcement personnel, including prosecutors, investigating magistrates and customs personnel, and other personnel charged with the prevention, detection and control of the offences covered by this Convention. Such programs may include secondments and exchanges of staff. Such programs shall deal, in particular and to the extent permitted by domestic law, with the following:

   (a) Methods used in the prevention, detection and control of the offences covered by this Convention;

   (b) Routes and techniques used by persons suspected of involvement in offences covered by this Convention, including in transit States, and appropriate countermeasures;

   (c) Monitoring of the movement of contraband;

   (d) Detection and monitoring of the movements of proceeds of crime, property, equipment or other instrumentalities and methods used for the transfer, concealment or disguise of such proceeds, property, equipment or other instrumentalities, as well as methods used in combating money-laundering and other financial crimes;

---

86 GAOR 55/25, *supra.*

87 GAOR 58/4, *supra.*

(e) Collection of evidence;
(f) Control techniques in free trade zones and free ports;
(g) Modern law enforcement equipment and techniques, including electronic surveillance, controlled deliveries and undercover operations;
(h) Methods used in combating transnational organized crime committed through the use of computers, telecommunications networks or other forms of modern technology;
(i) Methods used in the protection of victims and witnesses.

2. States Parties shall assist one another in planning and implementing research and training programs designed to share expertise in the areas referred to in paragraph 1 of this article and to that end shall also, when appropriate, use regional and international conferences and seminars to promote cooperation and to stimulate discussion on problems of mutual concern, including the special problems and needs of transit States.

3. States Parties shall promote training and technical assistance that will facilitate extradition and mutual legal assistance. Such training and technical assistance may include language training, secondments and exchanges between personnel in central authorities or agencies with relevant responsibilities.

4. In the case of existing bilateral and multilateral agreements or arrangements, States Parties shall strengthen, to the extent necessary, efforts to maximize operational and training activities within international and regional organizations and within other relevant bilateral and multilateral agreements or arrangements.

5. Each State Party shall, to the extent necessary, initiate, develop or improve specific training programs for its personnel responsible for preventing and combating corruption. Such training programs could deal, inter alia, with the following areas:
(a) Effective measures to prevent, detect, investigate, punish and control corruption, including the use of evidence-gathering and investigative methods;
(b) Building capacity in the development and planning of strategic anticorruption policy;
(c) Training competent authorities in the preparation of requests for mutual legal assistance that meet the requirements of this Convention;
(d) Evaluation and strengthening of institutions, public service management and the management of public finances, including public procurement, and the private sector;

(e) Preventing and combating the transfer of proceeds of offences established in accordance with this Convention and recovering such proceeds;
(f) Detecting and freezing of the transfer of proceeds of offences established in accordance with this Convention;
(g) Surveillance of the movement of proceeds of offences established in accordance with this Convention and of the methods used to transfer, conceal or disguise such proceeds;
(h) Appropriate and efficient legal and administrative mechanisms and methods for facilitating the return of proceeds of offences established in accordance with this Convention;
(i) Methods used in protecting victims and witnesses who cooperate with judicial authorities;
(j) Training in national and international regulations and in languages.

6. States Parties shall, according to their capacity, consider affording one another the widest measure of technical assistance, especially for the benefit of developing countries, in their respective plans and programs to combat corruption, including material support and training in the areas referred to in paragraph 1 of this article, and training and assistance and the mutual exchange of relevant experience and specialized knowledge, which will facilitate international cooperation between States Parties in the areas of extradition and mutual legal assistance.
7. States Parties shall strengthen, to the extent necessary, efforts to maximize operational and training activities in international and regional organizations and in the framework of relevant bilateral and multilateral agreements or arrangements.
8. States Parties shall consider assisting one another, upon request, in conducting evaluations, studies and research relating to the types, causes, effects and costs of corruption in their respective countries, with a view to developing, with the participation of competent authorities and society, strategies and action plans to combat corruption.
9. In order to facilitate the recovery of proceeds of offences established in accordance with this Convention, States Parties may cooperate in providing each other with the names of experts who could assist in achieving that objective.
10. States Parties shall consider using subregional, regional and international conferences and seminars to promote cooperation and technical assistance and to stimulate discussion on problems of mutual concern

between CTF actors, including the special problems and needs of developing countries and countries with economies in transition.

11. States Parties shall consider establishing voluntary mechanisms with a view to contributing financially to the efforts of developing countries and countries with economies in transition to apply this Convention through technical assistance programs and projects.

12. Each State Party shall consider making voluntary contributions to the United Nations Office on Drugs and Crime for the purpose of fostering, through the Office, programs and projects in developing countries with a view to implementing this Convention.

Article 60: Information Exchange and Training[88]

1. Law enforcement, immigration or other relevant authorities of States Parties shall, as appropriate, cooperate with one another by exchanging information, in accordance with their domestic law, to enable them to determine:
   (a) Whether individuals crossing or attempting to cross an international border with travel documents belonging to other persons or without travel documents are perpetrators or victims of trafficking in persons;
   (b) The types of travel document that individuals have used or attempted to use to cross an international border for the purpose of trafficking in persons;
   (c) The means and methods used by organized criminal groups for the purpose of trafficking in persons, including the recruitment and transportation of victims, routes and links between and among individuals and groups engaged in such trafficking, and possible measures for detecting them.

2. States Parties shall provide or strengthen training for law enforcement, immigration and other relevant officials in the prevention of trafficking in persons. The training should focus on methods used in preventing such trafficking, prosecuting the traffickers and protecting the rights of the victims, including protecting the victims from the traffickers. The training should also take into account the need to consider human rights and child- and gender-sensitive issues and it should encourage

88 GAOR 55/25, *supra*.

cooperation with nongovernmental organizations, other relevant organizations and other elements of civil society.

3. A State Party that receives information shall comply with any request by the State Party that transmitted the information that places restrictions on its use.

Article 61: International Cooperation and Coordination[89]

1. Contracting States shall cooperate within the scope of their capabilities to provide available technical assistance for preparing programs or holding joint training sessions with one or more Contracting State if the need arises for personnel required in the field of combating terrorism in order to improve their scientific and practical potential and upgrade their performance standards.
2. Contracting States shall cooperate with each other to undertake and exchange studies and researches on combating terrorist crimes as well as exchange of expertise in this field.
3. States Parties shall establish and enhance, where necessary, channels of communication between their competent authorities in order to facilitate the secure and rapid exchange of information concerning all aspects of the offences established in this Convention and in the international instruments of the United Nations related to terrorism.

Article 62: Cooperation between Fius[90,91]

1. A financial intelligence unit is hereby established that serves as a central, national agency responsible for receiving, requesting, analyzing and disseminating information concerning suspected proceeds of crime and potential financing of terrorism, as provided for by this law.
2. The head of the financial intelligence unit shall be appointed by the ministry. The composition, organization, operation and resources of the fi-

89 CICCIT (1999), *supra.*

90 Council of Europe Treaty Office *Council of Europe Convention on Laundering, Search, Seizure, and Confiscation of the Proceeds of Crime and on the Financing of Terrorism*, 15 May 2005, available from http://conventions.coe.int/Treaty/en/Treaties/Html/198.htm.

91 IMF (2005), *supra.*

nancial intelligence unit shall be established by decree, regulation, or other relevant legal instrument.

3. Parties shall ensure that FIUs, as defined in this Convention, shall cooperate for the purpose of combating money-laundering, to assemble and analyze, or, if appropriate, investigate within the FIU relevant information on any fact which might be an indication of money-laundering in accordance with their national powers.
4. For the purposes of paragraph 1, each Party shall ensure that FIUs exchange, spontaneously or on request and either in accordance with this Convention or in accordance with existing or future memoranda of understanding compatible with this Convention, any accessible information that may be relevant to the processing or analysis of information or, if appropriate, to investigation by the FIU regarding financial transactions related to money-laundering and the natural or legal persons involved.
5. Each Party shall ensure that the performance of the functions of the FIUs under this article shall not be affected by their internal status, regardless of whether they are administrative, law enforcement or judicial authorities.
6. Each request made under this article shall be accompanied by a brief statement of the relevant facts known to the requesting FIU. The FIU shall specify in the request how the information sought will be used.
7. When a request is made in accordance with this article, the requested FIU shall provide all relevant information, including accessible financial information and requested law enforcement data, sought in the request, without the need for a formal letter of request under applicable conventions or agreements between the Parties.
8. An FIU may refuse to divulge information which could lead to impairment of a criminal investigation being conducted in the requested Party or, in exceptional circumstances, where divulging the information would be clearly disproportionate to the legitimate interests of a natural or legal person or the Party concerned or would otherwise not be in accordance with fundamental principles of national law of the requested Party. Any such refusal shall be appropriately explained to the FIU requesting the information.
9. Information or documents obtained under this article shall only be used for the purposes laid down in paragraph 1. Information supplied by a counterpart FIU shall not be disseminated to a third party, nor be used by the receiving FIU for purposes other than analysis, without prior consent of the supplying FIU.

10. When transmitting information or documents pursuant to this article, the transmitting FIU may impose restrictions and conditions on the use of information for purposes other than those stipulated in paragraph 7. The receiving FIU shall comply with any such restrictions and conditions.
11. Where a Party wishes to use transmitted information or documents for criminal investigations or prosecutions for the purposes laid down in paragraph 7, the transmitting FIU may not refuse its consent to such use unless it does so on the basis of restrictions under its national law or conditions referred to in paragraph 6. Any refusal to grant consent shall be appropriately explained.
12. FIUs shall undertake all necessary measures, including security measures, to ensure that information submitted under this article is not accessible by any other authorities, agencies or departments.
13. The information submitted shall be protected, in conformity with international rules of confidentiality and protection of personal data as those that apply under the national legislation applicable to the requesting FIU.
14. The transmitting FIU may make reasonable enquiries as to the use made of information provided and the receiving FIU shall, whenever practicable, provide such feedback.
15. Parties shall indicate the unit which is an FIU within the meaning of this article.

Article 63: Access to Information[92]

1. In relation to any information it has received in accordance with its functions, the financial intelligence unit has the authority to obtain from any entity or person subject to the reporting obligation any additional information it deems useful for the accomplishment of its functions. The information requested shall be provided within the time limits set and the form specified by the financial intelligence unit.
2. The financial intelligence unit has the authority to access and review information on-site that belongs to or is in the custody of financial institutions and designated non-financial businesses and professions, which is necessary to the fulfilment of its functions.

92 IMF (2005), *supra*.

3. The financial intelligence unit may request in relation to any report it has received, any additional information it deems useful for the accomplishment of its functions from:
   (a) police departments;
   (b) authorities responsible for the supervision of the entities and persons subject to this law;
   (c) other administrative agencies of the State; in accordance with applicable procedures, judicial authorities.
4. The information requested shall be provided within the time limits set by the financial intelligence unit.
5. The financial intelligence unit may obtain the information referred to in paragraphs (1) through (3) pursuant to a request received from a foreign financial intelligence unit.
6. A Global Intelligence Unit shall be created to coordinate, exchange and gather information collected by FIUs for the purpose of Counter-terrorism financing.
7. A GFIU shall direct enforcement at the International Level in cooperation with the Alliance and related State Parties.

Article 64: Confidentiality[93]

The staff of the financial intelligence unit shall be required to keep confidential any information obtained within the scope of their duties, even after the cessation of those duties within the financial intelligence unit. Such information may only be used for the purposes provided for in accordance with the law.

Article 65: Relations with Foreign Counterpart Agency[94]

1. The financial intelligence unit may, spontaneously or upon request, share information with any foreign counterpart agency that performs similar functions and is subject to similar secrecy obligations, regardless of the nature of the agency, subject to reciprocity, or on the basis of cooperation arrangements.

93 IMF (2005), *supra*.
94 IMF (2005), *supra*.

2. For the purpose of paragraph (1) the financial intelligence unit may enter into an agreement or arrangement with a foreign counterpart agency that perform similar functions and is subject to similar secrecy obligations.
3. The information provided shall be used only for the purposes of combating money-laundering, predicate offences and financing of terrorism and only with the consent of the foreign counterpart agency.

Any breach of the obligation provided under this provision should be subject to penalties or sanctions.

Article 66: International Cooperation for Postponement of Suspicious Transactions[95]

1. Each Party shall adopt such legislative or other measures as may be necessary to permit urgent action to be initiated by a FIU, at the request of a foreign FIU, to suspend or withhold consent to a transaction going ahead for such periods and depending on the same conditions as apply in its domestic law in respect of the postponement of transactions.
2. The action referred to in paragraph 1 shall be taken where the requested FIU is satisfied, upon justification by the requesting FIU, that:
   (a) the transaction is related to terrorism-financing; and
   (b) the transaction would have been suspended, or consent to the transaction going ahead would have been withheld, if the transaction had been the subject of a domestic suspicious transaction report.

Article 67: Content of Request[96,97]

1. Any request for co-operation under this chapter shall specify:
   (a) the authority making the request and the authority carrying out the investigations or proceedings;
   (b) the object of and the reason for the request;

95 Search and Seizure (2005), *supra*.
96 Search and Seizure (2005), *supra*.
97 Proceeds from Crime, *supra*.

(c) the matters, including the relevant facts (such as date, place and circumstances of the offence) to which the investigations or proceedings relate, except in the case of a request for notification;
(d) in so far as the co-operation involves coercive action:
  (i) the text of the statutory provisions or, where this is not possible, a statement of the relevant law applicable; and
  (ii) an indication that the measure sought or any other measures having similar effects could be taken in the territory of the requesting Party under its own law;
(e) where necessary and in so far as possible:
  (i) details of the person or persons concerned, including name, date and place of birth, nationality and location, and, in the case of a legal person, its seat; and
  (ii) the property in relation to which co-operation is sought, its location, its connection with the person or persons concerned, any connection with the offence, as well as any available information about other persons, interests in the property; and
(f) any particular procedure the requesting Party wishes to be followed.

2. A request for provisional measures in relation to seizure of property on which a confiscation order consisting in the requirement to pay a sum of money may be realized shall also indicate a maximum amount for which recovery is sought in that property.

3. In addition to the indications mentioned in paragraph 1, any request shall contain:
(a) a certified true copy of the confiscation order made by the court in the requesting Party and a statement of the grounds on the basis of which the order was made, if they are not indicated in the order itself;
(b) an attestation by the competent authority of the requesting Party that the confiscation order is enforceable and not subject to ordinary means of appeal;
(c) information as to the extent to which the enforcement of the order is requested; and
(d) information as to the necessity of taking any provisional measures;
(e) a statement of the facts relied upon by the requesting Party sufficient to enable the requested Party to seek the order under its domestic law;
(f) when third parties have had the opportunity to claim rights, documents demonstrating that this has been the case.

Article 68: Requests for Information on Banking Transactions[98]

1. On request by another Party, the requested Party shall provide the particulars of specified bank accounts and of banking operations which have been carried out during a specified period through one or more accounts specified in the request, including the particulars of any sending or recipient account.
2. The obligation set out in this article shall apply only to the extent that the information is in the possession of the bank holding the account.
3. The requesting Party shall in its request indicate why it considers the requested information relevant for the purpose of the criminal investigation into the offence.
4. The requested Party may make the execution of such a request dependent on the same conditions as it applies in respect of requests for search and seizure.
5. Parties may extend this provision to accounts held in non-bank financial institutions. Such extension may be made subject to the principle of reciprocity.

Article 69: Requests for the Monitoring of Banking Transactions[99]

1. Each Party shall ensure that, at the request of another Party, it is able to monitor, during a specified period, the banking operations that are being carried out through one or more accounts specified in the request and communicate the results thereof to the requesting Party.
2. The requesting Party shall in its request indicate why it considers the requested information relevant for the purpose of the criminal investigation into the offence.
3. The decision to monitor shall be taken in each individual case by the competent authorities of the requested Party, with due regard for the national law of that Party.
4. The practical details regarding the monitoring shall be agreed between the competent authorities of the requesting and requested Parties.

---

98 Search and Seizure (2005), *supra*.

99 Search and Seizure (2005), *supra*.

5. Parties may extend this provision to accounts held in non-bank financial institutions.

Article 70: Plurality of Requests[100]

1. Where the requested Party receives more than one request in respect of the same person or property, the plurality of requests shall not prevent that Party from dealing with the requests involving the taking of provisional measures.
2. In the case of plurality of requests, the requested Party shall consider consulting the requesting Parties.

Article 71: Mutual Legal Assistance[101,102,103]

1. States Parties shall afford one another the widest measure of mutual legal assistance in investigations, prosecutions and judicial proceedings in relation to the offences covered by this Convention as provided for in article 3 and shall reciprocally extend to one another similar assistance where the requesting State Party has reasonable grounds to suspect that the offence referred to in article 3, is transnational in nature, including that victims, witnesses, proceeds, instrumentalities or evidence of such offences are located in the requested State Party and that the offence involves an organized criminal group.
2. Mutual legal assistance shall be afforded to the fullest extent possible under relevant laws, treaties, agreements and arrangements of the requested State Party with respect to investigations, prosecutions and judicial proceedings in relation to the offences for which a legal person may be held liable in the requesting State Party.
3. Mutual legal assistance to be afforded in accordance with this article may be requested for any of the following purposes:
   (a) Taking evidence or statements from persons;
   (b) Effecting service of judicial documents;

100 Search and Seizure (2005), *supra*.
101 GAOR 55/25, *supra*.
102 Proceeds from Crime, *supra*.
103 GAOR 58/4, *supra*.

(c) Executing searches and seizures, and freezing;
(d) Examining objects and sites;
(e) Providing information, evidentiary items and expert evaluations;
(f) Providing originals or certified copies of relevant documents and records, including government, bank, financial, corporate or business records;
(g) Identifying or tracing proceeds of crime, property, instrumentalities or other things for evidentiary purposes;
(h) Facilitating the voluntary appearance of persons in the requesting State Party;
(i) Any other type of assistance that is not contrary to the domestic law of the requested State Party.

4. Without prejudice to domestic law, the competent authorities of a State Party may, without prior request, transmit information relating to criminal matters to a competent authority in another State Party where they believe that such information could assist the authority in undertaking or successfully concluding inquiries and criminal proceedings or could result in a request formulated by the latter State Party pursuant to this Convention.
5. The transmission of information pursuant to paragraph 4 of this article shall be without prejudice to inquiries and criminal proceedings in the State of the competent authorities providing the information. The competent authorities receiving the information shall comply with a request that said information remain confidential, even temporarily, or with restrictions on its use. However, this shall not prevent the receiving State Party from disclosing in its proceedings information that is exculpatory to an accused person. In such a case, the receiving State Party shall notify the transmitting State Party prior to the disclosure and, if so requested, consult with the transmitting State Party. If, in an exceptional case, advance notice is not possible, the receiving State Party shall inform the transmitting State Party of the disclosure without delay.
6. The provisions of this article shall not affect the obligations under any other treaty, bilateral or multilateral, that governs or will govern, in whole or in part, mutual legal assistance.
7. If States Parties are bound by a mutual legal assistance treaty, the corresponding provisions of that treaty shall apply unless the States Parties agree to apply this article in lieu thereof. States Parties are strongly encouraged to apply these paragraphs if they facilitate cooperation.
8. States Parties shall not decline to render mutual legal assistance pursuant to this article on the ground of bank secrecy.

9. States Parties may decline to render mutual legal assistance pursuant to this article on the ground of absence of dual criminality. However, the requested State Party may, when it deems appropriate, provide assistance, to the extent it decides at its discretion, irrespective of whether the conduct would constitute an offence under the domestic law of the requested State Party.

10. A person who is being detained or is serving a sentence in the territory of one State Party whose presence in another State Party is requested for purposes of identification, testimony or otherwise providing assistance in obtaining evidence for investigations, prosecutions or judicial proceedings in relation to offences covered by this Convention may be transferred if the following conditions are met:
    (a) The person freely gives his or her informed consent;
    (b) The competent authorities of both States Parties agree, subject to such conditions as those States Parties may deem appropriate.

11. For the purposes of paragraph 10 of this article:
    (a) The State Party to which the person is transferred shall have the authority and obligation to keep the person transferred in custody, unless otherwise requested or authorized by the State Party from which the person was transferred;
    (b) The State Party to which the person is transferred shall without delay implement its obligation to return the person to the custody of the State Party from which the person was transferred as agreed beforehand, or as otherwise agreed, by the competent authorities of both States Parties;
    (c) The State Party to which the person is transferred shall not require the State Party from which the person was transferred to initiate extradition proceedings for the return of the person;
    (d) The person transferred shall receive credit for service of the sentence being served in the State from which he or she was transferred for time spent in the custody of the State Party to which he or she was transferred.

12. Unless the State Party from which a person is to be transferred in accordance with paragraphs 10 and 11 of this article so agrees, that person, whatever his or her nationality, shall not be prosecuted, detained, punished or subjected to any other restriction of his or her personal liberty in the territory of the State to which that person is transferred in respect of acts, omissions or convictions prior to his or her departure from the territory of the State from which he or she was transferred.

13. Each State Party shall designate a central authority that shall have the responsibility and power to receive requests for mutual legal assistance and either to execute them or to transmit them to the competent authorities for execution. Where a State Party has a special region or territory with a separate system of mutual legal assistance, it may designate a distinct central authority that shall have the same function for that region or territory. Central authorities shall ensure the speedy and proper execution or transmission of the requests received. Where the central authority transmits the request to a competent authority for execution, it shall encourage the speedy and proper execution of the request by the competent authority. The Secretary of the Alliance shall be notified of the central authority designated for this purpose at the time each State Party deposits its instrument of ratification, acceptance or approval of or accession to this Convention. Requests for mutual legal assistance and any communication related thereto shall be transmitted to the central authorities designated by the States Parties. This requirement shall be without prejudice to the right of a State Party to require that such requests and communications be addressed to it through diplomatic channels and, in urgent circumstances, where the States Parties agree, through the International Criminal Police Organization, if possible.
14. Requests shall be made in writing or, where possible, by any means capable of producing a written record, in a language acceptable to the requested State Party, under conditions allowing that State Party to establish authenticity. The Secretary of the Alliance shall be notified of the language or languages acceptable to each State Party at the time it deposits its instrument of ratification, acceptance or approval of or accession to this Convention. In urgent circumstances and where agreed by the States Parties, requests may be made orally, but shall be confirmed in writing forthwith.
15. A request for mutual legal assistance shall contain:
    (a) The identity of the authority making the request;
    (b) The subject matter and nature of the investigation, prosecution or judicial proceeding to which the request relates and the name and functions of the authority conducting the investigation, prosecution or judicial proceeding;
    (c) A summary of the relevant facts, except in relation to requests for the purpose of service of judicial documents;
    (d) A description of the assistance sought and details of any particular procedure that the requesting State Party wishes to be followed;

(e) Where possible, the identity, location and nationality of any person concerned;
(f) The purpose for which the evidence, information or action is sought.

16. The requested State Party may request additional information when it appears necessary for the execution of the request in accordance with its domestic law or when it can facilitate such execution.
17. A request shall be executed in accordance with the domestic law of the requested State Party and, to the extent not contrary to the domestic law of the requested State Party and where possible, in accordance with the procedures specified in the request.
18. Wherever possible and consistent with fundamental principles of domestic law, when an individual is in the territory of a State Party and has to be heard as a witness or expert by the judicial authorities of another State Party, the first State Party may, at the request of the other, permit the hearing to take place by video conference if it is not possible or desirable for the individual in question to appear in person in the territory of the requesting State Party. States Parties may agree that the hearing shall be conducted by a judicial authority of the requesting State Party and attended by a judicial authority of the requested State Party.
19. The requesting State Party shall not transmit or use information or evidence furnished by the requested State Party for investigations, prosecutions or judicial proceedings other than those stated in the request without the prior consent of the requested State Party. Nothing in this paragraph shall prevent the requesting State Party from disclosing in its proceedings information or evidence that is exculpatory to an accused person. In the latter case, the requesting State Party shall notify the requested State Party prior to the disclosure and, if so requested, consult with the requested State Party. If, in an exceptional case, advance notice is not possible, the requesting State Party shall inform the requested State Party of the disclosure without delay.
20. The requesting State Party may require that the requested State Party keep confidential the fact and substance of the request, except to the extent necessary to execute the request. If the requested State Party cannot comply with the requirement of confidentiality, it shall promptly inform the requesting State Party.
21. Mutual legal assistance may be refused:
(a) If the request is not made in conformity with the provisions of this article;

(b) If the requested State Party considers that execution of the request is likely to prejudice its sovereignty, security, *ordre public* or other essential interests;
(c) If the authorities of the requested State Party would be prohibited by its domestic law from carrying out the action requested with regard to any similar offence, had it been subject to investigation, prosecution or judicial proceedings under their own jurisdiction;
(d) If it would be contrary to the legal system of the requested State Party relating to mutual legal assistance for the request to be granted.

22. States Parties may not refuse a request for mutual legal assistance on the sole ground that the offence is also considered to involve fiscal matters.
23. Reasons shall be given for any refusal of mutual legal assistance.
24. The requested State Party shall execute the request for mutual legal assistance as soon as possible and shall take as full account as possible of any deadlines suggested by the requesting State Party and for which reasons are given, preferably in the request. The requested State Party shall respond to reasonable requests by the requesting State Party on progress of its handling of the request. The requesting State Party shall promptly inform the requested State Party when the assistance sought is no longer required.
25. Mutual legal assistance may be postponed by the requested State Party on the ground that it interferes with an ongoing investigation, prosecution or judicial proceeding.
26. Before refusing a request pursuant to paragraph 21 of this article or postponing its execution pursuant to paragraph 25 of this article, the requested State Party shall consult with the requesting State Party to consider whether assistance may be granted subject to such terms and conditions as it deems necessary. If the requesting State Party accepts assistance subject to those conditions, it shall comply with the conditions.
27. Without prejudice to the application of paragraph 12 of this article, a witness, expert or other person who, at the request of the requesting State Party, consents to give evidence in a proceeding or to assist in an investigation, prosecution or judicial proceeding in the territory of the requesting State Party shall not be prosecuted, detained, punished or subjected to any other restriction of his or her personal liberty in that territory in respect of acts, omissions or convictions prior to his or her departure from the territory of the requested State Party. Such safe conduct shall cease when the witness, expert or other person having had, for a period

of fifteen consecutive days or for any period agreed upon by the States Parties from the date on which he or she has been officially informed that his or her presence is no longer required by the judicial authorities, an opportunity of leaving, has nevertheless remained voluntarily in the territory of the requesting State Party or, having left it, has returned of his or her own free will.

28. The ordinary costs of executing a request shall be borne by the requested State Party, unless otherwise agreed by the States Parties concerned. If expenses of a substantial or extraordinary nature are or will be required to fulfil the request, the States Parties shall consult to determine the terms and conditions under which the request will be executed, as well as the manner in which the costs shall be borne.

29. The requested State Party:
    (a) Shall provide to the requesting State Party copies of government records, documents or information in its possession that under its domestic law are available to the general public;
    (b) May, at its discretion, provide to the requesting State Party in whole, in part or subject to such conditions as it deems appropriate, copies of any government records, documents or information in its possession that under its domestic law are not available to the general public.

30. States Parties shall consider, as may be necessary, the possibility of concluding bilateral or multilateral agreements or arrangements that would serve the purposes of, give practical effect to or enhance the provisions of this article.

31. Without prejudice to its own investigations or proceedings, a Party may without prior request forward to another Party information on instrumentalities and proceeds, when it considers that the disclosure of such information might assist the receiving Party in initiating or carrying out investigations or proceedings or might lead to a request by that Party under this chapter.

32. States Parties shall afford one another the greatest measure of assistance in connection with criminal proceedings brought in respect of the offences set forth in article 3, including the supply of evidence at their disposal necessary for the proceedings.

33. The State Party in which any of the crimes set forth in article 3 has been committed shall, if it has reason to believe that an alleged offender has fled from its territory, communicate to all other States concerned, directly or through the Alliance, all the pertinent facts regarding the crime committed and all available information regarding the identity of the alleged offender.

34. Whenever any of the crimes set in forth in article 3 has been committed against an internationally protected person, any State Party which has information concerning the victim and the circumstances of the crime shall endeavor to transmit it, under the conditions provided for in its internal law, fully and promptly to the State Party on whose behalf he was exercising his functions.
35. The law of the State requested shall apply in all cases. This provision shall not affect obligations under any other treaty, bilateral or multilateral, which governs or will govern, in whole or in part, mutual assistance in criminal matters.

Article 72: Border Measures[104,105]

1. The states parties, consistent with their respective domestic legal and administrative regimes, shall promote cooperation and the exchange of information in order to improve border and customs control measures to detect and prevent the international movement of terrorists and trafficking in arms or other materials intended to support terrorist activities.
2. In this context, they shall promote cooperation and the exchange of information to improve their controls on the issuance of travel and identity documents and to prevent their counterfeiting, forgery, or fraudulent use.
3. Such measures shall be carried out without prejudice to applicable international commitments in relation to the free movement of people and the facilitation of commerce.
4. Without prejudice to international commitments in relation to the free movement of people, States Parties shall strengthen, to the extent possible, such border controls as may be necessary to prevent and detect trafficking in persons.
5. Each State Party shall adopt legislative or other appropriate measures to prevent, to the extent possible, means of transport operated by commercial carriers from being used in the commission of offences.
6. Where appropriate, and without prejudice to applicable international conventions, such measures shall include establishing the obligation of commercial carriers, including any transportation company or the owner or operator of any means of transport, to ascertain that all passengers are

104 U.N. GAOR, *Inter-American Convention Against Terrorism*, AG/RES 1840, 3 June 2002, available from http://www.oas.org/xxxiiga/english/docs_en/docs_items/AGres1840_02.htm.

105 GAOR 55/25, *supra*.

in possession of the travel documents required for entry into the receiving State.

7. Each State Party shall take the necessary measures, in accordance with its domestic law, to provide for sanctions in cases of violation of the obligation set forth in this Convention.
8. Each State Party shall consider taking measures that permit, in accordance with its domestic law, the denial of entry or revocation of visas of persons implicated in the commission of offences established in accordance with this Protocol.
9. Without prejudice to this Convention, States Parties shall consider strengthening cooperation among border control agencies by, inter alia, establishing and maintaining direct channels of communication.

Article 73: Investigations[106,107]

1. Any State Party may, while recognizing the sovereign rights of States Parties in matters of criminal investigation, request any other State Party to carry out, with its assistance and cooperation, on the latter's territory, criminal investigations related to any judicial proceedings concerning alleged terrorist acts and, in particular:
   (a) the examination of witnesses and transcripts of statements made as evidence;
   (b) the opening of judicial information;
   (c) the initiation of investigation processes;
   (d) the collection of documents and recordings or, in their absence, authenticated copies thereof;
   (e) conducting inspections and tracing of assets for evidentiary purposes;
   (f) executing searches and seizures; and
   (g) service of judicial documents.
2. Each Contracting State pledges to promote cooperation with other contracting states and to extend assistance in the field of investigation procedures in terms of arresting escaped suspects or those convicted for terrorist crimes in accordance with the laws and regulations of each country.

106 OAU (1999), *supra.*
107 CICCIT (1999), *supra.*

Article 74: Joint Investigations[108]

States Parties shall consider concluding bilateral or multilateral agreements or arrangements whereby, in relation to matters that are the subject of investigations, prosecutions or judicial proceedings in one or more States, the competent authorities concerned may establish joint investigative bodies. In the absence of such agreements or arrangements, joint investigations may be undertaken by agreement on a case-by-case basis. The States Parties involved shall ensure that the sovereignty of the State Party in whose territory such investigation is to take place is fully respected.

Article 75: Special Investigative Powers and Techniques[109,110]

1. Each Party shall adopt such legislative and other measures as may be necessary to empower its courts or other competent authorities to order that bank, financial or commercial records be made available or be seized in order to carry out the actions referred to in Article 3. A Party shall not decline to act under the provisions of this article on grounds of bank secrecy.
2. Each Party shall consider adopting such legislative and other measures as may be necessary to enable it to use special investigative techniques facilitating the identification and tracing of proceeds and the gathering of evidence related thereto. Such techniques may include monitoring orders, observation, interception of telecommunications, access to computer systems and orders to produce specific documents.
3. If permitted by the basic principles of its domestic legal system, each State Party shall, within its possibilities and under the conditions prescribed by its domestic law, take the necessary measures to allow for the appropriate use of controlled delivery and, where it deems appropriate, for the use of other special investigative techniques, such as electronic or other forms of surveillance and undercover operations, by its competent authorities in its territory for the purpose of effectively combating organized crime.
4. For the purpose of investigating the offences covered by this Convention, States Parties are encouraged to conclude, when necessary, appropriate

108 GAOR 58/4, *supra*.
109 Proceeds from Crime, *supra*.
110 Search and Seizure (2005), *supra*.

bilateral or multilateral agreements or arrangements for using such special investigative techniques in the context of cooperation at the international level. Such agreements or arrangements shall be concluded and implemented in full compliance with the principle of sovereign equality of States and shall be carried out strictly in accordance with the terms of those agreements or arrangements.

5. In the absence of an agreement or arrangement, decisions to use such special investigative techniques at the international level shall be made on a case-by-case basis and may, when necessary, take into consideration financial arrangements and understandings with respect to the exercise of jurisdiction by the States Parties concerned.
6. Decisions to use controlled delivery at the international level may, with the consent of the States Parties concerned, include methods such as intercepting and allowing the goods to continue intact or be removed or replaced in whole or in part.
7. No cause of action shall lie in any court against any provider of a wire or electronic communication service, landlord, custodian, or other person (including any officer, employee, agent, or other specified person thereof) that furnishes any information, facilities, or technical assistance in accordance with a court order or request for emergency assistance under this Act.

Article 76: Prevention and Detection of Transfers of Proceeds of Crime[111]

1. Each State Party shall take such measures as may be necessary, in accordance with its domestic law, to require financial institutions within its jurisdiction to verify the identity of customers, to take reasonable steps to determine the identity of beneficial owners of funds deposited into high-value accounts and to conduct enhanced scrutiny of accounts sought or maintained by or on behalf of individuals who are, or have been, entrusted with prominent public functions and their family members and close associates. Such enhanced scrutiny shall be reasonably designed to detect suspicious transactions for the purpose of reporting to competent authorities and should not be so construed as to discourage or prohibit financial institutions from doing business with any legitimate customer.

111 GAOR 58/4, *supra*.

2. In order to facilitate implementation of the measures provided for in paragraph 1 of this article, each State Party, in accordance with its domestic law and inspired by relevant initiatives of regional, interregional and multilateral organizations against terrorist financing, shall:
   (a) Issue advisories regarding the types of natural or legal person to whose accounts financial institutions within its jurisdiction will be expected to apply enhanced scrutiny, the types of accounts and transactions to which to pay particular attention and appropriate account-opening, maintenance and recordkeeping measures to take concerning such accounts; and
   (b) Where appropriate, notify financial institutions within its jurisdiction, at the request of another State Party or on its own initiative, of the identity of particular natural or legal persons to whose accounts such institutions will be expected to apply enhanced scrutiny, in addition to those whom the financial institutions may otherwise identify.
3. In the context of paragraph 2 (a) of this article, each State Party shall implement measures to ensure that its financial institutions maintain adequate records, over an appropriate period of time, of accounts and transactions involving the persons mentioned in paragraph 1 of this article, which should, as a minimum, contain information relating to the identity of the customer as well as, as far as possible, of the beneficial owner.
4. With the aim of preventing and detecting transfers of proceeds of offences established in accordance with this Convention, each State Party shall implement appropriate and effective measures to prevent, with the help of its regulatory and oversight bodies, the establishment of banks that have no physical presence and that are not affiliated with a regulated financial group. Moreover, States Parties may consider requiring their financial institutions to refuse to enter into or continue a correspondent banking relationship with such institutions and to guard against establishing relations with foreign financial institutions that permit their accounts to be used by banks that have no physical presence and that are not affiliated with a regulated financial group.
5. Each State Party shall consider establishing, in accordance with its domestic law, effective financial disclosure systems for appropriate public officials and shall provide for appropriate sanctions for non-compliance. Each State Party shall also consider taking such measures as may be necessary to permit its competent authorities to share that information with the competent authorities in other States Parties when necessary to

investigate, claim and recover proceeds of offences established in accordance with this Convention.

6. Each State Party shall consider taking such measures as may be necessary, in accordance with its domestic law, to require appropriate public officials having an interest in or signature or other authority over a financial account in a foreign country to report that relationship to appropriate authorities and to maintain appropriate records related to such accounts. Such measures shall also provide for appropriate sanctions for non-compliance.

Article 77: Asset Freezing, Seizure, Confiscation & Recovery[112]

Each Party shall adopt such legislative and other measures as may be necessary to ensure that the measures to freeze, seize and confiscate also encompass:

(a) the property into which the proceeds have been transformed or converted;

(b) property acquired from legitimate sources, if proceeds have been intermingled, in whole or in part, with such property, up to the assessed value of the intermingled proceeds;

(c) income or other benefits derived from proceeds, from property into which proceeds of crime have been transformed or converted or from property with which proceeds of crime have been intermingled, up to the assessed value of the intermingled proceeds, in the same manner and to the same extent as proceeds.

Each State Party must take such measures as may be necessary to permit its competent authorities to give effect to an order of confiscation issued by a court of another state party.

Article 78: Seizure of Cash[113]

1. A customs officer or constable may seize any cash if he has reasonable grounds for suspecting that it is:
   (a) Recoverable property, or
   (b) Intended by any person for the use in unlawful conduct.

112 Search and Seizure (2005), *supra*.

113 PCA (2002), *supra*.

2. A customs officer or constable may also seize cash part of which he has reasonable grounds for suspecting to be-
   (a) Recoverable property, or
   (b) Intended by any person for the use in unlawful conduct,

If it is not reasonably practicable to seize only that part.

3. This section does not authorize the seizure of an amount of cash if it or, as the case may be, the part to which his suspicions relates, is less than the minimum amount.

Per this Convention, the requested State Party shall:

1. In the case of embezzlement of public funds or of laundering of embezzled public funds, return the confiscated property to the requesting State Party;
2. In the case of proceeds of any other offence covered by this Convention, return the confiscated property to the requesting State Party, when the requesting State Party reasonably establishes its prior ownership of such confiscated property to the requested State Party or when the requested State Party recognizes damage to the requesting State Party as a basis for returning the confiscated property;
3. In all other cases, give priority consideration to returning confiscated property to the requesting State Party, returning such property to its prior legitimate owners or compensating the victims of the crime.
4. Where appropriate, unless States Parties decide otherwise, requested States Parties may deduct reasonable expenses incurred in investigations, prosecutions or judicial proceedings leading to the return or disposition of confiscated property pursuant to this article.
5. Where appropriate, States Parties may also give special consideration to concluding agreements or mutually acceptable arrangements, on a case-by-case basis, for the final disposal of confiscated property.

Article 79: Obligation to Take Provisional Measures[114]

1. At the request of another Party which has instituted criminal proceedings or proceedings for the purpose of confiscation, a Party shall take the

114 Search and Seizure (2005), *supra*.

necessary provisional measures, such as freezing or seizing, to prevent any dealing in, transfer or disposal of property which, at a later stage, may be the subject of a request for confiscation or which might be such as to satisfy the request.

2. A Party which has received a request for confiscation shall, if so requested, take the measures mentioned in paragraph 1 of this article in respect of any property which is the subject of the request or which might be such as to satisfy the request.

Article 80: Execution of Provisional Measures[115]

1. The provisional measures shall be carried out as permitted by and in accordance with the domestic law of the requested Party and, to the extent not incompatible with such law, in accordance with the procedures specified in the request.
2. Before lifting any provisional measure taken pursuant to this article, the requested Party shall, wherever possible, give the requesting Party an opportunity to present its reasons in favor of continuing the measure.

Article 81: Freezing of Funds Associated with Financing of Terrorism[116]

1. The funds of terrorists, those who finance terrorism and terrorist organizations, designated by the Member State acting pursuant this Convention, shall be frozen by ministerial decree or other administrative decision. Such decree or decision shall define the terms, conditions and time limits applicable to the freezing, and shall be notified to the Secretary of the Alliance. The financial institutions and designated non-financial business and profession holding such funds shall immediately freeze them.
2. The financial institutions and designated non-financial business and profession shall report without delay to the financial intelligence unit or other competent authority the existence of funds linked to terrorists, terrorist organizations or individuals or entities associated with or that

115 Proceeds from Crime, *supra*.

116 IMF (2005), *supra*.

belong to such individuals or organizations in accordance with lists established by the United Nations, INTERPOL, the Alliance, and other related listing entities.

3. Failure to comply with the provisions of paragraphs (1) and (2) by a financial institution or a designated non-financial business and profession holding such funds shall be punishable by an administrative fine ranging from $50,000 to $150,000 and a fine ranging from $30,000 to $80,000 to other criminal sanctions.

Article 82: Obligation to Confiscate[117]

1. A Party, which has received a request made by another Party for confiscation concerning instrumentalities or proceeds, situated in its territory, shall:
   (a) enforce a confiscation order made by a court of a requesting Party in relation to such instrumentalities or proceeds; or
   (b) submit the request to its competent authorities for the purpose of obtaining an order of confiscation and, if such order is granted, enforce it.
2. For the purposes of applying paragraph 1.b of this article, any Party shall whenever necessary have competence to institute confiscation proceedings under its own law.
3. The provisions of paragraph 1 of this article shall also apply to confiscation consisting in a requirement to pay a sum of money corresponding to the value of proceeds, if property on which the confiscation can be enforced is located in the requested Party. In such cases, when enforcing confiscation pursuant to paragraph 1, the requested Party shall, if payment is not obtained, realize the claim on any property available for that purpose.
4. If a request for confiscation concerns a specific item of property, the Parties may agree that the requested Party may enforce the confiscation in the form of a requirement to pay a sum of money corresponding to the value of the property.

117 Search and Seizure (2005), *supra*.

Article 83: Confiscation Measures[118,119]

1. Proceeds of crime or property confiscated by a State Party shall be disposed of by that State Party in accordance with its domestic law and administrative procedures.
2. When acting on the request made by another State Party, States Parties shall, to the extent permitted by domestic law and if so requested, give priority consideration to returning the confiscated proceeds of crime or property to the requesting State Party so that it can give compensation to the victims of the crime or return such proceeds of crime or property to their legitimate owners.
3. When acting on the request made by another State Party, a State Party may give special consideration to concluding agreements or arrangements on:
   (a) Contributing the value of such proceeds of crime or property or funds derived from the sale of such proceeds of crime or property or a part thereof to the account designated in accordance with this Convention and to intergovernmental bodies specializing in the fight against organized crime;
   (b) Sharing with other States Parties, on a regular or case-by-case basis, such proceeds of crime or property, or funds derived from the sale of such proceeds of crime or property, in accordance with its domestic law or administrative procedures.
4. Each Party shall adopt such legislative and other measures as may be necessary to enable it to confiscate instrumentalities and proceeds or property the value of which corresponds to such proceeds.
5. Each Party may, at the time of signature or when depositing its instrument of ratification, acceptance, approval or accession, by a declaration addressed to the Secretary General of the Alliance, declare that paragraph 1 of this article applies only to offences or categories of offences specified in such declaration.
6. Each Party shall adopt such legislative and other measures as may be necessary to enable it to identify and trace property which is liable to confiscation, and to prevent any dealing in, transfer or disposal of such property.
7. Property confiscated by a Party, shall be disposed of by that Party in accordance with its domestic law and administrative procedures.

---

118 GAOR 55/25, *supra.*

119 Search and Seizure (2005), *supra.*

8. When acting on the request made by another Party, Parties shall, to the extent permitted by domestic law and if so requested, give priority consideration to returning the confiscated property to the requesting Party so that it can give compensation to the victims of the crime or return such property to their legitimate owners.
9. When acting on the request made by another Party, a Party may give special consideration to concluding agreements or arrangements on sharing with other Parties, on a regular or case-by-case basis, such property, in accordance with its domestic law or administrative procedures.
10. In the event of a conviction for actual or attempted money-laundering, an order shall be issued for the confiscation:
    (a) Of the property forming the subject of the offence, including income and other benefits obtained therefrom, against any person to whom they may belong, unless their owner can establish that he acquired them by actually paying a fair price or in return for the provision of services corresponding to their value or on any other legitimate grounds and that he was unaware of their illicit origin;
    (b) Of property belonging directly or indirectly to a person convicted of a laundering offence to his spouse, cohabitee or children, unless the parties concerned can establish the lawful origin thereof.

Moreover, if, in cases where an offence is established by the court, the perpetrator or perpetrators thereof cannot be convicted, the court may nevertheless order the confiscation of the property to which the offence related.

Article 84: Provisonal Measures and Confiscation[120]

Countries should adopt measures similar to those set forth in the Vienna and Palermo Conventions, including legislative measures, to enable their competent authorities to confiscate property laundered, proceeds from money-laundering or predicate offences, instrumentalities used in or intended for use in the commission of these offences, or property of corresponding value, without prejudicing the rights of bona fide third parties.

Such measures should include the authority to:

(a) identify, trace and evaluate property which is subject to confiscation;

120 FATF (1990), *supra*.

(b) carry out provisional measures, such as freezing and seizing, to prevent any dealing, transfer or disposal of such property;
(c) take steps that will prevent or void actions that prejudice the State's ability to recover property that is subject to confiscation;
(d) take any appropriate investigative measures.

Countries may consider adopting measures that allow such proceeds or instrumentalities to be confiscated without requiring a criminal conviction, or which require an offender to demonstrate the lawful origin of the property alleged to be liable to confiscation, to the extent that such a requirement is consistent with the principles of their domestic law.

Article 85: Confiscation and Seizure[121,122]

1. States Parties shall adopt, to the greatest extent possible within their domestic legal systems, such measures as may be necessary to enable confiscation of:
   (a) Proceeds of crime derived from offences covered by this Convention or property the value of which corresponds to that of such proceeds;
   (b) Property, equipment or other instrumentalities used in or destined for use in offences covered by this Convention.
2. States Parties shall adopt such measures as may be necessary to enable the identification, tracing, freezing or seizure of any item referred to in paragraph 1 of this article for the purpose of eventual confiscation.
3. If proceeds of crime have been transformed or converted, in part or in full, into other property, such property shall be liable to the measures referred to in this article instead of the proceeds.
4. If proceeds of crime have been intermingled with property acquired from legitimate sources, such property shall, without prejudice to any powers relating to freezing or seizure, be liable to confiscation up to the assessed value of the intermingled proceeds.
5. Income or other benefits derived from proceeds of crime, from property into which proceeds of crime have been transformed or converted or from property with which proceeds of crime have been intermingled

121 Search and Seizure (2005), *supra*.
122 GAOR 55/25, *supra*.

shall also be liable to the measures referred to in this article, in the same manner and to the same extent as proceeds of crime.

6. For the purposes of this Convention, each State Party shall empower its courts or other competent authorities to order that bank, financial or commercial records be made available or be seized. States Parties shall not decline to act under the provisions of this paragraph on the ground of bank secrecy.
7. States Parties may consider the possibility of requiring that an offender demonstrate the lawful origin of alleged proceeds of crime or other property liable to confiscation, to the extent that such a requirement is consistent with the principles of their domestic law and with the nature of the judicial and other proceedings.
8. The provisions of this article shall not be construed to prejudice the rights of *bona fide* third parties.
9. Nothing contained in this article shall affect the principle that the measures to which it refers shall be defined and implemented in accordance with and subject to the provisions of the domestic law of a State Party.

Article 86: Confiscation of Property of Criminal Organizations[123]

Property of which a criminal organization has power of disposal shall be confiscated if there is a connection between that property and the offence, unless the lawful origin of the property is established.

Article 87: Execution of Confiscation[124]

1. The procedures for obtaining and enforcing the confiscation shall be governed by the law of the requested Party.
2. The requested Party shall be bound by the findings as to the facts in so far as they are stated in a conviction or judicial decision of the requesting Party or in so far as such conviction or judicial decision is implicitly based on them.
3. Each Party may, at the time of signature or when depositing its instrument of ratification, acceptance, approval or accession, by a declaration addressed to the Secretary of the Alliance, declare that paragraph 2 of

123 IMLIN, *supra*.
124 Proceeds from Crime, *supra*.

this article applies only subject to its constitutional principles and the basic concepts of its legal system.

4. If the confiscation consists in the requirement to pay a sum of money, the competent authority of the requested Party shall convert the amount thereof into the currency of that Party at the rate of exchange ruling at the time when the decision to enforce the confiscation is taken.
5. The requesting Party alone shall have the right to decide on any application for review of the confiscation order.

Article 88: Confiscated Property[125]

Any property confiscated by the requested Party shall be disposed of by that Party in accordance with its domestic law, unless otherwise agreed by the Parties concerned.

Article 89: Right of Enforcement and Maximum Amount of Confiscation[126]

1. A request for confiscation does not affect the right of the requesting Party to enforce itself the confiscation order.
2. Nothing in this Convention shall be so interpreted as to permit the total value of the confiscation to exceed the amount of the sum of money specified in the confiscation order. If a Party finds that this might occur, the Parties concerned shall enter into consultations to avoid such an effect.
3. Nothing in this Convention shall be so interpreted as to permit the total value of the confiscation to exceed the amount of the sum of money specified in the confiscation order. If a Party finds that this might occur, the Parties concerned shall enter into consultations to avoid such an effect.
4. In the absence of mutual assistance treaties between countries regarding mutual assistance measures, States Parties shall afford each other assistance in accordance with their national law.

125 Proceeds from Crime, *supra*.

126 Proceeds from Crime, *supra*.

Article 90: Surrender of Property[127]

1. Within the limits authorized under the national legislation and subject to the rights of third parties, all property found in the territory of a Member State that has been acquired as a result of the offence committed or that may be required as evidence shall, if the requesting State so requests, be surrendered to the requesting State if extradition is granted.
2. The property in question may, if the requesting State so requests, be surrendered to the requesting State even if the extradition agreed to cannot be carried out.
3. Should that property be liable to seizure or confiscation in the territory of a Member State, the State may temporarily retain it or hand it over.
4. Where the national legislation or the rights of third parties so require, any property so surrendered shall be returned to the Member State free of charge, after the completion of the proceedings, if the Member State so requests.

Article 91: Forfeiture of Terrorist Cash[128]

1. This Convention provides a provision for enabling cash which:
   (a) is intended to be used for the purposes of terrorism;
   (b) consists of resources of an organization which is a proscribed organization; or
   (c) is, or represents, property obtained through terrorism.
2. The powers conferred by paragraph 1 is exercisable in relation to any cash whether or not any proceedings have been brought for an offence in connection with the cash.

Article 92: Disposal of Confiscated Proceeds of Crime or Property[129]

1. Proceeds of crime or property confiscated by a State Party shall be disposed of by that State Party in accordance with its domestic law and administrative procedures.

---

127 GAOR 55/25, *supra*.

128 Anti-terrorism, Crime and Security Act, 2001, c. 24, http://www.legislation.gov.uk/ukpga/2001/24/pdfs/ukpga_20010024_en.pdf.

129 GAOR 55/25, *supra*.

2. When acting on the request made by another State Party, States Parties shall, to the extent permitted by domestic law and if so requested, give priority consideration to returning the confiscated proceeds of crime or property to the requesting State Party so that it can give compensation to the victims of the crime or return such proceeds of crime or property to their legitimate owners.
3. When acting on the request made by another State Party, a State Party may give special consideration to concluding agreements or arrangements on:
   (a) Contributing the value of such proceeds of crime or property or funds derived from the sale of such proceeds of crime or property or a part thereof to the account designated and to intergovernmental bodies specializing in the fight against organized crime;
   (b) Sharing with other States Parties, on a regular or case-by-case basis, such proceeds of crime or property, or funds derived from the sale of such proceeds of crime or property, in accordance with its domestic law or administrative procedures.
4. Confiscated property and proceeds shall accrue to the State, which shall be empowered to allocate them to a fund for combating organized crime or drug trafficking. They shall remain encumbered, up to their value, by any rights in rem lawfully established in favor of third parties.
5. In cases where confiscation is ordered under a judgement by default, the confiscated property shall accrue to the State and be realized in accordance with the relevant procedures laid down. However, if the court, ruling on an application to set aside such judgement, acquits the person prosecuted, it shall order restitution to the value of the confiscated property by the State, unless it is established that such property is the proceeds of crime.

Article 93: Management of Seized Funds and Property[130]

1. The central authority of the Alliance for seizure and confiscation shall be responsible for the administration or management of seized assets in accordance with the feasible means available to it, with a view to returning or confiscating such assets in a condition reasonably comparable to their condition at the time of the seizure. The prosecutor's office or the judge overseeing investigations may authorize the sale of funds or property

130 IMF (2005), *supra*.

likely to incur significant depreciation as the result of management or for which the cost of preservation is unreasonably disproportional to its value. In such case, the value of the sale shall remain subject to the seizure.

2. The central authority of the Alliance for seizure and confiscation shall manage the sums of money seized unless they were already entrusted to a financial institution or private manager or were seized or blocked there.
3. In cases where confiscation is ordered under a judgment by default, countries should consider a provision to the effect that the court, ruling on an application to set aside such judgment, may order restitution to the value of the confiscated property by the State, unless it is established that such property is the proceeds of crime.

Article 94: Proceeds of Foreign Crimes[131]

State Members shall collect any foreign property, real or personal, within the jurisdiction of the Alliance, constituting, derived from, or traceable to, any proceeds obtained directly or indirectly from an offense against a foreign nation, or any property used to facilitate such an offense, if the offense involves the manufacture, importation, sale, or distribution of a controlled substance, or any other conduct considered unlawful.

Article 95: Return of Cash Necessary to Satisfy Essential Human Needs[132]

1. The power to detain goods under does not extend to, and the State Member must if practicable return immediately, cash seized if the State Member is satisfied that the cash is (or that things for which it might be exchanged are) necessary to satisfy the essential human needs:
   (a) of an individual from whom the cash has been seized; and
   (b) arising on, or within 7 days after, the date on which the detention would otherwise be effected.
2. Nothing in subsection (1) requires the State Members to return any cash that the Alliance is satisfied is not necessary for the purpose specified in that subsection.

---

131 Financial Crimes Enforcement Network, *USA Patriot Act*, FinCEN.gov, https://www.fincen.gov/resources/statutes-regulations/usa-patriot-act.

132 Terrorism Suppression Act 2002, No 34, 1 March 2017, available from http://www.legislation.govt.nz/act/public/2002/0034/latest/DLM151491.html.

Article 96: Review of Designation, Delisting and Unfreezing[133]

1. Identifying targets for designation should focus on recognizing those persons and entities that represent key elements of terrorist support networks in order to obtain maximum impact in preventing and suppressing acts of terrorism.
2. Member States receiving notification [of designation]…take, in accordance with their domestic laws and practices, all possible measures to notify or inform in a timely manner the listed individual or entity of the designation and to include with this notification a copy of the publicly releasable portion of the statement of case, any information on reasons for listing available on the Committee's website, a description of the effects of designation, as provided in the relevant resolutions, the Committee's procedures for considering delisting requests, and the provisions of UN resolution 1452 regarding available exemptions.
3. To inform designated persons and entities should be informed directly of:
   (a) The designation and its implications, in order to prevent any unintentional breaches on the part of themselves or related third parties;
   (b) The review procedure and information on the de-listing process, including a contact point within the government to address any questions regarding the process;
   (c) Publicly-releasable information concerning the reasons for designation.
4. To ensure procedural fairness both in administrative and judicial procedures for asset freezing, countries should make provision for any person or entity to apply for a review of the designation from the designating authority, with the ability to seek further review of an adverse.
5. Countries party to the Convention should also have procedures in place to allow, upon request, review of the designation decision before a court of other independent competent authority.
6. Availability of, and timely procedure for review of both national and supranational designations pursuant to this Convention, require Pursuant to the United Nations Resolution 1373, countries should have appropriate legal authorities and procedures or mechanisms to delist and unfreeze the funds or other assets of persons and entities that no longer meet the criteria for designation.
7. Concerning due process, including review, delisting and unfreezing, all reasonable efforts should be made by the designating country and

133 FATF (2012c), *supra.*

reviewed and (where appropriate or practicable) the country of residence, and by ASOP as soon as possible after the designation has taken effect.

8. Freezing should take place without delay. However, publication of the action should not take place until the freeze is in effect. This should be the case irrespective of whether the designation was made by a country on its own motion or upon acceptance of a designation request from another country.

Article 97: Establishment of a Central Authority for Seizure and Confiscation[134]

A central authority for seizure and confiscation shall be established under the management of ASOP and its representatives. It shall be responsible for assisting the competent law enforcement or judicial authorities investigating and prosecuting offences in identifying and tracing funds and property that may be subject to seizure and confiscation. It shall collect and maintain all data associated with its mission in accordance with the Data Protection International common legal standards. It shall manage seized assets in cooperation with the prosecutor's office or the judge overseeing investigations.

Article 98: Transfer of Criminal Proceedings[135]

States Parties shall consider the possibility of transferring to one another proceedings for the prosecution of an offence covered by this Convention in cases where such transfer is considered to be in the interests of the proper administration of justice, in particular in cases where several jurisdictions are involved, with a view to concentrating the prosecution.

Article 99: International Cooperation for Purposes of Confiscation[136]

1. A State Party that has received a request from another State Party having jurisdiction over an offence covered by this Convention for confiscation

134 Proceeds from Crime, *supra.*
135 GAOR 55/25, *supra.*
136 GAOR 55/25, *supra.*

of proceeds of crime, property, equipment or other instrumentalities situated in its territory shall, to the greatest extent possible within its domestic legal system:

(a) Submit the request to its competent authorities for the purpose of obtaining an order of confiscation and, if such an order is granted, give effect to it; or

(b) Submit to its competent authorities, with a view to giving effect to it to the extent requested, an order of confiscation issued by a court in the territory of the requesting State Party insofar as it relates to proceeds of crime, property, equipment or other instrumentalities situated in the territory of the requested State Party.

2. Following a request made by another State Party having jurisdiction over an offence covered by this Convention, the requested State Party shall take measures to identify, trace and freeze or seize proceeds of crime, property, equipment or other instrumentalities for the purpose of eventual confiscation to be ordered either by the requesting State Party or, pursuant to a request under paragraph 1 of this article, by the requested State Party.

3. Requests made pursuant to this article shall contain:

(a) a description of the property to be confiscated and a statement of the facts relied upon by the requesting State Party sufficient to enable the requested State Party to seek the order under its domestic law;

(b) a legally admissible copy of an order of confiscation upon which the request is based issued by the requesting State Party, a statement of the facts and information as to the extent to which execution of the order is requested;

(c) statement of the facts relied upon by the requesting State Party and a description of the actions requested.

4. The decisions or actions provided for in paragraphs 1 and 2 of this article shall be taken by the requested State Party in accordance with and subject to the provisions of its domestic law and its procedural rules or any bilateral or multilateral treaty, agreement or arrangement to which it may be bound in relation to the requesting State Party.

5. Each State Party shall furnish copies of its laws and regulations that give effect to this article and of any subsequent changes to such laws and regulations or a description thereof to the Secretary-General of the Alliance.

6. If a State Party elects to make the taking of the measures referred to in paragraphs 1 and 2 of this article conditional on the existence of a relevant treaty, that State Party shall consider this Convention the necessary and sufficient treaty basis.

7. Cooperation under this article may be refused by a State Party if the offence to which the request relates is not an offence covered by this Convention.
8. The provisions of this article shall not be construed to prejudice the rights of bona fide third parties.
9. States Parties shall consider concluding bilateral or multilateral treaties, agreements or arrangements to enhance the effectiveness of international cooperation undertaken pursuant to this article.

Article 100: Informational Gateways and Mutual Legal Assistance Treaties[137]

1. General provisions under this article pertain to the transference of information, evidence, and formal testimonies in reference to the pursuit, investigation, prosecution, forfeiture, recovery, and disposal of property comprised of those derived from or received in kind by means of monetary or any other tangible enrichment or benefit arising from the commission of any illicit act committed in concert with organized criminal enterprise transacting in a cross jurisdictional environment(s).
2. In the event of a formal investigation in the pursuit of a remedy by the requesting State an officially sanctioned Request for Mutual Legal Assistance must be ratified by the Alliance, and the highest Criminal Court of each jurisdiction with a material interest in the recovery.
   (a) The Subcommittee shall require that the requesting State's highest criminal court officially certify and sanction the intent and facts on the case on which the remedy and subsequent forfeiture is being sought.
   (b) The value of the asset sought for forfeiture and remedy by the requesting State shall be officially certified by the jurisdiction of residence no later than the 60th day post certification of facts.
   (c) The Subcommittee shall require that the requesting State post a bond to be held in trust by Alliance in the amount of not less than 1/3 of the total declared value of the asset sought.
3. All parties involved in the exchange or engaging in the pursuit and of the forfeiture and recovery related activities are subject to the governing laws of the requesting State.
   (a) All individuals participating in said matters in an evidentiary capacity are subject to formal certification as to fitness and character

137 Article 1 of the UK-Ireland-Canadian agreement.

for participation in the action by their resident jurisdiction's highest court.

(b) The resident jurisdiction will further be required to certify the existence of any relevant conflicts of interest inherent to the parties that would bar participation in the Action.

(c) The resident jurisdiction shall be required to post a bond held in trust by an independent certified third party for each participating individual who intends to provide material evidence for the forfeiture proceedings in the amount to 1/3 of the total certified present value of the asset sought.

4. Should at any time during the pursuit either party deem that they are unduly burdened by their participation in the investigation and seizure they may appeal to the Alliance for final determination of relief.

(a) Should the Governing body certify the existence of an undue burden the requesting Jurisdiction shall be offered a variance to allow for the appeal for certification of financial need. At such time that the certification is ratified the Alliance shall compel the International Monetary Fund to provide financial assistance related to participation in the form of a loan under customary present terms.

(b) Upon completion of the action and finalization of recovery and disposal all participating jurisdictions are required to submit an officially certified Request for Monetary Relief for expenses incurred during the course of the action.

(c) Upon recovery of the asset the requesting State shall be compelled to compensate all participating jurisdictions for incurred expenses not to exceed an amount totaling all jurisdictional payments of no greater than 75% of the forfeited items certified market value.

Article 101: Funds to Compensate Victims[138]

The Convention incites states to create mechanisms designed to allocate sums from asset confiscations to compensating victims of terrorist violations or their families. Its introduction would be based on national measures. Specific provisions should be introduced into National legislations to allocate the income from sanctions to the fund for the victims of terrorist acts.

138 GAOR 58/4, *supra*.

Article 102: Establishment of Criminal Record[139]

Each State Party may adopt such legislative or other measures as may be necessary to take into consideration, under such terms as and for the purpose that it deems appropriate, any previous conviction in another State of an alleged offender for the purpose of using such information in criminal proceedings relating to an offence covered by this Convention.

Article 103: Denial of Refugee Status[140]

Each State Party shall take appropriate measures, consistent with the relevant provisions of national and international law, for the purpose of ensuring that refugee status is not granted to any person in respect of whom there are serious reasons for considering that he or she has committed an offense established in this Convention.

Article 104: Enforcement[141]

Each State Party shall adopt such measures as may be necessary, including, where appropriate, domestic legislation, to ensure that criminal acts within the scope of this Convention, in particular where they are intended or calculated to provoke a state of terror in the general public or in a group of persons or particular persons, are under no circumstances justifiable by considerations of a political, philosophical, ideological, racial, ethnic, religious or other similar nature and are punished by penalties consistent with their grave nature.

Article 105: Penalties[142,143]

1. Each State Party, in accordance with its domestic legal principles, shall take the necessary measures to enable a legal entity located in its territory or organized under its laws to be held liable when a person responsible

---

139 GAOR 58/4, *supra.*

140 GAOR AG/RES 1840, *supra.*

141 U.N., *International Convention for The Suppression of Acts of Nuclear Terrorism*, (2005), available from https://treaties.un.org/doc/db/Terrorism/english-18-15.pdf.

142 GAOR 54/109, *supra.*

143 FATF (1990), *supra.*

for the management or control of that legal entity has, in that capacity, committed an offence set forth in article 3. Such liability may be criminal, civil or administrative.

2. Such liability is incurred without prejudice to the criminal liability of individuals having committed the offences.
3. Each State Party shall ensure, in particular, that legal entities liable in accordance with paragraph 1 above are subject to effective, proportionate and dissuasive criminal, civil or administrative sanctions. Such sanctions may include monetary sanctions.
4. The penalty of imprisonment of 3 to 5 and a fine of $25,000 to $80,000 and a fine of up to 5 times the amount of the laundered sums shall be imposed on anyone who commits a laundering offence. In case of money-laundering connected to terrorism-financing, where the person has knowledge and intention required for the purpose of this convention, the sentence is 15 years of imprisonment in a State decided by the Alliance.
5. An attempt to commit a laundering offence or aiding, abetting, facilitating or counselling the commission of any such offence shall be punishable as if the offence had been completed: shall be punishable by a penalty reduced by 1/4 in relation to the main penalty.
6. Countries should apply the crime of money-laundering to all serious offences, with a view to including the widest range of predicate offences. Predicate offences may be described by reference to all offences, or to a threshold linked either to a category of serious offences or to the penalty of imprisonment applicable to the predicate offence (threshold approach), or to a list of predicate offences, or a combination of these approaches.
7. Where countries apply a threshold approach, predicate offences should at a minimum comprise all offences that fall within the category of serious offences under their national law or should include offences which are punishable by a maximum penalty of more than one year's imprisonment or for those countries that have a minimum threshold for offences in their legal system, predicate offences should comprise all offences, which are punished by a minimum penalty of more than six months imprisonment.
8. Whichever approach is adopted, each country should at a minimum include a range of offences within each of the designated categories of offences.
9. Predicate offences for money-laundering should extend to conduct that occurred in another country, which constitutes an offence in that country,

and which would have constituted a predicate offence had it occurred domestically. Countries may provide that the only prerequisite is that the conduct would have constituted a predicate offence had it occurred domestically.

10. Countries may provide that the offence of money-laundering does not apply to persons who committed the predicate offence, where this is required by fundamental principles of their domestic law.

11. Countries should ensure that:
    (a) The intent and knowledge required to prove the offence of money-laundering is consistent with the standards set forth in the Vienna and Palermo Conventions, including the concept that such mental state may be inferred from objective factual circumstances.
    (b) Criminal liability, and, where that is not possible, civil or administrative liability, should apply to legal persons. This should not preclude parallel criminal, civil or administrative proceedings with respect to legal persons in countries in which such forms of liability.

12. Legal persons should be subject to effective, proportionate and dissuasive sanctions. Such measures should be without prejudice to the criminal liability of individuals. A legal person will be responsible for the crimes included in this article, the following sanctions will be applied:
    (a) Fine of two to five years, if the offence committed by the natural person brings with more than five years prison penalty.
    (b) Fine of one to three years, if the offence committed by the natural person brings with more than two years prisons penalty not included in the former subsection.

13. The Judges and Courts of Law may also impose the following penalties:
    (a) Dissolution of the legal person. The dissolution shall cause definitive loss of its legal personality, as well as of its capacity to act in any way in legal transactions, or to carry out any kind of activity, even if lawful.
    (b) Suspension of its activities for a term that may not exceed five years.
    (c) Closure of its premises and establishments for a term that may not exceed five years.
    (d) Prohibition to carry out the activities through which it has committed, favored or concealed the offence in the future. Such prohibition may be temporary or definitive. If temporary, the term may not exceed five years.

14. In countries which apply a threshold approach to specify ML predicate offences, the penalty for a TF offence should be set at a level above the

threshold required to be considered an ML predicate offence (or should be included in the category of serious offences which are ML predicates).

Article 106: Association or Conspiracy to Commit Terrorist Financing[144]

The same penalties shall apply to participation in an association or conspiracy to commit the offences referred to in article 3.

Article 107: Penalties Applicable to Legal Persons[145]

1. Any legal person other than the State on whose behalf or for whose benefit money-laundering and financing of terrorism has been committed by any natural person, acting either individually or as part of an organ of the legal person, who has a leading position within it, based on a power of representation of the legal person, an authority to take decisions on behalf of the legal person, or an authority to exercise control within the legal person, acting in such capacity, shall be punished by a fine of an amount equal to [indicate multiplier] times the fines specified for natural persons, irrespective of the conviction of those individuals as perpetrators of or accomplices to the offence.

The liability of the legal person does not preclude that of the natural person.

2. In addition to the cases already provided for in paragraph 1 of this article, a legal person may also be held liable where the lack of supervision or control over a natural person referred to in paragraph 1 has made possible the commission of money-laundering or financing of terrorism for the benefit of that legal person by a natural person acting under its authority.

Legal persons may additionally be:

(a) barred permanently or for a maximum period of [indicate number] years from directly or indirectly carrying on certain business activities;

144 IMLIN, *supra*.
145 Search and Seizure (2005), *supra*.

(b) placed under court supervision;
(c) ordered to close permanently or for a period of [indicate number] years their premises which were used for the commission of the offence;
(d) wound up;
(e) ordered to publicize the judgment.

Article 108: Penalties Applicable to Corporate Entities[146]

1. Corporate entities, other than the State, on whose behalf or for whose benefit a subsequent offence has been committed by one of their agents or representatives shall be liable to a fine of an amount equal to five times the fines specified for natural persons, without prejudice to the conviction of those individuals as perpetrators of the offence or accessories to it.
2. Corporate entities may additionally be:
   (a) Banned permanently or for a maximum period of five years from directly or indirectly carrying on certain business activities;
   (b) Ordered to close permanently or for a maximum period of five years their premises which were used for the commission of the offence;
   (c) Wound up if they had been established for the purpose of committing the offence in question;
   (d) Required to publicize the judgement in the press or by radio or television.

Article 109: Penalties Imposed by Disciplinary or Supervisory Authorities[147]

Where, as a result of a serious failure to exercise vigilance or a deficiency in the organization of internal anti-laundering procedures, a credit or financial institution or any other natural or legal person commits a breach of any of the obligations devolving upon it under the present law, the disciplinary or supervisory authority may act *ex officio* in conformity with the internal or administrative regulations.

146 IMLIN, *supra*.
147 IMLIN, *supra*.

Article 110: Statute of Limitations[148,149]

Any statute of limitations applicable to the offence of Terrorism and its Financing official shall allow an adequate period of time for the investigation and prosecution of this offence.

Article 111: Central Authority[150]

1. The Parties shall designate the Alliance as a central authority or, if necessary, other authorities, which shall be responsible for sending and answering requests, the execution of such requests or the transmission of them to the authorities competent for their execution.
2. Each Party shall, at the time of signature or when depositing its instrument of ratification, acceptance, approval or accession, communicate to the Secretary of the Alliance, the names and addresses of the authorities designated in pursuance of paragraph 1 of this article.

Article 112: Relationship to Other Conventions and Agreements[151]

1. This Convention does not affect the rights and undertakings derived from international multilateral conventions concerning special matters.
2. The Parties to the Convention may conclude bilateral or multilateral agreements with one another on the matters dealt with in this Convention, for purposes of supplementing or strengthening its provisions or facilitating the application of the principles embodied in it.
3. If two or more Parties have already concluded an agreement or treaty in respect of a subject which is dealt with in this Convention or otherwise have established their relations in respect of that subject, they shall be entitled to apply that agreement or treaty or to regulate those relations accordingly, in lieu of the present Convention, if it facilitates international co-operation.
4. Parties which are members of the Alliance shall, in their mutual relations, apply Community and European Union rules in so far as there are Community or European Union rules governing the particular subject

148 IMLIN, *supra.*
149 OECD, *supra.*
150 Search and Seizure (2005), *supra.*
151 Search and Seizure (2005), *supra.*

concerned and applicable to the specific case, without prejudice to the object and purpose of the present Convention and without prejudice to its full application with other Parties.

Article 113: Punishment Guidelines[152,153]

1. Financing the Grave Crime of Terrorism shall be make a punishable offence by each State Party under its National law.
2. Each State Party, in accordance with its domestic legal principles, shall take the necessary measures to enable a legal entity located in its territory or organized under its laws to be held liable when a person responsible for management or control of that legal entity has, in that capacity, committed an offence set forth in this Convention. Such liability may be criminal, civil or administrative.
3. Each State Party shall make the offences described in this Article 3 punishable by appropriate penalties which take into account their grave nature.
4. Each State Party shall ensure, in particular, that legal entities liable in accordance with paragraph 1 are subject to effective, proportionate and dissuasive criminal, civil or administrative sanctions. Such sanctions may include monetary sanctions.
5. Such liability is incurred without prejudice to the criminal liability of individuals having committed the offences.
6. Economic Sanctions/Boycott.

When deciding on the range of offences to be covered as predicate offences under each of the categories listed above, each Member State may decide, in accordance with its domestic law, how it will define those offences and the nature of any particular elements of those offences that make them serious offences.

Article 114: Recognition of Foreign Decisions[154]

1. When dealing with a request for co-operation, the requested Party shall recognize any judicial decision taken in the requesting Party regarding rights claimed by third parties.

---

152 GAOR 54/109, *supra*.
153 FATF (1990), *supra*.
154 Search and Seizure (2005), *supra*.

2. Recognition may be refused if:
   (a) third parties did not have adequate opportunity to assert their rights; or
   (b) the decision is incompatible with a decision already taken in the requested Party on the same matter; or
   (c) it is incompatible with the *ordre public* of the requested Party; or
   (d) the decision was taken contrary to provisions on exclusive jurisdiction provided for by the law of the requested Party.

Article 115: International Alliance Arrest Warrant[155]

Upon being satisfied that the circumstances so warrant, the State Party in whose territory the alleged offender is present shall take appropriate measures, including detention, under its national law to ensure his presence for the purpose of prosecution or extradition. Measures taken according to this article shall be notified without delay to the States required to establish jurisdiction pursuant to article 4 and, where appropriate, all other States concerned.

Such measures shall be notified without delay or through the Alliance to:

(a) The State where the crime was committed;
(b) The State or States of which the alleged offender is a national or, if he is a stateless person, in whose territory he permanently resides; and
(c) All other States concerned.

Article 116: Jurisdiction over Foreign Persons[156]

For purposes of adjudicating an action filed or enforcing a penalty ordered under this section, the district courts shall have jurisdiction over any foreign person, including any financial institution authorized under the laws of a foreign country, against whom the action is brought, if service of process upon the foreign person is made under the Federal Rules of Civil Procedure or the laws of the country in which the foreign person is found, and—

(a) the foreign person commits an offense involving a financial transaction that occurs in whole or in part in one of the Member States;

155 GAOR 54/109, *supra*.

156 Financial Crimes Enforcement Network, USA *Patriot Act*, FinCEN.gov, https://www.fincen.gov/resources/statutes-regulations/usa-patriot-act.

(b) the foreign person converts, to his or her own use, property in which one of the Member States has an ownership interest by virtue of the entry of an order of forfeiture by a court; or

(c) the foreign person is a financial institution that maintains a bank account at a financial institution in one of the Member States.

Article 117: Extradition[157,158,159]

1. The State Party in whose Territory the alleged offender is present shall, if it does not extradite him, submit, without exception whatsoever and without undue delay, the case to its competent authorities for the purpose of prosecution, tough proceedings in accordance with the laws of that State.
2. The States Parties shall undertake to extradite any person charged with or convicted of any terrorist act carried out on the territory of another State Party and whose extradition is requested by one of the States Parties in conformity with the rules and conditions provided for in this Convention or under extradition agreements between the States Parties and within the limits of their national laws.
3. If a State Party makes extradition conditional on the existence of a treaty receives a request for extradition from another State Party with which it has no extradition treaty, it may, if it decides to extradite, consider this Convention as the legal basis for extradition in respect of those crimes. Extradition shall be subject to the procedural provisions and the other conditions of the law of the requested State.
4. Extradition shall be subject to the other conditions provided by the law of the requested State.
5. States Parties which do not make extradition conditional on the existence of a treaty shall recognize the offences set forth in article 3 as extraditable offences between themselves, subject to the conditions provided by the law of the requested State.
6. The offences set forth in article 3 shall be deemed to be included as extraditable offences in any extradition treaty existing between any of the States Parties before the entry into force of this Convention. States Parties

157 U.N.T.S. 1973, *supra*.

158 GAOR 54/109, *supra*.

159 OAU (1999), *supra*.

undertake to include such offences as extraditable offences in every extradition treaty to be subsequently concluded between them.

7. Each State Party undertakes to include as an extraditable offence any terrorist act as defined in Article 3, in any extradition treaty existing between any of the States Parties before or after the entry into force of this Convention.
8. If necessary, the offences set forth in article 3 shall be treated, for the purposes of extradition between States Parties, as if they had been committed not only in the place in which they occurred but also in the territory of the States that have established jurisdiction.
9. The provisions of all extradition treaties and arrangements between States Parties with regard to offences set forth in article 3 shall be deemed to be modified as between States Parties to the extent that they are incompatible with this Convention.
10. Extradition shall not be granted if final judgement has been passed by a competent authority of the requested State upon the person in respect of the terrorist act or acts for which extradition is requested. Extradition may also be refused if the competent authority of the requested State has decided either not to institute or terminate proceedings in respect of the same act or acts.
11. A State Party in whose territory an alleged offender is present shall be obliged, whether or not the offence was committed in its territory, to submit the case without undue delay to its competent authorities for the purpose of prosecution if it does not extradite that person.
12. Nothing in this Convention shall be interpreted as imposing an obligation to extradite or to afford mutual legal assistance if the requested State Party has substantial grounds for believing that the request for extradition for offences set forth in article 3 or for mutual legal assistance with respect to such offences has been made for the purpose of prosecuting or punishing a person on account of that person's race, religion, nationality, ethnic origin or political opinion or that compliance with the request would cause prejudice to that person's position for any of these reasons.
13. None of the offences set forth in article 3 shall be regarded, for the purposes of extradition or mutual legal assistance, as a political offence or as an offence connected with a political offence or as an offence inspired by political motives. Accordingly, a request for extradition of mutual legal assistance based on such an offence may not be refused on the sole ground that it concerns a political offence, or an offence connected with a political offence or an offence inspired by political motives.

Article 118: Extradition Requests[160]

Exchange of extradition requests between the States Parties to this Convention shall be effected directly either through diplomatic channels or other appropriate organs in the concerned States.

1. Extradition requests shall be in writing, and shall be accompanied in particular by the following:
   (a) an original or authenticated copy of the sentence, warrant of arrest or any order or other judicial decision made, in accordance with the procedures laid down in the laws of the requesting State;
   (b) a statement describing the offences for which extradition is being requested, indicating the date and place of its commission, the offence committed, any convictions made and a copy of the provisions of the applicable law; and together with any other information which may assist in establishing the person's identity and nationality.
2. In urgent cases, the competent authority of the State making the extradition may, in writing, request that the State seized of the extradition request arrest the person in question provisionally. Such provisional arrest shall be for a reasonable period in accordance with the national law of the requested State.
3. Upon agreeing to extradite, States Parties shall seize and transmit all funds and related materials purportedly used in the commission of the terrorist act to the requesting State as well as relevant incriminating evidence.
4. Such funds, incriminating evidence and related materials, upon confirmation of their use in the terrorist act by the requested State, shall be transmitted to the requesting State even if, for reasons of death or escape of the accused, the extradition in question cannot take place.

Article 119: Detention and Transfer[161,162]

1. Upon being satisfied that the circumstances so warrant, any State Party in the territory of which the offender or the alleged offender is present, shall take that person into custody or take other measures to ensure that

160 OAU (1999), *supra*.
161 Maritime Navigation (1988), *supra*.
162 GAOR 54/109, *supra*.

person's presence. The custody and other measures shall be as provided in the law of that State but may only be continued for such time as is necessary to enable any criminal or extradition proceedings to be instituted.

Such State shall immediately make a preliminary enquiry into the facts.

2. The custody or other measures referred to in paragraph 1 of this article shall be notified without delay directly or through the Alliance to:
   (a) The State where the offence was committed;
   (b) The State against which compulsion has been directed or attempted;
   (c) The State of which the natural or juridical person against whom compulsion has been directed or attempted is a national;
   (d) The State of which the hostage is a national or in the territory of which he has his habitual residence;
   (e) The State of which the alleged offender is a national or, if he is a stateless person, in the territory of which he has his habitual residence;
   (f) The international intergovernmental organization against which compulsion has been directed or attempted;
   (g) All other States concerned.
3. Any person in custody pursuant to paragraph 1 of this Article shall be assisted in communicating immediately with the nearest appropriate representative of the State of which that person is a national.
4. When a State Party, pursuant to this Article, has taken a person into custody, it shall immediately notify the States Parties which have established jurisdiction under Article 4 and established jurisdiction and notified the Secretary of the Alliance and, if it considers it advisable, any other interested States of the fact that such person is in custody and of the circumstances which warrant that person's detention. The State Party which makes the preliminary enquiry contemplated in paragraph 2 of this Article shall promptly report its findings to the said State Parties and shall indicate whether it intends to exercise jurisdiction.
5. A person who is being detained or is serving a sentence in the territory of one State Party whose presence in another State Party is requested for purposes of testimony, identification or otherwise providing assistance in obtaining evidence for the investigation or prosecution of offences under this Convention may be transferred if the competent authorities of both States agree, subject to such conditions as those States may deem appropriate.

6. For the purposes of the present article:
   (a) The State to which the person is transferred shall have the authority and obligation to keep the person transferred in custody, unless otherwise requested or authorized by the State from which the person was transferred;
   (b) The State to which the person is transferred shall without delay implement its obligation to return the person to the custody of the State from which the person was transferred as agreed beforehand, or as otherwise agreed, by the competent authorities of both States;
   (c) The State to which the person is transferred shall not require the State from which the person was transferred to initiate extradition proceedings for the return of the person;
   (d) The person transferred shall receive credit for service of the sentence being served in the State from which he or she was transferred for time spent in the custody of the State to which he or she was transferred.
7. Unless the State Party from which a person is to be transferred in accordance with the present article so agrees, that person, whatever his or her nationality, shall not be prosecuted or detained or subjected to any other restriction of his or her personal liberty in the territory of the State to which that person is transferred in respect of acts or convictions anterior to his or her departure from the territory of the State from which such person was transferred.
8. Any person who is taken into custody, or regarding whom any other measures are taken or proceedings are being carried out pursuant to this Convention, shall be guaranteed fair treatment, including enjoyment of all rights and guarantees in conformity with the law of the State in the territory of which that person is present and applicable provisions of international law, including international human rights law.

Article 120: Criminalization of Obstruction of Justice[163]

Each State Party shall adopt such legislative and other measures as may be necessary to establish as criminal offences, when committed intentionally:

163 GAOR 55/25, *supra*.

1. The use of physical force, threats or intimidation or the promise, offering or giving of an undue advantage to induce false testimony or to interfere in the giving of testimony or the production of evidence in a proceeding in relation to the commission of offences covered by this Convention;
2. The use of physical force, threats or intimidation to interfere with the exercise of official duties by a justice or law enforcement official in relation to the commission of offences covered by this Convention. Nothing in this subparagraph shall prejudice the right of States Parties to have legislation that protects other categories of public officials.

Article 121: Double Criminality[164]

Under the present law, extradition shall be carried out only if the offence giving rise to extradition or a similar offence is provided for under the legislation of the requesting State and of another State Member of ASOP.

Article 122: Protection of Witnesses, Experts and Victims[165]

1. Each State Party shall take appropriate measures in accordance with its domestic legal system and within its means to provide effective protection from potential retaliation or intimidation for witnesses and experts who give testimony concerning offences established in accordance with this Convention and, as appropriate, for their relatives and other persons close to them.
2. The measures envisaged in paragraph 1 of this article may include, inter alia, without prejudice to the rights of the defendant, including the right to due process:
   (a) Establishing procedures for the physical protection of such persons, such as, to the extent necessary and feasible, relocating them and permitting, where appropriate, non-disclosure or limitations on the disclosure of information concerning the identity and whereabouts of such persons;
   (b) Providing evidentiary rules to permit witnesses and experts to give testimony in a manner that ensures the safety of such persons, such as permitting testimony to be given through the use of communications technology such as video or other adequate means.

164 IMLIN, *supra.*
165 GAOR 58/4, *supra.*

3. States Parties shall consider entering into agreements or arrangements with other States for the relocation of persons referred to in paragraph 1 of this article.
4. The provisions of this article shall also apply to victims insofar as they are witnesses.
5. Each State Party shall, subject to its domestic law, enable the views and concerns of victims to be presented and considered at appropriate stages of criminal proceedings against offenders in a manner not prejudicial to the rights of the defense.

Article 123: Assistance to and Protection of Victims[166,167]

1. Each State Party shall take appropriate measures within its means to provide assistance and protection to victims of offences covered by this Convention, in particular in cases of threat of retaliation or intimidation and to the need to protect the dignity and physical integrity of victims of terrorism, including during questioning and when testifying.
2. Each State Party shall offer support services that have the ability to provide assistance and support to victims of terrorism in accordance with their specific needs. The services shall be confidential, free of charge and easily accessible to all victims of terrorism. They shall include:
   (a) emotional and psychological support, such as trauma support and counselling;
   (b) provision of advice and information on any relevant legal, practical or financial matters, including facilitating the exercise of the right to information of victims of terrorism.
   (c) assistance with claims regarding compensation for victims of terrorism available under the national law of the Member State concerned.
   (d) adequate medical treatment to victims of terrorism immediately after a terrorist attack and for as long as necessary.
3. Each State Party shall establish appropriate procedures to provide access to compensation and restitution for victims of offences covered by this Convention.

166 GAOR 54/109, *supra*.

167 European Union, Directive (EU) *2017/541 of the European Parliament and of the Council of 15 March 2017 on combating terrorism and replacing Council Framework Decision 2002/475/ JHA* and amending Council Decision 2005/671/JHA, 15 March 2017, available from https:// eur-lex.europa.eu/legal-content/EN/TXT/PDF/?uri=CELEX:32017L0541&from=EN.

4. Each State Party shall, subject to its domestic law, enable views and concerns of victims to be presented and considered at appropriate stages of criminal proceedings against offenders in a manner not prejudicial to the rights of the defense.

Article 124: Protection of Reporting Persons[168]

Each State Party shall consider incorporating into its domestic legal system appropriate measures to provide protection against any unjustified treatment for any person who reports in good faith and on reasonable grounds to the competent authorities any facts concerning offences established in accordance with this Convention.

Article 125: Law Enforcement Cooperation[169]

1. States Parties shall cooperate closely with one another, consistent with their respective domestic legal and administrative systems, to enhance the effectiveness of law enforcement action to combat the offences covered by this Convention. Each State Party shall, in particular, adopt effective measures:
   (a) To enhance and, where necessary, to establish channels of communication between their competent authorities, agencies and services in order to facilitate the secure and rapid exchange of information concerning all aspects of the offences covered by this Convention, including, if the States Parties concerned deem it appropriate, links with other criminal activities;
   (b) To cooperate with other States Parties in conducting inquiries with respect to offences covered by this Convention concerning:
      (i) The identity, whereabouts and activities of persons suspected of involvement in such offences or the location of other persons concerned;
      (ii) The movement of proceeds of crime or property derived from the commission of such offences;

168 GAOR 54/109, *supra*.
169 GAOR 55/25, *supra*.

(iii) The movement of property, equipment or other instrumentalities used or intended for use in the commission of such offences;

(c) To provide, when appropriate, necessary items or quantities of substances for analytical or investigative purposes;

(d) To facilitate effective coordination between their competent authorities, agencies and services and to promote the exchange of personnel and other experts, including, subject to bilateral agreements or arrangements between the States Parties concerned, the posting of liaison officers;

(e) To exchange information with other States Parties on specific means and methods used by organized criminal groups, including, where applicable, routes and conveyances and the use of false identities, altered or false documents or other means of concealing their activities;

(f) To exchange information and coordinate administrative and other measures taken as appropriate for the purpose of early identification of the offences covered by this Convention.

2. With a view to giving effect to this Convention, States Parties shall consider entering into bilateral or multilateral agreements or arrangements on direct cooperation between their law enforcement agencies and, where such agreements or arrangements already exist, amending them. In the absence of such agreements or arrangements between the States Parties concerned, the Parties may consider this Convention as the basis for mutual law enforcement cooperation in respect of the offences covered by this Convention. Whenever appropriate, States Parties shall make full use of agreements or arrangements, including international or regional organizations, to enhance the cooperation between their law enforcement agencies.

3. States Parties shall endeavor to cooperate within their means to respond to transnational organized crime committed through the use of modern technology.

4. Each State Party shall consider providing for the possibility, in appropriate cases, of mitigating punishment of an accused person who provides substantial cooperation in the investigation or prosecution of an offence covered by this Convention.

5. Each State Party shall consider providing for the possibility, in accordance with fundamental principles of its domestic law, of granting immunity from prosecution to a person who provides substantial cooperation in the investigation or prosecution of an offence covered by this Convention.

Article 126: Responsible Authorities[170]

1. Member States shall ensure that their competent authorities inform ASOP of all administrative sanctions and measures imposed on credit institutions and financial institutions, including of any appeal in relation thereto and the outcome thereof.
2. Member States shall ensure that their competent authorities, in accordance with their national law, check the existence of a relevant conviction in the criminal record of the person concerned. Any exchange of information for those purposes shall be carried out in accordance with this Convention.
3. ASPOPI shall maintain a website with links to each competent authority's publication of administrative sanctions and measures imposed on credit institutions and financial institutions and shall show the time period for which each Member State publishes administrative sanctions and measures.

Article 127: Monitoring and Follow-up[171]

Any person regarding whom proceedings are being carried out in connection with any of the offences set forth in article 3 shall be guaranteed fair treatment at all stages of the proceedings.

Each State Party shall inform the depositary of its laws and regulations which give effect to this Convention. The depositary shall communicate such information periodically to all States Parties.

The State Party where an alleged offender is prosecuted shall, wherever practicable, first communicate the final outcome of the proceedings to the States directly concerned. The State Party shall also communicate the final outcome to the depositary who shall inform all States.

Article 128: Secretariat[172]

1. The Secretary of the Alliance shall provide the necessary secretariat services to the Conference of the Parties to the Convention.
2. The secretariat shall:

170 EU (2015), *supra*.

171 International Atomic Energy Agency, *Convention on the Physical Protection of Nuclear Material*, 26 October 1979, available from https://www.iaea.org/publications/documents/conventions/convention-physical-protection-nuclear-material.

172 GAOR 58/4, *supra*.

(a) Assist the Conference of the Parties make arrangements and provide the necessary services for the sessions of the Conference of the Parties;
(b) Upon request, assist States Parties in providing information to the Conference; and
(c) Ensure the necessary coordination with the secretariats of relevant international and regional organizations.

The Secretary of the Alliance must be constituted by 3 States which cannot be the same each calendar year.

The Secretary shall act as council for problem resolutions and dispute settlements.

The Secretary of the Alliance shall inform all States of signatures to this Convention, of the deposit of instruments of ratification or accession.

Article 129: Settlement of Disputes[173]

1. Any dispute between two or more States Parties concerning the interpretation or application of this Convention which is not settled by negotiation shall, at the request of one of them, be submitted to arbitration. If within six months from the date of the request for arbitration the parties are unable to agree on the organization of the arbitration, any one of those parties may refer the dispute to the International Court of Justice by request in conformity with the Statute of the Court.
2. Each State may at the time of signature or ratification of this Convention or accession thereto declare that it does not consider itself bound with respect to any State Party which has made a reservation.
3. Any State Party which has made a reservation in accordance with this article may at any time withdraw that reservation by notification to the Secretary of the Alliance.

Article 130: Amendment[174]

1. Any State Party may, within ninety days from the date of notification of a proposed amendment, transmit to the Alliance its comments. The

173 Maritime Navigation (1988), *supra*.

174 U.N., *Convention for the Suppression of Unlawful Acts Against the Safety of Civil Aviation*, Montreal, 23 September 1971, *U.N.T.S.*, vol. 974, no. 1-14118, available from http://www.un.org/zh/terrorism/pdf/1971E.pdf.

Alliance shall invite any State Party which comments on or objects to the proposed amendment to consult the Alliance Secretary.

2. The Alliance shall consider the views of States Parties made pursuant to the preceding paragraph and report to other Parties to this Convention. The Alliance, after consideration of the Secretary's report, and taking into account the nature of the amendment and the comments of States Parties, may propose the amendment to all States Parties for adoption.
3. If a proposed amendment has not been objected to by three or more States Parties by means of written notification to the Alliance within ninety days from the date of notification of the amendment by the Council, it shall be deemed to have been adopted, and shall enter into force one hundred and eighty days thereafter or after such other period as specified in the proposed amendment for States Parties not having expressly objected thereto.
4. States Parties having expressly objected to the proposed amendment may, subsequently, by any means of the deposit of an instrument of acceptance or approval, express their consent to be bound by the provisions of the amendment.
5. If five or more States Parties have objected to the proposed amendment, the Alliance shall refer it to the Secretary of the Alliance for further consideration.
6. If the proposed amendment has not been adopted, the Alliance may also convene a conference of all States Parties.

Article 131: Signature

This Convention is open for signature by all States until 31 December 2019 at the Alliance Headquarters in San Diego.

This Convention is subject to ratification. The instruments of ratification shall be deposited with the Secretary of the Alliance.

Article 132: Entry into Force

For each State accepting, approving, ratifying or acceding to the Convention after the deposit of the tenth instrument of ratification or accession, the Convention shall enter into force on the thirtieth day after deposit by such State of its instrument of acceptance, approval, ratification or accession.

Article 133: Denunciation

Any State may denounce this Convention by written notification to the Alliance.

Denunciation shall take effect one year following the date on which notification is received by the Secretary of the Alliance.

Article 134: Depository of Languages[175]

The original of this Convention, of which the Arabic, Chinese, English, French, Russian and Spanish texts are equally authentic, shall be deposited with the Alliance, who shall send certified copies thereof to all States.

IN WITNESS WHEREOF, the undersigned, being duly authorized thereto by their respective Governments, have signed this Convention, opened for signature at San Diego on 23 December 2018.

175 GAOR AG/RES 1840, *supra*.

CHAPTER 11

Ways to Strengthen Worldwide Detection, Prevention and Enforcement

This chapter provides recommendations for strengthening worldwide detection, prevention and enforcement, which demand closer consideration as there remain strong blockages to the current enforcement mechanisms. Actors' involvement and cooperation at the domestic and international levels, collaboration with the private sector, and the positive development of Global Financial Intelligence Units are essential to a new convention model.

A Actors' Involvement and Cooperation at the Domestic and International Levels

Money regularly crosses national borders, which raises the importance of effective intelligence and international cooperation to trace criminal assets and money flows. Recent terrorist events have led to the international community reconsidering a worldwide tool for CTF. Cheap terrorist events nowadays represent a greater threat since $10.000 or less, is sufficient to initiate a terrorist action, and illegal weapons trade is current in many countries, as part of Mafias or smaller organized criminal groups' daily activities. Financing terrorism in the case of Afghans coming to France amongst refugee groups with orders to stab people, should also refer to travelling, lodging, food expenses. It is hard to sanction the terrorist or potential terrorist, if the crime has not occurred yet. It is essential to keep a record of all the expenses made by the terrorist since he was enlisted. Expenses on his way to the attack scene, including transportation and living expenses should be retrieved to penalize the person responsible for financing the journey itself.

The layering of funds plays a key role in hiding the financers, who are usually at a much higher rank in society than the actual terrorists. The identity to protect in such cases, is not the terrorist's, but the financer's, as the terrorist wants to be known as a "soldier of his god" and has pride in his extremist ideology. The aim should be to increase cooperation both at the international and domestic levels through more effective exchanges of information for investigative, supervisory and prosecution purposes, while assisting countries in tracing, freezing and confiscating illicit assets.

 | DOI:10.1163/9789004409675_017

B Collaboration with the Private Sector

In its resolution 2199 (2015), the Security Council recognized the importance of the banking sector. Collaboration with the private sector is crucial in terms of the exchange of information and comprehension of the new trends they are facing, which can then be regulated in a more targeted manner. This can also help the private sector implement best practices as part of internal policies. The Financial Action Task Force is developing tools for its members to use as guidance in their collaboration with the private sector, which must be inserted into governments and financial institutions' policies for better implementation and efficiency. Red flags assist financial institutions and help them improve their internal policies including their monitoring and screening procedures.

The government plays a key role in promoting responsible self-regulation and involvement by industry through the creation of legal and regulatory incentives. Governments should form partnerships with financial institutions, such as banks, and other financial businesses, to identify terrorist fighters and prevent them from traveling by monitoring their financial endeavors. Financial institutions can use sophisticated algorithms and filters to discover cases requiring further investigation. Collaboration with the private sector should be enhanced to promote a better understanding of new ML/TF trends and thus, both actors can participate more effectively in their detection.

C The Positive Development of Global Financial Intelligence Units

FIUs ensure the flow of information between financial institutions and governments, helping to prevent ISIL and other groups from accessing the international financial system, while identifying and disrupting foreign terrorist fighter travel.[1] The main categories of indicators of TF contained in the "FIU's in Action Report" are: concealment within business structures, misuse of legitimate businesses, use of false identities, straw men, exploitation of international jurisdictional issues, the use of anonymous asset types and the effective use of intelligence exchanges. The application of intelligence and investigative techniques is a highly effective mean for discovering underlying activities from which the money for terrorism is derived, thereby being able to detect

1 U.N. SCOR, *Letter dated 2 September 2015 from the Chair of the Security Council Committee Established Pursuant to Resolution 1373 (2001) Concerning Counter-Terrorism Addressed to the President of the Security Council*, S/2015/683, 2 September 2015, available from http://www.un.org/en/sc/ctc/docs/2015/N1527297_EN.pdf.

and disrupt terrorist organizations and their activities.[2] Financial intelligence can play a crucial role in identifying foreign terrorist fighters and preventing their travel, yet, intelligence gathering should be carefully regulated by law, so as not to unjustifiably infringe upon human rights and the individuals' right to privacy. FIUs identify assets of suspect or possible fraud techniques.

According to the "FIU's in Action Report," actions taken by FIUs to respond to terrorist financing indicators consist of: cross-referencing with national and international law enforcement data bases, business document history, document timelines showing opening and closing of "representatives" offices, exchange of intelligence with foreign FIUs or with other FIUs through Egmont, liaising with foreign FIUs to recover citizens' funds, examining financial records for evidence of fund movement and/or for signs of travel expenses along with clues as to the location of the suspect. The idea of Global Financial Intelligence Units (GFIU) has been in the spotlight for many years, yet the implementation of such an ambitious initiative has not convinced all the international community's key players. Only a centralization of intelligence and investigation powers can lead to more efficiency on the part of financial units.

2 Egmont Group, *About,* 2018, https://egmontgroup.org/.

Conclusion

Terrorism Financing is a growing concern. Indeed, it is clear that financing an attack can cost very small amounts of money, which can easily be laundered or simply passed on to evade the financial system. The evolution of new technologies makes spotting TF quite a challenge. Gathering funds is becoming ever easier using a catalogue of well-known strategies, sometimes derived from financial crime activities. Since TF works in the opposite way to ML, this makes it more complex for financial institutions, businesses, and law enforcement to meet the burden of proof to demonstrate terrorist acts. It is especially difficult for prosecutors to explain the intention and full *modus operandi* of the individuals charged with TF when the crime hasn't yet been committed.

As the cost of ML/TF is estimated as being between 2 and 5% of global GDP,[1] the importance of deterring TF not only lies in the prevention of the violent crime itself, but also in the capturing of funds that are on the loose. Fighting the war against terrorism requires powerful tools.[2] If applied, the new Convention model would enable national authorities to take more effective action against ML and TF at all levels, from the identification of bank customers opening an account through to investigation, prosecution and forfeiture of assets, as well as promote better cooperation between actors and the private sector, both nationally and internationally. It should indeed strengthen the requirements for higher risk situations and allow countries to take a more targeted risk-based approach.

It can be expected that the model of the Alliance will provide a set of rules to prevent and deter terrorist financing, while increasing the ability to foresee future acts. Whilst the application of intelligence and investigation techniques can be a robust way of detecting and disrupting the activities of terrorists and terrorist organizations, the highest levels of cooperation and coordination among law enforcement and intelligence agencies around the globe is required to fight TF most effectively. Greater attention by the authorities should be on establishing international standards, overcoming political disagreement, and creating some connections between countries to improve cooperation.

---

1 Financial Action Task Force (FATF), *FATF steps up the fight against money-laundering and terrorist financing*, 2012, available from http://www.fatf-gafi.org/topics/fatfrecommendations/documents/fatfstepsupthefightagainstmoneylaunderingandterroristfinancing.html.

2 Dennis Lormel, *Terrorism Financing Operations Section FBI 2002*, available from http://www.fbi.gov/news/testimony/usa-patriot-act-terrorism-financing-operations-section.

 | DOI:10.1163/9789004409675_018

Criminals are always a step ahead of law enforcement, and the development of new technologies make the legitimate use of payment products a continual challenge for authorities. Countries and financial institutions should also take appropriate measures to manage and mitigate those risk by identifying and assessing the money-laundering or terrorist financing risks that may arise in relation to the development of new products and new business practices, including new delivery mechanisms, and the use of new or developing technologies for both new and pre-existing products. Risk assessment should take place prior to the launch of the new products, business practices or the use of new or developing technology.

Areas in which CTF measures can still be enhanced, but were found outside of the scope of the new Convention model, that could be added later as annexes, are measures to counter the financing of the proliferation of weapons of mass destruction as well as addressing the laundering of the proceeds of corruption and tax crimes more thoroughly. Criminals can undermine the integrity and stability of financial institutions and systems, discourage foreign investment, and distort international capital flows. In particular, they can exploit the vulnerabilities of financial systems with poor regulation and enforcement mechanisms, thus being attracted to such countries, where they can move their funds easily without being detected. The integrity and stability of national financial sectors are essential to the financial sector and macroeconomic stability, both on a national and international level.[3] Solid AML/CFT regimes allow for countries integration into the international financial system.

---

3 International Monetary Fund, *IMF and the Fight Against Money-Laundering and the Financing of Terrorism*, 30 October 2017, available from http://www.imf.org/external/np/exr/facts/aml.htm.

PART 5

Matters for Further Consideration

Introduction to Part 5

Billions of dollars transit every year worldwide to finance criminal organizations and terrorists. Whilst it seems obvious that the international community should fight TF, the question of the cost-effectiveness of deterring it will require much more data and analysis. Evidently, the money retrieved by States confiscating and collecting assets derived from illicit activities can serve to finance police units, an international system for CTF, and national enforcement systems. However, investigations can take years and fail to recognize terrorists' assets or seize them, which should make the international community wonder whether the money collected is sufficient to justify such involvement with TF.

Another core issue remains regarding CTF, which necessitates further consideration and study. That is, the international community should address how to lift the barriers to the implementation of a New Convention and promote international cooperation between the main actors involved in fighting TF, whilst also supporting international privacy rights. Fortunately, after 9/11, countries finally seemed to understand the stakes of this issue. The main reason why people cooperate in mutual legal assistance and information sharing regarding AML/CTF is that they are scared for their own country's future. This is the reason why countries like the US and the UK felt the need to incorporate more protective measures into their domestic laws. The US created the Patriot Act and the UK the Counter Terrorist Financing Act, for example. Whichever international system of financial scrutiny and CTF is put into place, it seems quite certain the world is advancing in finding a better way to deal with AML/CFT since terrorism is becoming an international priority and countries want to defeat such evil activity.

Reuniting the principal AML/CTF actors to produce a worldwide system might be imminent, but to be more efficient than most UN Conventions and Resolutions, countries need to first agree on common data protection regulations and align their national policies accordingly. It is always a difficult task to bind many states to an international set of standards. In a few countries, bribing public officials is a custom, if not an obligation when doing business. These countries will not wish to sign up to fight financial crimes and obey international rules.

Some nations are not prone to cooperation as much as others, mainly as it can be in politicians' interests to favour the financing illicit wars and terror. The main problem nowadays in international law is enforcement, for some countries are not scared of being "named and shamed" by their neighbors as non-compliant with international standards. Sometimes, they do not care about any

 | DOI:10.1163/9789004409675_019

embargo on their business-related activities. At present, no punishment mechanism seems to be enough to make countries want to join the AML/CTF team. Regulations are getting more specific and could help prevent ML/TF, but nothing forces countries to apply such rules even when having signed Conventions. Moreover, it will be hard to exploit efficiently the provisions of CTF or even contribute to mutual legal assistance and information sharing for counties with different data protection laws. CTF can continue to evolve, but in order to efficiently work, harmonization is necessary at the international level. An International Commission such as that proposed in Chapter 9 must also be appointed to deal with AML/CTF more adequately.

Whilst many actors in the CTF field are doing a remarkable work, it can be discouraging at the end of the day to realize that the current enforcement system in place is inappropriate. A better worldwide solution should be found regarding this issue. Countries should try to incorporate international organizations' work related to AML/CTF best practice into their national laws, thereby supporting the efforts of these institutions worldwide. An ongoing problem will be that new technologies tend to facilitate ML and TF, which is the main reason why countries should work together towards the implementation of worldwide regulations and always be aware of new threats in this area so as to be constantly able to respond quickly together. Unfortunately, we are reaching a point where all these measures are considered a great breach of human rights as wherever you go, whatever you do, someone will be notified of your actions. All these measures appear to be necessary to provide the international community with the maximum security and to defeat organize crime and terrorism, but at the cost of our freedom.

Annexes

Annex 1: United States Departments and agencies Involved In Combating Terrorism (Chapter 1 D)

Here are the most famous U.S. departments and agencies involved in combating terrorism[1]:

- Department of Justice (Criminal Division; Federal Bureau of Investigation; Bureau of Alcohol, Tobacco, Firearms, and Explosives; Drug Enforcement Administration);
- Department of the Treasury (Executive Office of Terrorist Financing and Financial Crime, Office of Foreign Assets Control, Financial Crimes Enforcement Network, Internal Revenue Service (IRS), and the Office of International Affairs);
- Department of Homeland Security (Bureau of Immigration and Customs Enforcement);
- Department of State (Office of the Coordinator for Counterterrorism, Bureau of International Narcotics and Law Enforcement Affairs, and Bureau of Economic and Business Affairs);
- Department of Defense (Office of the Secretary of Defense, Office of Naval Intelligence, Defense Intelligence Agency); Appendix I: Objectives, Scope, and Methodology Appendix I: Objectives, Scope, and Methodology
- Central Intelligence Agency;
- Congressional Research Service;
- U.S. Mission to the United Nations;
- U.S. Embassy in Belgium (political and economic officers, Department of Homeland Security (Customs), Drug Enforcement Administration, Federal Bureau of Investigation, Defense);
- U.S. Embassy in France (Department of Homeland Security (Customs), Federal Bureau of Investigation);
- U.S. Mission to the European Union; and
- U.S. representatives to INTERPOL. We also reviewed and assessed available documentation and interviewed officials from the following international entities:
- United Nations;
- INTERPOL;

1 U.S. GAO, *Terrorist Financing: U.S. Agencies Should Systematically Assess Terrorists' Use of Alternative Financing Mechanisms*, GAO-04-163, November 2003, available from http://www.gao.gov/new.items/d04163.pdf.

 | DOI:10.1163/9789004409675_019

- Financial Action Task Force on Money-laundering;
- World Customs Organization;
- European Union;
- Charities Commission on England and Wales; and
- Supreme Headquarters Allied Powers Europe (one of the North Atlantic Treaty Organization's military commands).

Annex 2: "FIUs In Action", 100 Cases from the Egmont Group (Chapter 3B & 11 C)

Indicators of Terrorist Financing activities listed in the FIU's in action Report include:

- Account activity atypical for account holder
- Atypical wealth compared to client profile
- Atypical Nature of currency/notes
- Atypical or uneconomical fund movements (within accounts) or fund transfer to or from foreign jurisdiction
- Atypical account behaviour (size and nature of business)
- Attempts to avoid identifying final beneficiaries of accounts
- Attempts to encourage bank staff to facilitate transaction by reference to higher authorities in the regulatory or supervisory system
- Changing explanation for fund origin
- Concealment of beneficial owner of funds
- Change of account behaviour without explanation
- Complex fund structure – why pay for commodities in such a way
- Documentation issued by an unfamiliar financial institution
- Deliberate concealment of fund ownership
- Deposits at a variety of branches and times for no logical reason (possible evidence of 'smurfing')
- Defensive stance to questioning
- Early repayment of loans
- Evidence of untruthfulness on part of client
- Fund movements to unknown third parties
- High level of cash deposits atypical of expected business profile
- High value transactions atypical of customer business history
- Illogical business activity: Why send multiple cheques for cashing at a higher charge? Why would a wealthy and successful businessman need to approach a small bank and without any supporting financial documentation? Why was a bank clerk not willing to use the simpler method of his own financial institution for financial affairs?

- International fund transfers at level just below threshold
- Insufficient explanation for source of funds
- Large and/or rapid movements of funds
- Large amount of cash used to open new account
- Large number of low denomination bills
- Last minute alteration to fund movement instructions
- Lack of knowledge by individual atypical to trade practitioners
- Lack of rational business explanation for financial activity
- Large scale cash transactions
- Lack of underlying business rationale
- Media coverage on accountholders activities
- Missing account activity – the accounts were not used to pay any of the normal running costs of a business that may be expected.
- Missing documentation normally to be expected from a legitimate business
- Multiple currency cash format
- Multiple use of money transmission services
- Multiple repeat movements of funds (between accounts)
- Multiple cash transactions below threshold
- Multiple transfers into a personal account
- Multiple transactions below threshold
- Multiple account openings within narrow timescale
- Multiple transactions in a short time period with no underlying business rationale
- Multiple unlinked transactions benefiting the same individual
- Multiple amounts paid into personal account without explanation
- New customer attempting large transactions with no supporting rationale
- Over complex movement of funds between accounts/companies
- Presence of low-denomination bills
- Possible client relationship to previous crimes
- Questionable rationale of underlying business – importing used consumer goods from Africa to Europe is unusual
- Questions over identification documents
- Rapid inter-bank transfer with little explanation
- Rapid creation and withdrawal of funds from accounts
- Rapid off shore transfer after funds deposited
- Rapid and contradictory changes to account names and/or beneficiaries
- Re-activation of dormant accounts
- Repeated exchange of currencies with no underlying business explanation
- Rounded sums transferred to pay for commodities – market multiples usually result in 'untidy' amount
- Suspicious activity of client associates

- Transactions structured to fall below mandatory reporting requirements (smurfing)
- Transfer of assets at well below (or above) market rates
- Unconnected companies channeling funds to a single account
- Unusual underlying business action (cross-border travel to undertake simple transaction)
- Unusually high rates of return for a low risk business activity
- Unrealistic business turnover
- Unrealistic wealth compared to clients profile
- Unrealistic explanation given by customer for account activity
- Unreasonable promises of returns on investment
- Unusual currency form
- Unusual business activity – transfer into relatives account
- Unusual background information
- Unusual client activity (multiple loans in short period)
- Unexplained dispersal of funds to multiple beneficiaries
- Unusual explanation for business/account activity
- Unusually complex method of purchasing financial products
- Unwarranted high security risk – personal transfer of valuable asset
- Use of multiple accounts without explanation
- Use of unusual banking material – banking certificates of deposit have a history of attempted use within frauds
- Use of 'unofficial loan repayments' as a cover story for funds
- Use of same branch or similar branches on multiple instances when a single transaction would be more efficient
- Use of accounts by apparently unconnected third parties
- Use of company name designed to resemble the name of an established company
- Use of false identification documents

Annex 3: Questionnaire (Chapter 8)

The Efficiency of Current Counter-terrorism Financing Regulations

I *Background Information*

Which category do you belong to?

- ◻ Governmental Agencies
- ◻ Military
- ◻ Police
- ◻ FIU
- ◻ International Organization
- ◻ Tribunal/law firm
- ◻ Consulting
- ◻ Bank
- ◻ Insurance
- ◻ Financial Institution

Which company do you work at?

What is your job title?

Do you wish to remain anonymous in this study?

II *Current CTF Regulations*

Which CTF tools and regulations are useful in relation to you work?

- ◻ Company's Internal rules
- ◻ Consulting Guidelines
- ◻ Recommendations provided by International Organizations
- ◻ EU directive
- ◻ Applicable National Law
- ◻ United Nations Conventions

Which CTF tools and regulations do you work with daily?

- ◻ Company's Internal rules
- ◻ Consulting Guidelines
- ◻ Recommendations provided by International Organizations
- ◻ EU directive
- ◻ Applicable National Law

- ☐ United Nations Conventions

According to you, are existing regulatory and advisory tools efficient?

- ☐ Yes
- ☐ No

What are the pros of current CTF regulatory tools (if any)?

What are the cons of current CTF regulatory tools (if any)?

Do you believe there is a need for a more appropriate CTF monitoring tool that would benefit all sectors?

- ☐ Yes
- ☐ No

III *Privacy*

Would you consider privacy as an important factor to incorporate in a new CTF tool?

- ☐ Yes
- ☐ No

Why?

IV *Procedures*

Which CTF preventive and reporting procedures are you familiar with?

- ☐ Customer Due Diligence
- ☐ Enhanced Due Diligence
- ☐ Currency Transaction Reports
- ☐ Suspicious Activity Reports
- ☐ National Security Letters
- ☐ None

Which CTF procedure do you use at work?

- ☐ Customer Due Diligence
- ☐ Enhanced Due Diligence
- ☐ Currency Transaction Reports
- ☐ Suspicious Activity Reports
- ☐ National Security Letters

- ☐ None
- ☐ Others, please specify: ______________________________

Are you in close connection with reporting entities?

- ☐ Yes
- ☐ No
- ☐ You are the reporting entity
- ☐ N/A

What are the most current CTF related procedural/paperwork problems you or your co-workers encounter?

Do you feel CTF procedures are too burdensome?

- ☐ If Yes, how?
- ☐ No

Do you believe CTF procedures are too slow?

- ☐ If Yes, how?
- ☐ No

Do you believe CTF procedures are often misused?

- ☐ If Yes, how?
- ☐ No

Do you trust that people working in CTF have sufficient and adequate training?

- ☐ Yes
- ☐ No

Do you feel like current CTF procedures are useless or inappropriate?

- ☐ If Yes, why?
- ☐ No

V *Cooperation*

Which Institutions do you frequently deal with?

- ☐ Governmental Agencies
- ☐ Military
- ☐ Police
- ☐ FIU
- ☐ International Organization

- ☐ Tribunal/law firm
- ☐ Consulting
- ☐ Bank
- ☐ Insurance
- ☐ Financial Institution
- ☐ Other, please specify: ____

Which CTF actors do you most often encounter Cooperation problems with?

In your opinion, what are the main problems faced by CTF actors while dealing with other agencies and actors?

Do you believe collaboration with the private sector is a suitable idea?

- ☐ Yes
- ☐ No

If Yes, how could this link with the private sector be established?

VI *Financial Intelligence Units*

Do you find the work of FIUs efficient?

- ☐ Yes
- ☐ No
- ☐ N/A

Why?

Do you feel that the efficacy of the work of FIUs could be improved?

- ☐ Yes
- ☐ No
- ☐ N/A

If Yes, how?

Where do you believe the main blockages in the effectiveness of FIUs' work remain?

Do you believe there is a lack of communications between FIUs and other CTF actors?

How could communication between key players be improved in your opinion?

VII *Cross-border Enforcement*

Is cross-border enforcement possible dealing with CTF?

According to you, what are the limits of CTF enforcement efforts?

How could enforcement worldwide be improved?

VIII *Cost-benefit of Monitoring*

Do you strongly believe that the price of confiscated assets for Terrorism Financing exceeds the cost of investigation?

- □ Yes
- □ No

Have you encounter evidences during your work that investigation in fact costs more than the confiscated assets in most cases?

- □ Yes
- □ No
- □ N/A

Could you provide such evidences or numbers that would help the purpose of this study?

- □ Yes, please specify:____
- □ No
- □ N/A

____

____

____

____

Personal Comments:

Please email back your questionnaire at: reben@tjsl.edu

Feel free to contact me if you wish to discuss certain aspects of the questions furthermore.
Thank you very much for your time and consideration for my work and collective effort to enhance CTF worldwide.

Bibliography

Admiralty and Maritime Law Guide, International Conventions, *Protocol for the Suppression of Unlawful Acts against the Safety of Fixed Platforms Located on the Continental Shelf*, 10 Mar. 1988, available from http://www.admiraltylawguide.com/conven/fixedplatforms1988.html.

Alderman, Liz, *France Investigates Lafarge Executives for Terrorist Financing*, N.Y. Times, 8 Dec. 2017, https://www.nytimes.com/2017/12/08/business/lafarge-syria-eric-olsen.html.

Anderson, Kerby, *Terrorism*, Probe Ministries, 1992, http://www.leaderu.com/orgs/probe/docs/terror.html.

Anti-Money-Laundering, (last visited 5 July 2014), http://www.antimoneylaundering.ukf.net/papers/solicitor.htm.

Anti-Money-Laundering and Counter-Terrorism Financing Amendment Bill 2017, available from http://parlinfo.aph.gov.au/parlInfo/download/legislation/bills/r5952_aspassed/toc_pdf/17177b01.pdf;fileType=application%2Fpdf.

Anti-terrorism, Crime and Security Act, 2001, c. 24, http://www.legislation.gov.uk/ukpga/2001/24/pdfs/ukpga_20010024_en.pdf.

Apuzzo, Matt & LaFraniere, Sharon, *13 Russians Indicted as Mueller Reveals Effort to Aid Trump Campaign*, N.Y. Times, 16 Feb. 2018, https://www.nytimes.com/2018/02/16/us/politics/russians-indicted-mueller-election-interference.html?ribbon-ad-idx=3&src=trending&module=ArrowsNav&contentCollection=Business%20Day&action=swipe&region=FixedRight&pgtype=article. Subsequent citations: Apuzzo, *supra*, at page.

Australian Government Federal Register of Legislation, *Anti-Money-Laundering and Counter-Terrorism Financing Act 2006 No. 169*, 2006, available from https://www.legislation.gov.au/Details/C2006A00169.

Australian Government Federal Register of Legislation, *Anti-Money-Laundering and Counter-Terrorism Financing Rules Instrument 2007 (No. 1)*, 10 Apr. 2007, available from https://www.legislation.gov.au/Details/F2007L01000/Html/Text.

Bank for International Settlements, *Consolidated KYC Risk Management - Consultative Document*, Aug. 2003, available from http://www.bis.org/publ/bcbs101.htm.

Bank for International Settlements, *Customer Due Diligence for Banks*, Oct. 2001, available from http://www.bis.org/publ/bcbs85.htm.

Bank for International Settlements, *Sharing of Financial Records Between Jurisdictions in Connection with the Fight Against Terrorist Financing*, Apr. 2002, http://www.bis.org/publ/bcbs89.htm.

Bank for International Settlements, *Sound Management of Risks Related to Money-Laundering and Financing of Terrorism*, Jan. 2014, http://www.bis.org/publ/bcbs275.htm.

Barnes, Joe, *Bitcoin Warning: ISIS Using Cryptocurrency to Fund Reign of Terror as Bitcoin Price Soars*, Sunday Express, 17 Dec. 2017, available at https://www.express.co.uk/finance/city/893151/Bitcoin-price-latest-news-ISIS-terror-cryptocurrency.

BBC News, *Jet Airways India Flight Attendant Held for Smuggling Money*, 9 Jan. 2018, http://www.bbc.com/news/world-asia-india-42617388.

Brisard, Jean-Charles & Damien Martinez, *Islamic State: The Economy-Based Terrorist Funding*, Oct. 2014, http://cat-int.org/wp-content/uploads/2016/06/White-Paper-IS-Funding_Final.pdf.

Bryan, Kenza, Home News, *Saudi Arabia Funding Linked to Terror in UK by Britain's Former Ambassador to Riyadh*, The Independent, 14 July 2017), http://www.independent.co.uk/news/uk/home-news/saudi-arabia-terror-funding-uk-extremism-islamist-william-patey-former-ambassador-home-office-qatar-a7840406.html.

de Carbonnel, Alissa, *EU Agrees Stricter Bitcoin Rules Against Money-Laundering, Terrorist Financing*, Reuters, 15 Dec. 2017, http://uk.businessinsider.com/r-eu-agrees-stricter-bitcoin-rules-against-money-laundering-terrorist-financing-2017-12?IR=T.

Central Bank of Ireland, (last visited 5 July 2014), http://www.centralbank.ie/regulation/processes/anti-money-laundering/Documents/IFIA%20Draft%20AML%20Procedures.

Commonwealth Model Law for the Prohibition of Money-Laundering, 1996, http://www.imolin.org/pdf/imolin/Comsecml.pdf.

Convention of the Islamic Conference on Combatting International Terrorism, available from www.oic-cdpu.org/en/getdoc/?dID=13.

Council of Europe, *Committee of Experts on the Evaluation of Anti-Money-Laundering Measures and the Financing of Terrorism*, 30 Jan. 2018, available from http://www.coe.int/web/moneyval.

Council of Europe, *Committee of Experts on the Evaluation of Anti-Money-Laundering Measures and the Financing of Terrorism, Politically Exposed Persons – COE*, 2018, available from http://www.coe.int/t/dghl/monitoring/moneyval/Web_ressources/WB_PEPs_en.pdf.

Council of Europe Treaty Office, *Convention on Laundering, Search, Seizure and Confiscation of the Proceeds from Crime*, available from http://www.coe.int/web/conventions/full-list/-/conventions/treaty/141.

Council of Europe Treaty Office, *Council of Europe Convention on Laundering, Search, Seizure, and Confiscation of the Proceeds of Crime and on the Financing of Terrorism*, 15 May 2005, available from http://conventions.coe.int/Treaty/en/Treaties/Html/198.htm.

Counter-Terrorism Act 2008, c. 28, available from http://www.legislation.gov.uk/ukpga/2008/28/pdfs/ukpga_20080028_en.pdf.

Cryer, Robert et al., *An Introduction to International Criminal Law and Procedure* 341 (2nd ed. 2010).

Deen, Thalif, *U.N. Remains Deadlocked on Defining Terrorism*, 23 Nov. 2010, available from http://www.ipsnews.net/2010/11/un-remains-deadlocked-on-defining-terrorism/.

Egmont Group, *About*, 2018, (last visited 5 July 2014), https://egmontgroup.org/.

Egmont Group, *Egmont Group of Financial Intelligence Units Principles for Information Exchange Between Financial Intelligence Units*, 28 Oct. 2013, available from https://sic.gov.lb/intorg/EG%20Principles%20for%20Information%20Exchange%20(2013).pdf.

Egmont Group, *Financial Intelligence Units (FIUs)*, http://www.egmontgroup.org/about/financial-intelligence-units-fius, (last visited 5 July 2014).

Egmont Group, *Money-Laundering and the Financing of Terrorism*, (last visited 5 July 2014), https://egmontgroup.org/en/content/money-laundering-and-financing-terrorism.

Electronic Privacy Information Center (EPIC), National Security Letters, available from http://epic.org/privacy/nsl/.

European Union, *Directive 2005/60/EC of the European Parliament and of the Council of 26 Oct. 2005 on the prevention of the use of the financial system for the purpose of money-laundering and terrorist financing*, 26 Oct. 2005, available from http://eur-lex.europa.eu/legal-content/EN/TXT/?uri=CELEX%3A32005L0060.

European Union, *Directive (EU) 2015/849 of the European Parliament and of the Council of 20 May 2015 on the prevention of the use of the financial system for the purposes of money-laundering or terrorist financing, amending Regulation (EU) No 648/2012 of the European Parliament and of the Council, and repealing Directive 2005/60/EC of the European Parliament and of the Council and Commission Directive 2006/70/EC*, 20 May 2015, available from http://eur-lex.europa.eu/legal-content/EN/TXT/?uri=CELEX%3A32015L0849.

European Union, *Directive (EU) 2017/541 of the European Parliament and of the Council of 15 March 2017 on combating terrorism and replacing Council Framework Decision 2002/475/JHA and amending Council Decision 2005/671/JHA*, 15 March 2017, available fromhttps://eur-lex.europa.eu/legal-content/EN/TXT/PDF/?uri=CELEX:32017L0541&from=EN.

European Union, *Directive (EU) 2018/843 of the European Parliament and of the Council of 30 May 2018 amending Directive (EU) 2015/849 on the prevention of the use of the financial system for the purposes of money-laundering or terrorist financing, and amending Directives 2009/138/EC and 2013/36/EU*, 30 May 2018, available from https://eur-lex.europa.eu/legal-content/EN/TXT/PDF/?uri=CELEX:32018L0843&from=EN.

European Union, *Directive of the European Parliament and of the Council on combating terrorism and replacing Council Framework Decision 2002/475/JHA on combating terrorism*, 12 Feb. 2015, available from https://ec.europa.eu/home-affairs/sites/

homeaffairs/files/what-we-do/policies/european-agenda-security/legislative-documents/docs/20151202_directive_on_combatting_terrorism_en.pdf.

European Parliament, *The Charter of Fundamental Rights of the European Union*, Oct. 2017, available from http://www.europarl.europa.eu/atyourservice/en/displayFtu.html?ftuId=FTU_4.1.2.html.

Federal Bank, *KYC Norms*, http://www.federalbank.co.in/kyc-norms.

Federal Deposit Insurance Corporation FDIC, *Bank Secrecy Act*, (last visited Jul 5, 2014), FDIC, http://www.fdic.gov/regulations/examinations/bsa/bsa_13.html.

Federal Deposit Insurance Corporation FDIC, *Bank Secrecy Act and Anti-Money-Laundering*, 20 Feb. 2009, available from http://www.fdic.gov/regulations/examinations/bsa/index.html.

Federal Deposit Insurance Corporation, *Bank Secrecy Act, Anti-Money-Laundering, And Office of Foreign Assets Control Introduction to the Bank Secrecy Act* §8.1, Dec. 2004, available from https://www.fdic.gov/regulations/safety/manual/section8-1.html.

Federal Financial Institutions Examination Council, *Bank Secrecy Act/Anti-Money-Laundering Examination Manual*, available from https://www.ffiec.gov/bsa%5Faml%5Finfobase/pages_manual/manual_online.htm.

Federal Reserve System Division of Banking Supervision and Regulation, *Bank Secrecy Act Examination Manual*, Sept. 1997, available from http://www.federalreserve.gov/boarddocs/supmanual/bsa/7-00bsaman.pdf.

Filipkowski, Wojciech, *Cyber Laundering: An Analysis of Typology and Techniques*, 3.1 Int. J. Crim. Just. Sci., 15–27, 2008, available from http://www.sascv.org/ijcjs/wojciech.html.

Financial Action Task Force (FATF), *Criminalising Terrorist Financing (Recommendation 5)*, Oct. 2016, available from http://www.fatf-gafi.org/media/fatf/documents/reports/Guidance-Criminalising-Terrorist-Financing.pdf.

Financial Action Task Force (FATF), *Emerging Terrorist Financing Risks*, Oct. 2015, available from http://www.fatf-gafi.org/media/fatf/documents/reports/Emerging-Terrorist-Financing-Risks.pdf.

Financial Action Task Force (FATF), *FATF steps up the fight against money-laundering and terrorist financing*, 2012, available from http://www.fatf-gafi.org/topics/fatf recommendations/documents/fatfstepsupthefightagainstmoneylaundering andterroristfinancing.html.

Financial Action Task Force (FATF), *Global Money-Laundering & Terrorist Financing Threat Assessment*, July 2010, http://www.fatf-gafi.org/media/fatf/documents/reports/Global%20Threat%20assessment.pdf.

Financial Action Task Force (FATF), *Glossary*, (last visited 5 July 2014), http://www.fatf-gafi.org/glossary/0,3414,en_32250379_32236930_35433764_1_1_1_1,00.html#34285860.

Financial Action Task Force (FATF), *Guidance for a Risk-Based Approach: The Banking Sector* Oct. 2014, available from http://www.fatf-gafi.org/media/fatf/documents/reports/Risk-Based-Approach-Banking-Sector.pdf.

Financial Action Task Force (FATF), *International Best Practices: Detecting and Preventing the Illicit Cross-Border Transportation of Cash and Bearer Negotiable Instruments,* 19 Feb. 2010, available from http://www.fatf-gafi.org/media/fatf/documents/recommendations/International%20BPP%20Detecting%20and%20Preventing%20illicit%20cross-border%20transportation%20SR%20IX%20%20COVER%202012.pdf.

Financial Action Task Force (FATF), *International Best Practices: Targeted Financial Sanctions Related to Terrorism and Terrorist Financing (Recommendation 6),* 2012, available from http://www.fatf-gafi.org/publications/fatfrecommendations/documents/bpp-finsanctions-tf-r6.html.

Financial Action Task Force (FATF), *International Standards On Combating Money-Laundering and the Financing of Terrorism & Proliferation,* Feb. 2012, http://www.fatf-gafi.org/media/fatf/documents/recommendations/pdfs/FATF_Recommendations.pdf.

Financial Action Task Force (FATF), *Measures to be Taken by Financial Institutions and Non-Financial Business and Professions to Prevent Money-Laundering and Terrorist Financing,* 2006, available from http://www.un.org/en/sc/ctc/docs/bestpractices/fatf/40recs-moneylaundering/fatf-reco6.pdf.

Financial Action Task Force (FATF), *Methodology for Assessing Technical Compliance with the FATF Recommendations and the Effectiveness of AML/CFT Systems,* Nov. 2017, available from http://www.fatf-gafi.org/media/fatf/documents/methodology/FATF%20Methodology%2022%20Feb%202013.pdf.

Financial Action Task Force (FATF), *Money-Laundering Using New Payment Methods,* Oct. 2010, available from http://www.fatf-gafi.org/media/fatf/documents/reports/ML%20using%20New%20Payment%20Methods.pdf.

Financial Action Task Force (FATF), *Report on Financing of the Terrorist Organization Islamic State in Iraq and the Levant* (ISIL), (2015), available from http://www.fatf-gafi.org/media/fatf/documents/reports/Financing-of-the-terrorist-organisation-ISIL.pdf.

Financial Action Task Force (FATF) on Money-Laundering, *The Forty Recommendations,* (1990), available from http://www.fatf-gafi.org/media/fatf/documents/recommendations/pdfs/FATF%20Recommendations%201990.pdf.

Financial Action Task Force (FATF) on Money-Laundering, *The Forty Recommendations,* 20 June 2003, available from http://www.fatf-gafi.org/media/fatf/documents/recommendations/pdfs/FATF%20Recommendations%202003.pdf.

Financial Action Task Force (FATF), *Typologies,* (last visited 5 July 2014), http://www.apgml.org/frameworks/docs/5/FATF%20Typologies%20rpt%201998-99.pdf.

Financial Crimes Enforcement Network, *USA Patriot Act*, FinCEN.gov, (last visited 5 July 2014), https://www.fincen.gov/resources/statutes-regulations/usa-patriot-act.

Financial Industry Regulatory Authority (FINRA), *Anti-Money-Laundering Template for Small Firms*, 1 Jan. 2010, available from http://www.finra.org/industry/anti-money-laundering-template-small-firms.

FIUs in Action, *100 Cases from the Egmont Group*, (last visited 5 July 2014), http://www.u4.no/recommended-reading/fius-in-action-100-cases-from-the-egmont-group/.

Fontevecchia, Agustino, *HSBC Helped Terrorists, Iran, Mexican Drug Cartels Launder Money, Senate Report Says*, Forbes, 16 July 2012, available from https://www.forbes.com/sites/afontevecchia/2012/07/16/hsbc-helped-terrorists-iran-mexican-drug-cartels-launder-money-senate-report-says/#69ad011a5712.

Friesen, Connie M., *US and UK Anti-Money-Laundering Requirements Compared*, International Law Office, 5 Sept. 2008, available from http://www.internationallawoffice.com/newsletters/detail.aspx?g=5e143642-6dd9-4b32-8d4e-cab33d724eea.

Guarascio, Francesco, Foreign Exchange Analysis, *EU Agrees Clampdown on Bitcoin Platforms to Tackle Money-Laundering*, Reuters, 15 Dec. 2017, https://www.reuters.com/article/uk-eu-moneylaundering/eu-agrees-clampdown-on-bitcoin-platforms-to-tackle-money-laundering-idUSKBN1E928M.

Haig, Samuel, *Europol and Interpol to Increase Measures Against BTC Laundering*, Bitcoin.com 30 Jan. 2018, https://news.bitcoin.com/105481-2/.

Hastings, Kirsten, *Rothschild Fined €9m Over 1MDB Failings*, Fund Selector Asia, 22 June 2017, https://fundselectorasia.com/rothschild-fined-eur9m-1mdb-failings/.

Interlocutory Decision on the Applicable Law: Terrorism, Conspiracy, Homicide, Perpetration, Cumulative Charging, Case No. STL-11-01/I (Feb. 16, 2011), (last visited 5 June 2014), http://www.stl-tsl.org/x/file/TheRegistry/Library/CaseFiles/chambers/20110216_STL-11-01_R176bis_F0010_AC_Interlocutory_D...

International Atomic Energy Agency, *Convention on the Physical Protection of Nuclear Material*, 26 Oct. 1979, available from https://www.iaea.org/publications/documents/conventions/convention-physical-protection-nuclear-material.

International Centre for Asset Recovery, *Alternative Remittance Systems*, (last visited 5 July 2014), available from http://www.assetrecovery.org/kc/node/22849190-bd32-11dc-bb7d-ebf2eb5e792a.0;jsessionid=70C2FBB8CEDA3B036D3C64D31E733234.

International Environmental Agreements (IEA) Database Project, *Convention for The Suppression of Unlawful Acts Against The Safety Of Maritime Navigation*, 10 Mar. 1988, available from http://iea.uoregon.edu/treaty-text/1988-unlawfulacts safetymaritimenavigationentxt.

International Monetary Fund, *Anti-Money-Laundering/Combating the Financing of Terrorism - Topics*, 2000, available from http://www.imf.org/external/np/leg/amlcft/eng/aml1.htm.

International Monetary Fund, *IMF and the Fight Against Money-Laundering and the Financing of Terrorism*, 30 Oct. 2017, available from http://www.imf.org/external/np/exr/facts/aml.htm.

International Money-Laundering Information Network, Global Programme Against Money-Laundering, *Model legislation on laundering, confiscation and international cooperation in relation to the proceeds of crime*, 1999, available from http://www.imolin.org/imolin/en/ml99eng.html.

Irish, John, *France to Press U.S. on 'Low-Cost' Terror Financing*, Reuters, 17 Dec. 2015, http://www.reuters.com/article/us-mideast-crisis-financing-france-idUSKBN0U02MZ20151217.

Kaplan, Eben, Council on Foreign Relations, *Tracking Down Terrorist Financing*, 4 Apr. 2006, available from https://www.cfr.org/backgrounder/tracking-down-terrorist-financing.

Keatinge, Tom, Centre for Financial Crime and Security Studies, *Why Qatar is the Focus of Terrorism Claims*, BBC News, 13 June 2017, http://www.bbc.com/news/world-middle-east-40246734.

Knecht, Eric, World News, *U.S., Qatar Agree to Further Curbs on Terrorist Financing*, Reuters, 30 Oct. 2017, https://www.reuters.com/article/us-qatar-usa-security/u-s-qatar-agree-to-further-curbs-on-terrorist-financing-idUSKBN1CZ2I7.

Kollewe, Julia, *Bitcoin: UK and EU Plan Crackdown Amid Crime and Tax Evasion Fears*, The Guardian, 4 Dec. 2017, https://www.theguardian.com/technology/2017/dec/04/bitcoin-uk-eu-plan-cryptocurrency-price-traders-anonymity.

Kyriakos-Saad, Nadim et al., *Islamic Finance and Anti-Money-Laundering and Combating the Financing of Terrorism (AML/CFT)*, 2016, available from https://www.imf.org/external/pubs/ft/wp/2016/wp1642.pdf.

LexisNexis Risk Division, *Emerging Anti-Money-Laundering Risks to Financial Institutions*, 2007, available from http://www.scribd.com/doc/3941706/AntiMoney-Laundering-Risks-to-Financial-Institutions.

Lexis PSL, *Anti-money-laundering and counter-terrorist financing*, 2013, http://lexisweb.co.uk/sub-topics/anti-money-laundering-and-counter-terrorist-financing.

Lormel, Dennis, *Terrorism Financing Operations Section FBI 2002*, available from http://www.fbi.gov/news/testimony/usa-patriot-act-terrorism-financing-operations-section.

Molander, Roger C. et al., *Cyberpayments and Money-Laundering*, 1998, available from http://www.rand.org/content/dam/rand/pubs/monograph_reports/1998/MR965.sum.pdf.

MENAFATF, (last visited 5 July 2014), www.menafatf.org/Linkcounter.asp?rid.

Money-Laundering, Sept. 2007, available from http://www.justice.gov/usao/eousa/foia_reading_room/usab5505.pdf.

New Zealand Ministry of Justice, *Justice Sector & Policy*, available from http://www.justice.govt.nz/policy/criminal-justice/aml-cft/about.

New Zealand Police, *Financial Intelligence Unit (FIU)*, (last visited 5 July 2014), http://www.police.govt.nz/advice/businesses-and-organisations/fiu.

Organisation for Economic Co-Operation and Development (OECD), (last visited 5 July 2014), www.oecd.org/dataoecd/31/50/34043689.pdf.

Organisation for Economic Co-Operation and Development (OECD), *OECD Convention on Combating Bribery of Foreign Public Officials in International Business Transactions*, 17 Dec. 1997, available from http://www.oecd.org/corruption/oecdantibriberyconvention.htm.

Organization of African Unity, *Convention on the Prevention and Combating of Terrorism, (1999)*, 14 July 1999, available from http://treaties.un.org/doc/db/Terrorism/OAU-english.pdf.

Parliamentary Counsel Office, New Zealand Legislation, *Financial Transactions Reporting Act 1996, No 9*, 1 Apr. 2017, available from http://www.legislation.govt.nz/act/public/1996/0009/latest/DLM373804.html.

Pistole, John S., *Terrorism Financing: Origination, Organization, and Prevention, FBI*, 2003, available from http://www.fbi.gov/news/testimony/terrorism-financing-origination-organization-and-prevention.

Proceeds of Crime Act 2002, available from http://www.legislation.gov.uk/ukpga/2002/29/contents.

Prohibition on Funding of Unlawful Internet Gambling, 31 C.F.R. §§ 132.2 (2012), available from https://www.law.cornell.edu/cfr/text/31/132.2.

Redman, Jamie, *Research Says Claims of Terrorism Financed With Bitcoin Are Exaggerated*, Bitcoin.com, 10 Mar. 2017, https://news.bitcoin.com/report-financing-terrorism-bitcoin-exaggerated/.

Regulation (EU) No 648/2012 of the European Parliament and of the Council of 4 July 2012 on OTC derivatives, central counterparties and trade repositories Text with EEA relevance, 4 July 2012, available from http://data.europa.eu/eli/reg/2012/648/oj.

Reports Analysis Centre of Canada, (last visited 5 July 2014), http://fintrac.gc.ca/publications/brochure/06-2008/1-eng.asp.

Reports Analysis Centre of Canada, *Money-Laundering and Terrorist Financing Typologies and Trends in Canadian Banking*, May 2009, available from http://www.fintrac.gc.ca/publications/typologies/2009-05-01-eng.asp.

Roth, John et al., National Commission on Terrorist Attacks Upon the United States, *Monograph on Terrorist Financing, Staff Report to the Commission*, 2004, available from https://govinfo.library.unt.edu/911/staff_statements/911_TerrFin_Monograph.pdf.

Saravalle, Edoardo & Elizabeth Rosenberg, *Bitcoin Can Help Terrorists Secretly Fund Their Deadly Attacks*, Fox News, 9 Jan. 2018, available from http://www.foxnews.com/opinion/2018/01/09/bitcoin-can-help-terrorists-secretly-fund-their-deadly-attacks.html.

Scheinin, Martin, U.N. GAOR, *Report of the Special Rapporteur on the Promotion and Protection of Human Rights and Fundamental Freedoms While Countering Terrorism*, A/HRC/13/37, 28 Dec. 2009, available from http://www2.ohchr.org/english/bodies/hrcouncil/docs/13session/A-HRC-13-37.pdf.

Serious Organised Crime and Police Act 2005, available from http://www.legislation.gov.uk/ukpga/2005/15/pdfs/ukpga_20050015_en.pdf.

Seymour, Gerald, *Harry's Game: A Novel* (1975).

Terrorism Act 2000, available from http://www.legislation.gov.uk/ukpga/2000/11/contents.

Terrorism Act 2006, available from http://www.legislation.gov.uk/ukpga/2006/11/section/1.

Terrorism Suppression Act 2002, No 34, 1 Mar. 2017, available from http://www.legislation.govt.nz/act/public/2002/0034/latest/DLM151491.html.

Tritten, Travis J., *The Dark Side of Bitcoin: Terror Financing and Sanctions Evasion*, Washington Examiner, 16 Jan. 2018, available from http://www.washingtonexaminer.com/the-dark-side-of-bitcoin-terror-financing-and-sanctions-evasion/article/2646118#!.

U.K. Financial Services Authority, *Banks' Management of High Money-Laundering Risk Situations*, June 2011, available from www.fsa.gov.uk/pubs/other/aml_final_report.pdf.

U.N., Commission on Narcotic Drugs and the Economic and Social Council, *United Nations Convention Against Illicit Traffic in Narcotic Drugs and Psychotropic Substances*, 25 May 1988, available from http://www.unodc.org/pdf/convention_1988_en.pdf.

U.N., *Convention for the Suppression of Unlawful Acts Against the Safety of Civil Aviation*, Montreal, 23 Sept. 1971, *U.N.T.S.*, vol. 974, no. 1-14118, available from http://www.un.org/zh/terrorism/pdf/1971E.pdf.

U.N., *Convention for the Suppression of Unlawful Seizure of Aircraft*, 16 Dec. 1970, *U.N.T.S. 1973*, available from http://www.refworld.org/docid/3ddcaa774.html.

U.N., *Convention on the Prevention and Punishment of Crimes against Internationally Protected Persons, U.N.T.S. 1973*, available from http://legal.un.org/ilc/texts/instruments/english/conventions/9_4_1973.pdf.

U.N., *Counter-Terrorism Strategy*, (last visited 5 July 2014), www.un.org/terrorism/strategy-counter-terrorism.shtml.

U.N., *International Convention against the Taking of Hostages*, New York, 17 December 1979, available from http://www.unodc.org/documents/treaties/Special/1979%20

International%20Convention%20against%20the%20Taking%20of%20Hostages.pdf.

U.N., *Protocol for the Suppression of Unlawful Acts of Violence at Airports Serving International Civil Aviation, supplementary to the Convention for the Suppression of Unlawful Acts against the Safety of Civil Aviation*, 24 Feb. 1988, *U.N.T.S 1990*, available from http://www.refworld.org/docid/3ddcac634.html.

U.N. GAOR, *Inter-American Convention Against Terrorism*, AG/RES 1840, 3 June 2002, available from http://www.oas.org/xxxiiga/english/docs_en/docs_items/AGres1840_02.htm.

U.N. GAOR, *International Convention for the Suppression of Terrorist Bombings*, A/52/653, 25 Nov. 1997, available from http://www.un.org/law/cod/terroris.htm.

U.N. GAOR, *Situation of human rights in the Democratic People's Republic of Korea: Report of the Secretary-General*, A/63/332, 26 Aug. 2008, available from undocs.org/A/63/332.

U.N. GAOR resolution 45/95, *Guidelines for the Regulation of Computerized Personal Data Files*, A/RES/45/95, 14 Dec. 1990, available from http://www.un.org/documents/ga/res/45/a45r095.htm.

U.N. GAOR resolution 54/109 *International Convention for the Suppression of the Financing of Terrorism*, 9 Dec. 1999, available from http://www.un.org/law/cod/finterr.htm.

U.N. GAOR resolution 55/25, *Convention on Transnational Organized Crime and the Protocols Thereto*, Article 14, 15 Nov. 2000, available from https://www.unodc.org/documents/middleeastandnorthafrica/organised-crime/united_nations_convention_against_transnational_organized_crime_and_the_protocols_thereto.pdf.

U.N. GAOR resolution 58/4, *Convention Against Corruption*, Article 54, 31 Oct. 2003, http://www.unodc.org/unodc/en/corruption/uncac.html.

U.N. GAOR resolution 3067 (XXVIII), *Convention on the Law of the Sea*, 19 November 1973, available from http://www.un.org/depts/los/convention_agreements/texts/unclos/unclos_e.pdf.

U.N. High Commissioner for Refugees (UNHCR), *Letter dated 2 Sept. 2015 from the Chair of the Security Council Committee established pursuant to resolution 1373 (2001) concerning counter-terrorism addressed to the President of the Security Council*, S/2015/683, 2 Sept. 2015, available from http://www.refworld.org/docid/5616128d4.html.

U.N. Human Rights Council, *Annual Report of the United Nations High Commissioner for Human Rights and Reports of the Office of the High Commissioner and the Secretary General*, A/HRC/28/28 ¶ 53, 19 Dec. 2014, http://undocs.org/en/A/HRC/28/28.

U.N. Human Rights Council, *The Right to Privacy in the Digital Age*, A/HRC/27/37, ¶ 24, 30 June 2014, available from http://www.ohchr.org/EN/HRBodies/HRC/RegularSessions/Session27/Documents/A.HRC.27.37_en.pdf.

U.N. International Civil Aviation Organization, *Convention on Offences and Certain Other Acts Committed on Board Aircraft*, 14 Sept. 1963, *U.N.T.S.*, No. 10106, available from http://treaties.un.org/doc/db/Terrorism/Conv1-english.pdf.

U.N., *International Convention for The Suppression of Acts of Nuclear Terrorism*, (2005), available from https://treaties.un.org/doc/db/Terrorism/english-18-15.pdf.

U.N. International Explosives Technical Commission, *Convention on the Marking of Plastic Explosives for the Purpose of Detection,* 1 Mar. 1991, available from http://www.un.org/en/sc/ctc/docs/conventions/Conv10.pdf.

U.N. Meetings Coverage and Press Releases, *Adopting Resolution 2195 (2014), Urges International Action to Break Links between Terrorists, Transnational Organized Crime,* S/2015/683, 2 Sept. 2015, available from http://www.un.org/press/en/2014/sc11717.doc.htm.

U.N. Meetings Coverage and Press Releases, *Security Council Adopts Resolution 2170 (2014) Condemning Gross, Widespread Abuse of Human Rights by Extremist Groups in Iraq, Syria,* SC 11520, 15 Aug. 2014, available from http://www.un.org/press/en/2014/sc11520.doc.htm.

U.N. Meetings Coverage and Press Releases, *Security Council Unanimously Adopts Resolution Condemning Violent Extremism, Underscoring Need to Prevent Travel, Support for Foreign Terrorist Fighters,* SC 11580, 24 Sept. 2014, available from http://www.un.org/press/en/2014/sc11580.doc.htm.

U.N. Meetings Coverage and Press Releases, *Unanimously Adopting Resolution 2199 (2015), Security Council Condemns Trade with Al-Qaida Associated Groups, Threatens Further Targeted Sanctions,* SC 11775, 12 Feb. 2015, available from http://www.un.org/press/en/2015/sc11775.doc.htm.

U.N. Office of Counter-Terrorism, *Action to Counter Terrorism,* 2017, available from http://www.un.org/terrorism/.

U.N. Office on Drugs and Crime, *Model Legislation on Money-Laundering and Financing of Terrorism,* 1 Dec. 2005, available from http://www.imf.org/external/np/leg/amlcft/eng/pdf/amlml05.pdf.

U.N. Office on Drugs and Crime, *Model Provisions on Money-Laundering, Terrorist Financing, Preventative Measures and Proceeds of Crime,* Apr. 2009, available from http://www.imolin.org/pdf/imolin/Model_Provisions_Final.pdf.

U.N. Office on Drugs and Crime, GAOR resolution 55/25, *Convention Against Transnational Organized Crime,* New York, 15 Nov. 2000, available from https://www.unodc.org/documents/treaties/UNTOC/Publications/TOC%20Convention/TOCebook-e.pdf.

U.N. Office on Drugs and Crime, GAOR resolution 58/4, *Convention Against Corruption,* New York, 31 Oct. 2003, available from https://www.unodc.org/documents/brussels/UN_Convention_Against_Corruption.pdf.

U.N., *Protocol Supplementary to the Convention for the Suppression of Unlawful Seizure of Aircraft*, Beijing, 10 September 2010, available from https://www.icao.int/secretariat/legal/Administrative%20Packages/Beijing_protocol_EN.pdf.

U.N. SCOR, *Letter dated 2 Sept. 2015 from the Chair of the Security Council Committee Established Pursuant to Resolution 1373 (2001) Concerning Counter-Terrorism Addressed to the President of the Security Council,* S/2015/683, 2 Sept. 2015, available from http://www.un.org/en/sc/ctc/docs/2015/N1527297_EN.pdf.

U.N. SCOR, Counter-Terrorism Committee, *Security Council Resolutions Pertaining to Terrorism,* 29 Jan. 2016, available from https://www.un.org/en/sc/ctc/resources/res-sc.html.

U.N. SCOR, *Resolution 1373*, S/RES/1373, 28 Sept. 2001, available from http://www.un.org/en/sc/ctc/specialmeetings/2012/docs/United%20Nations%20Security%20Council%20Resolution%201373%20(2001).pdf.

U.N. SCOR, *Resolution 1566,* S/RES/1566, 8 Oct. 2004, available from https://www.scribd.com/document/63963034/UNSCR-1566-2004.

U.N. SCOR, *Resolution 2178,* 24 Sept. 2014, available from http://www.un.org/en/sc/ctc/docs/2015/SCR%202178_2014_EN.pdf.

U.N., *UN Instruments and International Standards on Money-Laundering and Terrorist Financing,* 2018, available from http://www.unodc.org/unodc/en/money-laundering/Instruments-Standards.html?ref=menuside#UN-Conventions.

U.N., *United Nations*, http://www.un.org/terrorism/.

U.S. Dep't. of Justice, Offices of the United States Attorneys, *Asset Forfeiture*, 10 Feb. 2016, available from http://www.justice.gov/usao/eousa/foia_reading_room/usab5506.pdf.

U.S. Dep't. of State, Bureau of International Security and Nonproliferation, *Protocol of 2005 to the Convention for the Suppression of Unlawful Acts Against the Safety of Maritime Navigation,* LEG/CONF.15/22, 1 Nov. 2005, available from https://www.state.gov/t/isn/trty/81728.htm.

U.S. Dep't. of State, *Money-Laundering*, (last visited 5 July 2014), http://www.state.gov/1997-2001-NOPDFS/policy_remarks/1998/980611_winer_mlaundering.html.

U.S. Dep't. of State, *U.N. Security Council Resolution 1373,* 28 Sept. 2001, available from https://2001-2009.state.gov/p/io/rls/othr/2001/5108.htm.

U.S. Dep't. of the Treasury, Financial Crimes Enforcement Network, (last visited 5 July 2014), http://www.fincen.gov/news_room/rp/advisory/html/advissu4.html.

U.S. Dep't. of the Treasury, Financial Crimes Enforcement Network, *FATF-VIII Money-Laundering Typologies Exercise Public Report*, Nov. 1996, available from http://www.fincen.gov/news_room/rp/files/fatf.pdf.

U.S. Dep't. of the Treasury, Financial Crimes Enforcement Network, *FinCEN Educational Pamphlet on the Currency Transaction Reporting Requirement,* available from https://www.fincen.gov/fincen-educational-pamphlet-currency-transaction-reporting-requirement.

U.S. Dep't. of the Treasury, Financial Crimes Enforcement Network, *Guidance on Preparing a Complete & Sufficient Suspicious Activity Report Narrative*, Nov. 2003, available from https://www.fincen.gov/sites/default/files/shared/sarnarrcomplet guidfinal_112003.pdf.

U.S. Dep't. of the Treasury, Financial Crimes Enforcement Network, *Notice to Customers: A CTR Reference Guide*, available from http://www.fincen.gov/whatsnew/pdf/CTRPamphletBW.pdf.

U.S. Dep't. of the Treasury, Financial Crimes Enforcement Network, *Red Flags*, (last visited 5 July 2014), available from http://www.fincen.gov/financial_institutions/msb/materials/en/prevention_guide.html#Red Flags.

U.S. Dep't. of the Treasury, Financial Crimes Enforcement Network, *Suggestions for Addressing Common Errors Noted in Suspicious Activity Reporting*, 10 Oct. 2007, available from https://www.fincen.gov/resources/statutes-regulations/guidance/suggestions-addressing-common-errors-noted-suspicious.

U.S. Dep't. of the Treasury, *Resource Center*, 15 Mar. 2017, available from https://www.treasury.gov/resource-center/sanctions/Programs/Pages/faq_10_page.aspx.

U.S. GAO, *Terrorist Financing: U.S. Agencies Should Systematically Assess Terrorists' Use of Alternative Financing Mechanisms*, GAO-04-163, Nov. 2003, available from http://www.gao.gov/new.items/d04163.pdf.

U.S. Legal, *Wire Transfer System Law and Legal Definition*, (last visited 5 July 2017), http://definitions.uslegal.com/w/wire-transfer-system/.

U.S. Patriot Act, *SEC. 312*, (last visited 5 July 2014), http://ithandbook.ffiec.gov/media/resources/3356/con-usa_patriot_act_section_312.pdf.

U.S. SEC, *Joint Final Rule: Customer Identification Programs for Mutual Funds*, 9 June 2003, available from https://www.sec.gov/rules/final/ic-26031.htm.

Verdugo-Yepes, Concepcion, Compliance with the AML/CFT International Standard: Lessons from a Cross-Country Analysis, International Monetary Fund, July 2011, available from http://www.imf.org/external/pubs/ft/wp/2011/wp11177.pdf.

Weinstein, Adam, *The Real Largest State Sponsor of Terrorism*, Huffington Post, 16 Mar. 2017, available from https://www.huffingtonpost.com/entry/the-real-largest-state-sponsor-of-terrorism_us_58cafc26e4b00705db4da8aa.

Winer, Jonathan, *Combating Money-Laundering*, 11 June 1998, available from http://www.fas.org/irp/congress/1998_hr/980611_winer_launder.htm.

Wolfsberg, *Anti-Money-Laundering Principles*, (last visited 5 July 2014), http://www.wolfsberg-principles.com/faq-persons.html.

Wolfsberg, *Anti-Money-Laundering Principles for Correspondent Banking*, (last visited 5 July 2014), http://www.wolfsberg-principles.com/pdf/standards/Wolfsberg-Correspondent-Banking-Principles-2014.pdf.

Wolfsberg, *Anti-Money-Laundering Principles for Private Banking*, (last visited 5 July 2014), available from http://www.wolfsberg-principles.com/pdf/Wolfsberg-Private-Banking-Prinicples-May-2012.pdf.

Wolfsberg, *Frequently Asked Questions ("FAQ's")*, (last visited 5 July 2014), available from http://www.wolfsberg-principles.com/pdf/Wolfsberg_PEP_FAQs_(2008).pdf.

Zenko, Micah, Politics, Power, and Preventive Action & Center for Preventive Action, *Bitcoin for Bombs*, Council on Foreign Relations, 17 Aug. 2017, available from https://www.cfr.org/blog/bitcoin-bombs.

Index

www.ingramcontent.com/pod-product-compliance
Lightning Source LLC
LaVergne TN
LVHW011105300926
849160LV00008B/288
* 9 7 8 9 0 0 4 4 0 9 6 6 8 *